Patrick Kavanagh

a reference guide

*A
Reference
Guide
to
Literature*

*Richard J. Finneran
Editor*

Patrick Kavanagh

a reference guide

JONATHAN ALLISON

G. K. Hall & Co.
An Imprint of Simon & Schuster Macmillan
New York

Prentice Hall International
London   Mexico City   New Delhi   Singapore   Sydney   Toronto

Copyright © 1996 by Jonathan Allison

All rights reserved. No part of this book may be reproduced or transmitted in any form or by any means, electronic or mechanical, including photocopying, recording, or by any information storage and retrieval system, without permission in writing from the Publisher.

G.K. Hall & Co.
An Imprint of Simon & Schuster Macmillan
1633 Broadway
New York, NY 10019

Library of Congress Catalog Number: 96-29255

Printed in the United States of America

Printing number
1 2 3 4 5 6 7 8 9 10

Library of Congress Cataloging-in-Publication Data

Allison, Jonathan, 1958–
   Patrick Kavanagh : a reference guide / Jonathan Allison.
     p.   cm.—(A reference guide to literature)
   Includes bibliographical references and indexes.
   ISBN 0-8161-7286-2 (alk. paper)
   1. Kavanagh, Patrick, 1904–1967—Bibliography. 2. Ireland in literature—Bibliography. I. Title. II. Series.
Z8460.875.A55   1996
[PR6021.A74]
016.821'914—dc20   96-29255
                                                                                                            CIP

The paper used in this publication meets the requirements of ANSI/NISO Z39.48—1992 (Permanence of Paper).

Contents

Foreword   vii

Preface   ix

Acknowledgments   xi

Introduction   xiii

Primary Materials   xxv

List of Abbreviations   xxvii

Writings about Patrick Kavanagh   1

Author Index   199

Subject Index   209

Note on the Author   219

Foreword

Patrick Kavanagh's place in the history of modern Irish poetry has become increasingly secure. It is evident by the entries in this bibliography that critical attention on the man and his work has increased in the last thirty years and shows no sign of lessening. He emerged as a poet in the fallow years after the deaths of W. B. Yeats and James Joyce, when Irish writers were under suspicion in a restrictive puritanical society. Kavanagh was one of a handful of poets of diverse talents, such as Austin Clarke, Brian Coffey, Denis Devlin, Padraic Fallon, and Louis MacNeice, who struggled to make a place for himself in an uncongenial time. Some of these poets worked within the founding assumption of the Irish Literary Revival that an indigenous literature in the English language could be developed through a creative engagement with Ireland's cultural and historical resources. Others, pursuing a more independent course and interested in linguistic innovation, were attracted to European literary and intellectual traditions. Kavanagh turned away from much of the subject matter of the Irish Literary Revival and concentrated, instead, on what he knew: life in a small community in County Monaghan.

In a mainly rural society, Kavanagh was virtually the only poet to write with authority and intimacy about Irish rural life. Because of this fact alone, his work was sharply different from that of the Irish Literary Revival and from that of W. B. Yeats. Yeats's knowledge of farming life and of the mentality of country people was limited: he romanticized their affinity with the spirit world and described the countryside in vague and imprecise terms. The predominant style of the Literary Revival did not accommodate the harsher realities of life on a farm and did not register the speech of the farming community. But Kavanagh knew the ways of country people and their habits of thought and speech. Kavanagh's semiautobiographical fiction in *The Green Fool* and *Tarry Flynn*, as well as his poetry, realistically depicted rural life—everyday events, ordinary people, and casual conversations.

His long poem, *The Great Hunger*, a meditation on life and death, is grounded on familiar details of men working the land. It dramatizes their interests and concerns, describes the landscape of field and furrow, and reveals the bond between man and the earth. At the center of the poem's comprehensive social range is the bewildered, complex figure of the farmer, Patrick Maguire, who dreams of love, trusts the peasant wisdom of self-preservation, and comforts himself with the notion that he can find satisfaction in tending the land to the exclusion of a wife and children. The tension between illusion and reality, between man's normal desire for fulfillment and man's fatal ability to deceive himself and to allow himself to be deceived, gives the poem its dimension of tragic comedy. Also, central to the poem's achievement is its metaphorical power by which apparently ordinary images from the natural world become emblematical of Maguire's spiritual condition.

It's Kavanagh's ability to transform reality that gives his lyrics their particular appeal. The light of the poet's imagination—playful, animating and spiritual—brings magic and mystery to his recovery of the edenic world in which he was born and raised. He turns the ordinary into the extraordinary and finds spiritual potential in the natural world.

In his concentration on the local, Kavanagh kept apart from the mythic method. Instinctively and courageously a poet of the local and the ordinary, he did not explore the Irish past nor did he adopt the magisterial Yeatsian persona. His persona, naturally irreverent and independent, speaks the language of ordinary men and keeps his feet on the ground. In this basic choice, Kavanagh affected the course of Irish poetry. His concentration on the local showed the way for younger poets like John Montague and Seamus Heaney, and his comic, anarchic spirit helped to liberate Irish poetry from some of the constraints of Yeats's more formal procedures.

This bibliography assembles the evidence for a life that was fragmentary and chaotic. There was the truculent figure who was always ready to engage in sweeping attacks, whether the victim was some local literary figure, Robert Frost being honored by the National University of Ireland, or one of the American academics assembled at Northwestern University. But behind that truculent presence was the delicate sensibility, the sensitive self, who wrote "Spraying the Potatoes," "A Christmas Childhood," "Bluebells for Love," "The Long Garden," and the deeply moving *The Great Hunger*. This bibliography brings back memories of quarrels fought in the letter columns of Irish newspapers, libel actions, controversies, reviews of his work and, gradually, the more reliable assessments and definitions, in articles and books, by which Kavanagh's true worth has been defined. The book will be a valuable resource for biographers, literary critics, social and cultural historians, and the ordinary reader.

Maurice Harmon
Emeritus Professor of Anglo-Irish Literature
University College Dublin

Preface

In this reference guide, I have gathered together and annotated most of the secondary material in the English language on Patrick Kavanagh during the years 1935–1995, including books, journal articles, reviews, newspaper articles, letters to editors, and radio and TV broadcasts. Acknowledgment of passing references to the author has been kept to a minimum, although some brief allusions have been noted to suggest the scope of the author's influence. Only those broadcasts which are on the BBC or RTE online catalogs are noted. It is possible that titles of certain broadcasts were not online; if so, information concerning them is inaccessible. As is the custom with the G. K. Hall Reference Guide series, there are no reviews of secondary material, unless the review is of particular interest from the viewpoint of the reception of Kavanagh. Every effort has been made to represent the major written responses in the English language to the poet's work since the late 1930s, although some items may inevitably remain fugitive, particularly short articles in newspapers and transient journals, and especially those for which no indexes are available. The listings are arranged chronologically by year, and alphabetically within each year. The brief, descriptive, nonevaluative style of annotation is the house style of the G. K. Hall Reference Guides.

All bibliographies are, to some extent, dependent on previous bibliographies, and this bibliography is no exception. The following pioneering bibliographies have proved indispensable as foundations for this reference guide: Peter Kavanagh, *Garden of the Golden Apples* (New York: Peter Kavanagh Hand Press, 1972); Alan Warner's "Patrick Kavanagh: A Checklist," in Alan Warner, *Clay is the Word* (New York: Humanities Press, 1973); the Selected Bibliography in John Nemo, *Patrick Kavanagh* (Boston: Twayne, 1979); Mary M. Fitzgerald, "Modern Poetry," in Richard J. Finneran, *Recent Research on Anglo-Irish Writers* (New York: MLA, 1983); Peter Kavanagh, "An Annotated Bibliography of Patrick Kavanagh" in Peter Kavanagh (ed.), *Patrick Kavanagh: Man and Poet* (Orono: National Poetry Foundation, 1986). Some materials listed in previous bibliographies, especially materials from Irish newspapers, were unobtainable for various reasons and thus are not listed here. In some cases, the unavailability of items was due to inaccurate citation details in earlier bibliographies. It should be noted that some items listed here, particularly newspaper articles, lack page references, since only the clippings have

Preface

been preserved in the Kavanagh Archive at UCD, dated but without page references, and pasted into large scrapbooks. It should also be noted that there are a number of items in the Kavanagh Archive which are undated and thus regrettably could not be listed here. Items referred to in this bibliography from the following publications are available for consultation at the Kavanagh Archive: *Agricultural Record, Anglo-Celt, Argus, Birmingham Post, Catholic Herald, Catholic Standard, Creation, Daily Telegraph, Dundalk Democrat, Evening Press, Ireland of the Welcomes, Irish Independent, Irish Post, Irish Press, Irish Times, Limerick Leader, National Catholic Reporter, Northern Standard, Profile, Radio Times, RTV Guide, Sunday Independent, Sunday Press, Sunday Times, Sunday Tribune, Times*. For a complete description of the contents of the Kavanagh Archive, however, readers should consult the Archive catalog, Special Collections, UCD library.

The following archives were consulted: the Kavanagh Archive in Special Collections at UCD Library, the Kavanagh files of *The Irish Times*, and the sound archives of RTE (Dublin) and BBC (Northern Ireland). According to RTE regulations, it was impossible to view RTE television programs on the poet, but notice has been given here of their general content. In addition, the following newspaper indexes were consulted: *Christian Science Monitor*, 1954–1992; *Los Angeles Times*, 1972–1992; *New York Times*, 1954–1992; *Times* (including *Sunday Times, Times Education Supplement, Times Higher Education Supplement, Times Literary Supplement*), 1935–1993; *Washington Post*, 1971–1992. The following Digests and Indexes were also consulted: *Book Review Digest*, 1935–1992; *Book Review Index*, 1965–1984; *British Humanities Index*, 1962–1992; *International Index to Periodicals; Social Sciences and Humanities Index; Humanities Index*, 1924–1992. For information on academic theses and dissertations, use was made of the *Dissertation Abstracts International*, the *Annual Bibliography of English Language and Literature* (London), and the annual *Index to Theses with abstracts accepted for higher degrees by the universities of Great Britain and Ireland and the Council for the National Academic Awards* (ASLIB, London), 1950–1994.

Acknowledgments

I wish to thank Richard J. Finneran, Series Editor, for advising me as I worked on this project, and Chris Agee, George Bornstein, Angela Bourke, Jack Gillespie, Maurice Harmon, and Liam and Rosie McAuley for advice, criticism, and materials. I am grateful to Noel Russell and Marshall Hopley of BBC Northern Ireland and Grainne Loughran of the Sound Archive at the Ulster Folk and Transport Museum, who assisted me in finding BBC radio broadcasts on the poet. I also thank Richard Pine, John Condon (Head of Programme Library), Don Kennedy (Sound Librarian), and Peter Doyle at RTE Dublin who helped me track down recordings of relevant RTE broadcasts. Many thanks to Norma Jessop of Special Collections at the Library, University College Dublin, who introduced me to the Patrick Kavanagh Archive, to Liam McAuley of the *Irish Times* who made available to me the newspaper's files on the poet, and to the staff members of Special Collections at Queen's University Library, Belfast; Belfast Central Library; Bangor Carnegie Library; University College Dublin; and the King Library, University of Kentucky. Labhras Draper translated Irish language materials listed here, and Tracy Taylor translated articles in French and German. Michael Durkan, Bernard Loughlin, Antoinette Quinn, and Kevin P. Reilly replied promptly to my letters of inquiry.

Many materials listed here were obtained by the University of Kentucky Inter-Library Loan Department, for which I thank the dedicated and inexhaustible staff, especially Barbara Hale and Janet Layman. I also thank my assiduous research assistant, Gavin Keulks, and the Dean of the College of Arts & Sciences at the University of Kentucky, for paying his salary. A series of summer research fellowships made completion of this bibliography possible, for which I am grateful to the Office of the Vice President for Research and Graduate Studies at the University of Kentucky.

This book is dedicated to my sister, Heather, and to Neil and Marita.

Introduction

Patrick Kavanagh was born in 1904 in the townland of Mucker, near Inniskeen, County Monaghan, the eldest son of a cobbler and small farmer. While his talents and ambitions as a farmer were apparently limited, Patrick Kavanagh demonstrated as a young man a considerable interest in writing poetry, or in "the poeming" as it was called in his home. He published his first poems in 1928, in the *Irish Weekly Independent*, and in 1929 in A. E.'s journal, the *Irish Statesman*. His first collection of poems, *Ploughman and Other Poems*, was published by Macmillan in 1936, and Kavanagh's career as poet and man of letters was launched. He settled in England for a brief period in the late thirties, where he was persuaded by Helen Waddell to write an autobiography. *The Green Fool* was published in 1938 and was warmly received on both sides of the Atlantic. A lawsuit stopped circulation of the book in 1939, because of an allegedly libelous remark about Oliver St. John Gogarty's supposed affair with his maid. However, an American edition appeared that year, with the libelous page removed.

Kavanagh moved to Dublin in 1939, where he began to establish himself as a writer and reviewer for the local press, including the *Irish Times*, the *Standard*, and the *Irish Independent*. His path-breaking poem *The Great Hunger* was published in 1942 and was applauded as a landmark in modern Irish poetry, despite a brief setback with the Irish police force, who found portions of the poem obscene. His next collection, *A Soul for Sale*, was published in 1947, and his semiautobiographical novel, *Tarry Flynn*, appeared the following year. Always drawn to the world of literary journalism, Kavanagh wrote a rather controversial column for *Envoy* in the early fifties. When that journal folded, however, he continued to vent his passionate hatred of many aspects of the Irish cultural scene in the thirteen weekly editions of *Kavanagh's Weekly*.

Kavanagh's career faced a major setback in 1954 when he sued *The Leader* for libel and he lost the suit. Worn down by ill health and exhaustion, he entered the Rialto hospital in Dublin the following year, where he had a cancerous lung removed and he spent much of the next twelve months recuperating from the surgery. Ironically, it was then, when he was at his most beaten, that he entered one of the most creative periods of his career, which resulted in the writing of his Canal Bank sonnets. Today, they remain his most widely admired poems. He returned to journalism in the late 1950s and wrote a weekly column for the *Irish Farmer's Journal* from 1958 to 1963 and a monthly column for the *National Observer* from 1959 to 1960. His fame as a poet continued to grow, however. His most popular book, *Come Dance With Kitty Stobling and Other Poems*, appeared in 1960 and was the Poetry Book Society choice of that year. By November of 1960, it had sold 2000 copies and was into its third printing. In 1962, Kavanagh presented his *Self Portrait* on national television, which was, in the opinion of one critic, "a little frightening, but in its way exciting" (1962.17). He recorded with Claddagh an LP record of selected poetry and prose in 1963 entitled *Almost Everything*. In 1964, *Collected Poems* was published, and critics began to make serious evaluations of the curve of his career as a whole. A dramatic adaptation of *Tarry Flynn* was produced by the Abbey Theatre in 1966. He married Katherine Barry Moloney in 1967. He died in November of that year.

Many critics during the last fifty years seemed to agree that Kavanagh was an "uneven" writer—a recurrent epithet in the corpus of criticism on the poet—although now most readers of his poetry agree that his greatest contributions to modern literature are *The Great Hunger*, *Tarry Flynn*, and the Canal Bank sonnets. The latter, in particular, are repeatedly invoked as the high point of his career in poetry, all the more welcome since the satirical poetry which immediately preceded them is often considered by critics to be his least successful work. *The Green Fool* is mostly admired, and many critics try to protect its reputation from Kavanagh's own damning later rejection of the book as "stage-Irish." *Come Dance with Kitty Stobling* was Kavanagh's most popular collection of poems, although some critics, most notably John Hewitt (1961.3), have objected to the element of "doggerel" in this collection.

Kavanagh is also known, of course, as a writer of controversial essays. Whereas the lack of logical coherence in his essays is frequently regretted—Hubert Butler likened Kavanagh's mind, as demonstrated in the essays, to "a monkey house at feeding time" (1951.1)—this is frequently accepted as part of the anger which fuels the criticism, and he has often been praised for his bracing critique of the Irish Revival, especially his criticism of Yeatsian mythologizing. *Kavanagh's Weekly* tends to be considered a very uneven production and slightly absurd in its antinomian passion, although it has been praised as a welcome challenge to the insularity and hypocrisy of postrevolutionary Ireland (1952.6). Kavanagh's essay on the distinction between provincialism and parochialism is, as one might expect, the most influential piece of prose that he had ever written, to judge by the frequency with which it is cited in relation to all aspects of Irish culture and with regard to a wide range of other Irish writers.

This reference guide contains 1,420 items, the majority of which were published between 1960 and the present. There has been a gradual increase in scholarly and journalistic output on the poet over the years, from 34 items published in the 1930s, to 115 items in the 1940s, including over 45 letters to the *Irish Times*, to 109 in the 1950s, to 247 in the 1960s, to 375 in the 1970s, to 385 in the 1980s, and to 155 items in the first five years of the nineties. Many items listed here are book reviews and accordingly, the reader will find that in the years in which Kavanagh was publishing, a large number of reviews appear. What is striking, however, is the

Introduction

considerable amount of writing which has continued after the author's death, some of which are reviews of posthumous publications or of new editions of older texts, and some of which are newspaper articles on the annual commemorations of the poet, but many of which are scholarly analyses and commentaries. Paul Durcan's prediction in 1978 that the future years will witness many "memorable monographs" on Kavanagh may not yet have come true, but there has been no shortage of scholarly as well as journalistic interest in the poet and his contribution to modern Irish culture (1978.8). According to my estimation, there are five scholarly books on Kavanagh, seven doctoral dissertations (plus eleven dissertations which are partly devoted to the poet), and a handful of M.Phil.s, M.Litt.s, and M.A.s. There are also over forty poems addressed to, concerned with, or inspired by Kavanagh, including nine in the 1960s, twenty-three in the 1970s, seven in the 1980s, and three in the 1990s. There have been, if official records are correct, approximately fourteen radio broadcasts and fifteen television programs on Kavanagh, or which feature him to a significant degree.

To consider the evolution of Kavanagh's reputation, decade by decade, is to witness the slow but sure emergence of one of Ireland's most influential modern poets from the shadowy status of a minor, post-Revival romantic. It all began in the thirties, the high points of which were the publication of *Ploughman and Other Poems* and *The Green Fool*, with some positive reviews of the former and an enormously favorable response to the latter. In 1937, he had a poem translated into Czech, oddly enough (1937.1), and was mentioned (albeit condescendingly), in a work of criticism by Cornelius Weygandt (1937.4). In 1938, the year in which Kavanagh made his radio debut, Harold Nicolson called him the "Robert Burns of Eire," a comparison which has been made repeatedly over the years (1938.6). The first major critical notice of Kavanagh came a little earlier, however, in 1935, when Sean O'Faolain observed that this "farmer" has a mind "aflame with images" (1935.1). Despite this promising beginning to the poet's reception, however, reviews of *Ploughman and Other Poems* published in the following year were mixed. It was objected that the poetry sometimes lapsed into prose and expressed a "modern tendency" which made one reviewer feel sick (1936.2). Yet this same reviewer felt able to admire the "deep spiritual calm" communicated by some poems in the collection. Several reviewers claimed the poems were not modern enough, but derivative and redolent of the Celtic twilight (a view which has been reiterated over the years.) The poetry is "over-schooled" (1937.3); the poet should be encouraged to forget his "archaic musings" (1936.1.)

The Green Fool was published in May 1938, although it was withdrawn from circulation in March 1939, following Gogarty's libel suit against the publisher Michael Joseph, because of Kavanagh's unfortunate remark about Gogarty's relationship to his maid. On March 21, 1939, the courts decided in favor of Gogarty, who was awarded 100 pounds for damages. Although withdrawn in Europe, 750 copies of *The Green Fool*, with the offending passage removed, were published in the U.S.A. by Harper and Brothers. Although Austin Clarke claimed Kavanagh's style was a pleasant relief from the "sordid realism" of much contemporary writing, a large number of reviewers praised the work for its realistic, unsentimental, and "Breughelesque" treatment of rural life, including Nicolson (1938.6), V. S. Pritchett

Introduction

(1938.7), Reid (1938.8), and O'Sheel (1939.12). Favorable comparisons were ventured. A number of reviewers compared Kavanagh to Robbie Burns, and two readers (or was it one reader in two separate reviews?) compared him to the Kentucky author Jesse Stuart (1939.6, 1939.16). V. S. Pritchett compared him to John Clare and Edward Thomas, while F. P. detected a similarity to A. E. Housman, although Kavanagh "was gayer than the Shropshire lad ever dreamed of being" (1939.13). The words "racy," "vivid," and "vivacious" cropped up repeatedly in reviews by Clarke (1938.1), Fallon (1938.2), and Reid (1938.8.) Mary Manning found the book "gay as the song of the cuckoo in spring" (1939.7). Negative notes were sounded by two American reviewers, however, who found Kavanagh's characters unsympathetic, un-Catholic, or un-Christian (1939.11, 1939.17). Sheehy-Skeffington complained that the book was "at times cynical, ultra-modern" (1938.9), while Sylvester, on the other hand, argued that it was stage-Irish, cute and quaint (1939.17). How these two views could be reconciled is questionable, although the latter viewpoint was, of course, echoed by Kavanagh himself in his *Self Portrait*, in 1964, in which he dismissed *The Green Fool* as insincere and Revivalist.

The forties, which were perhaps Kavanagh's most important decade, artistically, began with a flurry of controversial publicity surrounding his offhand rebuke of Maurice Walsh, the Ulster writer whose popular novel *The Hill is Mine* Kavanagh dismissed as redolent of the "Boy Scout mentality." Such offhand rebukes were to make Kavanagh many enemies and much renown in years to come. The extraordinary sequence of letters which the *Irish Times* published in the summer of 1940 makes interesting reading and adumbrates the mixture of distaste, outrage, admiration, and amusement which Kavanagh provoked among Dublin readers not only that summer but in many summers subsequently. In 1941, for example, a number of readers of the *Irish Times* took exception to his remarks about the Royal Hibernian Academy, producing yet another small stream of letters from irate critics, both professional and amateur. The 1942 issue of *Horizon*, which carried an excerpt from *The Great Hunger*, was seized by the police, censored because of alleged obscenity, and Kavanagh's poem, upon which his fame chiefly rests, achieved a level of visibility among civic guards which he later regretted. The author of *The Great Hunger* became a cause célèbre, not for the last time. Responses to the poem were mixed. The reviewer for the *Spectator*, in 1942, described the poem as "no glib narrative" (1942.6), a judgment with which few would disagree. For Robert Greacen, *The Great Hunger* expressed the voice of angry defiance against the draconian censorship laws in Southern Ireland; it voiced the "frustration complex" of Irish writers hampered by the insularity and intellectual provincialism born of Irish neutrality during the war (1942.2.). Despite the power of the poem, however, which owed much to the "Breughelesque realism" noted by Geoffrey Taylor (1942.7), the poem had technical problems, a looseness of expression, and an "occasionally unhappy" use of rhyme (Taylor); Indeed, the overall impression for one reviewer was that *The Great Hunger* was "like a good rough draft rather than a finished poem" (1942.5.) Even Greacen, who praised its defiant expressiveness, found it dull and trite in places. A number of these observations, not least the allegations of technical unevenness, have been heard repeatedly during

Introduction

the fifty years since publication, although it can still be said with confidence that this poem established Kavanagh as one of the most powerful writers and cultural critics of his generation. The centrality of the poem in Kavanagh's opus may be judged by the fact that what has been said about the poem has been said of the poet himself: it is uneven, yet powerful, and deeply influential.

The Great Hunger appeared again in *A Soul for Sale* (1947), which met with a largely positive reception. Although Salomon found the book aetherial enough to find in it "the Celtic spirit" (1947.12), most reviewers found the poetry tougher, stylistically, than Kavanagh's first collection, and most emphatically more earthy than what Padraic Colum called the "folk poetry" of Yeats and Hyde (1947.1): It was "austere" (1947.14), "wiry" (1947.2), "bitter" (1947.6), "harsh" (1947.5), and "hard and disillusioned" (1947.1.) However, at least one reader, Roibeard O'Farrachain, found the poetry "vague and clumsy," and he reiterated the accusation that *The Great Hunger* was "loose in texture," although, mostly, he found the poetry in this collection more satisfying formally than Kavanagh's earlier work (1947.9). The accusation of looseness found an echo in an American reviewer's complaint that the poetry is "shapeless" (1948.2.). Generally, however, the toughness of Kavanagh's voice was praised by reviewers, one of whom announced that the poet was "his own man" and that *A Soul for Sale* was the most important collection of Irish poetry since the death of Yeats (1947.14). David Marcus claimed *The Great Hunger* was a landmark in Irish poetry (1948.3.)

Parts of *Tarry Flynn* appeared in serial form in *The Bell* in 1947, and it was published as a novel in London by the Pilot Press in October 1948 and in the U.S.A. the following year by Devin-Adair. It was initially banned in Ireland for a brief time, which led to several outbursts of protest and disbelief among reviewers (1949.3, 1949.13, 1950.6), but once the publicity surrounding the censorship settled, it received a number of warm reviews. It was considered lifelike (1948.7), mystical (1949.1), vivid and realistic (1949.4). We are told J. M. Synge would have loved the book (1950.12) and that Tarry Flynn is as neurotic as Kafka and J. Alfred Prufrock (1950.6). On the other hand, the reviewer for the *New Yorker*, who was less enthusiastic about the novel, speculated that it had been written in great haste, "tossed off in a very bright moment" (1949.2), while Frances Hunter found the novel "meandering and aimless" (1949.5). It was highly subjective and therefore not really a novel at all (1949.6). It was Gaelic-centered, imitative, and dull (1949.11).

The 1950s was a decade of great publicity for the poet—not all of it good. In 1954, there was the disastrous libel trial, which received enormous publicity, and the appeal the following year. In 1955, there was illness, surgery, and slow recovery. During his recuperation, Kavanagh lounged on the banks of the Grand Canal, near Baggot Street Bridge, and having had a lung removed, began to feel a change of heart. He called this his "hegira," his deliverance. He began not to care about the world of Dublin letters anymore, he ceased to worry about publishers' and editors' deadlines, and he developed a philosophy of "not-caring," which was to form the basis of the Canal Bank sonnets. Kavanagh's Diary in *Envoy* provided him with the kind of platform from which he could launch the assaults upon other writers and critics for which, since his dismissal of Maurice Walsh in 1940, he had become notorious. When *Envoy* ceased publication, Kavanagh continued to publish contro-

Introduction

versial articles for *Kavanagh's Weekly*, much of which he wrote himself, along with his brother, Peter, who subsidized the enterprise. The copy published in *Kavanagh's Weekly* was felt to be at worst opinionated and abusive, and at best refreshingly uncompromising in its attacks upon what the Kavanaghs regarded as the mediocrity prevalent in Irish life at the time. Reviewers of the paper seemed to be mostly amused by it, and the critic for *The Guardian* came to see it as "the brightest bit of Irish journalism to come out of Ireland for a long time" (1952.6). The reviewer for the *Nationalist and Leinster Times* compared its impact on Dublin to that of "a blast from a shot gun" (1952.9). This tended to be attributed to the temperament of Patrick himself. The mid-1950s were surely Kavanagh's darkest years, although they were also his most famous years, owing to publicity surrounding the libel action. Kavanagh often referred to 1955 as the turning point of his career, if not of his life. In his personal mythology, it was the year of his deliverance from darkness, a year of revelation burning brightly in the center of the decade.

In the sixties, what we might call the Kavanagh industry begins to get into full swing. The decade saw the publication of over fifteen substantial critical articles or review essays on the poet by John Jordan (1960.12), John Montague (1960.20 and 1965.14), Basil Payne (1960.23), John Hewitt (1961.3), Alan Warner (1964.29, 1968.53, and 1969.17), Douglas Sealy (1965.21), John Rees Moore (1966.13), Ulick O'Connor (1966.14), Grattan Freyer (1968.13), Sean McMahon (1968.30), Paul Potts (1968.36), David Wright (1968.54), William Fahey (1969.1), and Tom McLaughlin (1969.12). In addition, Kavanagh's ongoing work was widely reviewed, including *Come Dance with Kitty Stobling and Other Poems* (1960), *Collected Poems* (1964), the production of *Tarry Flynn* at the Abbey Theatre (1966), and *Collected Pruse* (1967). The decade began with the publication of *Come Dance with Kitty Stobling*, and most of the reviews were positive, although several critics, including Alvarez (1960.2), Jordan (1960.12), and Kinsella (1960.15) remarked on Kavanagh's "erratic" talent and most readers disliked Kavanagh's satires, which were considered shallow, self-pitiful, and technically loose. The Canal Bank sonnets were singled out for praise, and several reviewers praised the honesty of Kavanagh's voice and his avoidance of cliché (1960.11), although Ian Sowton found the arguments of the poems "banal" (1961.7). The poet's growing popularity at home, however, may be judged by Alvarez's reference to Kavanagh's "cult status" in Ireland. And ironically, despite Kavanagh's often-voiced skepticism about Irishness in literature, a critic as reliable as Donald Hall found him a very "Celtic" poet (1960.11). A number of reviewers were particularly harsh, however, especially Hayden Carruth (1962.1) and Richard Kell (1960.14), while John Hewitt's essay "The Cobbler's Song" remains the most serious attack on Kavanagh's technical sloppiness to date (1961.3). Seamus Heaney's review essay on Kavanagh in *Hibernia* (1963.1) offers moderate praise for the poet, although his statement that there is no "major poet" alive in contemporary Ireland elicited an angry and vociferous response by the Kavanagh supporters James Liddy and Richard Weber on the letters page of *Hibernia*, providing dramatic evidence of the poet's popularity, if not indeed his "cult status" on the home turf (1963.3.)

The year 1964 was important for Kavanagh's reputation, since it witnessed the publication of the *Collected Poems*, which was accompanied by much retro-

Introduction

spective assessment of the poet's achievement by critics like Alvarez (1964.1), Fallon (1964.2), Jordan (1964.11), O'Connor (1964.17), Payne (1964.22), Ricks (1964.24), and Thwaite (1964.27). The poet was interviewed by Mairin O'Farrell in *Hibernia* (1964.18) and by Peter Duvall-Smith on BBC radio (1964.26). While words like "inconsistent" (Thwaite) and "hit-and-miss" (Ricks) were used repeatedly by critics of the collection, there was a general consensus that *Collected Poems* represented a considerable achievement. A number of critics regarded Kavanagh's early writing as "derivative" (Fallon) and "sentimental" (1964.3), although *The Great Hunger* was widely admired. Predictably, however, the Canal Bank sonnets were preferred over the later poems of the late 1950s and early 1960s, especially the satirical poems, which were dismissed as "near-doggerel" by the anonymous critic in the *Times Literary Supplement*. A number of writers praised Kavanagh's uncompromising integrity. He is "his own man" (1964.23). He is "completely himself" (1964.13.) Presumably it was this sort of integrity which Andrew Oldham, the manager of the Rolling Stones, had in mind when he said he wished Patrick Kavanagh had been his father (1965.1).

Kavanagh's death in 1967 was met with a large number of obituaries and commemorations. His work began to appear in Irish high-school examinations (1967.62). A memorial Canal Bank seat was erected in 1968, near to where he had enjoyed his recuperation after the lung operation in the mid-1950s (1968.1). A special issue of *Dublin Magazine* appeared (1968.3) as well as several full-scale articles elsewhere, and *Lapped Furrows* was published in 1969, the first of a number of publications by Peter Kavanagh on his Hand Press (1969.6).

During the seventies, criticism of Kavanagh boomed, producing no fewer than three books on the poet, by Warner (1973.46), O'Brien (1975.25), and Nemo (1979.35), Ph.D. dissertations by Nemo (1971.24), Druska (1974.3), and Grever (1973.10), and Bonner's TCD M.Litt. thesis (1975.3). Nemo's UCD dissertation formed the basis of his 1979 book. The work of Druska, Grever, and Bonner was never published, as far as I know, which is a pity. (Grever's dissertation in particular is a useful resource.) In 1970, Brendan Kennelly published an article on Kavanagh in *Ariel* (1970.12), which has had quite a long life, having been reprinted twice (1973.22 and 1994.7). A number of substantial articles also appeared (there were more than a dozen), including those by Jordan (1971.12), Kiely (1971.17), Nemo (1974.26), Allen (1975.1), Brown (1975.5), Casey (1976.2), Sheerin (1977.40), Foster (1979.11), Frazier (1979.13), Heaney (1979.16), and Thornton (1979.49). The myth of Kavanagh as the messianic wild man of peasant letters was kept alive during the 1970s by a number of RTE TV programs on the life of the poet, visual complements to John Ryan's and Anthony Cronin's colorful memoirs of bohemian Dublin and Kavanagh in the fifties, *Remembering How We Stood* (1975.30) and *Dead as Doornails* (1976.3). A special issue of the *Journal of Irish Literature*, guest edited by John Nemo, was published (1977.29). The publication of Peter Kavanagh's annotated bibliography, *Garden of the Golden Apples*, brought to readers' attention for the first time the volume of primary and secondary materials on Kavanagh (1972.19). Donal Foley was not far off the mark when he wrote in 1977 in the *Irish Times* that the Kavanagh industry has "a rosy future" (1977.10).

Introduction

During the eighties only one Ph.D. dissertation on Kavanagh was completed, that is, David O'Reilly's study of *Kavanagh's Weekly* (1983.22), although several dissertations were partly devoted to his writing, including Fleischmann (1983.12), Keane (1984.13), and Roberts-Burke's splendid UCLA dissertation (1987.40), which I hope will eventually be published in whole or in part. In addition, a number of theses on Kavanagh completed for M.A. and M.Phil. degrees appeared in the early years of the decade, including McMahon (1981.15), Collins (1983.5), McLaughlin (1983.19), Morrow (1983.20), Warren (1983.26), and Werne (1985.43). The fact that four of these were completed in Northern Ireland complicates the claim, which it is otherwise tempting to make, that most writing on Kavanagh is done in the Irish Republic and in the United States. Michael O'Loughlin's short book *After Kavanagh* appeared mid-decade (1985.31), and in the following year, Peter Kavanagh's capacious anthology of essays *Patrick Kavanagh: Man and Poet* brought together a wide range of previously published work on the poet which had been lying dormant and uncollected in the pages of newspapers and journals (1986.28). The significance of Kavanagh for modern Irish literary history as a counter-Revival poet forms the basis of Kenner's (1983.16), Garratt's (1986.19), and Johnston's (1985.19) discussions of the poet. More than forty substantial scholarly articles appeared during the eighties, which effectively established Kavanagh's reputation as the most influential Irish poet after Yeats, despite a rather uneven oeuvre. These included pieces by Alexander (1980.1), Frazier (1980.6), Heaney (1980.7), Karrer (1980.10), Kiberd (1980.12), Meir (1980.19), Montague (1980.20), Sheerin (1980.35), Garratt (1981.7), Grennan (1981.8), Reilly (1981.22), Baird (1982.1), Fodaski-Black (1982.3), Gunton (1982.5), Veldhuis (1982.28), Cantalupo (1983.3), Klejs (1983.17), Nemo (1983.21), Welch (1983.27), Dalsimer (1984.4), Heaney (1984.8), O'Connor (1984.16—a reprint of 1980.23), Waters (1984.19), Dilworth (1985.8), Duffy (1985.11), Grever (1985.14), Murphy (1985.27), Kiberd (1986.36), Fleischmann (1987.9), Heaney (1987.11), Brown (1988.8—a reprint of 1979.1 and 1980.3), Houston (1988.28), and Waters (1988.55). Much of the writing on Kavanagh in the 1980s and 1990s concerns the poet's enormous influence on contemporary literary culture. This is the main focus of articles by Bono (1989.3), Bradley (1989.4), Dawe (1989.11), Grennan (1989.17), Kiberd (1989.26), and Longley (1989.27). If Denis O'Driscoll was exaggerating a little when he wrote that "it is mandatory in any discussion of Irish poetry to quote Patrick Kavanagh as frequently as possible" (1989.33), the claim was nonetheless a very revealing half-truth about the enduring power of the Kavanagh aesthetic. In December 1986, accompanied by a fanfare of publicity, Peter Kavanagh sold the papers which became the Kavanagh Archive to UCD, after a long fund-raising campaign orchestrated by Augustine Martin and others (1986.58). The materials are now available for consultation by scholars, and a selection of documents was exhibited at the UCD library in 1988, described in a catalog compiled by Aoife Leonard, who has also completed the descriptive list of the holdings of the archive (1988.36-37). The twentieth anniversary of Kavanagh's death in 1987 was celebrated by a series of radio and television programs on RTE (1987.1, 1987.7, 1987.18, 1987.19, 1987.20, 1987.27). Interest in *The Great Hunger* was renewed in 1983, when Tom MacIntyre's dramatic adaptation of the

Introduction

poem was staged at the Peacock Theatre. The script was published, with explanatory and critical materials, five years later by Lilliput Press (1988.39), which coincided with Abbey productions of the play in Moscow and New York (1988.14, 1988.24, 1988.53).

Kavanagh studies have been sporadic during the early nineties, although in 1991, Antoinette Quinn, who is herself a native of Inniskeen, published the most comprehensive and incisive treatment of Kavanagh's work to date: *Patrick Kavanagh: Born-Again Romantic* (published in the U.S.A. by Syracuse University Press as *Patrick Kavanagh: A Critical Study* (1991.29–30). This is what Edna Longley called "the authoritative critical study for which lovers of Kavanagh have been waiting" (1992.21) and is likely to remain the definitive study for many years to come. There is a notable paucity of books on Kavanagh, despite the welter of critical and journalistic pieces in print, although we may find that more books will be written when the myth of his minor status has dissolved. It is difficult to imagine Kavanagh can remain "minor" when such large claims have been made for his influence. The paradox itself deserves further study.

There have been, in recent years, a number of substantial articles on the poet, most notably those by Jaquin, on *Tarry Flynn* (1990.18), Muri, on *The Great Hunger* (1990.23), O'Grady, also on *The Great Hunger* (1990.26), Popowich, on the sense of space in both *The Great Hunger* and *Tarry Flynn* (1991.27), Peacock, on Kavanagh and MacNeice (1992.32), and Moorman, who compares Kavanagh to both Beckett and Heaney (1993.15). Desmond O'Grady's two essays in *Poetry Ireland Review* (1992.29–30) constitute an intriguing memoir of the poet in later years. Kavanagh is also recalled in of Robert Greacen's memoir (1991.12) and in autobiographies by Benedict Kiely (1991.19) and Karl Miller (1993.14). Several earlier essays on the poet have been republished, including John Wilson Foster's 1979 essay (1991.11) and Brendan Kennelly's essay of 1970 (1994.7). A small number of interesting academic theses have appeared, including John Redmond's UCD M.A. thesis (1990.31) and Ph.D. dissertations by Eamonn Hughes (1990.17), Una Agnew (1991.1), Michael Howlett (1991.15) (both Agnew and Howlett examine Kavanagh's religious sensibility), and Rita Barnes (1994.1). Interestingly, these works have generally come out of Ireland or England, whereas the earliest wave of academic dissertations on the poet, in the 1970s and 1980s, tended to come from American graduate schools. There have also, of course, been a large number of passing references to the poet and his influence on modern and contemporary Irish poetry. Most of these allusions concern either Kavanagh's influence on Irish poetry in general (e.g., Fallon and Mahon [1990.15], Hirsch [1991.14], Boran [1992.9], and Grennan [1992.17]) or his influence on particular authors. It must be said that the author who is most commonly associated with Kavanagh's influence is Seamus Heaney, who has himself been the focus of an enormous and dynamic critical energy during the last two decades. Most books on Heaney include the statutory tribute to Heaney's precursors (e.g., Burris [1990.4] and Hart [1992.18]), but other examples of commentary on Kavanagh's influence on Heaney can be found, for example, in Ormsby (1990.27), Vance (1990.32), McDonald (1991.21), and Allen (1992.1).

It is not only critics who have argued for the enduring power of Kavanagh's example. Many poets have, themselves, claimed him as a liberating precursor.

Introduction

Seamus Heaney's articles, which are among the most distinguished essays in the entire corpus of Kavanagh criticism, make such a testament. So also do occasional pieces by Boland (1967.2, 1967.22, 1970.3, 1971.3, 1981.1), Durcan (1988.18)—see also his foreword to *Lough Derg* (1978.8)—Egan (1986.15), Liddy (1969.9 and 1971.19), Longley (1968.25), Mahon (1968.26), and Montague, who is the source of the claim that Kavanagh "liberated us into ignorance" (1965.14.) It is clear that for these writers Kavanagh's poetry represents an enabling counterexample to the delphic voice of Yeats. Quite a large number of poems have also been written about Kavanagh over the years, or in tribute to him, including those by Cronin (1988.15), Grennan (1986.24), O'Tuarisc (1981.19), Egan (1978.9), Longley (1977.24), Foley (1969.2), Kennelly (1968.23-24), Mahon (1968.27), McGurk (1968.28 and 1969.11), and O'Grady (1968.34)—and more recently there have been poems by Fainlight (1990.14), Durcan (1987.8 and 1991.10), and Foley (1994.4). It is also worth mentioning Eugene Platt's *Patrick Kavanagh Anthology*, a selection of poems of tribute (of varying quality, it must be said) by over twenty writers (1973.36). There are no poems of direct tribute by John Montague or Seamus Heaney, although there is a story that Heaney once claimed that his first book, *Death of a Naturalist* (1966), is a tribute to his precursor, and Kavanagh does appear, as a ghost, in *Station Island* (1984.9).

There has been, in the years since the poet's death, an effort to commemorate his memory in his native town. Shortly after his death, a group of friends and neighbors in Inniskeen founded the Kavanagh Society, which arranged an annual graveside commemoration of the poet, named a local football tournament after him (1970.8) and, began an annual poetry competition (1970.1). Out of this local activity emerged the desire for a "Kavanagh summer school" (1975.31), which did not come to pass, although, in 1978, the Kavanagh Society arranged a "Kavanagh week," from September 3 to September 10, at which a number of scholars and writers, including Seamus Heaney, Brendan Kennelly, John Ryan, and Alan Warner paid tribute to the poet (1978.25). By 1984, the "Yearly,"—part conference, part festival—began to be considered a regular social and cultural fixture, and it has received regular media attention for a decade (1984.12, 1986.27, 1987.39, 1988.43, 1989.22). It seems to have retained its vitality and energy into the nineties (see 1990.5, 1990.20, 1990.33-34, 1991.17, 1991.25).

There have been other kinds of commemoration, of course, ranging from the grand to the ridiculous: a memorial Canal Bank seat was unveiled in March 1968 (1968.1). By 1970, there were plans for a modest Kavanagh museum in Inniskeen (1970.23), which was actually created and later described by Michael Hand (1973.12). By 1971, there was a "Kavanagh Room" in a Dundalk hotel (1971.18) and a portrait in the Great Southern Hotel, Galway (1971.27). There have been plaques in Inniskeen (1972.6) and Dublin (1985.5, 1985.13, 1990.16 and 1990.24). There was even a plaque outside a public house in London, marking the spot where the poet would relieve himself, although it was soon removed by Peter Kavanagh and his sister (1973.6, and 1973.45). The owner of a Dublin fast-food restaurant named his establishment "The Great Hunger," a dubious and tasteless tribute to the memory of Patrick Maguire (let alone an insult to the famine victims of the 1840s) (1977.42). The poet's face was sandblasted on the wall of McNello's Pub,

Introduction

Inniskeen, and in 1991 a bronze statue of the poet on a seat by the Grand Canal was unveiled (1991.2), which has a certain dignity and appropriateness, despite the fact it was the subject of a satirical poem by Michael Foley (1994.4).

Kavanagh once remarked that he had not been much considered by English critics. While it may be objected that he had friends and admirers among the English literati, including Cyril Connolly, who edited *Horizon*, John Betjeman, and Harold Nicolson, it remains true that most of the writing, both scholarly and journalistic, has been produced in Ireland, where he is valued both as the authentic voice of the counter-Revival and as a bold and original poetic precursor, and in the United States, where much, but by no means all, of the scholarly writing has originated. In general, British critics have been more impressed by Yeats than by Kavanagh, and Donald Davie may be representative of a silent majority when he prefers Clarke to Kavanagh (1989.10). There are, of course, political reasons why the counter-revival might have enjoyed more popularity in Ireland than in England, but another reason for the large volume of writing on Kavanagh at home may be that much of it has not exclusively been a matter of literary criticism but has been mere gossip about the doings of the bohemian man of letters. Indeed, it is precisely this tendency to confuse evaluation of the literature with gossip about the man which has been lamented by the shrewder critics, and some of the best writing on this author has been very conscious of the need to separate judgment of the writing from opinion about the poet's colorful personal reputation.

Where will Kavanagh studies go from here? Much of the work on Kavanagh has been biographical and historical in orientation, and with the possibility of a full-scale biography appearing some day, we might expect further exploration in that vein. Antoinette Quinn's book offered a new trenchancy in close reading of the poet and novelist, and it is hoped that future critics will build upon her example. There is much work to be done on the subject of Kavanagh's manuscripts and on the status of the text of his *Collected Poems*. Indeed, Kavanagh studies offers a gold mine for editorial theorists, and perhaps there will, someday, be a variorum edition of the poems. The Kavanagh Archive at UCD will undoubtedly be a rich source of information for scholars in the coming years. There is also work to be done on the reception of Kavanagh and what the body of criticism and response adumbrated in this reference guide has to tell us about our cultural paradigms and our aesthetic expectations over the last fifty years.

Primary Materials: Major Publications

Ploughman and Other Poems. London: Macmillan, 1936.

The Green Fool. London: Michael Joseph, 1938.

"The Old Peasant." (First part of *The Great Hunger*.) In *Horizon*, January 1942.

The Great Hunger, Dublin: Cuala Hand Press, 1942.

A Soul for Sale. London: Macmillan, 1947.

Tarry Flynn. London: Pilot Press, 1948.

Kavanagh's Weekly. Dublin, (Weekly for 13 issues from 12 April to 15 July), 1952.

Recent Poems. New York: Peter Kavanagh Hand Press, 1958.

Come Dance with Kitty Stobling and Other Poems. London: Longmans, Green and Co., 1960.

"Almost Everything" (LP). Dublin: Claddagh Records, 1963.

Collected Poems. London: MacGibbon and Kee, 1964.

———. New York: Devin Adair, 1964.

Self Portrait. Dublin: Dolmen, 1964.

Collected Pruse. London: MacGibbon and Kee, 1967.

Lapped Furrows: Correspondence, 1933–67, Between Patrick and Peter Kavanagh. With Other Documents. Edited by Peter Kavanagh. New York: Kavanagh Hand Press, 1969.

November Haggard: Uncollected Prose and Verse of Patrick Kavanagh. Selected, arranged and edited by Peter Kavanagh. Illustrated. New York: Kavanagh Hand Press, 1971.

The Complete Poems of Patrick Kavanagh. Collected, arranged and edited by Peter Kavanagh. New York: Kavanagh Hand Press, 1972.

Primary Materials

By Night Unstarred. An Autobiographical Novel by Patrick Kavanagh. Edited by Peter Kavanagh. New York and Dublin:Kavanagh Hand Press and Goldsmith Press, 1977.

Lough Derg. Dublin: Goldsmith, Martin Brian & O'Keeffe, 1978.

List of Abbreviations

Publications

AntigR	Antigonish Review
CJIS	Canadian Journal of Irish Studies
ClQ	Colby Quarterly
DAI	Dissertation Abstracts International
DQ	Denver Quarterly
DQR	Dutch Quarterly Review
Eire	Eire-Ireland
EI	Études Irlandaises
ELWIU	Essays in Literature (Macomb, Ill.)
G	Georgia Review
HudR	Hudson Review
IUR	Irish University Review
JIL	Journal of Irish Literature
JJQ	James Joyce Quarterly
KR	Kenyon Review
MR	Massachusetts Review
PLL	Papers on Language and Literature
PNR	PN Review
PoetryR	Poetry Review
RES	Review of English Studies
SNNTS	Studies in the Novel (Denton, Tex.)

List of Abbreviations

SoR	Southern Review
SR	Sewanee Review
TLS	Times Literary Supplement
VQR	Virginia Quarterly Review

Institutions

BBC	British Broadcasting Corporation
QUB	Queen's University, Belfast
RTE	Radio Telefis Eireann
TCD	Trinity College Dublin
UCD	University College Dublin

Please note that an asterisk before an item number indicates that, for some reason, I have not been able to obtain the item in question, although there is strong evidence suggesting the item exists.

Patrick Kavanagh

a reference guide

Writings about Patrick Kavanagh

1935

1 O'FAOLAIN, SEAN. "Irish Poetry Since the War." *London Mercury* (April):545–552.
    Kavanagh is a farmer whose mind is "aflame with images." Quotes from "The Sower" with approval.

1936

1 MACDONAGH, DONAGH. "New Verse and Old." *Ireland Today* 1, no. 6:85–86.
    Review of *Ploughman and Other Poems*. Claims Kavanagh's poetry is marred by "prettiness and lack of force." Suggests that Kavanagh should read the later Yeats "and leave his archaic musings."

2 W., M. "Two New Irish Poets. Mr. Kavanagh's Work." *Irish Independent* (6 October):4.
    Review of several books, including *Ploughman and Other Poems*. Praises Kavanagh's lyrical skill, but condemns his "modern tendency," which leaves the reader with "a sense of blasphemy and nausea." Some of his poems, however, project "a deep spiritual calm."

1937

1 BABLER, O. F., ed. *Pisen o Neme Tvari. Anthologie basni o zviratech (Songs of a Dumb Face. Anthology of poems about animals)*. Hlasy SV.42, Svaty Kopecek. Olomonc.
    Czech anthology of poems, including Kavanagh's "The Goat of Slieve Donard" translated into Czech.

1938

2 MACM., F. "Two Poets." *Irish Press* (6 October):6.

Review of *Ploughman and Other Poems*, which is praised for its economical imagery and "wiry, sensitive" style, although it sometimes lapses into "chopped prose." Kavanagh is often bookish and derivative: "Echoes of the factitious Celtic mysticism of nature comes trailing like rags of gaudy gauze."

3 T., P. C. *Irish Book Lover* (London), (March/April):45.

Contains review of *Ploughman and Other Poems*. Finds Kavanagh's poetry disappointing, prosaic and "over-schooled." Quotes with disapproval "To a Late Poplar," which is in danger of lapsing into "flatfooted prose."

4 WEYGANDT, CORNELIUS. *The Time of Yeats: English Poetry of To-Day Against an American Background.* New York: D. Appleton-Century Co., Inc., pp. 441–442.

Kavanagh writes "with absolute simplicity of the little things of his life."

1938

1 CLARKE, AUSTIN. "Over the Hills and Far Away. An Irish Childhood." *Observer* (London), (26 June):4.

Review of *The Green Fool*, an "unusual autobiography." The world in Kavanagh's book is "scarcely touched by the shadow of the twentieth century." Kavanagh's writing differs from the "grim, sordid realism" of more recent Irish authors, yet he combines poetry with realism in his work. Praises the "vivacious characters and stories" in the book, and its meditative center. *The Green Fool* takes you "over the hills and far away."

2 FALLON, PADRAIC. "A Poet's Apprenticeship—Symbols of a Countryside." *Irish Times* (20 August):7.

Review of *The Green Fool*. The characters in *The Green Fool* "are not merely people, but symbols of a countryside." His book might be taken for "what somebody has called 'The Book of the People.'" His childhood is portrayed with delicacy, humor, lyricism and without sentimentality. Praises Kavanagh's "knowledge of his fellows," and claims that "what emerges from the book is not Mr. Kavanagh so much as his neighbourhood. He has made a sort of spirit-map of Mucker." He "is a living indictment of his time, when a poet is not at home in his own country."

3 ——. Review of *The Green Fool*. *Dublin Magazine* 13 (October):68–69.

Claims the book represents vividly "the sights and sounds of the Monaghan farmlands," although it is not "fine literature" from a "literary"

1938

point of view. Claims Kavanagh has objectivity and distance from his surroundings. Discusses the pagan beliefs of the Irish peasantry. Claims Kavanagh "rules out religion as a topic," although in his poems he seems to worship the god Pan.

4 "Irish Poet." *Times Literary Supplement* (22 October):680.
    Review of *The Green Fool*. Praises the autobiography as "highly original." Admires Kavanagh's depiction of the roving beggars of the countryside: Paddy the Bread, Barney the Bottle, and Mary Ann the Plantain. Claims he writes "with humour and vivacity" of the world of rural labor.

5 KING, RICHARD. "Life in Rural Ireland." *Tatler* (22 June):536.
    Review of *The Green Fool*, which has "real beauty" and "real human interest."

6 NICOLSON, HAROLD. "Young Poet Who May Become the Irish Robert Burns." *Daily Telegraph and Morning Post* (27 May):22.
    Review of *The Green Fool*. Claims Kavanagh may become "the Robert Burns of Eire." The book is a good study of the literary mind ("his fellows thought him a trifle mad"); an unromantic depiction of rural Ireland ("more satisfying than the Celtic crooning with which we have been nauseated"); and it contains good family portraits. Praises the "hidden loveliness" of the language.

7 PRITCHETT, V. S. "A Young Man Looks at Present-Day Europe—A London Letter." *Christian Science Monitor*. (Weekly Magazine section), (3 August):11.
    Review of several books, including *The Green Fool*. Compares Kavanagh to John Clare and Edward Thomas. Commends the work because it avoids the conventional condescending view of peasant life. Claims Kavanagh has the potential to be "one of the rustic masters."

8 REID, FORREST. "An Irish Peasant." *Guardian* (Manchester), (21 June):7.
    Review of *The Green Fool*. Praises the novel's realism and objectivity, with its "racy and picturesque" dialogue. Claims Kavanagh was a "tough youth," because he once boiled the eggs of a wood pigeon, and then returned them to their nest.

9 SHEEHY-SKEFFINGTON, HANNAH. "The Four-Leafed Shamrock." *Irish Press* Christmas number. UCD Archive.
    Review of *The Green Fool*, which is "at times cynical, ultra-modern." Concludes the protagonist is "not such a fool, after all."

1939

10 "Undiscovered Ulster." *Radio Times* (20 October). UCD Archive.
Announces Kavanagh's radio debut in an account of his "discoveries" in county Armagh.

1939

1 "Biography." *Booklist* 35, no. 15 (March):229.
Briefly describes several books, including *The Green Fool*.

2 "Dr. Gogarty's Libel Action." *Irish Times* (21 March):8.
Describes Gogarty's libel action against Michael Joseph Ltd. and William Brendon and Son, publisher and printer of *The Green Fool*, published in May, 1938. At the King's Bench Division, London, G. D. Roberts, K.C. was counsel for Gogarty. G. O. Slade acted for the defense. Describes the counsel's statement, Gogarty's evidence, and Slade's cross-examination of Gogarty. Justice MacNaughten decided against Slade.

3 "Dr. Gogarty's libel action. Judge's Award of 100 pounds." *Irish Times* (22 March):1.
Announces the conclusion of hearing and judgment.

4 "Dr. Gogarty's Libel Action." *Irish Times* (22 March):10.
Describes the conclusion of the Gogarty hearing. The plaintiff was awarded 100 pounds in damages. Describes the speech for the defense and the judge's summing up. Justice MacNaughten claimed that the offending passage in *The Green Fool* "imputed that Dr. Gogarty was a loose man who had a paramour, the publication was a gross libel, and Dr. Gogarty was entitled to bring the action out of respect for himself and his wife, and as a duty to the medical profession."

5 KERR, THERESA A. "Kavanagh of Ulster." *New York Times Book Review* (30 April):27.
Brief letter responding to Horace Reynolds' review (1939.16) and to O'Loughlen (1939.10), correcting the erroneous claim that Kavanagh lived in Louth.

6 "Late Plums." *Time* (27 February):80.
Brief review of two books, including *The Green Fool*: "The autobiography of a sort of Irish Jesse Stuart."

7 MANNING, MARY. "Poet and Peasant: Patrick Kavanagh, Known as a Poet, Turns Out a First-Rate Life Story." *Boston Evening Transcript* part four (4 March):2.

1939

Review of *The Green Fool*, which is "gay as the song of the cuckoo in spring." Claims Kavanagh was one of A. E.'s "discoveries," although Kavanagh has remained shy and reclusive. Criticizes Ireland's education system which deprived Kavanagh the chance of higher education.

8   NEEDHAM, WILBUR. "Young Irish Poet Writes Vividly of Lusty Rebel Life." *Los Angeles Times* part 3 (19 March):6.
    Review of *The Green Fool*. Claims that English reviewers have praised this novel, although the English tend to romanticize Irish life and writing. Claims the English readers have failed to realize that the novel is "consciously" accusing the English of having oppressed the Irish.

9   "New Books: A Reader's List." *New Republic* 95, no. 8 (March):147.
    Brief review of *The Green Fool*, an "engaging autobiography."

10 O'LOUGHLEN, CLEMENT. "Hail County Louth." *New York Times* (2 April):27.
    Brief letter responding to Reynolds (1939.16).

11 O'R., B. M. Review of *The Green Fool*. *Catholic World* 149 (April):120.
    Claims it is an overstatement to call Kavanagh the "Robert Burns of Eire," although the novel is "well written." Claims the Catholic faith does not seem to mean much to Kavanagh.

12 O'SHEEL, SHAEMAS [*sic*]. "Poetry and Peasantry." *New York Herald Tribune Books* (19 February):15.
    Review of *The Green Fool*. Agrees that Kavanagh is the "Burns of Eire," although also compares Kavanagh with Peter Breughel: his characters are "a peasantry as robust and earthy as ever the great Dutchman painted." Compares *The Green Fool* with Tomas O'Crohan's *The Islandman*, Peadar O'Donnell's *The Way It Was With Them*, Maurice O'Sullivan's *Twenty Years A-Growing* and Synge's *The Aran Islands*. However, Kavanagh's book is less romantic than these. His characters "have something of the vulgarity of slum dwellers," but they speak beautifully. Although the book is realistic, it is too grim.

13 P., F. *Saturday Review of Literature* (25 March):19–20.
    Review of *The Green Fool*, which is "one of the best books of its kind." Claims Kavanagh was "a bit of a queer fish" in his native Iniskeen. Compares the book to the poetry of A. E. Housman, although Kavanagh was "gayer than the Shropshire lad ever dreamed of being, and has a powerful Hibernian sneer that instantly eviscerates anything in its direction."

1940

14 Review of *The Green Fool*. *New Yorker* (18 February):72.
Claims *The Green Fool* concerns "a Burns-like poet's childhood and young manhood."

15 Review of *The Green Fool*. *Pratt Institute Free Library. Quarterly Booklist* (Autumn):26.
Brief mention of *The Green Fool*.

16 REYNOLDS, HORACE. "A Young Ulsterman's Autobiography." *New York Times Book Review* (26 February):4.
Review of *The Green Fool*. Compares Kavanagh with Kentucky author Jesse Stuart. Claims mistakenly that Kavanagh grew up in County Louth. Gives biographical sketch and alludes to some of the "escapades" in *The Green Fool*. "It is when he writes of these escapades and his travels that the slightly hard-boiled navvy note he affects intrudes itself into his writing." Mentions his meeting with A. E. and his friendship with O'Connor, O'Faolain and Higgins. Kavanagh is "as independent as a hog on ice, or the true Ulsterman he is. You can hardly call him gracious or grateful, but he has the great virtue of honesty, and his heresies are refreshing."

17 SYLVESTER, HARRY. Review of *The Green Fool*. *Commonweal* 29, no. 17 (March):585–586.
Claims Kavanagh is "more talented and more annoying" than Michael McLaverty. *The Green Fool* is too "desperately cute and quaint in spots." Claims Kavanagh is "Stage-Irish," but he has been at a disadvantage as a Catholic writer trying to get published in a Protestant and Communist publishing world. Laments the "unchristian" behavior of Kavanagh's characters. Claims it would have been a better book if Kavanagh told us less about himself, more about Sean O'Faolain.

1940

1 "'A. E.' Award." *Times Literary Supplement* (13 January):13.
Announces that Kavanagh has won the 1939 "A.E." Award of one hundred pounds. There were twenty-four applications for the 1939 Award.

2 "'A.E.' Memorial Award. Trustees Report." *Irish Times* (5 January):9.
Announces that Kavanagh won the 1940 "A.E." Memorial Award, and Brian O'Nolan was given a "special commendation."

3 J., F. L. "Literary Criticism." Letter. *Irish Times* (22 July):2.
Response to Kavanagh's recent review of Maurice Walsh's novel, *The Hill is Mine* (*Irish Times*, 20 July, p. 5.), in which Kavanagh makes derogato-

1941

ry remarks about the Boy Scouts and the "Scout mentality." Defends both *Gone with the Wind* and *The Hill is Mine* against Kavanagh's slur, and voices dismay at his attack on the Boy Scout movement. Further letters in the *Irish Times* by M. C. Ahern (26 July, p. 6), Bandar-Ka-Bai [pseud.] (3 August, p. 3), H. V. Briscoe (27 July, p. 8), Harold C. Brown (24 July, p. 3), N. C. (27 July, p. 8), Whit Cassidy (2 August, p. 6), Judy Clifford (27 July, p. 8), Harry Conroy (2 August, p. 6), CUS04 [pseud.] (31 July, p. 7), J. R. H. (1 August, p. 6), N. S. Harvey (25, 29 July, pp. 4, 2), Isotta Degli Atti [pseud.] (7 August, p. 6, which is the final letter in the correspondence), F. L. J. (24, 26 July, and 2 August, pp. 3, 6, 6), Frank F. Prenton Jones (24, 26 July, pp. 3, 6), W. H. Lambkin (30 July, p. 6), Oscar Love (23, 25, 27, 30 July, 2 August, pp. 6, 4, 8, 6, 6), E. A. Macdonald (1 August, p. 6), Ewart MacGonicle (31 July, p. 7), Eoin T. Macmurchadha (3 August, p. 3), John F. Manning (1 August, p. 6), David Meredith (25 July, p. 4), Ewart Milne (29 July, p. 2), Niall Montgomery (27 July, p. 8), Terence Mulvaney (5 August, p. 6), F. McEwe Obarn [pseud.] (3 August, p. 3), F. O'Brien (29 July, p. 2), Lir O'Connor (30 July, p. 6), Miss ("Alas") Luna O'Connor (5 August, p. 6), The O'Madan [pseud.] (31 July, p. 7), Jno O'Ruddy (30 July, 2 August, pp. 6, 6), Punch [pseud.] (30 July, p. 6), F. M. Q. (31 July, p. 7), R. H. S. (30 July, p. 6), South American Joe [pseud.] (2 August, p. 6), Sam Sullivan (1 August, p. 6), and Hilda Upshott (30 July, p. 6).

1941

1   "Abbey Theatre and the Poets: Mr. Patrick Kavanagh's View." *Irish Times* (6 February):6.

    Brief report on Kavanagh's speech at a meeting of the College Historical Society at Trinity College Dublin. The proposal under debate was: "The cinema is a better form of entertainment than the theatre." Kavanagh criticized the Abbey Theatre directors and suggested they should resign.

2   GANLEY, R.B. (ARHA). "Letters. The Hibernian Academy." *Irish Times* (2 April):3.

    Response to Kavanagh's scathing review in the *Irish Times* (1 April 1941) of the recent Royal Hibernian Academy Exhibition. Further letters in *Irish Times* by Art Lover [pseud.] (4 April), Niall O'Leary Curtis (7 April, p. 3), R. B. Ganley (8 April, p. 4), Stephen Gilbert (7 April, p. 3), L. S. Gogan (5 April, p. 6), John S. Jackson (7 April, p. 3), T. F. Harvey Jacob (9 April), Oscar Love (7 April, p. 3), Angelina McCaffey (3 April, p. 7), Norah McGuinness (3 April, p. 7), Elizabeth Milne (2 April, p. 3), Ewart Milne (8 April, p. 4), F. O'Brien (4 April, p. 6).

1942

3 "Trinity College Notes." *Irish Times* (8 February):4.
Brief reference to the previous week's meeting of the College Historical Society, at which debaters, including Patrick Kavanagh, discussed the motion "That the Cinema is Preferable to the Theatre."

1942

1 Announcement. *Horizon* 5, no. 29 (May):300.
Announces that the Irish number of *Horizon* has been banned in Dublin because it carried "The Old Peasant," an early version of *The Great Hunger*, parts of which were deemed obscene by the authorities.

2 GREACEN, ROBERT. Review of *The Great Hunger*. *Horizon* 6, no. 33 (September):217–219.
Criticizes post-Yeatsian Southern Irish literature as mediocre, but praises Ulster writers who are "unhampered by the introverted loyalties" of the South. Considers *The Great Hunger* a poem of defiance against Irish censorship. Patrick Maguire's frustration is emblematic of the "frustration-complex" of Southern Ireland, debilitated by neutrality and by "grandmotherly" censorship laws. Complains of too many "lapses into dullness and trite speech" in the poem, despite occasional "masterly passages of delicate lyricism." Suggests the only solution to the sterility of Irish writing is a military invasion of Southern Ireland.

3 O'CONNOR, FRANK. "The Future of Irish Literature." *Horizon* 5, no. 25 (January):55–63.
Briefly discusses *The Green Fool* as an example of a novel which shows the limitations of Ireland as a subject for Irish writers, and compares it to Gerald O'Donovan's *Father Ralph* and James Joyce's *A Portrait of the Artist as a Young Man*. Calls for Irish writers to reject Romanticism and embrace satire.

4 ———. "Letters. *Horizon*." *Irish Times* (25 February):2.
Response to R. O'Farrachain's recent review of the Irish number of *Horizon* (January). Defends Kavanagh against O'Farrachain's criticism. Kavanagh is "a real poet," not one of "the Woolworth bards." He "thinks of his subject and not of the impression he is creating."

5 O'FARRACHAIN, ROIBEARD. "The Irish Number of *Horizon*." *Irish Times* (21 February):5.
Reviews January, 1942 issue of *Horizon*, including Kavanagh's poem, "The Old Peasant," which is like "a good rough draft rather than a finished

poem." Laments "the intrusion of vague, bookish grandiosity into good, hard, sound peasant observation."

6 SHANNON, S. "New Poetry." *Spectator* (17 July):66–68.
Review of several books, including *The Great Hunger*, which is "no glib narrative."

7 TAYLOR, GEOFFREY. Review of *The Great Hunger*. *Bell* 4, no. 6 (September):448–450.
Dismisses the Cuala Press's comparison of *The Great Hunger* to *The Waste Land*, although considers the poem much better than Bloomfield's *Farmer Boy*. Praises Kavanagh's knowledge of technique and subject matter, the "love-life" of a peasant. Claims Kavanagh has "reverence" for nature, human nature, and "all that is beyond nature." Praises the "Brueghelesque realism" of the card-playing scene, although Kavanagh's use of rhyme is "occasionally unhappy."

1944

1 FIGGIS, R. R. "Letters. The New Art Patronage." *Irish Times* (26 August):3.
Response to debate about Kavanagh's recent article on the fine arts in Dublin, "The New Art Patronage."

2 "Letters. The New Art Patronage." *Irish Times* (22 August):3.
Response to Kavanagh's article, "The New Art Patronage."

3 MCDONAGH, DONAGH. Introduction to *Poems from Ireland*. Dublin: *Irish Times Publications* 1–3.
Kavanagh's poetry is "as recognisably Irish as turf-smoke."

4 SCOTT, KINGSLEY. "Letters. The New Art Patronage." *Irish Times* (22 August):3.
Approving response to Kavanagh's article, "The New Art Patronage."

5 SPEAIGHT, ROBERT. "Books on Trial." *Dublin Review* (July):93.
Review of *The Great Hunger*, "the most considerable poem to come out of Ireland since the death of Yeats." Compares it to Eliot's recent poems. It is a "strange and disquieting" poem and a reaction against the romanticization of the peasant. The poem "reminds us that a man may be obliterated by the mud as well as by the machine." Admires the poem's technique and "the varying, terse style." Although a realistic poem, it has "the awareness of universal things. An entire human situation is lit up in poor Maguire, stranded between the implacable earth and the immense hinterland of God."

1945

1 MCDONAGH, DONAGH. "A Tradition (for Patrick Kavanagh)." *Irish Times* (23 June):2.
   Poem dedicated to Kavanagh.

1946

1 IREMONGER, VALENTIN. "Aspects of Poetry Today." *Bell* (June):242–250.
   Claims that Donagh McDonagh, John Hewitt and Patrick Kavanagh were "the more important forerunners in the new movement" in modern Irish poetry.

1947

1 COLUM, PADRAIC. "The Tang of Sloes." *Saturday Review of Literature* (20 September):24.
   Review of *A Soul for Sale*. Claims that Kavanagh's view of the peasantry differs from that of Yeats or Hyde, and his poetry "has no longer a traditional lilt with the overtones of folk poetry." On the contrary, he sometimes seems "hard and disillusioned," and his work recalls Eliot's *The Waste Land*. He is in a transitional phase between celebration and satire and cannot decide which mode he prefers.

2 FITTS, DUDLEY. "Loving Evocation of Irish Life." *New York Times*, section 7 (24 August):10.
   Review of *A Soul for Sale*, the poetry of which is "wiry and aware, where so many of our moderns are nerveless and glib." It is an example of "rough Irish." Praises "Primrose" (which he compares with the work of Vaughan and Wordsworth), but in general, the collection is disappointing, and the poet does not know clearly what his aims are.

3 GREACEN, ROBERT. "The Way We Write Now." *Irish Writing* 2 (June): 86–94.
   Brief discussion of *The Great Hunger* in relation to Romanticism in contemporary Irish poetry.

4 MACGLYNN, LOCHLINN. "The World in the Window." *Irish Bookman* 2, no. 1 (September):33–34.
   Brief reference to *Ploughman and Other Poems*: "the first unforgettable promise from Patrick Kavanagh."

1947

5. MACM., M. J. "The Poetry of Patrick Kavanagh." *Irish Press* (27 February):7.
   Review of *A Soul for Sale*. Praises the sincerity of the poems, especially *The Great Hunger*. The poetry is "harsh," close to life, and the whole book sounds a note of "frustration and loss." Praises "Memory of Brother Michael," although claims it is historically inaccurate. Claims this is "one of the most striking books of Irish verse published in our time."

6. MERCIER, VIVIAN. "The Arts in Ireland." *Commonweal* (6 June):183–185.
   Discusses the arts in Dublin during and after the war: "London, as usual, has swallowed up most Irish talent." Announces the British publication of *A Soul for Sale* and calls Kavanagh "a sort of peasant Blake, dour, earthbound, bitter," with an "uneasy relationship with his Church and his country."

7. MILNE, EWART. "The Gallivanting Poet. An Open Letter to Patrick Kavanagh." *Irish Times* (8 December). UCD Archive.
   Response to Kavanagh's essay on F. R. Higgins, "The Gallivanting Poet."

8. ———. "The Gallivanting Poet." *Irish Times* (26 December). UCD Archive.
   Further response to Kavanagh's essay on Higgins.

9. O'FARRACHAIN, ROIBEARD. "Poetry." *Irish Library Bulletin* (June):107–108.
   Review of *A Soul for Sale*. Claims that Kavanagh's work lacks "tension," and that his feeling for form is "vague and clumsy," but that he is nonetheless "an important writer." Criticizes *The Great Hunger* for being too realistic and "loose in texture." His feeling for form has improved in *A Soul for Sale*. Praises "Pegasus," "Memory of Brother Michael" and "Temptation in Harvest."

10. Review of *A Soul for Sale*. *Cape Times* (Capetown, South Africa), (25 October). UCD Archive.
    Claims Kavanagh is a powerful writer, "but not a good poet." Praises his "restless questing activity."

11. Review of *A Soul for Sale*. *The Tiger's Eye* (USA) (October). UCD Archive.
    Notice and brief description of book.

12. SALOMON, I. L. "Contemporary Magic." *Voices* (Opus Press, Wigginton, Herts.), (October):45–48.
    Review of *A Soul for Sale*. Claims Kavanagh "takes his themes from the land." He expresses "the Celtic spirit" and his writing is "full of poet magic." His writing blends the mystical with the real, and is "as modern as Yeats

1948

without his poetic experience, as observant as Joyce without his all-seeing inner eye, and as clean in the handling of lines as Auden."

13 "The Dream and the Business." *Times Literary Supplement* (17 May):240.
    Review of *A Soul for Sale*. Praises Kavanagh's humour and "liveliness." Discusses *The Great Hunger* which is "full of intense realism and is told with fierceness and power."

14 W., B. "The Individual Talent." *Irish Times* (8 March):6.
    Review of *A Soul for Sale*. Praises the "honest creative purpose" and the technique of Kavanagh's poetry. Claims Kavanagh is free of influence and is "his own man." He despises the values of the market place, as "Pegasus" demonstrates. The poetry is simple, economical and at times, austere. Praises "A Christmas Childhood," "Candida," "Temptation in Harvest," and *The Great Hunger*, which expresses "a compressed and bitter philosophy." Although the poetry is bitter it does not voice despair but "sublime anger." Claims the book may not become popular because it is neither romantic nor nostalgic, but it is the most important collection of Irish poems since the death of Yeats.

1948

1 FARREN, ROBERT. *The Course of Irish Verse in English*. London: Sheed and Ward, pp. 166–169.
    Kavanagh is "possibly the first poet of several generations who literally broke Irish soil for seed."

2 GREGORY, HORACE. "Clearing Ground." *Poetry* 71, no. 6 (March):324–326.
    Review of *A Soul for Sale*. Dislikes the book's title and finds the poems within it "shapeless." Claims *The Great Hunger* has "an extremely inflated title," yet it is clear Kavanagh has "something to say," and is escaping the shadow of Yeats. Although it is not wholly successful, few long poems in English in the last decade equal *The Great Hunger*. Kavanagh should, however, beware of "the temptations of a fake poetic language." Compares Kavanagh with Sean O'Casey.

3 MARCUS, DAVID. "Reviews 1947." *Poetry Ireland* 1 (April):25–28.
    Reviews *A Soul for Sale*, which enhances Kavanagh's reputation as "the most considerable of the younger poets now writing in Ireland." Admires Kavanagh's seriousness and considers *The Great Hunger* a "landmark" poem for Irish poetry. Kavanagh's poetry is "centripetal" in relation to nature, but Roy McFadden's is "centrifugal." "Kavanagh curses, McFadden blesses."

1949

4 MILNE, EWART. "The Gallivanting Poet." *Irish Times* (5 January):5.
Further response to Kavanagh's recent essay on Higgins.

5 MORROW, LARRY. [The Bellman]. "Meet Mr. Patrick Kavanagh." *Bell* 16, no. 1 (April):5–11.
As with Frank Sinatra, Dylan Thomas and others, you can't be indifferent to Kavanagh. "You either scream for him or against him." Describes the enormous publicity surrounding Kavanagh's character. Describes in detail a conversation that he had with Kavanagh in a Dublin café in which Kavanagh boasted that "I'm the only man who has written in our time about rural Ireland from the inside."

6 O'FAOLAIN, SEAN. "Public Opinion. Coloured Balloons." *Bell* 15, no. 4 (January):61–62.
Letter, defending Frank O'Connor and himself against Kavanagh's accusation, (*The Bell*, 1947) that their work lacked realism. Kavanagh's weakness is that "he cannot rise an inch above the small farm . . . Always stuck in the old mud. Reality, reality, reality from start to finish. Dung from morning to night!" Further letters on this topic in *The Bell* 15, no. 5 (February), include those by Bryan Guinness (p. 62), Patricia O'Connor (pp. 57–58), Joan Robertshaw (p. 58–61), and Blanaid Salkeld (pp. 61–62).

7 W., B. "Country Matters." *Irish Times* (6 November):6.
Review of *Tarry Flynn*. Describes the novel's plot and praises the portrait of Tarry's mother—"a salty, vigorous life-sized character." The novel is warm and lifelike, depicting "the decline and fall of a very ancient civilisation."

1949

1 B., V. A. "Other New Fiction: Irish Selection." *Chicago Daily News* (12 October):28.
Brief review of *Tarry Flynn*. Claims Kavanagh "has a touch of the authentic mysticism of the great Irish writers."

2 "Briefly Noted." *New Yorker* (5 November):116–117.
Brief review of *Tarry Flynn*, which "has an air of having been carelessly tossed off in a very bright moment."

3 CRITIC [pseud.]. "An Irish Diary." *New Statesman* (29 January):97–98.
Laments and ridicules the Irish censorship laws by which a book is banned and often later "unbanned." Uses Kavanagh's *Tarry Flynn* as an example of this. Cannot understand why the novel, now selling well in Dublin, was banned in the first place.

1949

4 HARRITY, RICHARD. *New York Herald Tribune Book Review*: (13 November):32.
  Review of *Tarry Flynn*. Praises the author's "insight and sensitivity" and considers the novel "a vivid and realistic picture" of peasant life. Praises, in particular, the portrait of Tarry's mother.

5 HUNTER, FRANCES L. "The Poetic Irish." *Hartford Courant* (CT) (13 November).
  Review of *Tarry Flynn* (Devin Adair). Praises the realism of the novel, although sometimes it is realistic to an "almost revolting degree." Finds Mrs. Flynn unpleasant but convincing. Claims the plot is meandering and aimless.

6 M., H. L. "The Old Gentlemen Say 'Yes!'" *Irish Writing* (February):77–78.
  Review of *Tarry Flynn*, which should not be called a novel since it is heavily autobiographical. Claims it is a highly subjective book which Kavanagh needed to write in order to vent his anger at society before proceeding to write more substantial works.

7 MURRAY, GERARD MAJELLA. "'Tarry Flynn,' Novel in Poesy." *Brooklyn Eagle* (6 November):15.
  Review of *Tarry Flynn*. Claims Tarry is "as beguiling a character as ever graced the pages of Irish literature." Discusses theological problems inherent in Kavanagh's phrases "a new soul, brand new" and "wondering at the newly created world." Expresses reserve at the treatment of the church and priests in the novel.

8 O'DONNELL, DONAT. "The Unfallen." In *Envoy* 1, no. 1 (December):48.
  Review essay on books by O'Faolain and Arland Ussher, with brief references to Kavanagh.

9 Review of *Tarry Flynn*. *Commonweal* (2 December):254.
  Claims the novel "deals with Ireland in the O'Faolain manner." Finds the portrayal of Tarry realistic and "genuine" but the other characters less so.

10 RYAN, JOHN. Foreword to *Envoy* 1, no. 1 (December):1–7.
  Introduces Patrick Kavanagh's "Diary."

11 SANDROCK, MARY. "New Books." *Catholic World* 170 (December):235.
  Review of *Tarry Flynn*, which is "the *Tobacco Road* of County Cavan." It is "minor," "Gaelic-centred," and "imitative." The plot is dull: "Nothing much happens."

12 "Sense and Satire." *Irish Times* (10 September):6.
  Review of issue of *Horizon* which includes "The Paddiad," which the reviewer finds "intensely virile in its mocking anger."

1950

13 STERN, JAMES. "Wild Harps Playing." *New York Times*, section 7 (27 November):44.
  Review of *Tarry Flynn*. Expresses surprise that the novel was banned. Claims Kavanagh does not sufficiently allow Tarry Flynn to speak.

1950

1 BREIT, HARVEY. "Talk with Mr. Kavanagh." *New York Times*, section 7 (22 October):33.
  Interview with Peter Kavanagh in which he makes some comments about his brother, Patrick.

2 Foreword to *Envoy* 2, no. 5 (April):9–11.
  Claims Patrick Kavanagh is "Orpheus-like."

3 GERARD, PAUL. "Poetry in Ireland: 1930–1950." *Envoy* 3, no. 8 (July):65–74.
  Any discussion of Irish poetry from 1930 to 1950 "must to a very great extent be concerned with [Kavanagh's] achievement." Kavanagh is the only great poet of the period. He avoids "false romanticism" and is the only modern Irish poet to speak for the peasant, although he, himself, is not a true peasant but a poet. His realistic portrayal of rural life "achieves universality," and his satire has "more than local importance."

4 HOGAN, THOMAS. "Theatre." *Envoy* 1, no.4 (March):78–82.
  Brief references to Kavanagh.

5 JAMES, HILAIRE. "Letters to the Editor." *Envoy* 3, no. 10 (September): 90–93.
  Wonders why Kavanagh "is relegated to writing a prose diary?"

6 KIELY, BENEDICT. *Modern Irish Fiction. A Critique*. Dublin: Golden Eagle Books, pp. 40–41.
  Mentions the "censorship sentence for obscurity or indecency" against *Tarry Flynn*, which was later revoked. Compares Maguire, "the thwarted unmarried mother-dominated peasant" and Tarry Flynn to Kafka and J. Alfred Prufrock: "Tarry Flynn is in fact a neurotic." In *Tarry Flynn*, Kavanagh shows a "talent for caricature that can be comic without being spiteful."

7 MACDONNELL, JAMES. "Letters to the editor." *Envoy* 1, no. 3 (February):92–93.
  Praises Kavanagh's diary in *Envoy*, which is "generally provoking and is based on good sound judgement and fair criticism."

1950

8 MANNIN, ETHEL. "Letters to the editor." *Envoy* 2, no. 5 (April):93.
    Criticizes Kavanagh for his "typically aggressive and dogmatic" remark that no serious writer can make a living "entirely by writing." Claims she has done so, and suggests Kavanagh is "talking through his probably shabby hat."

9 MILNE, EWART. "Letters to the editor." *Envoy* 1, no. 3 (February):88.
    Discusses the plight of Irish authors (himself included) who publish their work in London, which Patrick Kavanagh had mentioned in his diary (*Envoy*, January 1950).

10 NA GCOPALEEN, MYLES. "Baudelaire and Kavanagh." *Envoy* 3, no. 12 (November):78–81.
    Compares Kavanagh's diary in *Envoy* with Baudelaire's diary, on the grounds that "both diaries seem to be occupied with the same problems, complaints and anxieties." For example, both authors have a distaste for commerce, newspapers, and journalists. Criticizes Kavanagh's disdain for Irish newspapers.

11 QUINN, OWEN. "No Garland for John Synge." In *Envoy* 3, no. 1 (October):44–51.
    Essay on Synge, with brief references to Kavanagh.

12 REYNOLDS, HORACE. Review of *Tarry Flynn*. *Saturday Review of Literature* (21 January):19.
    Finds more autobiographical detail in *Tarry Flynn* than in Kavanagh's supposed autobiography, *The Green Fool*. Describes the novel as a struggle within Tarry between the land, his mother and his aspirations to be a poet. Admires the portraits of Tarry and his mother. It is "written in the easy, natural style of all good Irish writers." Synge would have enjoyed it.

13 RIORDAN, JOHN. "Letters to the Editor." *Envoy* 2, no. 6 (May):95.
    Expresses shock at Kavanagh's diary in *Envoy*.

14 RYAN, JOHN. "Being Young and Foolish." Foreword to *Envoy* 1, no. 4 (March):9–11.
    Brief reference to Kavanagh, accompanied by cartoon of him.

15 SHERIDAN, JOHN D. "The Yeats Film." "Letters to the editor." *Envoy* 1, no. 3 (February):91–92.
    Begs to differ with Kavanagh's recent remarks in *Envoy* about the National Film Institute and its Yeats film under production. Claims "jingoistic" is a favorite word of Kavanagh's.

1951

1 BUTLER, HUBERT. "Envoy and Mr. Kavanagh." *Bell* 17, no. 6 (September):32–41.

Discusses contemporary Irish writing in light of the fact nationalism is no longer an urgent subject. Discusses *Envoy* whose objectives were violently stated in Kavanagh's diary. Claims "Mr. Kavanagh's mind, when he abandons poetry and fiction, is like a monkey house at feeding time." Defends Anglo-Irish writers of the Revival against Kavanagh's attacks upon them, and questions Kavanagh's attempt to equate Irishness with Catholicism. Criticizes Kavanagh for his "sloppy thinking."

2 BYRNS, RUTH KATHERINE. "Week End in Dublin." *Catholic World* 172 (March):436–440.

Describes meeting Kavanagh in Dublin. He is an expert with an air rifle. Claims everyone in the restaurant at which they dined greeted Kavanagh warmly.

3 CAREY, EDWARD PAT. "Letters to the Editor." *Envoy* 4, no. 16 (March):77–78.

Defends his friend, the late Senator Joseph Brennan, against Patrick Kavanagh's "unjust, unkind, and therefore ungentlemanly" accusations in the January *Envoy* that he lacks artistic taste.

4 "Envoi." *Envoy* 5, no. 20 (July):8–9.

Announces that this is the last issue of the journal. Claims Kavanagh has served "the cause of truth in Ireland" in his diary, and has cleared the air of false poetasters.

5 GRIFFITH, H. B. "Letters to the editor." *Envoy* 4, no. 15 (February):77–79.

Criticizes Kavanagh for his remarks on Rome in his diary in *Envoy*. Claims Kavanagh affects a bored, intellectual, cosmopolitan pose. Feels offended by Kavanagh's "sneering attitude" toward pilgrims in Rome. Kavanagh is a "culture snob."

6 MORGAN, MATTHEW. *Envoy* 4, no. 14 (January):92–95.

Refers to Kavanagh's diary, which he calls "facile," in context of discussion of Irish literary tradition.

7 O'LAOGHAIRE, COLM. "Letters to editor." *Envoy* 4, no. 18 (May):76–77.

Expresses puzzlement at Kavanagh's recent remarks in *Envoy* about photography. Alludes to Kavanagh's quarrel with the Cultural Relations Committee. Suggests that Kavanagh always says the exact opposite of what his opponents always say.

1952

8   SWIFT, PATRICK. "Portrait of Patrick Kavanagh." *Envoy* 4, no. 15 (February):40.
    Reproduction of Swift's painting.

9   Untitled. *Radio Times* (27 July). UCD Archive.
    Announces Kavanagh's talk on radio about Carleton.

1952

1   "Jottings." *Dublin Evening Mail* (10 April). UCD Archive.
    Discusses first issue of *Kavanagh's Weekly*.

2   "Jottings." *Dublin Evening Mail* (29 April). UCD Archive.
    Calls *Kavanagh's Weekly* "that darling of Irish journalism."

3   KAVANAGH, PETER. "My Wild Irish Weekly." *American Mercury* 75, no. 345, (September):87–91.
    Describes the origins, progress and decline of *Kavanagh's Weekly*, published by Peter and Patrick Kavanagh. Claims that although continually dogged by financial problems, the paper had a circulation of two thousand. Claims the Kavanaghs wrote most of the articles themselves, because the contributions sent in were so disappointing. Claims they ceased publication because of censorship pressure and because the minds of the Irish were corrupt and dull.

4   M., L. "Radio Record." *Dublin Evening Mail* (9 May). UCD Archive.
    Discusses Radio Telefis Eireann in light of attacks on it in *Kavanagh's Weekly*.

5   NICHEVO [pseud.]. "An Irishman's Diary." *Irish Times* (11 April):9.
    Discusses *Kavanagh's Weekly*. Praises Patrick Kavanagh as "among our most notable poets," who has "a touch of genius." Discusses Peter Kavanagh's recent article in the *American Mercury* (1952.3) Claims both brothers enjoy "being in a minority of one." Laments the fact that *Kavanagh's Weekly* is carelessly written. Warns that Patrick Kavanagh is in danger of becoming pompous.

6   "Our London Correspondence. A Weekly Gone." *Manchester Guardian* (3 July):6.
    Brief discussion of the demise of *Kavanagh's Weekly*—"the brightest bit of weekly journalism to come out of Ireland for a long time." Claims Patrick Kavanagh is "noisy and untidy, but passionately a poet and defender of Ireland against her evangelists of mediocrity."

1954

7 PLUNKETT, JAMES. "Pulled Weeds on the Ridge." *Bell* 17, no. 12 (March):69–78.
   Praises the "compression and unerring selection" of Kavanagh's poetry, and suggests his poetry was influenced by the technique of the cinema.

8 "Profile: Patrick Kavanagh." *Leader* (11 October):8–12.
   The parodic profile that led to the libel action.

9 Review of *Kavanagh's Weekly*. *Nationalist and Leinster Times* (19 April). UCD Archive.
   Claims the weekly hit Dublin "like a blast from a shotgun." It is "a bulletin of abuse and mockery."

10 Review of *Kavanagh's Weekly*. *Kilkenny People* (3 May). UCD Archive.
   Claims weekly is "a success beyond the expectations of the doubting Thomases."

1954

1 "An Irishman's Diary." *Irish Times* (9 February):5.
   Discusses the popularity and theatricality of the High Court hearing of the Kavanagh libel action.

2 "Ben Jonson Quoted in Libel Appeal." *Irish Times* (25 November):8.
   Discusses conclusion of preliminary arguments on behalf of Kavanagh in libel appeal.

3 "Counsel Claims Reasonable Jury Would have Found For Mr. Kavanagh." *Irish Times* (23 November):9.
   Discusses the reading of evidence and the charge of the trial judge in the High Court. Sir John Esmonde, S.C., claims the jury had been unduly influenced, and the Profile was defamatory.

4 "Court-Room Packed As Libel Action Enters Its Second Day. Mr. Patrick Kavanagh in the Witness Box." *Irish Times* (5 February):1, 3.
   Detailed account of second day of libel case, with photo. Further reports in *Irish Independent*, *Irish Press*, and *Cork Examiner*.

5 "Damages Sought By Journalist." *Irish Independent* (4 February). UCD Archive.
   Discusses Kavanagh's libel action against *The Leader* and the printer, Argus (1952) Ltd. Further reports in *Irish Press*, *Cork Examiner*, and *Irish Times* (4 February:1).

1954

6   "Defendants win Writer's Libel Action." *Irish Weekly Independent* (18 February). UCD Archive.
    Announces victory for defendants.

7   "Dublin Libel Action Expected To End To-Day. Judge to put eight questions to the jury." *Irish Times* (12 February):3.
    Detailed account of the libel action, with photos. Further reports in *Cork Examiner* (12 February), *Irish Independent* (12 February), and *Irish Press* (12 February).

*8 "First Bloomsday Commemoration." Radio Telefis Eireann TV program. Accession no. A0457. Recorded 16 June. Duration: 7 minutes, 35 seconds.
    Film documentary about the celebration of Bloomsday by Kavanagh and others at Dublin Quays, Grand Canal, Merrion Strand, and Goggins Public House, Monkstown.

9   "Further Cross-examination of Novelist in Libel Action. Mr. Patrick Kavanagh all day in witness box." *Irish Times* (9 February):3.
    Detailed account of the libel action, with photo. Further reports in *Irish Press* (9 February), *Irish Independent* (9 February), *Evening Herald* (9 February), and *Cork Examiner* (9 February).

10 "Mr. Patrick Kavanagh's Second Full Day in Witness Box. Permission to interrupt evidence refused." *Irish Times* (10 February):3.
    Detailed discussion of libel action. Further reports in *Cork Examiner* (10 February) *Irish Press* (10 February), and *Irish Independent* (10 February).

11 "Fund To Assist Kavanagh Appeal." *Irish Press* (6 March). UCD Archive.
    Brief paragraph on the Kavanagh Appeal Fund. Mentions meeting at Gresham Hotel to discuss the Fund.

12 "Grounds of Appeal in Libel Action." *Irish Independent* (10 March). UCD Archive.
    Announces that Kavanagh is to appeal the case. See also report in *Irish Press* (10 March).

13 "Journalist's libel claim before Supreme Court. Kavanagh Appeal is opened. 'Jury misdirected by trial judge.'" *Irish Press* (17 November). UCD Archive.
    Detailed discussion of Supreme Court hearing of Kavanagh's appeal. Further reports in *Irish Independent* (17 November:3).

14 "Judgement Reserved on Novelist's Appeal." *Irish Times* (27 November):11.
    Announces conclusion of seven-day hearing of the appeal.

1954

15 MACMILCHO, CAITLIN. "Letters to the Editor. A Reply to P. K." *Bell* 19, no. 5 (April):52.

   Satirical poem addressed to Patrick Kavanagh, concerning his attitude toward women.

16 "Mr. Kavanagh's Case Finished in Dublin Libel Action. Spent Thirteen Hours in Witness Box." *Irish Times* (11 February):3–4.

   Detailed account of libel case, with photo. See also reports in *Irish Press* (11 February), *Irish Independent* (11 February), and *Cork Examiner* (11 February).

17 "Mr. Kavanagh Not Libelled By Profile Article in The Leader. Jury Absent for 74 minutes." *Irish Times* (13 February):5.

   Detailed account of the seventh day of the libel action, with photo of Justice Teevan, the trial judge, and cartoon, "Poet's Pub," by Alan Reeve (first published in *Irish Times* in 1940). Further reports in *Irish Press* (13 February:9, 11), *Cork Examiner*, and *Irish Independent* (13 February).

18 "Mr. Kavanagh Lodges Notice of Appeal." *Irish Times* (10 March):4

   Announces that notice of appeal has been served on Patrick Kavanagh from the findings of the jury and judgment on the *Leader* libel case. The appeal is based on the claim that the trial "had been unsatisfactory" in a number of ways.

19 "Novelist Appeals Against Libel Action Findings." *Irish Times* (17 November):8.

   Discusses opening day of Kavanagh's Supreme Court Appeal.

20 "Novelist's Appeal. Complaint About Cross-examination." *Irish Times* (19 November):3.

   Discusses cross-examination of Kavanagh during the trial.

21 OLDEN, G. A. "A Journey That Was More Than Necessary." *Irish Times* (21 January):4.

   Review of Radio Eireann broadcast, "Return to Inniskeen," hosted by Patrick Kavanagh, a program "of extreme originality and daring." Kavanagh interviewed old friends and neighbors in Inniskeen, most of whom thought he was a lazy worker. Claims that Kavanagh affects "a certain pleasant awkwardness in speech."

22 "185 Pages of Evidence Read in Appeal." *Irish Times* (18 November):9.

   Discusses Supreme Court appeal. Further report in *Irish Independent* (18 November).

1955

23 "Reference to Yeats in Kavanagh case. Comments on Cartoon." *Irish Press* (25 November):5. UCD Archive.
    Discusses hearing of Kavanagh's appeal in Supreme Court.

24 WHITE, JACK. "The Kavanagh Case." *Spectator* (5 March):255–257.
    Discusses Kavanagh's libel action against the *Leader*, which increased sales of Dublin's daily newspapers. Claims Kavanagh is a "colourful" plaintiff and a "Literary Lion," and that defense counsel, Justice Teevan, and prosecutor, John A. Costello, are political opponents. Describes Costello's reputation as a fierce prosecutor, quoting excerpts from his cross-examination of Kavanagh. Kavanagh must raise 250 pounds to appeal the trial.

1955

1 "A good time was had by all." *Evening Press* (3 February). UCD Archive.
    Gives account of Kavanagh's discussion at the British Rail Staff Association Literary And Debating Society of the motion: "The 1916/21 War was not justified by the results achieved."

2 "By-line." *Irish Times* (5 March):1.
    Cartoon alluding to the Kavanagh case.

3 "Film talk 'downright rubbish.'" *Irish Press* (28 February). UCD Archive.
    Gives account of Kavanagh's talk at the Bray Literary and Debating Society symposium on the cinema.

4 "Kavanagh libel action settled." *Irish Times* (24 May):4.
    Discusses settlement of the libel case. Further report in *Irish Independent* (24 May).

5 *Law Case, 1955. Transcript. Ireland. High Court of Justice. Before Mr. Justice Teevan and a jury KAVANAGH V THE LEADER & Ors. Transcript of Evidence. Signed ARTHUR H. RAE*, 325 pp.
    Transcript of law case. UCD Kavanagh archive, Kav/B/69.

6 "Mr. Kavanagh wins 'profile' article appeal. New trial ordered: Supreme Court majority of one." *Irish Press* (5 March):7. UCD Archive.
    Describes the legal process by which Kavanagh was awarded his appeal. Claims the judge had unduly influenced the jury in their original decision. Meanwhile, Kavanagh is in hospital, after falling ill under cross-examination, during the trial, on February 10th. Further reports in *Irish Independent* (5 March), *Irish Press* (5 March, p. 1), and *Irish Times* (5 March).

1956

7 "Novelist Wins Appeal In Supreme Court Today. New Trial of Action for Alleged Libel. Plea That Jury's Verdict Was Perverse. Costs Allowed." *Evening Herald* (4 March):1.
   Discusses Kavanagh's appeal victory. Further reports in *Dublin Evening Mail* (4 March) and *Evening Press* (4 March:1). UCD Archive.

8 "Settlement in Kavanagh libel action." *Irish Press* (24 May). UCD Archive.
   Libel action settled, although "terms were not disclosed."

9 "The Talks at UCD." *Evening Press* (22 February). UCD Archive.
   Discusses Kavanagh's recent lecture at UCD.

1956

1 CRONIN, ANTHONY. "Innocence and Experience, The Poetry of Patrick Kavanagh." *Nimbus* 3, no. 4 (Winter):20–23.
   Claims Kavanagh's poetry expresses "the dialectic of innocence and experience." In the early poems, he sees the world with childlike "intensity of vision." Kavanagh does not care about the "importance" of his subject matter, but confers significance on ordinary experience, as in *The Great Hunger*. Kavanagh's Dublin satires also constitute "the dialectic of innocence and experience," contrasting "vision" with the "barrenness" the poet sees around him. These later poems, written since 1947, are direct and honest, and contain an element of irony absent in his earlier work.

2 KIELY, BENEDICT. "The Writer's Map." *Spectator* (20 April):535.
   Claims Kavanagh's weekly lecture at University College Dublin, has been more popular than Beckett's *Waiting for Godot* as a "theatrical attraction."

3 MILNE, EWART. "Notes from a Journal." *Irish Writing* 35 (Summer): 95–113.
   Claims Kavanagh worships W. H. Auden, although Kavanagh is greater than Auden. Recalls meeting Kavanagh in London.

4 MULLIGAN, ARTHUR. "Irish Poet Gives Out With Everything But." *New York Daily News* (28 December):28.
   Discusses Press conference in New York on December 27, 1956 with Kavanagh, who criticized the English, expressed reservations about the Irish Republican Army, dismissed Churchill and praised Eisenhower.

1957

5 "University College Dublin. Board of Extra-Mural Studies. Series of Dublin Lectures by Mr. Patrick Kavanagh." *Irish Times* (21 February):5.

Announcement of venue, dates, and times of Kavanagh's UCD lectures, from February to May 1956.

6 WEBER, RICHARD. "The Poetry of Patrick Kavanagh." *Icarus* (TCD), no. 6, (May):22–25.

Criticizes "Pegasus" for its use of forced rhyme and its lack of symbolism. *The Great Hunger*, which is inferior to *The Deserted Village*, lacks the narrative form of Shakespeare's *Venus and Adonis* and is marred by journalistic clichés, nursery-rhyme ditties, and prosaic rhythms.

7 "World is Ruled by Idiots." *Evening Press* (28 December). UCD Archive.

Records some of Kavanagh's recent political statements.

1957

1 MONTAGUE, JOHN. "Letter from Dublin." *Poetry* 90, no. 5 (August): 310–315.

Considers Kavanagh "unquestionably our finest poet." Although he appears to be "the comic Irishman of tradition," he is sincere. His recent poems are sometimes awkward but a few, such as "Auditors In" and "Prelude," are worth noting and reminiscent of Swift's "On the Death of the Dean."

1958

1 DONOGHUE, DENIS. "Irische Literatur nach Yeats und Joyce." *Dokumente* 14, no. 3 (June):233–235. (German language.)

Describes Irish writers after Yeats and Joyce as "average." They are amateur, carefree bards, sometimes inspired, but more usually "awkward and unsure" in their use of language. At times they write with "raw vitality," though usually they write like "vulgar anti-intellectuals," full of mockery and crude jokes. Brendan Behan and Patrick Kavanagh demonstrate this tendency.

2 GALVIN, PATRICK. "Correspondence." *Delta* (Cambridge), 15 (Summer): 25–26.

Letter response to Weber's recent article in *Delta* (1958.7). Claims Weber's views on Kavanagh are "sheer nonsense." Praises *A Soul For Sale*.

3 MACDONAGH, DONAGH, and ROBINSON, LENNOX, eds. Introduction to *The Oxford Book of Irish Verse*. Oxford University Press, pp. xxi–xxii.

Describes Kavanagh as "the articulate voice of the inarticulate small farmer, the poet of commonplace beauty."

4   MONTAGUE, JOHN. "Contemporary Verse: A Short Chronicle." *Studies* 47, no. 188 (Winter):441–449.

Claims that Austin Clarke's "The Loss of Strength," a long poem in his collection *Too Great a Vine* (1958), is "the best poem by an Irishman since *The Great Hunger*." Quotes Kavanagh on the difficulties faced by the Irish writer.

5   PHILIPS, McCANDLISH. "Irish Mythology Book Turned Out By Hand on Home-Made Press by 29th Street 'King.'" *New York Times* (8 September):23.

Discusses Peter Kavanagh's Hand Press and his new book of Irish mythology. Brief reference to Patrick Kavanagh.

6   TRACY, HONOR. *Mind You, I've Said Nothing*. New York: British Book Center, p. 76.

Describes meeting Kavanagh in the Pearl Bar: "He launched, in his beautiful voice, a diatribe against Ireland and all her works, her passion for mediocrity, her crucifixion of genius."

7   WEBER, RICHARD. "Poetic Potential in Ireland." *Delta* (Cambridge), 14, (Spring):13–16.

Discusses contemporary Irish poetry scene. Expresses dislike of Kavanagh because of "the parochial elevation of his work by his admirers to the level of great poetry." Praises Kavanagh's criticism, but not his criticism of Irish writing.

1959

1   DEALE, EDGAR M. "Kavanagh and Dr. Schweitzer." *National Observer* (Dublin) 2, no. 6 (December):8.

A letter to the editor complaining about Kavanagh's "loutish and almost incoherent article" on Albert Schweitzer, printed in a previous issue of the journal.

2   MONTAGUE, JOHN. "Isolation and Cunning: Recent Irish Verse." *Poetry* 94, no. 4, (July):264–270.

Review of several books of Irish poetry, including Kavanagh's *Recent Poems*. Claims the book is merely "an interim report, a sign of continuing life." Claims the poems are technically loose, "as though the poet had reached that stage of enlightenment where doggerel can signify spiritual truth." Praises "Epic." Also praises Kavanagh's weekly column in the *Farmer's Journal*,

1960

which he compares to Kenneth Rexroth's "Sunday morning broadcasts in San Francisco."

3 "Mr. Kavanagh and 'nonplus.'" *Irish Press* (17 October):6. UCD Archive.
   Review of a Kavanagh essay in the first issue of a new quarterly, *Nonplus*: "Mr. Kavanagh literally cuts the ground from under his nonplussed neighbours."

4 RYAN, STEPHEN P. "Literary Life in Dublin." *Commonweal* (18 December):347–349.
   Claims Dublin literary life is dead or dormant. Those promising authors of the forties who were expected to produce "a second revival"—especially Kavanagh—have stopped writing or write seldom.

1960

1 "Alive and Kicking." *Times Literary Supplement* (12 August):514.
   Review of several books, including *Come Dance with Kitty Stobling*. Notes that Kavanagh is "generally thought of by the better judges among his countrymen as the best Irish poet since Yeats." Notes points of contrast between Kavanagh and Yeats: Yeats is self-dramatizing; Kavanagh is more like Wordsworth. Compares Kavanagh's love of nature to Hopkins' attitude toward nature, although Kavanagh's humor and self-irony distinguish him from both Hopkins and Wordsworth. Discusses Kavanagh's satires on Ireland's "cult of the small poet." Praises his "honest poetic personality."

2 ALVAREZ, A. "The Slimmest Volume." *Observer* (10 July):27.
   Review of *Come Dance with Kitty Stobling*. Claims Kavanagh is a distinguished but "uneven" poet. Claims the book shows a "concentration which transforms outer and inner worlds into a single, compelling and fresh poetic whole." Kavanagh's best work has a "pausing, almost clumsy movement which preserves him from blarney." Kavanagh is "a latter-day Edward Thomas." Dislikes Kavanagh's later satires, spoiled by "mud-in-your eye posturing." Praises his later sonnets. Thinks Kavanagh is "the most controlled, original and least pretentious Irish poet since Yeats."

3 ARMSTRONG, ROBERT. "Celt and Saxon." *Poetry Review* 51:234.
   Review of *Come Dance with Kitty Stobling*. Praises the poetry's "Celtic flame and humour and the gift of astringent imagery."

4 BARRETT, MARY L. "Poetry." *Library Journal* 85, no. 15 (November): 4150.

1960

Review of *Come Dance with Kitty Stobling and Other Poems*. Describes Kavanagh as "one of the best [to some critics, the best] of the young British poets of Irish descent." Praises the technical achievement of the poems. Dislikes "the self-consciousness of the author, both as man and as poet."

5 BODKIN, THOMAS. "An Irish Poet." *Birmingham Post* (22 November). UCD Archive.
    Review of *Come Dance with Kitty Stobling*. Claims the poems are "singularly beautiful and original," and "intensely Irish in their inspiration."

6 CRONIN, ANTHONY. "A Choice of Poetry." *Daily Telegraph and Morning Post* (18 November):20.
    Review of *Come Dance with Kitty Stobling*, in which Kavanagh has found his true poetic self. Praises the "astonishingly direct" technique. Claims the poems are often "records of intense moments of communion with simple images."

7 DELAHANTY, JAMES. "The Bell: 1940–1954 (2)." *Kilkenny Magazine* (Autumn):32–38.
    Discusses *The Bell*, 1940–1954. Recalls that the periodical published four long extracts from *Tarry Flynn*, which was "exciting." Praises the unsentimentality of Kavanagh's fiction, "unequalled since Carleton."

8 "Enjoying Words That State And Words That Sing." *Times* (London), (25 August):11.
    Review of *Come Dance with Kitty Stobling and Other Poems* (Longman). Claims Kavanagh is "primarily an expressive poet." He lacks the poetic range of Auden, but he is a powerful poet and is "at one with himself."

9 FREYER, GRATTAN. "Ireland's Contribution." *The Modern Age*. Edited by Boris Ford. Harmondsworth: Penguin, pp. 204–223.
    The Great Hunger contains "passages of savage, humourless satire," reminiscent of the work of D. H. Lawrence, who is an important influence on Kavanagh.

10 GRUBB, FREDERICK. "To look on is enough." *Journal of the Working Men's College* (London) 37, no. 487 (November):31–33.
    Recalls his first meeting with Kavanagh in Dublin. Compares Kavanagh to Dylan Thomas. Review of *Come Dance With Kitty Stobling*, which is "an antidote to 'Behanitis' which seems to have conquered London." Kavanagh's inspiration is "an unsophisticated muse, who languishes and droops in the artificial atmosphere of the city." However, the poems lack the vigor of his prose.

1960

11 HALL, DONALD. "Imagination and Effort." *New Statesman* (2 July):27–28.
Review of several books, including *Come Dance with Kitty Stobling and Other Poems*. Contrasts Kavanagh with Charles Tomlinson, although they share "a feeling for what is right in language." Calls Kavanagh "a Celtic Philip Larkin, or a drinking man's R. S. Thomas." Admires the book because of the absence of cliché and phoniness.

12 JORDAN, JOHN. "Mr. Kavanagh's Progress." *Studies* 49 (Autumn): 295–304.
Review essay, culminating in a review of *Come Dance with Kitty Stobling and Other Poems*. Claims Kavanagh's genius is "fragmentary and erratic." Considers *Ploughman and Other Poems* to have been "evidence of a small but pure talent." Discusses *The Green Fool*—"Kavanagh's most successful attempt at sustained prose narrative"—and *A Soul for Sale*. Discusses more extensively *The Great Hunger*. Argues that Kavanagh's religious beliefs in the poem seem unorthodox, even "vaguely pantheistic." Discusses the "cult" status of Kavanagh in Ireland, "based largely on his wild, uninformed and deliberately provocative generalizations." Claims the best poems in *Come Dance with Kitty Stobling* are attempts to find "self-knowledge," but the theme of the book is "love for life." Admires "Auditors In," "The Hospital," "Prelude," and others. Finds the poet sentimental when writing about "the Eternal Feminine" or when trying to "re-burnish" the banal. Other faults include: "over-reliance on portentous abstractions, the mandarin platitude," and "an uneasy acquaintance with Greek mythology." Claims that Kavanagh's career has a pattern "of departure, disillusion and bewilderment, enrichment and return." The new book represents "the illumined return." Hopes Kavanagh will write another long poem at least as good as *The Great Hunger*.

13 KAVANAGH, PETER. *Hermeneutics of Kednaminsha*. New York: Peter Kavanagh Hand Press. UCD Kavanagh Archive.
Includes brief reference to *Kavanagh's Weekly*.

14 KELL, RICHARD. "Commonsense and sensibility." *Guardian* (Manchester) (29 July):4.
Review of *Come Dance with Kitty Stobling*. Claims many of the poems are concerned with "self examination" and the need to "clarify artistic purposes." A mystical element in the poetry is undermined by "romantic posturing." Expresses misgivings about the poet's occasional tone of rapture and his "concern with poetic attitudes." Finds the more didactic poems "trite."

15 KINSELLA, THOMAS. "Song at Fifty." *Irish Times* (9 July):8.
Review of *Come Dance with Kitty Stobling and Other Poems*. Claims that Kavanagh has always been an inconsistent poet, and remains so, but his

new book contains some surprises. Discusses how Kavanagh's poem, "The Hospital," evidenced "a kind of rebirth," also indicated by the sonnets, which combine the "simple directness" of early Kavanagh with the "dryish, hobbled verse" of the satirical years. Discusses how "Canal Bank Walk" transcends his earlier themes of meanness and injustice. This poem and others "leaven the whole book, and indeed the whole of Mr. Kavanagh's work."

16 KRAUSE, DAVID. *Sean O'Casey: The Man and his Work*. London, New York: Macmillan, pp. 301–302.

O'Casey liked "Kerr's Ass" and *The Great Hunger*. The final lines of the latter poem prompted O'Casey to talk about the Labor leader Jim Larkin: "There it is again, the hungry fiend, in Mucker or in Dublin, and it takes the rage of a poet to put it right. Larkin was the poet of the people."

17 MACCAIG, NORMAN. "Peering and Seeing." *Spectator* (5 August):223.

Review of several books, including *Come Dance with Kitty Stobling*. Criticizes the lack of rigorous thought in Kavanagh's poetry, but praises his use of off-rhyme and his avoidance of falseness: "He is an Irishman all right, but he wears no Syngeing robes."

18 MACLIAMMOIR, MICHEAL. "Poetry from Dublin." *Sunday Times* (London), Magazine Section (24 July):25.

Review of *Come Dance with Kitty Stobling*. Claims Kavanagh's "ploughboy" rusticity is no mask, but is genuine. Prefers the nonattitudinizing poetry, since Kavanagh is more poet than philosopher. Regrets Kavanagh's preoccupation with the literati of Dublin pubs. Prefers to think of Kavanagh's loves rather than his hates. Praises "Auditors In" but dislikes "The Paddiad."

19 MCALERNON, DON. "Patrick Kavanagh." *Focus* (September):7.

Claims that Kavanagh came to Dublin in 1936, "a rebel against rationality, an imagination enthusing over the dandelions." In *The Great Hunger* Kavanagh "established a claim to be one of the most striking of contemporary Irish poets." *Tarry Flynn* is the best Irish prose "since Carleton," although parts of it are carelessly written. In *Come Dance with Kitty Stobling*, "his poetry has the quick pulse of life, not the hollow sigh of weariness so fashionable among contemporary poets." His latest work has a certain astringency, although his satires are not memorable. He has "a magnificent, unfettered religious sense."

20 MONTAGUE, JOHN. "From Monaghan to the Grand Canal." *Hibernia* (August).

Review of *Come Dance with Kitty Stobling*.

1960

21 MORAES, DOM. "Come Dance with Mr. Kavanagh." *Time and Tide* (30 July).
   Review of *Come Dance with Kitty Stobling*. "The acrid, self-mocking wit, the energy, the passion and the completely unliterary quality of these poems mark them as some of the most valuable poetry produced since the last war."

22 P., B. "Alive, Alive O!" *National Observer* (Dublin), 3, no. 1 (September):2. UCD Archive.
   Review of *Come Dance with Kitty Stobling and Other Poems*. Claims every society and generation needs a poet, because the poet provides "spiritual synthesis." Kavanagh is "Ireland's best living poet." Claims that Kavanagh has learned to accept life, and many poems in this book "are poems of sublime acceptance." Praises Kavanagh's note of "assured calmness."

23 PAYNE, BASIL. "The Poetry of Patrick Kavanagh." *Studies* 49 (Autumn):279–294.
   Claims to be a "reassessment" of Kavanagh. Discusses *Ploughman and Other Poems* ("slight work of honest, unpretentious competence"), *A Soul for Sale* and *Come Dance with Kitty Stobling*. Claims Kavanagh is a religious poet, comparable to the later Eliot. Discusses his treatment of Catholicism, including "Father Mat." Praises "Temptation in Harvest" as the best poem in *A Soul for Sale*. Claims the later poetry is "more direct, subtle, humorous and generous." Praises the "concentrated precision" of the sonnets in *Come Dance with Kitty Stobling*, although finds the satirical poems like "The Paddiad" banal. Claims love is the "fundamental concern" of the later poetry.

24 POTTS, PAUL. *Dante Called You Beatrice*. London: Eyre and Spottiswoode, p. 214.
   Brief reference to Kavanagh.

25 ———. "Homer's ghost came whispering." *John O'London's: for books and the arts* (London), 21 (July):79. UCD Archive.
   Review of two books, including *Come Dance with Kitty Stobling and Other Poems*. Kavanagh is "the most important Irish poet since Yeats." He is "very protestant, with a small p, for an Irish Catholic. Perhaps it is not for nothing that he comes from Ulster." Although uneven, some of the poetry is "worthy of Milton or of Blake."

26 ———. "Potts on Kavanagh." *John O'London's* (18 August). UCD Archive.
   Letter about Kavanagh in response to recent letter by Ewart Milne.

*27 SWAN, THOMAS D. *"The Great Hunger": A Critical Study of the Poem by Patrick Kavanagh*. M.A. thesis, UCD.
   Thesis on Kavanagh.

1961

1 CLARKE, AUSTIN. *Poetry in Modern Ireland.* Second edition. Illustrations by Louis Le Broquy. Cork: Mercier Press, for Irish Cultural Relations Committee, pp. 47–52.

Considers *The Green Fool* too idyllic, but Kavanagh's later work, especially *The Great Hunger*, represents a welcome reaction against "the cult of the wonderful peasant." The rough free verse in *The Great Hunger* "suits the mood of disillusion." Compares the poem to the realistic novel in its expression of discontent with rural life.

2 "Guinness Prizes for Poetry." *Daily Telegraph* (1 November):13.

Kavanagh was a judge in the Guinness Poetry Award.

3 HEWITT, JOHN. "The Cobbler's Song." *Threshold* 5, no. 1 (Spring/Summer):42–51.

Claims the "essence" of Kavanagh's work can be found in *A Soul for Sale* and *Tarry Flynn*, the latter of which "provides a rich and illuminating gloss upon the poems." Praises *The Great Hunger* ("Its social comment is disturbingly valid"), although its technical roughness is noted. Compares the plight of the isolated Kavanagh to that of other "peasant poets," who became "displaced" persons, including John Clare, Stephen Duck, Robert Bloomfield, and James Woodhouse. Complains that much of *Come Dance with Kitty Stobling* is "doggerel." The meter and line length is irregular, the rhymes are uneven, and the diction is poor.

4 HOLLOWAY, JOHN. "Book Reviews." *London Magazine* 8, no. 1 (January):74–78.

Review of several poetry collections, including *Come Dance with Kitty Stobling and Other Poems*. Claims Kavanagh has learned "a fluent dryness" from Swift's poetry, but his poetry is marred by a tendency toward cliché.

5 POTTS, PAUL. "P.E.N. Poets' Choice." *Sunday Times*, Magazine Section (12 November):30.

Laments the absence of Kavanagh's poetry in the PEN Club's annual anthology, *New Poetry, 1961*.

6 Press statement from McConnell's, Public Relations Department, 10–11 Pearse St., Dublin. UCD Kavanagh Archive.

Announces that from May 30 to June 3, 1961, the National Ballet, in association with Radio Eireann, will perform a ballet entitled "Gamble No Gamble"—"the thoughts of poet Patrick Kavanagh will be expressed by actor T. P. McKenna and dancer Charles Schuller who are both appearing as guest artists with the National Ballet."

1962

7   SOWTON, IAN. "Poetry To No One Else: Six Gestures of Lyric Response." *Queen's Quarterly* 68, (Summer):344–350. UCD Archive.
    Review of six poetry books, including *Come Dance with Kitty Stobling and Other Poems*. Considers the poetry "a simple Irish variation on the cliché version of Wordsworthianism; the common man-philosopher-bard." Claims Kavanagh lectures too much, although his argument is often "ludicrously banal."

1962

1   CARRUTH, HAYDEN. "Problems of Maturity." *Poetry* 101, no. 3 (December):205–207.
    Review of three books, including *Come Dance with Kitty Stobling and Other Poems*. Kavanagh has failed to find "the delicate, dynamic balance of substance and style." The poems are "roughshod," sometimes "close to doggerel." Criticizes Kavanagh's un-Yeatsian indifference to felicitous form. Finds Kavanagh's philosophical outlook merely a conventional liberal, sentimental Christianity. Claims Kavanagh began with great talent but has failed to live up to his potential.

2   COLUM, PADRAIC. "A Note on P. K." *Kilkenny Magazine* no. 7 (Summer):47–48.
    Defends himself against Kavanagh's claim (made in a postscript to his essay "William Butler Yeats" in *Kilkenny Magazine* (Spring 1962), that Colum's style was derived from Synge. Colum points out that he published some of his poetry before Synge could have influenced him.

3   DELAHANTY, JAMES. Review of John Montague's *Poisoned Lands and Other Poems*. *Kilkenny Magazine* no. 6 (Spring):49.
    Claims he prefers "Kavanagh's earthy outspoken ridicule to Montague's sophisticated half-insult."

4   HOLOHAN, LEO. "T. E. Tonight." *RTV Guide* (26 October). UCD Archive.
    Profile of Kavanagh. Announces the forthcoming *Self Portrait* program to be broadcast on October 30.

5   "Kathleen ni Houlihan" [pseud.]. "Letters to the Editor. Debunking Yeats." *Irish Times* (7 April):12.
    Response to Payne (1962.12).

6   LIDDY, JAMES. "Letters to the Editor. Debunking Yeats." *Irish Times* (4 April):7.

1962

Response to Payne (1962.12). Defends both Kavanagh and Yeats. "Anyone who knows Mr. Kavanagh would realise that he would not lend himself to a small-minded attack on the work of Yeats."

7   MACALERNON, DON. "Books." *Focus* (December):283. UCD Archive.
    Review of *Brendan Behan's Island* (1962). "Mr. Behan is like Paddy Kavanagh, only more so. On the whole, if an opinion is unpopular, he holds it."

8   MERCIER, VIVIAN. *The Irish Comic Tradition*. London, New York: Oxford University Press, pp. 201, 208.
    Kavanagh's satirical work shows the influence of Swift. Praises the satire of *A Soul for Sale*.

9   MOONEY, DONAL. "Poetry Ireland." *St. Stephen's* (UCD), Michaelmas, pp. 6–8.
    Briefly discusses Kavanagh's "emotional intensity."

10 O'CONAILL, DONAL. "Spectrum, T. E.'s new show, has much promise, few faults." *Irish Press* (3 November):13. UCD Archive.
    Discusses several current television programs, including Kavanagh's *Self Portrait*, which he praises highly: "Every sentence was alive." Remarks this "anti-humbug personality" has the courage to be himself.

11 O'FAOLAIN, SEAN. "Fifty Years of Irish Writing." *Studies* 51, no. 201 (Spring):93–105.
    Briefly mentions Kavanagh in the context of recent poetry. Claims all Irish writers must find a universal vision based in local detail, as Joyce and Kavanagh have done.

12 PAYNE, BASIL. "Letters to the Editor. Debunking Yeats." *Irish Times* (31 March):9.
    Letter on the Irish reception of Yeats. Refers to Kavanagh's views on Yeats.

13 ———. "Letters to the Editor. Debunking Yeats." *Irish Times* (7 April):7, 12.
    Letter response to Liddy (1962.6).

14 S., T. J. M. "Television. The Inimitable Kavanagh." *Pioneer* (November). UCD Archive.
    Positive review of *Self Portrait*.

1963

*15 SHEEDY, LARRY. "How Kavanagh Told His Story." *Irish Farmer's Journal* (18 August). UCD Archive.

16 STUART, FRANCIS. "National Gallery, Patrick Kavanagh." *Development, Agriculture and Industry*, no. 39 (January):16. UCD Archive.
    Profile of Kavanagh, who is in the tradition of "outcast" poets, such as Rimbaud, Baudelaire, Poe, and Villon. He writes against "the cult of mediocrity."

17 "TV Round-Up: Patrick Kavanagh was too big for television." *Evening Herald* (1 November). UCD Archive.
    Review of *Self Portrait* on RTE. Claims Kavanagh "took the small screen by the throat, threw it out of the window." *Self Portrait* was "a little frightening, but in its way exciting."

18 WHITE, TERENCE DE VERE. "The Road to Parnassus." *Irish Times* (15 September).
    Review of *X* magazine 2, no. 3, which contains "an inimitable account of horse-dealing by Patrick Kavanagh."

1963

1 HEANEY, SEAMUS. "The Immortal Newsmen." *Hibernia* (July):17.
    Review of several books of poems, including *Come Dance with Kitty Stobling and Other Poems*. Claims there are no major poets in contemporary Ireland. Provides an outline of Kavanagh's poetic career from his "naturalistic" novels to *The Great Hunger*, which is "one of our best Irish poems." In *Come Dance with Kitty Stobling*, Kavanagh "has been driven to the pose of disgruntled bard, hard-headed and sharp-tongued, who occasionally capitalises rather than particularises the concepts of Life, Art, Time and Love." Looks forward to the *Collected Poems*.

2 ———. "Letters. Poets Protest." *Hibernia* (September):2.
    Heaney's response to Liddy, Hartnett and Weber (1963.3, 1963.5). Claims he did not "refuse commendation" to Clarke and Kavanagh, but questions whether they are and will be "major—for all time in all places."

3 LIDDY, JAMES, and MICHAEL HARTNETT. "Letters. Poets Protest." *Hibernia* (August):2.
    Protests Seamus Heaney's apparent refusal to commend the poetry of Kavanagh and Austin Clarke.

1964

4 POTTS, PAUL. "Patrick Kavanagh, The Poems and the Poet." *London Magazine* 2, no. 11 (February):78–81.

Claims Kavanagh is the best Irish poet since Yeats. Discusses the poem "Sanctity." Compares Kavanagh to Spinoza, Pound, Hugh McDiarmid, Blake, Van Gogh, et al.

5 WEBER, RICHARD. "Letters. Poets Protest." *Hibernia* (August):2.

Claims that Seamus Heaney in his recent *Hibernia* review suffers from "a national inferiority complex." Challenges Heaney's claim that a test of poetic worth is being read abroad by foreign readers.

6 ———. "Letters. Poets Protest." *Hibernia* (October):2.
Response to Seamus Heaney's letter (1963.2).

7 WOLLMAN, MAURICE. *Ten Contemporary Poets*. London: Harrap, p. 91.

Brief biographical introduction to Kavanagh, preceding a selection of his poems.

1964

1 ALVAREZ, A. "The Irish Gadfly." *Observer* (26 July).

Review of several books, including Kavanagh's *Collected Poems* (MacGibbon and Kee). Considers Kavanagh "the best poet Ireland now has." He is now "the gadfly of Irish letters." Claims the book is "an achievement more of personality than of poetry." Divides Kavanagh's career into three parts: the romantic lyricist, the realist, and the satirist. Praises *The Great Hunger*. Dismisses the later poems as poems that are "mostly too prattling to have much poetic impact," but praises them as "an expression of a personality."

2 FALLON, PADRAIC. "The Sage of Monaghan." *Irish Times* (15 August):8.

Review of *Collected Poems* (Macgibbon and Kee). Claims that in his early poems, Kavanagh had "a vast respect for the timeless soul of man" but this did not necessarily make good poetry. He was open to "religious illumination," rather than "poetic experience." He is "a poet of moments." Most of his early work was a romantic, derivative echo of a former age. It was technically more polished than the later "manic-impressive utterances and the ranker satires." Praises *The Great Hunger*. Wishes Kavanagh had written another novel.

3 "Going Through the Emotions." *Times Literary Supplement* (27 August):766.

Review of *Collected Poems*. Considers Kavanagh "an alternately poker-faced and lachrymose knockabout." Mentions Kavanagh's self-con-

1964

sciousness as a poet and public figure. Claims Kavanagh is most successful when showing an "ironic edge," blending the conversational with the lyrical. His main themes are "the tension between regretting and justifying his loneliness (more specifically a barren emotional and sexual life), his sense of vocation as a poet, and the damaging effect on this of apparent failure." Finds these themes limited in range. Wishes Kavanagh could show more self-pity in his poems. Regrets the near doggerel of Kavanagh's satires, and contrasts them with those of George Barker. Finds the early poems "anachronistic and sentimental."

4 GOLDWYN GIRLS. "Letterbox. Cheers for Kavanagh." *RTV Guide* (24 May). UCD Archive.
  Complains that Kavanagh, film critic for *RTV Guide*, is stuck in "the old days." Films have changed, "but Kavanagh has not."

5 H., T. *Kilkenny Magazine* (Spring):118.
  Brief review of *Self Portrait*. Claims Kavanagh is very unpredictable. Refers to interview with the poet in *Hibernia* (1964.18).

6 HARMAN, M. A. "Letters. Kavanagh challenged." *Hibernia* (July–August):7
  Response to Kavanagh's interview in *Hibernia* (1964.18). Offers criticism of Kavanagh's view of poetry as "saying things."

7 HIGGINS, BRIAN. "Ironic Dublin Poet." *Daily Telegraph and Morning Post* (20 August):18.
  Review of *Collected Poems*. Claims Kavanagh "can stand alongside Hugh MacDiarmid, Roy Campbell, W. H. Auden and George Barker." He is "the ironic master of the Dublin scene." Praises his love poems and defends him against charges of technical sloppiness.

8 HORGAN, JOHN. "Reproach to Irish Poets." *Catholic Herald* (October). UCD Archive.
  Review of *Collected Poems*. Admires *The Great Hunger*, as well as Kavanagh's later humorous poems and ballads.

9 "Image of a Poet." *RTV Guide:* (9 October). UCD Archive.
  Profile of Kavanagh, who is to be "the subject of Monday's *Image* programme," which will be broadcast on RTV.

10 "Irish Poet." *Times Literary Supplement* (9 July):587.
  Review of *Self Portrait*. Describes Kavanagh's background in Monaghan and his views on *The Green Fool* and *The Great Hunger*. "The booklet is illustrated with six photographs of Mr. Kavanagh in characteristic attitudes."

1964

11 JORDAN, JOHN. "A Few Thoughts about P. K." *Poetry Ireland* 4 (Summer):123–126.

Discusses Kavanagh's *Collected Poems*, which is "a confusing compromise between a 'collected' edition, and an amateur 'critical' edition," although it is the first attempt to produce a "Kavanagh verse canon, albeit an incomplete one." Laments some omissions. Kavanagh is "one of the most original minds writing verse today," whose work is marked by "an unmistakableness of attitude, a unity in contrariness." Claims *The Great Hunger* is an "aberration" from Kavanagh's "quest for self-knowledge." He is a Wordsworthian "poet of the Self."

12 KENNEDY, MAURICE. "Appetiser." *Irish Times* (28 March):8.

Review of *Self Portrait*, which is "not so much a self-portrait as a typical exercise in self-concealment." Claims Kavanagh is highly selective in his self-portrait, thus leaves much out that could be included. For instance, his views on films. Praises his film criticism. Regrets that Kavanagh has not written much of late, and hopes he will write a fuller autobiography.

13 KENNELLY, BRENDAN. "Books." *Dubliner* (Winter):70–71.

Review of *Collected Poems*. Discusses Kavanagh's later dismissal of *The Great Hunger*. Claims Kavanagh's career was a journey "toward the authority of wisdom and the gaiety of youth." Praises Kavanagh for always being "completely himself."

14 LIDDY, JAMES. "Poetry in Ireland." *Hibernia* (December):19.

Brief reference to the poet, with photo of Kavanagh, et al.

15 ———. "Patrick Kavanagh's Dublin." *In a Blue Smoke*. Dublin: Dolmen, Oxford: Oxford University Press, p. 7.

Poem addressed to or inspired by Kavanagh.

16 LOFTUS, RICHARD. *Nationalism in Modern Anglo-Irish Poetry*. Madison and Milwaukee: University of Wisconsin Press, p. 19.

Quotes from "Memory of Brother Michael," and claims Kavanagh "condemns Ireland's romantic nostalgia for the past."

17 O'CONNOR, FRANK. "Awkward But Alive." *Spectator* (31 July). 159.

Review of *Collected Poems*. Recalls how George Russell (AE) thought the poems of Kavanagh's first volume were "fake," but claims that Kavanagh is a much better poet than AE. Praises the sonnets in particular. Discusses "Inniskeen Road: July Evening," "Stony Grey Soil" (a watershed poem), and *The Great Hunger*. Believes Kavanagh's second and third collections contain his best work. Recalls his pleasure upon first reading *The Great Hunger*. Discusses response of "Irish middle-class society" to the self-educated coun-

1964

try poet. Finds Kavanagh's later work "confused" and too subjective, although he is "our best living poet."

18 O'FARRELL, MAIRIN. "Poetry is not really an Art." *Hibernia* (May):16.
Interview with Kavanagh.

19 ———. "A Dublin Literary Pub." *Hibernia* (July–August):12.
Interview with Paddy O'Brien, head bartender in McDaid's pub. Refers to Kavanagh's contribution to the pub's fame: "Another thing that put McDaid's on its feet was Kavanagh's libel action. They were coming here sightseeing at the time."

20 O'GLAISNE, RISTEARD. "Books." *Focus* (May):116.
Review of *Self Portrait*. Prefers Kavanagh's work on paper to his work on television. Thinks it is "a lot of blather," but thought provoking. Now that it is in print "one can rage quietly at its arrogant excesses and respond to its occasional insights."

21 O'REILLY, P. O. "If computers write poetry." *Evening Herald* (22 October). UCD Archive.
Refers to letter from "Oscar" in *Evening Herald* concerning Kavanagh's recent interview on Telefis Eireann. Praises Kavanagh and the interview. Kavanagh "isn't a failure."

22 PAYNE, BASIL. "Love and the Irish. Portrait of the poet as prophet." *Hibernia* (April):1–3.
Review of *Self Portrait*. Claims Kavanagh is exception to Camille Bourniquel's theory that Irish artists have "discovered how to glorify reality." Kavanagh is neglected in Ireland, but predicts he "will be recognised posthumously . . . as our greatest poet since Yeats, and a greater (because truer) voice than Yeats's."

23 ———. "Kavanagh Incorporated." *Hibernia* (September):14.
Review of *Collected Poems*. Kavanagh cannot be "typed" for he is "his own man." If you like Kavanagh, "you have the bug for life." He is humble, and religious—"our poetic high priest."

24 RICKS, CHRISTOPHER. "Twin Ironies." *New Statesman* (31 July):152.
Review of *Self-Portrait* and *Collected Poems*. Admires the personal note of Kavanagh's poems. Discusses the selection of poems for *Collected Poems*, and regrets that weaker poems "clog up" the collection. Prefers Kavanagh's early works to his late poems, although some early poems are marred by "a religiose whimsy." Kavanagh is "obsessed with failure," and *The Great Hunger* examines different kinds of failure. Compares the poem to

1964

the work of George Crabbe. Finds the late satires "parochial and long-winded." Kavanagh is "a hit-and-miss poet."

25 ROCHE, EMER. "Letterbox. Cheers for Kavanagh." *RTV Guide* (24 May). UCD Archive.
    Praises Kavanagh as film critic for *RTV Guide*.

26 SMITH, PETER DUVALL, and PATRICK KAVANAGH. Interview with Patrick Kavanagh. BBC radio broadcast, transmitted 18 August. Duration 9 minutes 12 seconds.
    Smith interviews Kavanagh about his poetry and his life in Ireland.

27 THWAITE, ANTHONY. Review of *Collected Poems*. *Listener* 13 (August). 243.
    Comments on Kavanagh's legendary status in Ireland despite being little known in England. Claims he is an inconsistent poet and the early verse was "trite." The poetry of *The Great Hunger* and *A Soul for Sale* is his best work. Praises the "innocence" and "stoicism" of these poems, but finds Kavanagh's later satires weak, because he has little to say, "except that he doesn't like the Irish being Irish, doesn't like scholars and reviewers, and distrusts reason." Concludes he is original but not major.

28 TORCHIANA, DONALD. "Contemporary Irish Poetry." *Chicago Review* 17, nos. 2 and 3:152–168.
    Although Kavanagh is "frequently a windbag, a bore and even an opportunist," he is possibly the strongest Irish poet since Yeats, especially in his later sonnets, "when he surrenders himself to the ensorcelling greenery of Dublin's canals and parks." Criticizes the "humorless, self-righteous, self-flagellating" note of much of *A Soul for Sale* and *Come Dance with Kitty Stobling*. Compares Kavanagh to Patrick Collins, the painter, who are both, when at their best, "unrivalled in Ireland."

29 WARNER, ALAN. "A Poet of the Countryside. *Review of English Literature* 5, no. 3 (July):79–86.
    Although Kavanagh's early style was "Georgian pastoral," *The Great Hunger* represents the development of "a more powerful and individual voice." Contrasts the poem with Goldsmith's *The Deserted Village* and Thomson's *Seasons,* which idealized rural life. *The Great Hunger*, which is an "ironic antidote" to romanticism, has an occasionally strident note but remains "profoundly moving," combining "colloquial ease" with "vivid imagery." Contrasts Kavanagh with Crabbe. Even in Dublin, Kavanagh "can still praise the commonplace," as in "The Hospital." Discusses Kavanagh's change of tone after his lung operation, observing "a note of prayer and praise" in his late poetry.

1965

30 ——. "Introducing Patrick Kavanagh." *Acorn* no. 7 (Autumn). UCD Archive.
Essay on the poet. Discusses *Tarry Flynn, The Ploughman and Other Poems, The Great Hunger, Kavanagh's Weekly*, and Kavanagh's diary in *Envoy*.

1965

1 "A world in which parents can pre-select their children." *Queen* (London), (6 October). UCD Archive.
Andrew Oldham, manager of the Rolling Stones, would choose Patrick Kavanagh for a father.

2 BOGAN, LOUISE. "Verse." *New Yorker* (10 April):194.
Review of three books, including Kavanagh's *Collected Poems*. Mentions the early poetry, including *The Great Hunger*. Claims there is a sense of disillusionment in his later poetry. Discusses Kavanagh's hatred of stage Irishry. Claims the poems in *Collected Poems* were selected by Martin Green. Contrasts Kavanagh with "the more official and solemn post-Yeatsians." Praises his wildness.

3 BOLAND, EAVAN. Review of *Tarry Flynn. Dublin Magazine* (Summer): 84–85.
Claims the novel works on two levels: the daily life of Tarry and Tarry's "feeling for the earth, his disturbed and lyrical communion with it." Praises MacGibbon & Kee edition of novel.

4 BRAYBROOKE, NEVILLE. "The Schizophrenic Novel." *Spectator* (19 March):369.
Review of several novels, including *Tarry Flynn*, which he compares and contrasts to *Snake Water* (1965), by Alan Williams. Finds Kavanagh's prose humorous and lyrical.

5 HAMILTON, IAIN. "Recent Fiction: Elegy for the Peasant Life." *Daily Telegraph and Morning Post* (8 April):22.
Review of *Tarry Flynn*. Praises the book's "hard-edged precision, lack of sentimentality," and irony. The novel is "an elegy for the old life on the southerly slopes of Ulster," and Kavanagh is a "rural O'Casey" or "a mountainy Joyce." Discusses character of Tarry.

6 KAVANAGH, PATRICK, THOMAS KINSELLA, W. D. SNODGRASS, and STEPHEN SPENDER. "Poetry Since Yeats: An Exchange of Views." *TriQuarterly* 4 (Autumn):100–111.

Four talks by the above poets on poetry after Yeats. A heated debate follows Kavanagh's final contribution. Kinsella concludes: "We are in total and utter and irretrievable disagreement on the bench here."

7   KIELY, BENEDICT. "That Old Triangle: A Memory of Brendan Behan." *Hollins Critic* 11, no. 1 (February):1–12.
    Recalls that Brendan Behan once painted Kavanagh's apartment all black as a joke.

8   KINSELLA, THOMAS. "A Yeats Festival on the shores of Lake Michigan." *Hibernia* (June):9.
    Account of the Yeats centenary celebrations at Northwestern University. Refers to Kavanagh's disruptive contribution.

9   LENNON, ANTHONY. "Kavanagh's Record." *Irish Times* (19 June):8.
    Brief review of Kavanagh's LP record, *Almost Everything*, edited and produced by Proinsias Mac Aonghusa.

10 LIDDY, JAMES. "Prolegomenon." *Kilkenny Magazine* (Spring):35–38.
    Brief reference to Kavanagh.

11 "London Letter: Fashionable Set." *Irish Times* (22 April):9.
    Mentions that Kavanagh drinks regularly in the Bloomsbury pub, "The Plough."

12 MARTIN, AUGUSTINE. "The Rediscovery of Austin Clarke." *Studies* 54, no. 216 (Winter):408–434.
    "Ten years ago Kavanagh was regarded as Ireland's leading poet, just as surely as Austin Clarke is now considered to have taken his place." Discusses the power of *The Great Hunger*. Discusses the rising reputation of Clarke, but notes that Basil Payne and Al Alvarez consider Kavanagh the better poet.

13 MCMAHON, SEAN. "Backgrounds For the Study of Irish Literature." *Eire* (Spring):83.
    Briefly mentions *Tarry Flynn*.

14 MONTAGUE, JOHN. "Under Ben Bulben." *Shenandoah* 16, no. 4 (Summer):21–24.
    In a discussion of post-Yeatsian poetry, remarks that Kavanagh's honest voice "has liberated us into ignorance: he has literally nothing to say."

1965

15 MURPHY, RICHARD. "New Beauty from Old Clay." *New York Times*, section 7 (23 May):4.

    Review of *Collected Poems*. Discusses Kavanagh's early background and *The Great Hunger*, which was "a moral poem," showing humor and compassion. Discusses the comic "legend" of Kavanagh in Dublin. Mentions "The Paddiad" and claims the satires are weaker than his other poems. Praises the Canal Bank sonnets, in which "the voice of his own personality speaks."

16 NEWTON, J. M. "Patrick Kavanagh's Imagination." *Delta* (Cambridge) 37 (Autumn):4–8.

    Review of *Tarry Flynn*. Identifies the protagonist as a thinly-disguised version of Kavanagh himself. Discusses the character of Tarry and the novel's action. Finds *The Green Fool* "more vigorously written" than *Tarry Flynn*, and prefers *The Great Hunger* to *Tarry Flynn*, although it is also "unconvincing and untragic." Praises Kavanagh's briefer, simpler poems, such as "Beech Tree," although none of his poetry is perfect because he "simply hasn't any urgent concern to get the poem perfectly right." Yet Kavanagh is a good poet, better than Philip Larkin.

17 "Notes on Current Books." *VQR* (Autumn):cxxiv.

    Brief review of *Collected Poems*. Compares Kavanagh to Yeats and claims his poetry moves from the earth "into beautiful free flight."

18 O'DONOGHUE, FLORENCE. "Second Sight." *Tablet* (18 September): 1034–1035.

    Brief review of the reprint of *Tarry Flynn*.

19 PAYNE, BASIL. "Cheers all round: the real Kavanagh." *Hibernia* (Dublin), (June):13.

    Review of Kavanagh's LP record, *Almost Everything*. Finds the record "compellingly original, yet surprisingly restful." Praises the richness of the autobiographical pieces collected on side one, and of the nineteen poems on side two of the record. Claims that love is Kavanagh's central theme.

20 Review of *Collected Poems*. *Choice* 2 (November):580.

    Praises the poetry's "rushing vigor" and "rude force."

21 SEALY, DOUGLAS. "The Writings of Patrick Kavanagh." *Dublin Magazine* 4, nos. 3–4 (Autumn/Winter):5–27.

    Claims *Ploughman and Other Poems* was influenced by the Revival and by Padraic Colum's *Wild Earth*. Notes resemblance between *The Green Fool* and *Tarry Flynn*, the latter of which is "Kavanagh's *Goodbye to All That*." Discusses *The Great Hunger*, *A Soul for Sale*, and Kavanagh's

1965

Weekly, which seems to have been "a waste of talent." Argues that Kavanagh found peace in *Come Dance with Kitty Stobling,* although some of the poems are awkward and slovenly, "like a sort of automatic writing." Concludes that the later work is inferior and that Kavanagh's reputation rests on *The Great Hunger* and *A Soul for Sale.*

22 SKELTON, ROBIN. "Life at Work." *Poetry* 106 (June):234–236.
    Review of *Self Portrait, Come Dance with Kitty Stobling*, and *Collected Poems*. Praises the simplicity of Kavanagh's early poetry, although notes they are conventional. Praises *The Great Hunger* as Kavanagh's greatest work, comparing its mood to that of Van Gogh's "Potato-Eaters." Discusses Kavanagh's "rebirth" in 1955, and considers much of the subsequent writing "idiosyncratic light verse." Laments the casualness of his recent poems, yet he is still "his own man."

23 TAUBMAN, ROBERT. "Style-Spotting." *New Statesman* (19 March):456.
    Review of *Tarry Flynn*. Claims that Kavanagh's "sketches of an Irish village in the thirties are a matter of old women and their hens, a young man hardly awakened at the age of thirty, and the compost of ideas in a Catholic community."

24 TORCHIANA, DONALD. "Some Dublin Afterthoughts." *TriQuarterly* 4 (Autumn): 140–145.
    Discusses the planning of the 1965 Yeats festival at Northwestern University. Finds Kavanagh's caustic attack on Yeats and the academic treatment of poetry to have been "the usual stale Kavanagh clichés: Yeats was not Irish, most contemporary poets are dull. American criticism is loony."

25 "Touchliner." *Observer*, Weekend Review (25 April):23.
    Announces Kavanagh's appearance at Yeats symposium at Northwestern University. Claims he is "rarely seen in public in London, except perhaps on the touchline, watching Battersea Park, the young publishers' football team."

26 WHITE, TERENCE DE VERE. "Patrick's Morning." *Irish Times* (20 March):8.
    Review of reprint of *Tarry Flynn*, which he claims was neglected when first published. Praises the novel as a deceptively simple "tiny epic," one of the few great Irish books of its time. Concludes: "To be Irish and not to read it is to sin against the light."

1966

1 "Back room boys play rough." *Chicago Daily News* (2 January). UCD Archive.
   Account of Kavanagh's contribution to Yeats symposium at Northwestern University.

2 BENCE-JONES, MARK. *The Remarkable Irish*. New York: David McKay, pp. 131, 141–142, 194.
   Claims Kavanagh's poetry "has an air of no-nonsense." Discusses "The Paddiad."

3 BRESLIN, JIMMY. "In a Dublin Pub. Poetry and People." *New York Herald Tribune* (13 April):23.
   Profile of Kavanagh: "Rude and rough and delightful and profane." The Dublin pub is McDaid's.

4 CALLAGHAN, BARRY. "One Forgotten Old Man." *Telegram* (Toronto), *Showcase* (supplement), (7 May):5.
   Profile of Kavanagh and discussion of *The Great Hunger*. Finds Patrick Maguire "one of the most compelling figures in English language poetry." Claims Kavanagh is "unknown in North America, and his work is read only by a few in Ireland and England," although he is the best Irish poet since Yeats. Gives account of recent conversation between poet and George Barker in London pub, The Plough.

5 CARROLL, NIALL. "'I'd love to meet Ian Paisley,' says Patrick Kavanagh." *Irish Press* (November). Undated. UCD Kavanagh Archive.
   Announces that Kavanagh will be the subject of a forthcoming RTE program, in which he will be interviewed by Proinsias MacAonghusa. Kavanagh admires The Beatles, Sean O'Casey, and Ian Paisley.

6 CURTAYNE, ALICE. "Darker gleam of rural life." *Hibernia* (June):13.
   Compares Seamus Heaney, author of *Death of a Naturalist*, to Patrick Kavanagh.

7 HARSCH, SANDOL. "Letters to the Editor. Carping at Kavanagh." *Hibernia* (August):2.
   Letter to the editor. Responds to Kavanagh's interview in *Hibernia* (1966.8). Claims Kavanagh has a prejudiced and distorted view of America.

8 "Kavanagh's America." *Hibernia* (July):11.

1966

Interview with Kavanagh concerning his part in the Yeats Festival at Northwestern University. Questions Kavanagh about his view of modern American writing and American life in general.

*9 KENNELLY, BRENDAN. "Markings: Patrick Kavanagh." *RTV Guide* (26 November):8–9.
    Remarks on Kavanagh.

10 MAX [pseud.]. "Shows Abroad. *Tarry Flynn*." *Variety* (14 December):62.
    Review of Abbey Theatre production of *Tarry Flynn*, written by P. J. O'Connor. Praises Kavanagh's *Tarry Flynn*, and claims that O'Connor "has preserved the original dialog faithfully." Discusses the main actors.

11 MCMAHON, SEAN. "The Ireland in The Heart." *Eire* (Fall):84–85
    Briefly discusses two Kavanagh poems, "Memory of Brother Michael" and "Epic."

12 MONTAGUE, JOHN. "Living under Ben Bulben." *Kilkenny Magazine* 14 (Spring–Summer):44–47.
    Reprint of Montague (1965.14).

13 MOORE, JOHN REES. "Now Yeats Has Gone: Three Irish Poets." *Hollins Critic* 3, no. 2 (April):6–12.
    Kavanagh is "a rugged individualist." Discusses antiromantic iconoclasm of *Self Portrait* and *The Great Hunger*. Contrasts Maguire with the "man with the hoe" in a poem by Edward Markham. In his later poetry, Kavanagh is carefree, but the poems are merely "light verse."

14 O'CONNOR, ULICK. "Patrick Kavanagh: Poet." *Creation* (August). UCD Archive.
    Refers to Patrick O'Connor's sculpture of Kavanagh's head—"one of the important pieces of Irish sculpture." Profile of Kavanagh, who "has the constitution of a Tibetan snowhorse." Comments on Kavanagh's recovery from cancer: "He recovered to write his best poetry."

15 O'HAODHA, MICHAEL. "Patrick Kavanagh." First Night Program, *Tarry Flynn* (adapted by P. J. O'Connor), Abbey Theatre, 22 November. UCD Archive.
    Brief introduction to poet.

16 "QUIDNUNC." "An Irishman's Diary." *Irish Times* (26 January):9.
    Alludes to O'Connor's portraits of Kavanagh in oil and clay.

1967

17 SEALY, DOUGLAS. "Irish Poets of the Sixties." *Irish Times* (24 January):8.
   Discusses Kavanagh's claim that the usual number of Irish poets "seldom falls below the figure of 10,000." Contemporary Irish poetry, including Kinsella's and Montague's, "does a little to offset the gloomy impression caused by Kavanagh's remark."

18 "'Tarry Flynn' at the Abbey." *Hibernia* (December):32.
   Review of the first night of P. J. O'Connor's dramatization of *Tarry Flynn* at the Abbey Theatre. Claims the theater company has made of the play an affectionate and delightful "dramatic comedy." The novel on the other hand was "a ruthless picture of a bad society." The reviewer disliked the set.

19 Untitled. *National Catholic Reporter* (30 March). UCD Archive.
   Describes meeting Kavanagh in Dublin pub.

1967

1 "A Poet Comes Home." *Young Citizen. Civics Bulletin for Schools* (December). UCD Archive.
   Obituary notice of Kavanagh's death.

2 BOLAND, EAVAN. "In Praise of Praise." *Irish Times* (24 March):8.
   Review of reprint of *The Great Hunger* (MacGibbon and Kee). Claims the poem communicates at two separate levels: as a social protest and as "a protest about the human condition." The poem is also "a praise of human freedom" and a "celebration of possibility." Discusses the themes of love and joy in the poem.

3 ——. Review of *Collected Pruse. Dublin Magazine* (Autumn):85–86.
   Claims Kavanagh is a highly individual poet, but his writing has been limited by an unwillingness to adopt the "disguise of drama," a "Yeatsian anti-self." The egotism which humanizes his poetry spoils his prose, marked by unimpressive "quarrelsome sweeps of his imagination." Nevertheless, Boland finds the collection a moving one.

4 BRACKEN, T. "Patrick Kavanagh." *Evening Herald* (7 December):9. UCD Archive.
   Expression of appreciation of poet.

5 BURGESS, ANTHONY. "A buuk" [sic]. *Observer* (London) (12 March):26.
   Review of *Collected Pruse*. Disapproves of Kavanagh's whimsical title, and thinks little of his critical acumen: "Perhaps the best of contemporary Irish poets, he has few critical qualifications except candour."

1967

6   CANDIDA [pseud.]. "An Irish Woman's Diary." *Irish Times* (11 December):7.
    Briefly discusses *Kavanagh's Weekly* and mentions the memorial seat at the Grand Canal.

7   CLEEVE, BRIAN. *Dictionary of Irish Writers*. First Series. Cork: Mercier Press, p. 67.
    Biographical entry on the poet.

8   CRAVEN, JIM. "Patrick Kavanagh." *Dundalk Democrat* (9 December). UCD Archive.
    Tribute to Kavanagh: "Already his fame seems assured."

9   Death Notice. *Time* (8 December):108.
    Announces death of Kavanagh, who was "better known for his acid tongue than for his lyric poetry."

10 "Death of a Noted Poet." *Irish Press* (1 December). UCD Archive.
    Obituary and profile.

11 "Death of leading Irish poet." *Irish Independent* (1 December):11. UCD Archive.
    Obituary notice and profile.

12 "Death of Patrick Kavanagh." *Evening Press* (30 November). UCD Archive.
    Announces death.

13 "Death of Poet Paddy Kavanagh." *Evening Herald* (30 November). UCD Archive.
    Obituary.

14 "Deaths Elsewhere." *Philadelphia Inquirer* (1 December):28. UCD Archive.
    Short obituary of Kavanagh, "a farm-bred, rough-tongued man who hated intellectual philistines and status seekers."

15 FISHER, JONATHAN. "Kavanagh and Wilde Busts on Offer." *Irish Times* (6 November):8.
    Announces that Patrick O'Connor's bust of Kavanagh is for sale at Christie's in London. The artist's father, Andrew O'Connor, drew the designs for the bust.

1967

16 FOLEY, DONAL. "Patrick Kavanagh is Buried at Inniskeen." *Irish Times* (4 December):6.

Describes Kavanagh's funeral, at which there were "300 to 400 people present." Leo Holohan spoke at the graveside, and poems were read by John Montague, Seamus Heaney, David Wright, and Richard Reardon. Lists other mourners. See further reports in *Irish Independent* (4 December) and *Irish Press* (4 December).

17 "Funeral Takes Place Today." *Irish Times* (2 December):6.

Gives details of Kavanagh's funeral and of a special commemorative program on RTE that will be broadcast December 3. The audience of the evening's performance of *Tarry Flynn* in the Abbey Theatre on December 1st were asked to stand for a minute's silence.

18 "Greatest poet since Yeats: last tribute." *Sunday Press* (3 December). UCD Archive.

Tribute to the poet.

19 HAYMAN, RONALD. *Encounter* 29 (December):88–89.

Review of reprint of Kavanagh's *The Great Hunger*, "a very simple and very solid narrative." Claims Kavanagh "deserves to be taken more seriously, especially by himself." Mistakenly attributes the book *On the Way to the Depot* to Patrick Kavanagh.

20 HOLOHAN, LEO. "A Tribute." *Irish Times* (1 December):14.

Recycles several anecdotes about the "continuously humorous" Kavanagh. Recalls a conversation with him about the waning power of Catholicism. Like Swift, he became "a legend in his lifetime." Notes the performance of *Tarry Flynn* at the Peacock Theatre was canceled on November 30 "as a mark of respect."

21 HORGAN, JOHN. "An Ear to the North." *Irish Times* (7 December).

Discusses RTE's use of radio archives and mentions a recent commemorative program on Kavanagh broadcasted on December 3.

22 Interview. *Sunday Press* (29 October). UCD Archive.

Interview with Eavan Boland, who praises Kavanagh.

23 "Irish Poet Dies." *London Evening News* (30 November). UCD Archive.

Death notice.

24 "Irishman in Soho." *Times Literary Supplement* (4 May):381.

Review of *Collected Pruse*. Discusses the fifty-seven pages of court proceedings from the *Leader* trial, printed in *Collected Pruse*. Considers the

1967

proceedings fair, and argues that Kavanagh expects special privileges just because he is a poet. Dislikes much of the book. Suggests it should not have been published, except for the "sketches of life in rural Monaghan." Claims Kavanagh lacks the ability to reason systematically, even though he has written "ten or twelve good poems, and *Tarry Flynn*."

25 JORDAN, JOHN. "The voice of love." *Hibernia* (April):19.
Review of *Collected Pruse*, which is "a kind of patchwork autobiography, ingeniously stitched together by an unnamed hand." Claims Kavanagh "revels in the idiosyncratic vowel sounds of Northern speech." Discusses *Self Portrait* and the 1954 libel action. Claims Kavanagh is "not a critic in any received sense of the word," although his opinions are passionately held.

26 "Kavanagh Completes the Cycle." *Evening Press* (2 December). UCD Archive.
Appreciation of Kavanagh. Announces forthcoming RTE radio tribute to Kavanagh on December 3, 1967.

27 "Kavanagh: Master of the Rural Ode." *Irish Times* (1 December):14.
Obituary of Kavanagh, with biographical sketch.

28 KEANE, JOHN B. "Patrick Kavanagh." *Evening Press* (30 November). UCD Archive.
Memoir of Kavanagh.

29 KELLY, JAMES W. Untitled poem. *Hibernia* (April):19.
Describes Dublin landmarks, including "Kavanagh's canal."

*30 KENNELLY, T. B. *Modern Irish Poets and the Irish Epic*. Ph.D. thesis, TCD.
Thesis on modern Irish poetry.

31 M., S. "Patrick Kavanagh." *Clogher Diocesan Review: The Witness* (December):3. UCD Archive.
Memoir of Kavanagh. Remembers playing football with him.

32 MAC AONGHUSA, PROINSIAS. "Kavanagh, A Truly Great Poet." *Sunday Independent* (3 December):8. UCD Archive.
Obituary and profile. Claims Kavanagh will be remembered in 100 years as "one of the finest lyric poets in the English language," and that *The Great Hunger* "will be counted among the greatest works that have come out of Ireland."

33 ——. "Obituary: Patrick Kavanagh." *New Statesman* (8 December):818–819.
Praises Kavanagh as a very original poet, with no debts to Yeats, Synge, or AE. Discusses life and background. Discusses the banning of *The Great*

1967

Hunger when published in *Horizon* in 1942. Claims Kavanagh could be personally difficult, yet he always thought of himself as "a comic character." *Kavanagh's Weekly* was "the funniest paper ever produced in Ireland."

34 MARTIN, AUGUSTINE. "Poet's pruse." *Irish Press:* (18 March):10.
Review of *Collected Pruse*. Claims it is a valuable book insofar as it throws light on Kavanagh's poetry. However, as criticism the essays are very disappointing.

35 ———. "Tribute to Patrick Kavanagh." *Irish Independent* (1 December). UCD Archive.
An appreciation of Kavanagh.

36 MCGOWAN, GARRETT. "Patrick Kavanagh." *Dundalk Democrat* (9 December). UCD Archive.
Tribute to Kavanagh, the "greatest Irish poet since Yeats."

37 MCNEICE, W. G. "Poem." *Irish Independent* (9 December). UCD Archive.
Poem about Kavanagh.

38 MONTAGUE, JOHN. "A Tribute to Patrick Kavanagh." *Irish Times* (2 December).
Recalls meeting Kavanagh for the first time in Dublin. He was "clearly a genius." Discusses *The Great Hunger*: "The ripples from that extraordinary work are still spreading." Discusses the "energetic simplicity" of his later sonnets.

39 "Notes and Comments." *New Yorker* (9 December):51–52.
Notes the death of "the premier poet of Ireland." Discusses Kavanagh's drinking habits and his "powers of invective." Compares Kavanagh to Brendan Behan for his "superb vocabulary of scatological abuse." Quotes from a television appearance in which Kavanagh lambasted "peasant quality." Recounts an anecdote about meeting Kavanagh in New York.

40 "Obituary. Mr Patrick Kavanagh: An outstanding Irish poet." *Times* (London), (1 December):12.
Obituary notice. Discusses Kavanagh's early life and background. Claims that after *The Great Hunger*, Kavanagh became an "eloquent and irascible" Dublin character—"a tourist attraction." Discusses the *Leader* trial. Kavanagh's reputation will rest on *The Great Hunger* and some later poems. Although his work can be casual, perfunctory, even trivial, his whole opus communicates a sense of "remarkable integrity."

1967

41 O'CONNOR, FRANK. *The Backward Look.* London: Macmillan; and New York: Putnam's, pp. 213, 224, 229.

Sean O'Faolain's influence is "most strongly marked" on the poetry of Kavanagh, who was a "genius." Mentions the censorship of *The Great Hunger* when it was printed in *Horizon.* O'Connor, O'Faolain, Clarke, and Kavanagh were "the strayed revellers of the Irish literary revival," which was finished by 1940.

42 O'FAOLAIN, NUALA. Review of *Collected Pruse. Studies* 56, no. 223 (Autumn):324–326.

Kavanagh's 1954 trial was "a locus classicus of the confrontation of the philistine and artist." *Collected Pruse* shows Kavanagh's authenticity and sincerity. There is no sentimentality in the book. However, the book lacks "any kind of formulated philosophy," because Kavanagh is interested not in generalities but in details.

43 O'HAODHA, MICHAEL. "Patrick Kavanagh." *RTV Guide:* (8 December). UCD Archive.

Tribute to Kavanagh.

*44 O'MUIRITHE, DIARMUID. "Feach. Death of Patrick Kavanagh." RTE TV program. Transmitted 3 December. Duration: 6 minutes.

O'Muirithe talks to old friends of Kavanagh at McDaid's pub: Thomas McGowan, Tomas Toibin, Hayden Murphy, and Dr. O'Riordain.

45 "Patrick Kavanagh." *Variety* (6 December):63.
Brief obituary of the poet.

46 "Patrick Kavanagh." *Newsweek:* (11 December):61.
Obituary of the poet, "virtually a living landmark on Dublin's list of tourist attractions."

47 "Patrick Kavanagh—Film Philosopher." *Catholic Standard* (8 December). UCD Archive.

An appreciation of Kavanagh. Claims that large numbers of American students came to the library of the *Catholic Standard* to read Kavanagh's film criticism for the paper. "He distrusted crowds and admired those who walked alone."

48 "Patrick Kavanagh comes home to Inniskeen." *Dundalk Democrat* (9 December). UCD Archive.

Describes the poet's funeral.

1967

49 "Patrick Kavanagh, 1905-1967." *Studies* 56, no. 224 (Winter):368.
    Announces the death of Kavanagh. Reprints two sonnets by the poet which were published in the journal in 1958 and 1959.

50 "Patrick Kavanagh, Irish Poet and Playwright, Dies in Dublin. Reputation for Eccentricity Said to Have Overshadowed Literary Achievements." *New York Times* (1 December):47.
    Obituary. Mentions Kavanagh's recent marriage to Katherine Maloney, "a niece of Kevin Barry, the Irish boy patriot, who was executed by the British in 1918." Some poets who knew Kavanagh "believed he would have attained great fame if he had been more conventional in his behavior." Kavanagh's antisocial behavior at a New York party is cited as typical of his character. Discusses Kavanagh's tendency to dismiss canonical writers, like Whitman, Emerson, and Yeats.

51 "Poet laid to rest in his native soil." *Sunday Independent* (3 December). UCD Archive.
    Describes the poet's funeral.

52 "Poet Paddy weds niece of Kevin Barry." *Evening Herald* (19 April). UCD Archive.
    Announcement of Kavanagh's marriage to Katherine Maloney shortly before his death.

53 "Poets' Corner." *Sunday Press* (8 October). UCD Archive.
    Claims British Arts Council awarded Kavanagh a bursary of twelve hundred pounds.

54 POTTS, PAUL. "A Note on Patrick Kavanagh's Greatness." *Evening Herald* (9 December). UCD Archive.
    Tribute to Kavanagh.

55 *Publisher's Weekly: The Book Industry Journal* (New York) 192, no. 25 (December):35.
    Brief obituary. Notes the New York publication of *Tarry Flynn*, which was dramatized by the Abbey Theatre, Dublin, and *Collected Poems* (1964).

56 "Mr. P. Kavanagh." *Times* (London), (8 December):12.
    Brief additional obituary to Kavanagh. Praises Kavanagh, and claims he was "a holy poet without being a religious one."

57 "QUIDNUNC." "An Irishman's Diary." *Irish Times* (25 November):11.
    Briefly discusses a reviewer's mistaking Patrick for P. J. Kavanagh.

1967

58 ROSENTHAL, M. L. *The New Poets*. New York: Oxford University Press, pp. 275–283.
Discusses Kavanagh as antipastoral poet.

59 RYAN, JOHN. "Back to the fields of his youth." *Sunday Press* (3 December). UCD Archive.
Memoir of his recent meeting with Kavanagh, and profile.

60 SEALY, DOUGLAS. "Pruse Gleanings." *Irish Times* (24 March):8.
Review of *Collected Pruse*. Discusses the *Leader* trial proceedings which "makes astonishing and distasteful reading." Claims Kavanagh's criticism is not built on reasonable arguments but is highly subjective. Claims the parts of the book make up a large jigsaw puzzle, although the prose is inferior to his poetry.

61 "6,000 Pounds in Poetry Bursaries." *Times* (London), (6 October):9.
Announces that Kavanagh is one of five winners of poetry bursaries, worth twelve hundred pounds each.

62 "Sweeping Changes in Inter-Cert." *Sunday Press* (18 June). UCD Archive.
Discusses inclusion of Irish writers, including Kavanagh, in English studies in Irish secondary schools.

63 "The poet's last journey." *Sunday Press* (3 December). UCD Archive.
Describes funeral.

64 "To honour Patrick Kavanagh." *Irish Times* (12 December):8.
Mentions plans to commemorate Kavanagh with a dramatic tribute, to be performed at the Abbey Theatre and a seat at the Grand Canal.

65 Untitled. *Daily Telegraph* (5 October):19.
British Arts Council awarded Kavanagh a bursary worth twelve hundred pounds.

66 WEBB, W. L. "Patrick Kavanagh: an appreciation." *Guardian* (Manchester) (1 December):7.
Obituary. Claims that *The Great Hunger*, Kavanagh's best work, had the "same sort of influential underground reputation among young poets as the first novel of his contemporary Flann O'Brien."

67 WHITE, TERENCE DE VERE. "Patrick Kavanagh is Dead." *Irish Times* (30 November):1.
Announces death of poet. Gives biographical summary. Considers *The Great Hunger* "the highest point in Kavanagh's poetic development" and

"probably the greatest epic poem to appear in Ireland in this century." Discusses his journalism in *Envoy* and *Kavanagh's Weekly*: "The general tone of these writings was denigratory." Refers to the 1952 libel case, his lung operation, and his appearance at Northwestern University, where "he exhibited his familiar refusal to fit in with protocol." Kavanagh was "a more tragic Burns."

1968

1 "A Canal-Bank Seat. A Wish Fulfilled." *Irish Times* (18 March):13.
   Describes unveiling of the memorial Grand Canal Bank seat on March 17. Kavanagh's widow and three sisters were in attendance. Senator Eoin Ryan and John Ryan addressed the audience. Three priests blessed the seat: "I must say we never miss a trick," said Father Tom Stack. Describes Senator Ryan's speech, who praised Kavanagh's originality, independence of judgment, and sense of beauty. A photograph of Mrs. Katherine Kavanagh sitting on the seat accompanies the article.

2 ADAMS, MICHAEL. *Censorship: The Irish Experience*. Dublin: Scepter Books, p. 228.
   Reference to Kavanagh's libel action against *The Leader*.

3 CAREW, RIVERS, and TIMOTHY BROWNLOW. "Editorial: Patrick Kavanagh." *Dublin Magazine* (Spring):3–5.
   Except perhaps for Austin Clarke, Kavanagh was the "most notable" Irish poet since Yeats. Discusses his nonacademic background, which was an asset to the poet, because it gave him a clear vision. He possessed "a kind of innocence" which helped him write directly and freshly. He was well known as an eccentric character and became "the victim of his own image" in the 1954 libel case. He was unable "fully to realise his potential," but some of his work was great.

4 CASSEN, BERNARD. "Poètes irlandais d'aujourd'hui." *Le Monde* (21 December):7.
   Accompanies translations by Patrick Rafroidi of poems by Kavanagh, Clarke, Montague, Heaney, and Kennelly. General discussion of the contemporary Irish poetry scene, with brief references to the influence of Kavanagh.

5 CHILDS, SISTER MARYANNA. "P. K.: A Green Memory." *Catholic World* 206, no. 1236 (March):269–270.
   Obituary. Claims Kavanagh was a "character" who had the courage, faith and individuality of St. Patrick. Recalls seeing Kavanagh in Dublin.

Alludes to Torchiana essay (1965.24) and discusses Kavanagh's behavior at the Chicago Yeats Festival.

6 CLARKE, AUSTIN. *A Penny in the Clouds: More Memories of Ireland and England.* London: Routledge & Kegan Paul, p. 71.
    Brief reference to Kavanagh.

7 CRONIN, SEAN. "Baggot Street Bard." *Commonweal* (12 January):447.
    Announces Kavanagh's death, who was "perhaps Ireland's greatest living poet." He was "a peasant poet in the Burns tradition . . . anti-materialist, anti-bourgeois, anti-humbug, anti-sham." Praises *Tarry Flynn*'s authenticity. Kavanagh "honoured Ireland by his work and despite his criticism, never deserted her."

8 "Cross now marks Irish poet's grave." *Irish Independent* (22 August):7, 15. UCD Archive.
    Describes the cross on Kavanagh's grave.

9 "Editor's Notes." *Eire* 3, no. 1 (Spring):3.
    Announces the death of Kavanagh. Admires Sean Cronin's obituary piece in *Commonweal* (1968.7). Praises Garech Browne for having recorded Kavanagh's voice for Claddagh Records.

10 "Epitaph to a poet." *Irish Press* (21 August). UCD Archive.
    Describes how Peter Kavanagh used shale stones from the Inniskeen area to flag Patrick's grave.

11 FALLER, KEVIN. "Kavanagh and Others." *Irish Independent* (15 June). UCD Archive.
    Review of special issue of *Dublin Magazine* devoted to Kavanagh.

12 FITZ-SIMON, CHRISTOPHER. "Patrick Kavanagh and Tarry Flynn." Program for *Tarry Flynn*, Lyric Theatre, Belfast, 1968. UCD Archive.
    Brief introduction to the play. Challenges Kavanagh's renunciation of his early work, which Fitz-simon admires.

13 FREYER, GRATTAN. "Patrick Kavanagh." *Eire* 3, no. 4 (Winter):17–23.
    Considers Kavanagh to have been the most original Irish poet since Yeats. Discusses Kavanagh's background, observing that although Monaghan is "not tourist Ireland," Kavanagh bestows upon it "all the magic of Yeats's Sligo." Compares *The Great Hunger* to Eliot's *The Waste Land* in its "despair and simultaneous yearning for faith," to Hopkins's *The Wreck of the Deutschland*, and to D. H. Lawrence's realistic fiction. Considers the "hunger"

1968

of the poem's title to refer both to the "hunger of the peasant for land" and to the "Circean hunger of the land for men." Mentions Kavanagh's years in London and Dublin in the forties and his sexual frustration, and examines his "rasping denunciations" of his fellow Irishmen in *Kavanagh's Weekly*. Mentions "Profile," the trial, and the 1955 "religious experience" which transformed Kavanagh. Cites two Canal Bank sonnets and *In Memory of My Mother* as examples of his later "serenity."

14 "Give me a play on today!" *Sunday Independent* (1 December):26. UCD Archive.
Review of Lyric Theatre's (Belfast) production of *Tarry Flynn*, which had "enough sparkle to please the large audience."

15 GREEN, MARTIN. "Patrick Kavanagh." *Two Rivers* 1, no. 1 (Winter):27.
Poem addressed to Kavanagh.

16 ——, and PAUL DURCAN. "Editorial Note." *Two Rivers* 1, no. 1 (Winter):6.
Refers to Kavanagh's remark about *The Great Hunger* that poetry should not be noticeable by the police.

17 HAND, MICHAEL. "Patrick Kavanagh." *Sunday Press* (22 July). UCD Archive.
Appreciation of poet.

18 HARMON, MAURICE. *Modern Irish Literature 1800–1967: A Reader's Guide*. Chester Springs, PA.: Dufour, p. 43.
Brief reference to Kavanagh.

19 HARTNETT, MICHAEL. "The Dublin Literary World." *Irish Times* (13 November):6.
Recalls being introduced to Kavanagh in the Bailey in 1962 and being called an "insolent pup."

20 HOGAN, ROBERT. *After the Irish Renaissance. A Critical History of the Irish Drama since "The Plough and the Stars."* London, Melbourne: Macmillan, p. 256.
Reference to O'Connor's stage adaptation of *Tarry Flynn*.

21 JORDAN, JOHN. "Tribute to Patrick Kavanagh." *Hibernia* (January):25.
Compares Kavanagh to Alceste in Moliere's *Le Misanthrope*. Remembers his feeling of "utter desolation" at the news of Kavanagh's death: "A bereavement of almost familial intensity." Despite the competition for his

friendship, Kavanagh had a "basic distrust of discipleship." Claims he loved Kavanagh, despite his distaste for the poet's "points of view."

22 "Kavanagh, the farmer's poet." *Limerick Leader* (23 March). UCD Archive.
  Profile of Kavanagh. Refers to Canal Bank seat on Grand Canal, which was newly unveiled on March 17. Claims it was "only among the farming stock that Kavanagh was truly in his element, because he himself was typical of the countless small farmers" in Ireland.

23 KENNELLY, BRENDAN. "A Man I Knew (For Patrick Kavanagh)." *Dublin Magazine* 7, no. 1 (Spring):10–11.
  Elegy, presenting Kavanagh as "the epitome of chivalry."

24 ———. "Tribute to Patrick Kavanagh." *Hibernia* (January):25.
  Long poem addressed to Kavanagh, the "Man of Monaghan," who "scorned the measured mind."

25 LONGLEY, MICHAEL. "Patrick Kavanagh." *Dublin Magazine* (Spring):9–10.
  Recalls his first impressions of reading Kavanagh's verse, which "seemed rough and tough, awkward even." Admires the "passionate and precise detail" of the poetry and its innocence. Claims most of his contemporaries have heard "the voice of authority" in Kavanagh and "stay quiet but near."

26 MAHON, DEREK. "Patrick Kavanagh." *Dublin Magazine* (Spring):6–8.
  Much of Kavanagh's work is "cheerfully awful" but "nobody minds at all." Kavanagh possessed the strong character, stamina and humour to do what he wanted. Claims Kavanagh resembled in appearance "those enormous jazzmen" of New Orleans in the 1920s, "working off the frustrations of their people in great sweaty orgies of delicate rhythm and humorous pathos." Considers Kavanagh the best Irish poet since Yeats, using "Irish poet" to mean "involved in the Irish situation, and usually mauled by it."

27 ———. "Patrick Kavanagh: An Epitaph." *Dublin Magazine* (Spring):12.
  Imagines Kavanagh buried "in the hungry soil of Monaghan."

28 McGURK, TOM. "A Tribute to Patrick Kavanagh." *Dublin Magazine* (Spring):11–12.
  Poem addressed to Kavanagh.

29 MCKEOWN, PATRICK D. "Patrick Kavanagh—Anniversary Thoughts." *Dundalk Democrat* (30 November):17. UCD Archive.
  Claims Monaghan people were ignorant of Patrick's work through the 1950s. First discovered *A Soul For Sale* in the Galway County Library mis-

1968

takenly shelved with music texts. Disliked the stage adaptations of *Tarry Flynn*.

30 MCMAHON, SEAN. "The Parish and the Universe: A Consideration of Tarry Flynn." *Eire* 3, no. 3 (Autumn):157–169.

Finds Kavanagh's poetry after 1955 "less interesting" than the earlier work. Praises the "documentary realism" of *Tarry Flynn*. Compares Tarry to Huckleberry Finn and Holden Caulfield: "the class of solitary, benighted youth who, without the ability to put their mission into words, are all in quest of the Grail." Praises the novel's realistic portrayal of rural life and of Tarry's recurrent sense of the beauty of the land. The language is "tough, pungent, vulgar." Tarry Flynn is the "doppelganger" of Patrick Maguire of *The Great Hunger*. Although Kavanagh is a famous poet, he is more well known as the author of *Tarry Flynn*.

31 MONTAGUE, JOHN. "Homage on a Canal Bank." *Guardian* (Manchester), (19 March):6.

Discusses Baggott Street Bridge, comparing Kavanagh's fondness for it with that of George Moore, who "cried that the sun setting over Baggott Street Bridge was the most peaceful sight in the world." Describes unveiling of the Canal Bank memorial seat to Kavanagh on Sunday, March 17, and lists some of those present. Criticizes the destruction of Georgian Dublin and the "relentless commercialism of modern Ireland."

32 "My Brother Patrick: Peter Kavanagh talks about the poet who loved the hills and potato fields of Inniskeen." *Sunday Press* (28 July). UCD Archive.

Discusses Peter Kavanagh and his relationship with Patrick. Interviews some of Patrick's Inniskeen neighbors.

33 O'BEOLAIN, ART. "Patrick Kavanagh." *Comhar* (Irish language article), (February):15–18. .

Praises Kavanagh's poetry in *The Bell* in the 1940s, which proved that he was a true poet. Also praises *The Great Hunger,* in which "there is clay in the mouth of the poet." Admires Kavanagh's later poetry written after 1955, although only time will tell if he was truly a "great poet." Always individualist, Kavanagh "walked his own path from beginning to end."

34 O'GRADY, DESMOND. "Tribute to Patrick Kavanagh." *Hibernia* (January):25.

Poem in response to the death of Kavanagh.

35 "Poet commemorated by Grand Canal seat." *Irish Independent* (18 March). UCD Archive.

Describes unveiling of the commemorative Canal Bank seat.

1968

36 POTTS, PAUL. "Instead of a Wake, / In Memoriam: 1905–1967 / (For Mrs. Patrick Kavanagh)." *Hibernia* (January):25.
   Kavanagh wrote several poems that are equal to the best poems in English in this century. Like Blake, he was holy but not religious. Like Davitt, he expressed the beauty of the Irish Catholic peasantry.

37 ———. "Patrick Kavanagh." *Twentieth Century* (London), 176, no. 1038:48–51.
   Compares Kavanagh to Blake, Clare, Dante, Einstein, Eliot, Herbert, MacDiarmid, O'Casey, Pasternak, Pound, Spinoza, Van Gogh, Henry Vaughan, and others. Claims Kavanagh's mind was broader than Yeats's and deeper than Eliot's. Wonders why he was not better known and concludes that Kavanagh's art, like Whitman's and Blake's, will take time to find an audience. Compares Kavanagh to Michael Davitt, as spokesman for "peasant Gaelic Catholic Ireland," just as Yeats and Parnell expressed the Anglo-Irish. Claims Kavanagh's poetry "gives stature to the country, as did Conor Cruise O'Brien's conduct at the United Nations," although "only in a few poems" did Kavanagh achieve greatness.

38 "PRO-QUIDNUNC." "An Irishman's Diary." *Irish Times* (19 March):9.
   Describes public dedication of the Canal Bank seat in honor of Kavanagh. Mentions the priests' blessing of the seat.

39 R., E. O. "Tribute to Patrick Kavanagh." *An Muinteoir Naisiunta* (Official Journal of the Irish National Teachers' Organization), 12, no. 9 (January). UCD Archive.
   Appreciation of Kavanagh. Author had been a teacher with Peter Kavanagh at Westland Row Christian Brothers School in the 1930s. At that time, Patrick seemed to be "a rather disgruntled young man." Praises his achievements.

40 Review of *Tarry Flynn*. *Sunday Independent* (1 December):25. UCD Archive.
   Review of Belfast Festival's production of *Tarry Flynn* at the Lyric Theatre.

41 ROSENFIELD, RAY. "Loving Appreciation of Kavanagh's Work." *Irish Times* (22 November):12.
   Kavanagh was commemorated at Festival '68 in Belfast by Basil Payne, who called him "a good religious poet, in the sense that Shakespeare, Blake and Keats were religious poets." In his later work, Kavanagh "transcended suffering."

1968

42 ——. "Tarry Flynn Goes North to the Lyric." *Irish Times* (27 November):17.
Reviews performance of *Tarry Flynn* at Belfast's Lyric Theatre. Barney McCaughney as Tarry was "a beautifully conceived characterisation of the Irish Robby Burns."

43 RUSTIC [pseud.]. "In Memory of Patrick Kavanagh." *Dundalk Democrat* (January). UCD Archive.
Elegy to Patrick Kavanagh.

44 RYAN, JOHN. "Editorial". "Patrick Kavanagh: A Tribute in Poetry and Prose." *Dublin Magazine* 7, no. 1 (Spring):3–5.
Introduction to special Kavanagh issue.

45 ——. "From Inniskeen to Baggot Street Bridge." *RTE Guide* (13 September). UCD Archive.
Memoir of Kavanagh, and announcement of forthcoming "special commemorative program on Patrick Kavanagh" (1968.46).

*46 ——. "Patrick Kavanagh Memorial." RTE TV program. Accession no. P611/68. Recorded 17 March. Duration: 11 minutes, 41 seconds.
Interview with John Ryan. Also features Niall Toibin, Siobhan McKenna and T. P. McKenna.

47 SHEEHY, MICHAEL. *Is Ireland Dying? Culture and the Church in Modern Ireland*. New York: Taplinger, p. 203.
Brief reference to "the cynical view of women" presented in *The Great Hunger*.

48 SISSMAN, L. E. "Patrick Kavanagh, an Annotated Exequy." (Poem). *New Yorker* (4 May):51.
A humorous elegy to Kavanagh which alludes to some of Kavanagh's self-descriptions in his later poems and which concludes that Kavanagh loved all things and had a poetic talent "transcending all / Obituaries which record your fall."

49 "Sitting Out the Siege." *Tablet* (6 January):5–6.
Announces the death of Kavanagh. Claims he was "the greatest poet that we had," although he gained recognition in Ireland late in his career. Claims he was personally unpretentious, honest, gruff and sometimes "frightening."

50 SLEVIN, GERARD. "Irish Families: The Kavanaghs." *Ireland of the Welcomes* 17, no. 3 (September):31–33.
Discusses the Irish Kavanagh family, whose origins are in Kilcavan, Wexford. Mentions Patrick Kavanagh.

1969

51 "Tarry Flynn." *Sunday Press* (24 March). UCD Archive.
Announces production of *Tarry Flynn* by Listowel Players.

52 "Tarry Flynn." *Sunday Press* (4 February). UCD Archive.
Discusses recording of song called "Tarry Flynn" by Johnny McEvoy (written by Shay Healey). Claims that "a portion of the royalties will go to Patrick Kavanagh's widow."

53 WARNER, ALAN. "An Angry Foghorn: Patrick Kavanagh as Critic." *Dublin Magazine* 7, no. 1 (Spring):13–23.
Discusses Kavanagh's reception in Ireland and the U.S. Claims he was "a powerful if uneven poet" and "not an orderly or systematic critic." Notes that Kavanagh called his voice "my angry foghorn." Kavanagh's passionate honesty and courage gives life to his journalism. "His own daimon is too strong to be suppressed." Discusses his writing for *Envoy* and *Kavanagh's Weekly*, which Kavanagh described as "the best autobiography of the years when I was violent and funny." Compares and contrasts Kavanagh's critique of modern Ireland with that of Yeats in "September 1913." Discusses Kavanagh's criticism of Synge ("unfair"), Yeats ("curiously ambivalent and equivocal"), and Joyce. Discusses Kavanagh's favorite books and his eccentric dismissal of Lawrence, Ibsen, and Austen.

54 WRIGHT, DAVID. "Patrick Kavanagh. 1905–67." *London Magazine* 8, no. 1 (April):22–29.
Describes a personal visit to Inniskeen, which he found dilapidated and reminiscent of "some remote rural backwater of Portugal." Believes this background was influential on Kavanagh. Discusses Kavanagh's hatred of "Irishness," and his plain, unsentimental style in *Tarry Flynn* and *The Great Hunger*. The two works together "make a stereoscopic vignette of the reality of the human condition": the former is tragic, the latter is comic. Praises Kavanagh's "ordinary, spoken, live idiom with the singing lift and beat of lyric versification" with reference to "Epic" and "The Hospital." Discusses the poetry as resistant to university study, although not lacking intellectual or emotional complexity. Claims that in England Kavanagh remained relatively unknown until 1960, when *Come Dance with Kitty Stobling* became Poetry Book Society Choice. Compares Kavanagh to Dr. Johnson.

1969

1 FAHEY, WILLIAM A. "Patrick Kavanaugh: A Comment" [sic]. *Renascence* 21, no. 2 (Winter):81–87.
Discusses how Kavanagh, although "enjoying a middle-aged recrudescence," rages against his earlier work, as in *Self Portrait*. Agrees with Kavanagh

1969

that "his weakest work is that of his mid-career," but admires "Shancoduff," "To the Man after the Harrow," and "Plough Horses." Objects to "an artificial pumped up ecstasy" in *Ploughman*. In such poems, Kavanagh played "the ploughboy poet, a kind of imitation Irish Burns," full of artificial passion. This is the reason for the failure of *The Great Hunger*. Agrees with Kavanagh that *The Great Hunger* is "not poetry," even though it is, at times, beautiful, antipicturesque, and antiromantic. Contrasts Kavanagh with Yeats, whose peasants "are more lunar than Irish." *The Great Hunger* contains some disappointingly flat lines and platitudinous statements, reminiscent of "Burns at his worst." Praises Canal Bank sonnets, but finds *Come Dance With Kitty Stobling* (1960) uneven. His late satire shows the negative influence of Betjeman.

2 FOLEY, MICHAEL. "Morning Stroll (After Patrick Kavanagh)." *Honest Ulsterman* (November):13.

Humorous poem in tribute to Kavanagh's style.

3 GREACEN, ROBERT. *Even Without Irene: An Autobiography*. Dublin: Dolmen, p. 100.

Recalls meeting Kavanagh in Dublin. Describes him as "a massive, lumbering, awkwardly honest, foghorned-voiced fellow from Monaghan, who impressed with the sheer naked strength both of his poetry and personality."

4 HENNIGAN, AIDAN. "Kavanagh Tribute." *Irish Press* 18 (December). UCD Archive.

Gives account of recent tribute to Kavanagh at Irish Embassy, London.

5 HOGAN, JAMES. "Death and Contacts." *Lace Curtain*, no. 1:35–38.

Discusses the state of Irish poetry. Brief reference to Kavanagh, to whom he attributes the remark "a poet has a head start if has a pain in the stomach."

6 KAVANAGH, PETER. Editor. *Lapped Furrows. Correspondence 1933–1967 Between Patrick And Peter Kavanagh: With Other Documents*. New York: Peter Kavanagh Hand Press. 307 pp.

Consists of Patrick Kavanagh's letters to and from Peter and sister Celia, from the early thirties on, interleaved with biographical commentary and diary entries by Peter. Includes a biographical introduction by Peter and a memoir by Celia. Concludes with Patrick's unposted letters to editors.

7 KENNELLY, BRENDAN. "Contemporary Irish Poetry." *Tablet* (15 March):264–265.

Discusses post-Yeatsian Irish poetry, including Kavanagh's, whose work "is so pure, so profound and sincere, yet so simple that one never doubts that here, at his best, is a poet who ranks with Blake and Yeats."

8 ——. "The Rebirth of Irish Poetry." *Hibernia* (August/September):13.
Occasional references to Kavanagh, "the best Irish poet since Yeats."

9 LIDDY, JAMES. "Open Letter to the Young About Patrick Kavanagh." *Lace Curtain* no. 1:55–57.
Whereas Yeats has little to say, the poetry of Eliot and Kavanagh is "related to what you feel on the streets and the connection made or escaped." Praises Kavanagh's criticism of Yeats, and claims his poetic landscape is "Yeats's great dream infested by swinishness." Compares Kavanagh to a saint.

10 MACAONGHUSA, PROINSIAS. "Personally Speaking." *Hibernia* (December):28.
Brief anecdote about Kavanagh in Dublin's Pearl Bar.

11 MCGURK, TOM. "Kavanagh's Arrival (I. M. Patrick Kavanagh)." *Threshold* 22 (Summer):70.
A short poem about Kavanagh.

12 McLAUGHLIN, TOM. "Patrick Kavanagh and the 'Ireland' Myth." *Honest Ulsterman*, no. 13 (May):41–44.
Claims Kavanagh's writing deteriorated when he lived in Dublin, becoming increasingly self-conscious and contrived. Praises Kavanagh's critique of "the Ireland myth," the romantic view of rural Ireland bequeathed to us by the Revival. Claims too many contemporary readers and writers have a taste for a "backward-looking" romantic Irishness.

13 PRESS, JOHN. "Ted Walker, Seamus Heaney, and Kenneth White: Three New Poets." *Southern Review* (July):673–688.
Refers to Heaney's admiration for *The Great Hunger*.

14 RICHARDSON, KENNETH, ed. *Twentieth Century Writing*. London: Newnes Books, p. 342.
Biographical sketch of the poet.

15 SIMMONS, JAMES. Review of "Almost Everything." *Honest Ulsterman* (August):23.
Review of Kavanagh's LP record, "Almost Everything." Finds the record disappointing. "Patrick Kavanagh is a contender for the title of Best Irish Poet Since Yeats; but there is a distance between his speech and his verse that makes it hard to take him seriously." Finds the prose "boring." Praises the "loose realism" of *The Great Hunger*.

1970

16 SULLIVAN, KEVIN. "Literature in Modern Ireland." In *Conor Cruise O'Brien Introduces Ireland*. Edited by Owen Dudley Edwards. London: Deutsch, New York: McGraw-Hill, pp. 135–147.

Kavanagh and Austin Clarke are the most notable recent Irish poets. Kavanagh's work seems so "spontaneous" that it appears to have avoided all literary influences, including that of Yeats. *The Great Hunger* and *Tarry Flynn* are reminiscent of Carleton.

17 WARNER, ALAN. "The Poet as Watcher." *Threshold* (Belfast) 22, (Summer):64–70.

Discusses notion of poet as outsider and watcher, and compares *The Great Hunger* with poems by R. S. Thomas and Edward Thomas. *The Great Hunger* differs from most rural poems because Kavanagh was once a farmer himself: "Does he now stand inside or outside that rural community? Is he a watcher or a participant?" As a member of a rural farming community, Kavanagh felt that Synge's portrayal of peasant life was artificial, "observed from the outside." However, in the end, Kavanagh also became an "outsider," detached from his community.

18 ———. "The Poetry of Patrick Kavanagh (1904–1967)." *English* 18, no. 102 (Autumn):98–103.

Biographical sketch of poet. Describes "Ploughman" as unoriginal, although *The Great Hunger* alone shows the poet to be an original, antipastoral voice. Compares Kavanagh to Wordsworth, although the former "had his feet more firmly planted in the dung and clay than Wordsworth." The later work suggests that Kavanagh's inspiration dried up. Kavanagh was not an Irish Burns, despite Harold Nicholson's claims to the contrary, because he was not linked to an oral folk tradition as Burns was. However, Kavanagh may be "the last of the peasant poets."

19 WEYGANDT, CORNELIUS. *The Time of Yeats: English Poetry of To-Day against an American Background*. New York: Russell & Russell, 1937, 1969, pp. 441–442.

Reprint of Weygandt (1937.4).

1970

1 "Award for Writers." *Sunday Press* (6 December). UCD Archive.
Announces establishment of Kavanagh Society Award.

*2 BARDWELL, LELAND. "Poetry in the Sixties." Dublin Arts Festival 1970. Official Program.

1970

3   BOLAND, EAVAN, SEAMUS HEANEY, MICHAEL HARTNETT, and LIAM MILLER. "The Future of Irish Poetry: A Discussion." *Irish Times* (5 February):14.
    Discusses Kavanagh's influence. Liam Miller argues that *The Great Hunger* was a watershed in Irish poetry. Boland argues that the poem was new in its unselfconscious representation of peasant life, and thus "made a new reality." Heaney suggests that Kavanagh's long poem influenced John Montague's *The Rough Field*.

4   CALLINAN, BRIAN. "Beautiful Prose." *Hibernia* (28 August):23.
    Review of Paul Potts, *To Keep a Promise* (1970.24). Refers to Potts's "obvious enthusiasm for Patrick Kavanagh."

5   "Ceremony at Graveside of Monaghan Poet." *Anglo-Celt* (Cavan), (4 December). UCD Archive.
    Describes Inniskeen commemoration of Kavanagh.

6   "Famous forge closes." *Sunday Press* (8 February). UCD Archive.
    Concerns a forge in Monaghan which Kavanagh used to visit.

7   HAND, MICHAEL. "Kavanagh brother's new book." *Sunday Press* (26 July). UCD Archive.
    Discusses Peter's plan to publish new book on Patrick. Also discusses *Lapped Furrows*. Interviews Peter Kavanagh and Frank Cassidy of Inniskeen.

8   "Inniskeen Senior Football Tournament Semi-Final, Patrick Kavanagh Memorial Cup." *Democrat and People's Journal* (18 July). UCD Archive.
    Announces football trophy named after poet.

9   JORDAN, JOHN. "Joyce Without Fears: A Personal Journey." In *A Bash in the Tunnel*. Edited by John Ryan and Myles Na Gopaleen. London: Clifton Books, pp. 135–146.
    Personal memoir, with brief references to Kavanagh. Claims Kavanagh once boasted he had read *Ulysses* twenty times: "I disbelieved him."

10 KANE, MICHAEL. "A Letter from Zurich." *Lace Curtain* 2 (Spring):42–44.
    Claims Joyce "invented" Dublin, whereas Kavanagh "populated" it: "Between them, they created a city in which artists can live."

11 "Kavanagh Society plans weekend ceremony." *Dundalk Democrat* (22 November). UCD Archive.
    Announces ceremony in Inniskeen to mark Kavanagh's death.

1970

12 KENNELLY, BRENDAN. "Patrick Kavanagh." *Ariel* 1, no. 3, (July):7–28.

Claims that throughout his work, Kavanagh sought a comic vision and in so doing, became a model of sanity. Argues that Kavanagh's sense of "detachment," and his religious faith contributed to his achievement of a comic voice. Examines the blend of pagan and Christian in *The Great Hunger*, the sense of freedom in *A Soul for Sale*, and the sense of comedy in the Canal Bank sonnets. Kavanagh lacked a mythology, which at times hindered his poetry.

13 ———. ed. Introduction to *The Penguin Book of Irish Verse*. Harmondsworth: Penguin, pp. 29–42.

Brief references to Kavanagh. Compares *The Great Hunger* to early Irish poetry, which is characterized by "a hard, simple, virile, rhetorical clarity." Compares Kavanagh's belief in the Comic Muse to the later Yeats's notion of "gaiety."

14 "Memories of Patrick Kavanagh." *Limerick Leader* (December). UCD Archive.

Mrs. Paul Barry of Shannon recalls her late husband's friendship with Kavanagh.

15 MATTHEWS, JAMES H. "History to Literature: Alternatives to History in Modern Irish Literature." In *Literature and History*, edited by I. E. Cadenhead. Tulsa: University of Tulsa Press, pp. 73–87.

Claims Kavanagh's social criticism was "violently lyrical." Praises *The Great Hunger* as Kavanagh's best poem. Claims Maguire is "the Irish Prufrock," a "eunuch" dominated by his mother. He is a representative figure of Ireland. The later poetry of *A Soul for Sale* is "more strident, less sympathetic." Kavanagh and Clarke cleared a space for later Irish poets.

16 O'CONNOR, ULICK. *Brendan Behan*. London: Hamish Hamilton, pp. 89, 91–92, 109, 147, 163, 164–165, 288.

Recounts several anecdotes about Kavanagh. Discusses Kavanagh's friendship with and then hatred for Behan. Quotes Behan's letter to Sindbad Vail in which he refers to "Paddy the wanker, poet and peasant." Claims when Kavanagh died, "he was virtually unknown in America."

17 O'KEEFE, TIMOTHY. "God is Good to Patrick Kavanagh." *Two Rivers* 1 (Spring):71–74.

Review of *Lapped Furrows*, (correspondence between Patrick and Peter Kavanagh), which "provides the hard details of living as a poet." The editor, Peter, fails to provide any indication of his principle of selection of material. Compares the intimacy of the brothers to that of John and George Keats. They were conspirers together, "two gladiators contra mundum," and both believed in Patrick's genius. Compares the libel action to Oscar Wilde's. Mentions Kavanagh's late dismissal of his earlier work, including *The Great Hunger*, which is compared to the work of Langland. Concludes it's "a splendid, terrible book."

18 "Of bards and goals." *Sunday Press* (26 July). UCD Archive.
   Describes visit to Inniskeen. Accompanied by photo by Brian Barron of Peter Kavanagh at Patrick's graveside.

19 "Patrick Kavanagh." *Ireland of the Welcomes* 17, no. 4 (November–December). UCD Archive.
   Biographical sketch of Kavanagh.

20 "Patrick Kavanagh Commemoration." *Irish Times* (30 November):10.
   Announces that a graveside commemoration was held for Kavanagh in Inniskeen on November 29. Plans are announced for a monument to the poet, as well as a museum and library.

21 "Patrick Kavanagh remembered." *Northern Standard* (4 December). UCD Archive.
   Describes annual Kavanagh memorial.

22 "Patrick Kavanagh remembered at Inniskeen." *Dundalk Democrat* (5 December). UCD Archive.
   Describes annual Kavanagh memorial ceremonies.

23 "Plans for Kavanagh museum." *Sunday Press* (29 November). UCD Archive.
   Announces graveside commemoration of Kavanagh and mentions plans to establish a Kavanagh museum in Inniskeen.

24 POTTS, PAUL. "More than One Magnificence." In Paul Potts, *To Keep a Promise*. London: MacGibbon & Kee, pp. 56–65.
   Reprint of Potts (1968.36).

25 "Requests no vulgar display." *Sunday Independent* (16 November). UCD Archive.
   Announces ceremony in Inniskeen to mark Kavanagh's death.

26 "Rests in sight of life's miracles." *Sunday Independent* (25 October). UCD Archive.
   Author recalls his last meeting with Kavanagh.

1971

27 "Salute to old friend." *Dundalk Democrat* (5 December). UCD Archive.
Reproduction of photo of John Lennon (not the rock star), a friend of the poet, laying a wreath at his grave.

28 SLATTERY, FINBAR. "A Letter from Paddy Kavanagh." *Agricultural Record* (September). UCD Archive.
Discusses a letter of Kavanagh's published in *Lapped Furrows*.

29 SMITH, MICHAEL, and TREVOR JOYCE. Editorial of *Lace Curtain*, no. 2 (Spring):2.
Claims *Lace Curtain* "salutes the living spirit of these two great writers," Patrick Kavanagh and Flann O'Brien.

30 ———. "Irish Poetry and Penguin Verse." Editorial of *Lace Curtain*, no. 3 (Summer):3–10.
Review of Kennelly's *Penguin Book of Irish Verse*. Praises the independence of Kavanagh's voice.

31 WARD, A. C., ed. *Longman Companion to Twentieth Century Literature*. London: Longman, p. 293.
Biographical entry on the poet.

1971

1 "Appreciation of Literary Endeavour." *Sunday Independent* (7 March):19. UCD Archive.
Discusses the Patrick Kavanagh Society.

2 ARNOLD, BRUCE. "A Gathering of the Sussex Irish." *Sunday Press* (4 July). UCD Archive.
Gives account of Cyril Connolly anecdote about Kavanagh.

3 BOLAND, EAVAN. "Patrick Kavanagh: Tragedy into Comedy." *Irish Times* (15 June):10.
Essay on Kavanagh as a comic writer. Claims that "environment and comedy are inextricable in Kavanagh's work." Discusses *The Great Hunger*, *Tarry Flynn*, "Pygmalion," "Innocence," and the Canal Bank poems.

4 BOLAND, JOHN. "Still the Indomitable Irishry." *Hibernia* (27 August):17.
Discusses the state of modern poetry: "The degree to which many younger practitioners of poetry revere a figure like Kavanagh is frightening, the reverence applying anyway more to the image of the boozy poet than to the poetry."

1971

5 BOYLE, PATRICK. "The Poet Emerging." *Hibernia* (5 November):13.
   Review of *The Green Fool*. Describes the book's first publication in 1938 and Gogarty's libel suit. It is "a marvellous book. Better even than Tarry Flynn . . . Out of this earthy background, the figure of the poet struggles for emergence."

6 CLARKE, AUSTIN. "The Thirties." *The Lace Curtain* 4 (Summer):87–92.
   Recalls Kavanagh's visits to his house—"a simple, unsophisticated country lad with a lost air about him which was attractive." Discusses his bitter rivalry with Brendan Behan. Recalls how Kavanagh once took shelter from an angry Behan in a confessional box in St Andrew's church, Westland Row.

7 COOPER, WILLIAM. "Recent Fiction." *Daily Telegraph* (28 October):9.
   Review of reissue of *The Green Fool*. Praises the book as "harmless, delightfully humorous and ironic, with an underlying vein of sadness." Expresses surprise that it was ever withdrawn following Gogarty's libel suit.

8 CRONIN, ANTHONY. "The Great Poetry Boom, 1970s." *Dublin Magazine* (Summer):116–117.
   A satirical poem on the Irish literature industry and Ireland's treatment of its authors. Makes several references to Kavanagh.

9 ———. "The Decade of Derision: Anthony Cronin Discusses the Literary Journals of the 1930s." *Hibernia* (10 September):18.
   Occasional references to Kavanagh.

10 DOWNEY, P. K. "Giving Kavanagh His Rightful Place." *Irish Times* (24 May):27.
   Discusses the relative obscurity of Kavanagh during his lifetime and the fame surrounding his name, posthumously. Discusses Kennelly (1970.12).

11 "Green fool." *Times* (London), (10 June):14.
   Announces republication of *The Green Fool* by Martin, Brian, and O'Keeffe.

12 JORDAN, JOHN. "P.K.'s Point of View—1." *Hibernia* (22 October):13.
   Mentions *November Haggard* (1971.15), and questions Peter Kavanagh's accuracy in dating the material, yet he admires Peter for his "pietas." In *Collected Pruse*, Patrick Kavanagh is "alternately aggressive and humble, dogmatic and sceptic, curmudgeonly and tender, fascist and anarchist." Claims Kavanagh once said the three great living authors were Auden, Gide, and Ludovic Kennedy. Kavanagh's viewpoint was "not always coherently or temperately expressed."

1971

13 ——. "P. K.'s Point of View—2." *Hibernia* (5 November):12.
Discusses Patrick's UCD lectures, which "make compelling, if often exasperating reading." The lectures contained "outrageous and provocative attacks on the Liberal Establishment." Concludes Kavanagh displays "Johnsonian arrogance" blended with humility.

14 ——. "From a small townland in Monaghan." *Irish Independent* (6 November):6.
Review of *The Green Fool*. Comparing his first impressions of the novel in 1938 with his present impressions, it now seems "a genuinely innocent book." Although it's partly autobiographical, it also "tells the story of an almost vanished culture, vestigially Gaelic."

15 KAVANAGH, PETER. Preface to *November Haggard*. Uncollected Prose and Verse of Patrick Kavanagh. Edited by Peter Kavanagh. New York: Peter Kavanagh Hand Press. 229 pp.
Briefly lists the Kavanagh holdings which still remain unpublished.

16 KENNELLY, BRENDAN. "Kavanagh's Kind of Loving Laughter." *Sunday Independent* (9 May). UCD Archive.
Review of November Haggard (1971.15): "It will be the most splendid, moving and memorable book of 1971."

17 KIELY, BENEDICT. "In Kavanagh Country—I. A Journey to the Quiet Island." *Irish Times* (8 October):14.
Describes traveling the Monaghan countryside, on the road from Carrickmacross to Inniskeen ("The Quiet Island.") Recalls his first reading about Kavanagh in *The Irish Press* in 1936 or 1937, and the impact Kavanagh had on him when young. Remembers Kavanagh complain in 1947 about the smugglers of Monaghan.

18 ——. "In Kavanagh Country—2. The Star over Cassidy's Hill." *Irish Times* (21 October):12.
Continues his description of a visit to Inniskeen. Mentions that there is a Functions room called the "Kavanagh Room" in a Dundalk hotel. Describes Kavanagh's usual journey, by train, from Dublin to Monaghan and how Kavanagh and his mother once got lost in the woods near Inniskeen.

19 LIDDY, JAMES. *Homage to Patrick Kavanagh*. Edited by Trevor Joyce. VERSHEET 3. Dublin: New Writers' Press. 6 pp.
Divides modern Irish literature into "closed periods when the bosses rule" and "open periods" when they don't. Yeats was a boss, but after his death, "we see the anti-boss, the man who hates cultural authority," such as Kavanagh, who "gave a whole world of love and faith" to younger writers.

Satire "enabled Kavanagh to convert the self-pity of 'The Great Hunger' into impersonal suffering" and gave him an entry to his "beautiful casualness." Dislikes the "stiff and solemn foolery" of "The Paddiad." Kavanagh was "apostle of poetry and one of the Dublin saints."

20 "London Day by Day. Unburnt relics" *Daily Telegraph* (28 April):14.
   The Dublin pub, The Bailey, had a fire, but the portrait of Kavanagh was unharmed.

21 MACGORIS, MARY. "Hillside tribute to a great poet." *Irish Independent* (29 November):9.
   Describes fourth annual Kavanagh memorial ceremonies.

22 MCCARTEN, JOHN. "The Locks That Are Threatened With Rape." *New Yorker* (20 November):190–197.
   Briefly discusses Kavanagh's Canal Bank seat in an essay on the municipal threat to develop Dublin's canal system.

23 "Monaghan Aid for Kavanagh Award." *Argus* (6 August). UCD Archive.
   Describes presentation of check to Patrick Kavanagh Poetry Society.

*24 NEMO, JOHN. *Patrick Kavanagh*. Ph.D. dissertation, UCD. See Aslib Index to Theses (London), vol. 22, 1971–1972.
   Ph.D. thesis on Kavanagh.

25 "Now it can be told!" *Sunday Independent* (31 October). UCD Archive.
   Describes the emergence of a literary "cult" surrounding Kavanagh, and announces republication of *The Green Fool*.

26 OSBORNE, CHARLES. "Patrick Kavanagh." In *Penguin Companion to English Literature*. Edited by David Daiches. Harmondsworth: Penguin, New York: McGraw-Hill, p. 289.
   Gives brief account of the poet's work, which "appears not to have undergone any significant poetic development."

27 PAYNE, BASIL. "Kavanagh a la carte." *Hibernia* (25 June):21.
   Poem about Patrick Swift's portrait of Kavanagh in the dining room of Galway's Great Southern Hotel. See Platt (1973.36).

28 "People, Places, Pastimes." *Observer* (London), (12 December):27.
   Brief discussion of *The Green Fool*. Praises the freshness of the writing and claims "it is just that there should be a revival of interest in [Kavanagh] in Ireland."

1971

29 "QUIDNUNC." "An Irishman's Diary." *Irish Times* (13 November):11.
Calls for aspiring poets to submit entries for annual Patrick Kavanagh Poetry Award.

30 Review of *The Green Fool*. *Times* (London) (18 November):10.
Points out the irony that the passage which led to Oliver St. John Gogarty's libel action against Kavanagh is now reprinted on the book jacket. The book presents "a good picture of a young mind growing up."

31 SISSON, C. H. *English Poetry, 1900–1950: An Assessment*. London: Rupert Hart-Davis, pp. 251–254.
Discusses Kavanagh's poetry of the 1940s in the context of British poetry in that decade, although believes his late work was his best. Gives biographical sketch of the poet and finds *The Great Hunger* "too directly autobiographical." It increased Kavanagh's reputation, although "more on account of its Irishness than its literary qualities." Finds his "Lines to Yeats" excellent criticism of Yeats and evidence of Kavanagh's fine intelligence.

32 SMITH, MICHAEL. "Irish Poetry Since Yeats: Notes Towards A Corrected History." *DQ* 5, no. 4 (Winter):1–26.
Discusses Yeats, the Revival, and the post-Yeatsian generation of Irish poets. Gives an account of contemporary scene. Argues that literary history is more complex than usually thought, since the work of a number of poets is regularly ignored, including Samuel Beckett, Charles Donnelly, Thomas MacGreevy, Denis Devlin, Brian Coffey, Niall Montgomery, and Patrick Kavanagh. These poets opposed the Yeatsian tradition of "literary nationalism." Claims Kavanagh was "one of the healthiest influences on Irish poetry of the 1950s and 1960s."

33 ———. "Michael Smith asks Mervyn Wall Some Questions about the Thirties." *Lace Curtain* 4 (Summer):77–86.
Wall contrasts the cultural background of urban writers like himself and that of rural writers like Kavanagh. Claims Kavanagh had an anxiety to be accepted as a writer, and "once swept all the books out of Hannah's window, and started to set up his own books in their place."

34 SWEENEY, MAURICE. "Bookchat." *Hibernia* (16 April):7.
Announces projected publication of Platt's *Patrick Kavanagh Anthology* (1973.36). Call for poems to be included.

35 TRACY, HONOR. "Prose and Cons." *Sunday Telegraph* (21 November). UCD Archive.
Review of *The Green Fool*. Claims "the book wears well."

36 WALKER, DOROTHY. "Irish Imagination." *Hibernia* (3 December):14.
Reproduction of Patrick Swift's "marvellous, glowering portrait of Patrick Kavanagh" at the Irish Imagination Exhibition at Dublin's Municipal Gallery—under review here.

1972

1 "A Selected List of Recent Reprints." *Times Literary Supplement* (18 February):201.
Mentions the Martin Brian and O'Keefe reprint of *The Green Fool*, which makes "a welcome reappearance."

2 "Art." *Sunday Bulletin* (Philadelphia), (10 September). UCD Archive.
Reproduction of Patrick Swift's portrait of Kavanagh.

3 "Auction." *Irish Independent* (17 May). UCD Archive.
Estate Agent's advertisement of sale of McNello's pub in Inniskeen village, described as "heart of the Kavanagh county."

4 BATES, DAVID R. "New Ireland." *Irish Times* (15 May):11.
Letter which claims the phrase "New Ireland" was first coined in *The Green Fool*.

5 BOLAND, JOHN. "The Poetry of W. R. Rodgers." *Hibernia* (21 January):10.
Brief references to Kavanagh.

6 ———. "Poet honoured in home town. Kavanagh plaque unveiled." *Irish Press* (27 November):3.
Describes unveiling of a copper holograph plaque (containing the poem "Thank You, Thank You") in memory of Kavanagh, in Inniskeen. A sister of Kavanagh unveiled the plaque, and Benedict Kiely gave an address.

7 BOYLAN, FRANCIS. *Ishmael* (Biarritz) 1 (Winter–Spring):26–62.
Claims Kavanagh's poetry has been neglected. Compares and contrasts Kavanagh with Eliot, Pound, Yeats, Jean Cocteau, and Swift. Discusses Kavanagh's lectures at University College Dublin, which were "kaleidoscopic." Praises *The Great Hunger*, "Auditors In," and the Canal Bank sonnets. Claims Kavanagh had "moral vision." In his later work, we see "the hollowing out of a spirit to such an extent that it uttered statements of a simplicity and profundity not easily plumbed."

1972

8 BOYLE, PATRICK. "Christmas Books: Personal Book Choice." *Hibernia* (15 December):13.
   Chooses *The Green Fool* as a favorite book.

9 BROWN, MALCOLM. *The Politics of Irish Literature*. Seattle: University of Washington Press, pp. 11, 14, 16, 250, 296.
   Makes occasional references to Kavanagh. In *Tarry Flynn*, Kavanagh uses "Balzac's mode with striking success."

10 CHAMBERS, HARRY. "The Little Magazine and the Small Press." In *British Poetry Since 1960: A Critical Survey*, edited by Michael Schmidt and Grevel Lindop. Manchester: Carcanet, pp. 85–91.
   Employs Kavanagh's distinction between provincialism and parochialism in relation to the "metropolitan reviewers" of poetry in London.

11 "Echoes of Kavanagh—Shakespearean Accompaniment." *RTE Guide* (22 September). UCD Archive.
   Describes a new musical work by Seoirse Bodley, *Meditations on Lines from Patrick Kavanagh*.

12 FELTON, KEITH. "14-Carat Verses From the Emerald Isle." *Los Angeles Times* Calendar Section (16 April):45.
   Review of *Poems from Ireland* by William Cole. Brief mention of Kavanagh.

13 FOLEY, MICHAEL. "Review." *Honest Ulsterman* 34 (June–August):38–40.
   Review of *The Green Fool*. Claims that reading Kavanagh when young produces a pleasing "shock" in the reader. Kavanagh was a "profound critic," although not of his own work, which he foolishly rejected. Compares and contrasts *The Green Fool* with *Tarry Flynn*. Kavanagh was surrounded by "insensitive brutes" in London and Dublin.

14 GREEN, MARTIN. "Patrick Kavanagh: Monaghan Poet." *Ireland of the Welcomes* (Dublin) 20, no. 5:34–36.
   Gives biographical background. Claims Kavanagh's childhood was "full of wonder and magic." States that *The Green Fool* "must surely be one of the gayest autobiographies ever written . . . a kind of prose map of places named in the poems." Kavanagh is popular in Ireland, and printed in school anthologies. There is even a "Patrick Kavanagh Bar" in a Galway hotel.

15 HEANEY, SEAMUS. "After the Synge-song: Seamus Heaney on the Writings of Patrick Kavanagh." *Listener* (13 January):55–56.
   Describes Kavanagh's life and career, from *The Green Fool*, which is "an act of piety towards the terrain of childhood," to the late verse, in which

1972

he had finally broken his connection with Monaghan and "could talk poetry out of anywhere." Claims he was reborn as a poet in 1955.

16 "Inniskeen News: Their Night Out." *Dundalk Democrat* (20 May). UCD Archive.
    Cast of Inniskeen production of *Tarry Flynn* had a night out.

17 JUDE THE OBSCURE [pseud.]. "The H. U. Business Section." *Honest Ulsterman* 32 (January/February):28–33.
    Discussion of Dublin mockery of Kavanagh in the 1940s.

18 KAVANAGH, PETER. "Letters." *Irish Independent* (11 April). UCD Archive.
    Letter from Peter Kavanagh concerning a Patrick Kavanagh bibliography, *The Garden of Golden Apples*, which he is planning.

19 ———. *The Garden of the Golden Apples*. New York: Kavanagh Hand Press. Limited Edition.
    Bibliography of primary and secondary materials on Kavanagh.

20 "Kavanagh Day." *Dundalk Democrat* (9 December):9. UCD Archive.
    Describes "Kavanagh Day" at Inniskeen, the 5th annual commemoration of his death, and the unveiling of a plaque "on the wall outside the village school."

21 "Kavanagh memorial plaque unveiled." *Irish Times* (27 November):8.
    Describes unveiling of Kavanagh plaque at Inniskeen on November 26. Anne Kavanagh, the poet's sister, unveiled the plaque.

22 KELLEHER, TERRY. "Booknews." *Hibernia* (14 July): 17.
    Announces forthcoming publication of Platt anthology (1973.36).

23 KENNELLY, BRENDAN. "The Poet Kavanagh, Complete." *Sunday Independent* (12 March). UCD Archive.
    Review of *Complete Poems* (Peter Kavanagh Hand Press, 1972). Praises Peter's "vision, daring and stamina." Claims that "all of Kavanagh is here—the great, the good, the bad."

24 KENNELLY, BRENDAN. "Review." *Sunday Independent* (26 November).
    Review of Peter Kavanagh's *The Garden of the Golden Apples*.

1972

25 MILLER, LIAM. "The Heirs of Saint Columba: Publishing in Ireland." *Times Literary Supplement* (17 March):315–316.
   In a discussion of the "rise of the small presses" in Ireland, mentions 1942 publication by Cuala Press of *The Great Hunger*, which was a milestone in Irish poetry. Claims Kavanagh remains very influential.

26 MONTAGUE, JOHN. "Order in Donnybrook Fair." *Times Literary Supplement* (17 March):313.
   Although "melodramatically titled," *The Great Hunger* is "probably the best long poem by an Irishman since 'The Deserted Village' or 'The Midnight Court,' if one includes Irish." Praises the early lyrics and late sonnets. Kavanagh has had a strong influence on other Irish poets, e.g., Brendan Kennelly, but not always positively: "A more permanently damaging aspect of the Kavanagh legend is that it cuts young poets off from any wider context." Dispraises "Kavanagh idolators."

27 O'CONNOR, ULICK. *Brendan Behan*. London: Coronet Books.
   Reprint of O'Connor (1970.16).

28 "Plaque to honour poet." *Sunday Press* (26 November). UCD Archive.
   Announces unveiling of Kavanagh plaque at Inniskeen.

29 "QUIDNUNC." "An Irishman's Diary." *Irish Times* (28 September):11.
   Interview with Paddy O'Brien, veteran barman at McDaid's. Discusses Behan and Kavanagh in the pub. Kavanagh was "a fierce man for rows and for insulting Americans."

30 "The Irelands of Austin Clarke." *Times Literary Supplement* (1 December):1459–1460.
   Compares Clarke to Kavanagh. Claims both poets shared with Denis Devlin an anger at Irish provincialism. Kavanagh channeled this anger into "acts of self-commemoration in which the local detail of the poem was charged with the current of the poet's personality." Kavanagh learned the "theme of the personality" from Yeats.

31 QUIGLEY, ISABEL. "Painting the self-image." *Spectator* (22 January):119.
   Brief review of *The Green Fool*, which was originally withdrawn because of "an improbable, glancing half-libel or might-be libel." Prefers the early part of the book to the latter. Claims the Irish, in general, write gracefully if not miraculously.

32 RAFROIDI, PATRICK. *L'Irlande et le Romantisme*. Paris: Editions Universitaries, pp. 3, 355, 397, 473.
   Brief references to Kavanagh.

33 "Review." *Argus* (Dundalk), (21 April). UCD Archive.
   Review of local production of *Tarry Flynn*.

34 ROGERS, W. R. "AE (George Russell)." In *Irish Literary Portraits*. London: BBC, pp. 200–201.
   Mentions that AE first published Kavanagh's poetry. Quotes Kavanagh's memory of meeting AE.

35 RUSHE, DESMOND. "Tatler's Parade: An Old Target Steps out of the Line of Fire!" *Irish Independent* (6 January):10. UCD Archive.
   Discusses Archbishop McQuaid and makes reference to his kindness to Kavanagh.

36 SHARE, BERNARD. "Minority Report. A Soul for Sale." *Hibernia* (22 September):13.
   Discusses *Kavanagh's Weekly*, and laments the demise of such low-budget journalism. Claims to have been on editorial and publishing staff of the weekly, which "exceeded by excess, failing to find anything remotely good to say about anyone or anything."

37 "Tarry Flynn Drew the Crowds." *Argus* (Dundalk), (14 April). UCD Archive.
   Describes Inniskeen production of *Tarry Flynn*.

38 "Tribute to Patrick Kavanagh." *Irish Press* (5 November). UCD Archive.
   Announces a reading of Kavanagh's works in the Lyric Theatre, Belfast, by the McArdle brothers and Eugene McCabe.

39 Untitled. *Irish Independent* (6 January). UCD Archive.
   Describes Archbishop McQuaid's kindness to Kavanagh.

40 "What's on today." *Sunday Press* (26 November). UCD Archive.
   Announces Kavanagh commemorative service at Inniskeen.

1973

1 "A Pearl of Taverns in Dublin is Doomed." *New York Times* (4 March):14.
   Brief references to Kavanagh.

2 BOLAND, EAVAN. "Decline in Dignity." *Hibernia* (30 November):24.
   Discusses issue of financial support for Irish writers. Claims Kavanagh was good example of an underpaid poet, although he managed to keep his dignity, despite poverty.

1973

3 BOLAND, JOHN. "In Praise of a Truthsayer from Monaghan." *Hibernia* (19 October):19–20.
   Praises the "forthrightness of expression" and "simplicity and rapture" of Kavanagh's poetry. Argues that Kavanagh has not had the critical acclaim he deserves, because his poetry is unfashionably life-affirming, even though many of the poems express his "sense of rejection."

4 "By the graveside of the poet Kavanagh." *Irish Times* (1 December):12.
   Account of annual commemoration.

5 CAHILL, SUSAN and THOMAS CAHILL. *A Literary Guide to Ireland*. Dublin: Wolfhound, pp. 192, 252, 295, 311.
   Brief descriptions of Kavanagh in relation to Inniskeen and Dublin.

6 "Cascades from Kavanagh." *The Sunday Press* (8 April). UCD Archive.
   Describes the plaque erected near London pub (The Plough) to mark the place where the poet urinated.

7 CRONIN, ANTHONY. "The Man Under the Black Hat." *Irish Times* (17 August):10.
   Discusses Flann O'Brien, who allegedly called Patrick Kavanagh "the Monaghan toucher."

8 DOWNEY, P. K. "Radio. Poets Make Their Own Importance." *Irish Times* (16 April):12.
   Discusses McGurk's radio broadcast about Kavanagh (1973.28).

9 GRANT, DAMIAN. "Body Poetic: The Function of a Metaphor in Three Irish Poets." *Poetry Nation* (Manchester) 1:112–135.
   Discusses the personification of Ireland in poetry, which Kavanagh protested vehemently, with particular reference to the work of Seamus Heaney, John Montague, and Paul Muldoon. Briefly mentions the influence of Kavanagh on Heaney.

10 GREVER, GLENN ALBERT. *The Poetic Achievement of Patrick Kavanagh (1904–1967)*. Ph.D. dissertation. University of Illinois at Urbana-Champagne. 377 pp. DAI-A 34/01 (July):314.
   Consists of nine chapters on aspects of the poet, including Kavanagh as "national character," his poetic principles, his influences and his exploration of various themes, including the land, the city, and the role of the poet. Also provides history of the critical reception of Kavanagh. Begins with description of life and career, and the distinction between the "character" and the poet. Argues that he is an uneven but perceptive critic, influenced by poets as

various as Eliot, Wordsworth, AE, and Joseph Campbell. In his Dublin poems, "his position was anti-Establishment, anti-bourgeois, and anti-nationalist." Since he was a very self-conscious poet, he often drew self-portraits in his poems and mused often about poetry as a vocation. Considers the blend of Revival, Georgian, and Imagist influences on poems in *Ploughman*, and Kavanagh's characteristic use of simple diction and masculine rhyme. Discusses origins of *The Great Hunger* in three early poems from the thirties: "Peasant," "Plough," and "Hired Boy." Provides a detailed critique of the long poem, under four headings: "Seasonal Cycle," "Personal, Familial, Communal Activities," "Maguire's Thoughts," and "Key Images." In *A Soul For Sale*, Kavanagh describes ordinary life but avoids the idyllic pastoral of *Ploughman*, and the language and imagery are clearer, more original, and more controlled. In his final poems, of which the Canal Bank sonnets are the climax, the "message" is one of love. Concludes with discussion of Kavanagh's influence, which is considerable, despite the fact he is less a craftsman than Devlin, Clarke, or Kinsella.

11 HAMBURGER, MICHAEL. *A Mug's Game. Intermittent Memoirs, 1924–1954*. Cheadle, Cheshire: Carcanet, pp. 240, 283.
    Remembers meeting Kavanagh in London, "but had little communication with him beyond requests for more whisky." Reading *Tarry Flynn* made him think: "The Irish still have a sense of grass roots—the advantage of being a 'backward' nation."

12 HAND, MICHAEL. "Where old ghosts meet: Kavanagh museum will move to old church." *Sunday Press* (22 April). UCD Archive.
    Discusses the Patrick Kavanagh museum at Inniskeen.

*13 ———. "Sunday Sports Show. GAA Hurling and Soccer." RTE TV program. Accession no. P395/73. Transmitted 30 December. Duration: 13 minutes 38 seconds.
    Michael Hand discusses Kavanagh the Hurler (4 minutes 51 seconds).

14 JOHNSTON, JENNIFER. "Christmas Books. Personal Book Choice." *Hibernia* (14 December):18.
    Finds *The Green Fool* "a wry and beautiful book."

15 JORDAN, JOHN. "To Kill a Mockingbird." *Hibernia* (30 November):14.
    Discusses the article on Kavanagh in *The Bell* (1948) and the profile in *Leader* (October 1952). Believes that Kavanagh overreacted to the article in *Leader*, but claims that the profile and the subsequent defense of it by many Dublin intellectuals was "a classic case of moral and intellectual sadism."

1973

16 "Kavanagh: Jordan to Tell (Almost) All." *Sunday Independent* (9 September). UCD Archive.
    Announces forthcoming talk on Kavanagh by John Jordan.

17 "Kavanagh Commemoration." *Dundalk Democrat* (1 December). UCD Archive.
    Account of annual commemoration at Inniskeen.

18 "Kavanagh Memorial." *Irish Independent* (30 March). UCD Archive.
    Describes the Kavanagh memorial plaque near The Plough.

19 KAVANAGH, PETER. "Bernard Canon Maguire, Parish Priest of Inniskeen, 1869–1948." *Dundalk Democrat* (19 May). UCD Archive.
    Memoir. Brief references to Patrick Kavanagh.

20 "Kavanagh's Explosive Legacy." *Profile*. Incorporating *This Week* 4, no. 14 (June). UCD Archive.
    Claims *Lapped Furrows* "may ultimately explode the pretensions of many in Dublin's literary and pseudo-literary circles."

21 "Kavanagh to be remembered." *Sunday Press* (25 November). UCD Archive.
    Announcement of annual commemoration.

22 KENNELLY, BRENDAN. "Patrick Kavanagh." In Lucy (1973.25), pp. 159–184.
    Reprint of Kennelly (1970.12).

23 KIELY, BENEDICT. "The Poets and the Prosemen." In Lucy (1973.25), pp. 118–130.
    Both *Tarry Flynn* and the *Piers Plowman* column show the tendency of Kavanagh's prose to "flower into verse," which is allegedly a typical quality of Irish writing in general.

24 KINSELLA, THOMAS. "The Divided Mind." In Lucy (1973.25), pp. 208–218.
    On Kavanagh's public rejection of *The Great Hunger*: "his self-knowledge was punishing, and his self-judgement heroic."

25 LUCY, SEAN, ed. *Irish Poets in English: The Thomas Davis Lectures on Anglo-Irish Poetry*. Cork and Dublin: Mercier Press, 227 pp.
    Includes Kennelly (1973.22), Kiely (1973.23), Kinsella (1973.24), Lucy (1973.26), Mcmahon (1973.29), and Montague (1973.30).

26 ——. "What is Anglo-Irish Poetry?" In Lucy (1973.25), pp. 13–29.

Discusses Kavanagh's hatred of "the cult of literary Irishness" in relation to "Memory of Brother Michael." Claims Kavanagh's poetry is totally Irish although he owes little to the Gaelic literary tradition itself.

*27 MARTIN, AUGUSTINE. "Telefis Scoile. The Irish Poet and Tradition." RTE TV program. Accession no. P22/73. Transmitted 26 January. Duration: 23 minutes 25 seconds.
Augustine Martin interviews Thomas Kinsella and Austin Clarke. References to, and film footage of Kavanagh.

28 MCGURK, TOM. "Gods make their own importance. Documentary on Patrick Kavanagh." RTE radio broadcast. Accession no. 288/73. Recorded 7 April. Presented by Tom McGurk, produced by Kieran Sheedy.
Biographical sketches of the poet. Kavanagh's Inniskeen neighbors recount numerous anecdotes about the poet.

29 MCMAHON, BRYAN. "Place and People into Poetry." In Lucy (1973.25), pp. 60–74.
Praises Kavanagh's courage in treating the fundamental questions of existence while also testifying to the beauty of nature.

30 MONTAGUE, JOHN. "The Impact of International Modern Poetry on Irish Writing." In Lucy (1973.25), pp. 144–158.
Like Dylan Thomas, Kavanagh was so preoccupied by his "private vision" that he sought only to protect that vision.

31 NEMO, JOHN. "A Bibliography of Materials by and about Patrick Kavanagh." *Irish University Review* (Spring):80–106.
Bibliography of primary and seconday materials.

32 NYE, ROBERT. "Irishmen and others." *Times* (London) (15 February):16.
Recalls meeting Kavanagh once. Kavanagh told him he had cancer. Admires the poetry contained in the reprint of *Collected Poems* (Martin, Brian, and O'Keeffe). "Intuitive, epigrammatic, shrewd, Kavanagh is always the peasant, seeing how much he can get away with, returning again and again to a handful of themes perceived as underlying all creation."

33 O'BRIEN, EAMON. "Patrick Kavanagh." *Profile* (September). UCD Archive.
Letter in response to earlier article on Kavanagh in *Profile*.

34 O'SULLIVAN, T. F. "Sweet Athy." *Irish Times*17 October):14.
Refers to Kavanagh's memorial bench on Grand Canal.

1973

35 "Plaque that Marks a Convenient Spot." *Irish Post* (17 March). UCD Archive.
Describes the Kavanagh memorial plaque near The Plough.

36 PLATT, EUGENE ROBERT, ed. *A Patrick Kavanagh Anthology*. Dublin: Commedia Publishing Company, 50 pp.
Contains foreword by Platt and poems addressed to or inspired by Kavanagh by the following poets (in order of appearance): Michael Roberts, Desmond Egan, Basil Payne, Francis Harvey, Thomas Tessier, Cecilia Parsons Miller, Thomas Dillon Redshaw, Dorothy W. McCartney, Jim Craven, Paul Durcan, L. E. Sissman, David Wright, F. X. Sherwin, James Liddy, Brendan Kennelly, Desmond O'Grady, Aurora Gonella, Derek Mahon, Eugene Platt, Rudi Holzapfel, Martin Green, Hayden Murphy, and Peter Fallon.

37 POLLAK, ANDREW. "Booknews." *Hibernia* (30 March):18.
Describes the Kavanagh memorial plaque near The Plough.

38 POTTS, PAUL. "Poet of Two Cultures." *Catholic Herald* (1 June). UCD Archive.
Praises Kavanagh as a great poet.

39 Review of *Patrick Kavanagh at the King's Head. Profile* (October). UCD Archive.
Review of LP record (Elektra K32003), consisting of thirty-one Kavanagh poems read by Patrick Magee and John Welsh at a live pub performance.

40 RUSHE, DESMOND. "The Night that the Buck Was Stretched." *Irish Independent* (5 October). UCD Archive.
Review of Ulick O'Connor's one-man show on Gogarty. Refers to Gogarty's libel action against Kavanagh.

41 SAMPSON, GEORGE. *The Concise Cambridge History of English Literature*. Third Edition. Revised by R. C. Churchill. Cambridge: Cambridge University press, p. 726.
Briefly refers to Kavanagh as one of Yeats's successors in the "'Celtic Daylight' mood."

42 SEYMOUR-SMITH, MARTIN. *Guide to Modern World Literature*. London: Wolfe Publishing, p. 318.
Gives brief description of Kavanagh's life and work. Praises *The Great Hunger* and *Tarry Flynn*. His best work combines "self-satire" with lyricism.

1973

43 SIMMONS, JAMES. "In Lieu of an Answer: Patrick Kavanagh's Poetry." *Honest Ulsterman*, no. 38:42–50.

Review of *Collected Poems* (Martin Brian & O'Keeffe), paper reprint of MacGibbon & Kee hardback of 1964. Claims Kavanagh is "involved in a romantic quest. His life is full of epiphanies." Finds similarities between Kavanagh's creative impulses and those which started *The Honest Ulsterman*. By the age of forty-three, Kavanagh had written "a more impressive body of poems than Yeats had at the same age." Admires some, although not all, of the later satirical poems. Generally in his poetry, we find "rock-hard passion."

44 "Speaker says Yeats ahead of his time." *Irish Times* (20 August):9.

Describes Michael Longley's lecture on Kavanagh at Yeats Summer School in Sligo.

45 WALKER, MARTIN. "P for Poet." *Guardian* (28 December):11.

Describes removal of Kavanagh memorial plaque in London, by, he supposes, brother Peter Kavanagh, sister Cecilia, and Peter's two daughters. Inscribed on the plaque were the words "Is ioma steall do chaith se annso," translated as: "Multifarious were the cascades that he threw at this spot."

46 WARNER, ALAN. *Clay is the Word: Patrick Kavanagh, 1904–1967*. Dublin: Dolmen Press, 144 pp.

Admires "Ploughman" and "Shancoduff" in the first collection, although many of the early poems were strongly influenced by Georgian conventions. Contrasts these poems with *The Great Hunger*, which is powerful, despite its occasional rawness and grating stridency. Compares and contrasts the poem with *The Deserted Village* and Wordsworth's "Michael." Claims Kavanagh has a dualistic emotion toward the land, torn between love and hate, although love usually wins. His Monaghan poems, including "Innocence," "Peace," and others, express his love for the rural landscape he had left behind, "without any straining or standing on tiptoe to catch a glimpse of wonder." Discusses *Collected Poems* and argues that Kavanagh's weakest poems come at the beginning and the end of his career. His satires are his least impressive poems. Praises Kavanagh's surprising ability to write about nature in a vital, original way in the Monaghan poems and Canal Bank sonnets, which are his finest works.

47 ——. "Inside the Monkey House." *Hibernia* (2 November):17.

Review of *Collected Pruse* (Martin, Brian, and O'Keeffe), a reprint of earlier edition published by MacGibbon and Kee, 1967. Expresses gratitude for the collection, but criticizes the selection and editing, which "leaves much to be desired." Wishes the whole of *Kavanagh's Weekly* (not just selections) could have been reproduced. Although some think his criticism "absurd,

1974

chaotic and impertinent" (e.g., Hubert Butler and Anthony Burgess), Warner finds it "thought-provoking." He finds Kavanagh's views on Yeats unacceptable but stimulating.

48 WEBB, E. T. "Patrick Kavanagh." In *Cassell's Encyclopedia of World Literature*, vol. 2. Edited by S. H. Steinburg. London: Cassell and Co. 1953, 1973, p. 782.
Biographical entry on Kavanagh: "*The Great Hunger* suffers from a certain indiscipline and a need to strike attitudes."

49 "Wreath Placed at Kavanagh's Grave." *Irish Times* (26 November):16.
Account of annual commemoration.

1974

1 "An Irishman's Diary." *Irish Times* (20 July):11.
Interview with Paddy O'Brien, head bartender at McDaid's. Discusses the way Kavanagh acted when he was in McDaid's. "He was a great character—the greatest character of all time," said O'Brien.

2 BRAZIL, DAVID. "Kavanagh Plaque 'Raid.'" *Irish Press* (3 January). UCD Archive.
Describes how Peter Kavanagh removed the memorial wall plaque in London. Claims Peter wrote letter to *The Irish Press* claiming responsibility for the plaque's removal.

3 DRUSKA, JOHN ANDREW. *The Way It Happened and the Way It Is: A Study of Patrick Kavanagh's Poetry*. Ph.D. dissertation, University of Cincinatti. 223 pp. See DAI-A 34/08 (February):5166A.
Argues that Kavanagh's poetry has great vitality and that critics have unjustifiably neglected Kavanagh's work. Consists of five chapters: (1) an introduction to the poems, (2) a study of the comic vision of his early work, (3) a chapter on *The Great Hunger* as a tragedy, (4) a study of "tension between town and country and the growth of a satiric impulse," and (5) "radical innocence: the comic achievement of the late poetry." Argues that his most successful poems are "comic" because they are personal and self-revealing. Although very successful, *The Great Hunger* is Kavanagh's least personal poem and is insufficiently close to the poet's personal experience to avoid becoming a simplistic version of his view of rural life. The poem was a necessary "tragic" phase in the development of Kavanagh's comic poetic. The middle period, 1942–1955, was the "most chaotic" portion of Kavanagh's life. During this period, he worked in Dublin as a journalist, wrote urban satires and evocations of pastoral childhood and developed a legendary repu-

tation as a local character. Many poems in this period, especially the satires, are "aberrations" in his career as a poet of the comic impulse. The final period witnessed the flowering of this comic vision of radical innocence.

4   ELLMANN, RICHARD. "Irish Verse." *New Review* 1, no. 4 (July):70–71.
    Review of *Faber Book of Irish Verse*, edited by John Montague, who is "rightly most respectful of Clarke and Kavanagh."

5   FOLEY, DONAL. "The Kindness of Four Writers: Patrick Kavanagh." *Irish Times* (5 June):10.
    Anecdotes about four authors (O'Cadhain, O'Casey, Behan, and Kavanagh), and a memoir of Kavanagh's visits to the London office of the *Irish Times* on Fleet Street. When Foley's mother died, Kavanagh comforted him.

6   HALPERN, SUSAN. *Austin Clarke: His Life and Works*. Dublin: Dolmen, pp. 19, 40.
    Briefly refers to Kavanagh in a general consideration of Irish writers of the 1930s and 1940s.

7   HARMON, MAURICE. Introduction to *Irish University Review* 4, nos. 1–2 (Spring/Autumn):12.
    Contrasts Kavanagh's poetic "direction" to that of Clarke.

8   "Has replica of Kavanagh plaque." *Irish Independent* (5 January). UCD Archive.
    Dubliner Jimmy Bourke "displayed a replica of the Patrick Kavanagh memorial plaque . . . which caused a stir in London this week when the poet's brother had it removed."

9   HEANEY, SEAMUS. "Explorations. The Long Garden." BBC radio broadcast. Sound Archive, Ulster Folk and Transport Museum, #BBC TBE49/UE305. Transmitted 31 January. Duration: 20 minutes. Produced by David Hammond, introduced and narrated by Seamus Heaney.
    Discusses childhood and childhood memories, in relation to Kavanagh's "The Long Garden" and other literary texts.

10 "He's too crude, they said, but Kipling of the water front has last laugh!" *Sunday Independent* (14 July). UCD Archive.
    Discusses Frank Sherwin, author of two poems on Kavanagh published in 1973 Platt anthology (1973.36).

11 Irish Leaving Certificate Examination. Higher Level. UCD Archive.
    Exam question on Kavanagh's poetry.

1974

12   Irish Leaving Certificate Examination. Ordinary Level. UCD Archive.
      Exam question about "Lines on a Seat on the Grand Canal, Dublin."

13   "Irish poet's 'obscene' plaque removed." *Evening Herald* (3 January). UCD Archive.
      Describes removal of Kavanagh memorial plaque in London.

*14   JONES, K. *The Complete Poems of Patrick Kavanagh: A Developing Maturity.* M.A. thesis, UCD.
      Thesis on Kavanagh.

15   JORDAN, JOHN. "A partial portrait of Kavanagh." *Irish Independent* (2 March). UCD Archive.
      Review of Alan Warner's *Clay is the Word* (1973.46). Praises Warner's perseverance in writing the book, despite lack of encouragement from Kavanagh and his family. Suffers from lack of biographical details, yet is "admirable in its lucidity, courtesy and moderation." Claims it is an unoriginal critique.

16   KAVANAGH, PETER. Postscript to *Love's Tortured Headland*: A Sequel to *Lapped Furrows.* New York: Peter Kavanagh Hand Press.
      Contains remarks concerning Kavanagh's final conversation with his sister on his deathbed.

17   KENNELLY, BRENDAN. "One of the signs of a great poet." *Sunday Independent* (7 April). UCD Archive.
      Review of Alan Warner's *Clay is the Word*. Claims Kavanagh is "one of the most sophisticated, profound and visionary poets of modern times." Warner's book "succeeds remarkably well."

18   KENNY, HERBERT A. *Literary Dublin: A History.* Dublin: Gill & Macmillan. New York: Taplinger, pp. 231–233, 277–278, 291, 294–298, 300–301, 322–323.
      Recounts several personal anecdotes concerning Kavanagh. Describes him as "one of those mythic Protean creatures Yeats dreamed of, only half emerged from the soil, as knotty as trees, somehow slightly primordial." Considers him a "perfectionist" in his poetry. Claims he is little known in England and America. Praises the poem "Who Killed James Joyce?" Claims Kavanagh was personally troublesome and "antagonistic."

19   KINSELLA, THOMAS. "The Poetic Career of Austin Clarke." *Irish University Review* 4, nos. 1–2 (Spring/Autumn):128, 132.
      Brief references to Kavanagh. Claims "we . . . responded with startled pleasure to Kavanagh's brief fulfillment in *Come Dance With Kitty Stobling.*"

1974

20 LAMBERT, HUGH. "The Diary. If Kavanagh Were Alive Now." *Sunday Press* (24 November). UCD Archive.
Interview with Paul Durcan, winner of Kavanagh Poetry Award.

21 LENNON, PETER. "Draft of Irish." *Sunday Times* (28 April):39.
Review of *Collected Pruse*. Considers Kavanagh a major poet but also "quite a joker." Finds especially interesting the proceedings of the *Leader* trial. Considers the symbolism of the courtroom confrontation as "the broken and physically suffering, but defiantly articulate poet facing a counsel who had been a Prime Minister of Ireland, John A. Costello."

22 LIDDY, JAMES. "An Introduction to the Poetry of James Clarence Mangan." *Lace Curtain* 5 (Spring): 55–56.
Briefly compares Kavanagh to Mangan.

23 MCGURK, TOM. "Jungle of Pembroke Road. Documentary on Patrick Kavanagh." RTE broadcast. Presented by Tom McGurk, produced by Kieran Sheedy. Recorded 5 October. Duration: 58 minutes 15 seconds. RTE sound archive, accession no. 87/74.
A number of Kavanagh's friends and acquaintances, including Benedict Kiely, Anthony Cronin, Niall Sheridan, and John A. Costello recall their impressions of the poet during the *Leader* trial and up to the time of his illness in 1955.

24 MCINERNEY, MICHAEL. *Peadar O'Donnell: Irish Social Rebel*. Dublin: O'Brien Press, pp. 191–192.
Peadar O'Donnell claimed that Kavanagh was "the man of greatest genius among us. He was much more sensitive to his environment than any other. One might even consider his philosophy of life shallow, but one forgot all that, in the magic of his words." O'Donnell claimed Kavanagh was a difficult person, but likeable. He also praised his discipline as a writer, despite his "explosive and sometimes irresponsible" manner of speech. *Tarry Flynn* was, in O'Donnell's view, an authentic account of rural Ireland.

25 MONTAGUE, JOHN, ed. "In the Irish Grain." *The Book of Irish Verse*. London: Faber, pp. 21–39.
Considers *The Great Hunger* to be "one of the better long poems of our time, and its releasing influence on other writers, from R. S. Thomas to Seamus Heaney, has still to be estimated."

26 NEMO, JOHN. "The Green Knight: Patrick Kavanagh's Venture into Criticism." *Studies* 63 (Autumn):282–294.
Discusses trends in Kavanagh's criticism, especially of the forties and fifties. Claims Kavanagh's prose lacks logical order, which reflected an

1975

"essentially romantic approach" to life. He came to believe he had created, through his criticism, an audience receptive to his views on his two main subjects—the nature of literary art and the function of the poet and critic. Kavanagh believed happiness depended on "sympathy with the poetic spirit" and that poetry had a religious dimension. He was scathing about sport and nationalism as subjects for poetry (except for Carleton and Joyce). Discusses his egotistical intolerance of other writers.

27 "No Plaque for Kavanagh." *Sunday Independent* (24 February). UCD Archive.
   Claims Timothy O'Keeffe and Maureen Pryor each have replicas of the Kavanagh memorial plaque, which was removed by Peter, although they do not intend to replace it.

28 "'Obscene' Plaque is Removed." *Irish Independent* (4 January). UCD Archive.
   Describes removal of Kavanagh memorial plaque in London.

29 SMITH, MICHAEL. "Patrick Kavanagh and the loss of innocence." *Education Times* (Irish Times Publications) (17 October):16.
   Discusses theme of loss of innocence in the poem "Advent."

30 SZANTO, PIROSKA. "Patrick Kavanagh in Rome. Drawing." *Era*, no. 1:13.
   Reproduction of drawing of the poet.

1975

1 ALLEN, MICHAEL. "Provincialism and Recent Irish Poetry: The Importance of Patrick Kavanagh." In Dunn (1975.10), pp. 23–36.
   Contrasts Matthew Arnold's view of provincialism with Hardy's and Faulkner's, arguing that Kavanagh's position resembles Hardy's, whereas Yeats's position resembles Arnold's. Compares Hardy's ambivalence toward London with Kavanagh's toward Dublin, and examines Kavanagh's distinction between the parochial and provincial in relation to "Shancoduff" and other poems. Claims *The Great Hunger* lacks "a formal centre of control and judgement." Dislikes the satires of the fifties, which display the provincialism which Kavanagh attacks elsewhere. Compares the treatment of Kavanagh during the *Leader* trial to the rough treatment of Hardy over the publication of *Jude the Obscure*. Discusses Kavanagh's influence on Heaney and Montague.

2 BOLAND, JOHN. "The Age of the Banned and the Great Put-Down." *Evening Press* (2 September). UCD Archive.
   Claims the problems for Irish artists remain the same today as in Kavanagh's day.

1975

*3 BONNER, H. *Patrick Kavanagh and the Development of a Comic Vision*. M. Litt. thesis, TCD. See Aslib *Index to Theses* (London), vol. 25, 1976–1977. UCD Archive.

4 "Briefing: Paperbacks." *Observer* (London), (28 September):22.
    Brief discussion of the Penguin reprint of *The Green Fool*. Praises the book's "pleasing but non-whimsical close-ups of Irish village life."

5 BROWN, TERENCE. "Conclusion: With Kavanagh in Mind." In *Northern Voices: Poets from Ulster*. Totowa, N.J.: Rowman and Littlefield, pp. 215–221.
    Describes Ulster as a colonial space which inhibits imagination, and claims much Ulster poetry is a reaction against this oppressive condition. MacNeice and Kavanagh were exceptional in their ability to transcend this situation, although *The Great Hunger* was a poem of reaction. Discusses Kavanagh's notion of the parochial, and claims his major achievement was that he "transcended the provincial-urban waste of spirit" in his late sonnets, which are written to celebrate life, not to solve problems.

6 BUTTEL, ROBERT. *Seamus Heaney*. Lewisburg: Bucknell University Press, London: Associated University Press, pp. 14–15, 25, 45.
    Discusses Kavanagh's distinction between parochial and provincial, and concludes that Seamus Heaney is in this sense a parochial poet. Mentions Kavanagh's influence on Heaney, especially *The Great Hunger*.

7 COGHLAN, DENIS. "Peter Kavanagh: His Brother's Keeper. Denis Coghlan talked to the poet's brother about his self-appointed task to make the name of Patrick Kavanagh known and honoured, and about his own life." *Irish Times* (10 September):10.
    Describes Peter Kavanagh's life and work, including his foundation of the Peter Kavanagh Hand Press, which he assembled "from scratch along the lines of the medieval masters." Discusses his supportive relationship with Patrick. Peter recalls the day of Patrick's death. Claims the second part of *Lapped Furrows* (the letters) will be published in twenty-five to thirty years.

8 "Culchie versus Jackeen Syndrome." *Irish Independent* (9 March). UCD Archive.
    Discusses the antipathy between Kavanagh and Brendan Behan.

9 DEANE, SEAMUS. "Irish Poetry and Irish Nationalism." In Dunn (1975.10), pp. 4–22.
    Argues that, although Kavanagh is "a lesser poet than Yeats," he is actually more influential than Yeats in Ireland. Describes Kavanagh as the emancipated voice of the parochial, and therefore as regional, and "bare-faced."

1975

Describes Kavanagh's influence on John Montague, both of whom have a religious sense of place.

10 DUNN, DOUGLAS, ed. *Two Decades of Irish Writing: A Critical Survey*. Edited by Douglas Dunn. Chester Springs: Dufour Editions, 260 pp.
    Includes Allen (1975.1), Deane (1975.9), Heaney (1975.14), Longley (1975.21), and Smith (1975.32).

11 GILL, BRENDAN. *Here at the New Yorker*. New York: Random House, p. 3.
    Quotes Kavanagh, who allegedly "said of the peasantry from which he sprang that they live in the dark cave of the unconscious and they scream when they see the light." Compares *New Yorker* writers to Irish peasants.

12 HEANEY, SEAMUS. "Patrick Kavanagh." *New Review* 1, no. 10 (January):57–62.
    Argues that Kavanagh contributed significantly to the Irish literary tradition through his rejection of the Revival and of Yeats's idea of the peasant. Finds Kavanagh technically adept but believes he relies often on "prospector's luck." Reads *The Great Hunger* as a mixture of tragic and comic modes, foreshadowing the comic vision of *Tarry Flynn*. Finds the satires mostly opportunistic, self-pitying "doggerel." Contrasts Kavanagh's lack of a system with Yeats's ritualizing poetic, and concludes that after he "had consumed the roughage of his Monaghan experience, he ate his heart out."

13 ———. *The Ministry of Fear*. North. London: Faber,:63.
    A poem, which borrows from the first line of Kavanagh's "Epic."

14 ———. "The Poetry of Patrick Kavanagh: From Monaghan to the Grand Canal." In Dunn (1975.10) pp. 105–117.
    Reprint of Heaney (1975.12).

15 "Inniskeen Remembers Patrick Kavanagh." *Northern Standard* (5 December). UCD Archive.
    Describes annual Kavanagh commemoration, with photo of French Ambassador at Inniskeen.

16 "Kavanagh Lecture." Argus (13 March). UCD Archive.
    Announces forthcoming lecture on Kavanagh by Daniel J. Casey (of SUNY) in Dundalk Regional College Theatre.

17 KERSNOWSKI, FRANK. *The Outsiders: Poets of Contemporary Ireland*. Fort Worth, Texas: Texas Christian University Press, 202 pp.
    A study of Irish poetry from 1939 to the present. In an introductory chapter, claims Kavanagh's early poetry was maudlin and merely picturesque.

The Great Hunger is "a long, ironic Irish in-joke." Concludes that Kavanagh was a minor talent. However, claims that in the 1950s Kavanagh was "a rallying point for many who would strike a new note, an un-Yeatsian note." Examines other poets' indebtedness to Kavanagh, including Anthony Cronin, Michael Hartnett, Seamus Heaney, John Hewitt, Brendan Kennelly, James Liddy, Derek Mahon, and Ewart Milne.

18 KRAUSE, DAVID. *Sean O'Casey. The Man and His Work.* Enlarged edition. New York: Macmillan. London: Collier.
   Reprint of Krause (1960.16).

19 L., P. "Recollections of the First Production." Abbey Theatre program for *Tarry Flynn* (June). UCD Archive.
   Describes the day Kavanagh attended the performance.

20 LEONARD, HUGH. "A memorial with smaltz." *Irish Independent* (14 September). UCD Archive.
   Recalls meeting Kavanagh at Parson's bookstore, Dublin.

21 LONGLEY, EDNA. "Searching the Darkness: The Poetry of Richard Murphy, Thomas Kinsella, John Montague, and James Simmons." In Dunn (1975.10), pp. 118–153.
   Briefly refers to Kavanagh, who attempted to yoke Corkery's "Hidden Ireland" to his own imaginative, Romantic concerns.

22 MAHON-SMITH, WALTER. Letter. *Honest Ulsterman* (February):55.
   Letter concerning Patrick Kavanagh Society. Recounts an amusing anecdote about Kavanagh's noisy departure from a cosmetics company luncheon in the 1940s.

23 NEMO, JOHN. "A Joust With the Philistines: Patrick Kavanagh's Cultural Criticism." *JIL* 4, no. 2 (May): 65–75.
   Discusses Kavanagh's self-portrait in his short sketch "The Lay of the Crooked Knight" and claims that by 1945, Kavanagh had "in his own eyes become a sort of Green Knight" attacking "the fake and the mediocre." Claims that *The Great Hunger* was the best of Kavanagh's social criticism, and it showed he was a better poet than novelist or critic. *The Great Hunger* was an antiromantic, antipastoral analysis of rural Ireland, showing how "the psychological conditions under which (Maguire) functions also contribute to his failure to achieve a full life." No one could deny the poem's "postive influence" on writers. Discusses Kavanagh's "crusade" against philistinism in the 1940s and his verse satires of 1947–1953. Repeats material from Nemo (1974.26).

1975

24 ——. "William Carleton: a Monaghan View." *Carleton Newsletter* (Gainsville, Fla.), no. 5, pp. 11–12.

Discusses Kavanagh's inconsistent attitude toward Carleton. In 1945, Kavanagh expressed reservations about him. In 1951, he wrote his brother, Peter, that he thought Carleton was "no good," and yet, later that year, he praised him in a BBC broadcast. Throughout his career, he praised Carleton as one of Ireland's most accomplished writers, and he wrote a positive assessment of him for the 1968 MacGibbon & Kee edition of Carleton's autobiography. His alternating viewpoint was due to his "critical feistiness" in the early 1950s. After his lung cancer operation, he grew to like Carleton again.

25 O'BRIEN, DARCY. *Patrick Kavanagh.* Lewisburg: Bucknell University Press, 72 pp.

Contains four chapters: "The Great Hunger," "Stony Grey Soil," "Adventures in the Bohemian Jungle," and "Freedom." Discusses Kavanagh's hatred of abstract nationalism and his poetic of the "universal particular," which emerged as part of his reaction against "mythopoeic notions of Irishness." Finds *The Great Hunger* a very didactic poem and polemicizes "against sentimental literary lies about the land." Examines the departure from Inniskeen and the Dublin years. Concludes that Kavanagh's life is reminiscent of that of a Beckett character like Molloy, who sheds all his possessions and enters a realm of pure contemplation: his own last years were marked by an interest in poetic mysticism. Discusses his influence on younger Irish poets.

26 O'CASEY, SEAN. *The Letters of Sean O'Casey, 1910–1941.* Vol. I. Edited by David Krause. New York: Macmillan, pp. 684, 856.

O'Casey ordered *Ploughman and Other Poems* from Macmillan, in a letter of November 2, 1937. In a letter of March 31, 1940 to Horace Reynolds, O'Casey laments: "It will be a long time, I'm afraid, before Ireland gets another Lady G; & longer before she gets another W. B.; though there is a young poet rising in P[atrick] Cavanagh, I think."

27 "Patrick Kavanagh Award." *Democrat and People's Journal* (29 November). UCD Archive.

Announces that John Ennis won award, to be presented at annual Kavanagh commemoration at Inniskeen.

28 "Patrick Kavanagh Remembered in Inniskeen." *Democrat and People's Journal* (6 December). UCD Archive.

Describes annual commemoration of Kavanagh at Inniskeen.

29 "QUIDNUNC." "An Irishman's Diary." *Irish Times* (29 November):11.

1975

Announces annual Kavanagh commemoration at Inniskeen, which the French Ambassador and his wife will attend. John Ennis has won the 1975 Kavanagh Poetry Award.

30 RYAN, JOHN. *Remembering How We Stood*. Dublin: Gill and Macmillan, New York: Taplinger, 168 pp.

Provides many anecdotes about Kavanagh's life and career, especially in chapter ten, "Paddy Kavanagh", in which he discusses the poet's friendships with Betjeman, who urged Kavanagh to join the British Secret Service, Harold and Maurice Macmillan, and the Earl of Iveagh, the Guinness magnate. Discusses his meetings with Ezra Pound and Dylan Thomas and his 1954 trial and cancer operation. Kavanagh was "the last authentic pastoral voice to produce great poetry."

31 "School of Kavanagh." *Irish Press* (1 December). UCD Archive.

Describes plans for a Kavanagh summer school at Inniskeen. Contains photo of French Ambassador at the Kavanagh's grave.

32 SMITH, MICHAEL. "The Contemporary Situation in Irish Poetry." In Dunn (1975.10), pp. 160–161.

Argues that Kavanagh influenced James Liddy.

33 STUART, FRANCIS. "Earthy Visionary." *Hibernia* (25 July):21.

Contrasts Yeats with Kavanagh; "to think of [Yeats] having a bet on a horse-race or entering a Dublin pub would have been impossible." Kavanagh was one of the "outcasts" like Baudelaire, Rimbaud, Poe, and Villon. His "deep integrity has made him the enemy of all Literary Establishments, especially the Irish one." Kavanagh "presented existent Reality in a more immediate and tangible way than ever before, but, not being prophet or visionary, he did not reveal an alternative reality." Kavanagh, Beckett, and O'Faolain were part of a realistic, antiromantic countercurrent after Irish independence. *The Great Hunger* was "mildly disturbing only on the surface with its fashionable criticism of rural Irish puritanism," but "showed no sign of a current counter to the native stream; the disuptive, imaginative passion that was to impell what was still deepening in the high mountain lake of Kavanagh's psyche." In his life and art, Kavanagh achieved a "unity" which Yeats did not.

34 SUMMERFIELD, HENRY. *That Myriad-Minded Man: A Biography of George William Russell "A.E." 1867–1935*. Totowa, New Jersey: Rowman and Littlefield, p. 263.

Describes Kavanagh's arrival at AE's door on December 20, 1931, and AE's hospitality to the traveler from Monaghan. "He was the last of the long line of poets whom AE discovered."

1976

35 SWAN, DESMOND. "Caring Too Much: Autobiograpy in *The Great Hunger*." *Era* no. 2:29–31.

Claims Kavanagh's purpose was "to drown in a cold shower of realism the lingering rainbows of Celtic twilightry." Claims *The Great Hunger* was a landmark in Irish poetry, and praises the poem's authenticity: "in reading it we find ourselves." Yet, the poem is marred by too much autobiographical content—Maguire is a thin mask for Kavanagh himself. Claims Maguire's despair with rural life expressed Kavanagh's desire to outgrow his adolescent self. Finds the poem's conclusion unconvincing and "overdone."

36 WAKEMAN, JOHN, ed. *World Authors, 1950–1970*. New York: H.W. Wilson, pp. 753–754.

Biographical entry on Kavanagh.

37 WALSH, CAROLINE. "The Saturday Interview: Caroline Walsh Talks to Seamus Heaney." *Irish Times* (6 December):5

Heaney claims "Kavanagh's great achievement was to make our sub-culture—the rural outback—a cultural resource for us all."

1976

1 ANDERS, JAROSLAW, and PIOTR SOMMER. "Patrick Kavanagh Przelozyl Jaroslav Anders. 'Wielki Glod' (fragmenty)." In *Literatura Na Swiece*. Warsaw Kwiecien. Miesiecznik 4 (60):66–72.

Translations into Polish of *The Great Hunger* I and IX by Anders, and of "Shancoduff" by Sommer.

2 CASEY, DANIEL J. "Kavanagh's Calculations and Miscalculations." *Colby Quarterly* 12, no. 2 (June):65–82.

Kavanagh's reputation in Irish literature is "secure," thanks to about twenty poems. Discusses early poems, including "Shancoduff" and "To a Blackbird" and *The Green Fool*. "The autobiography of a good-natured country liar." *The Great Hunger* is "a masterful diatribe against the woeful state of the peasantry and their acceptance of divine apathy." It is a savage, unheroic "indictment of indignities that infest the lives of the Irish country poor." Disagrees with Kavanagh's conclusion that the poem was "a humourless failure." Discusses *A Soul for Sale*, 1947, and *Tarry Flynn*, which "never makes top grade as a novel." Praises *Come Dance with Kitty Stobling*, especially the Canal Bank sonnets, which are worthy of Shakespeare and are "a denial of 'The Great Hunger' and 'Pegasus' and 'The Paddiad'." Kavanagh is the most influential Irish poet after Yeats.

1976

3 CRONIN, ANTHONY. *Dead as Doornails.* Dublin: Dolmen, in association with the Talbot Press, 201 pp.

A memoir of postwar bohemian Dublin, focusing on Kavanagh, Behan, and Flann O'Brien. Describes literary Dublin's first impressions of Kavanagh, his work at *Envoy*, his friends and detractors at the Palace bar and McDaid's, his continuing battle with Behan, and his addiction to horse racing. Discusses Kavanagh during the time of the libel trial, his subsequent illness and recovery. Recalls his last conversation with the poet.

4 ———. "The Coming of Kavanagh. The third excerpt from Anthony Cronin's literary biography, 'Dead as Doornails.'" *Irish Times* (14 August):10.

Describes the literary milieu of the late forties surrounding the Palace Bar, McDaid's, and *Envoy* magazine. Describes relationship between Kavanagh and Dublin's editors and journalists in this period and his reputation in these circles as a "maladroit, mannerless oaf." Considers Kavanagh a genius. Describes his relations with neighbors on the Pembroke Road and his longing for fame in London. Mentions Kavanagh's alcoholism in his later years. Describes Kavanagh's pride in his acquaintance with Betjeman, V. S. Pritchett, Cyril Connolly, and Maurice Macmillan.

5 DOWNEY, GERRY. "Faces of Ireland." BBC radio broadcast. Sound Archive, Ulster Folk and Transport Museum, #BBC (BBE02/14QU031). Produced by Paul Muldoon. Transmitted 18 January. Duration 39 minutes 45 seconds.

Gerry Downey discusses the Irish at work and play, in light of poems, songs, and prose pieces. Considers *The Great Hunger* to be "among the best descriptions of the Irishman's intimate relationship with the soil."

6 FINNERAN, RICHARD, ed. *Anglo-Irish Literature: A Review of Research.* New York: MLA, pp. 18, 34, 153, 248, 475, 495.

Brief references to Kavanagh as poet and critic.

7 GREACEN, ROBERT. "Encounters with Kavanagh." *Irish Times* (16 January):8.

Describes the circumstances leading to his being asked to review *The Great Hunger* for *Horizon* (see 1942.2). Recalls how impressed he was by the power of the poem: "this was raw, disturbing work." Recalls with affection his later meetings with the poet in Dublin. Considers Kavanagh a loud, dogmatic, reincarnated Dr. Johnson. Claims there are many legends about him, which "will grow with the passing of time." Thinks of Kavanagh as basically "an unhappy man."

1976

8   HUTCHINS, PATRICIA. "Letters. Encounters with Kavanagh." *Irish Times* (29 January):11.
    Response to Greacen (1976.7) and Mahon-Smith (1976.13),

9   "Kavanagh commemoration." *Irish Times* (29 November):11.
    Describes wreath laying in Kavanagh's memory at Inniskeen on November 28. Former President Cearbhall O'Dalaigh was in attendance. Aidan Matthews won the 1976 Kavanagh Poetry Award.

10 KEHOE, KIERAN. "Ryan's Monument." *St Stephen's* 3, no. 3:60–61.
    Review of Ryan, *Remembering How We Stood* (1975.30). Considers Kavanagh "the hero of the book."

11 KERSNOWSKI, FRANK, C. W. SPINKS, and LAIRD LOOMIS (editors). *Bibliography of Modern Irish and Anglo-Irish Literature*. San Antonio, Tex.: Trinity College Press, pp. 64–66.
    Contains primary Kavanagh bibliography and two items of criticism.

*12 KINSELLA, THOMAS. "Writer in Profile. Thomas Kinsella." RTE TV program. Accession no. LB101. Transmitted 20 September. Duration: 26 minutes 17 seconds. Produced by James Plunkett.
    Augustine Martin interviews Kinsella, who talks of his respect for Kavanagh and other writers.

13 MAHON-SMITH, WALTER. "Letters. Encounters with Kavanagh." *Irish Times* (24 January):9.
    Response to Greacen (1976.7).

14 MCINERNY, MICHAEL. "The man who resisted greatness." *Irish Times* (6 January):5.
    Obituary of John A. Costello. Alludes to his role in the 1954 Kavanagh trial.

15 MONTAGUE, JOHN. "In the Irish Grain." *The Book of Irish Verse*. New York: Macmillan, First American Edition, pp. 21–39.
    Reprint of Montague (1974.25).

16 O'CONNOR, KEVIN. "Fleeting City. The London Years of Patrick Kavanagh." RTE radio broadcast. Presented and produced by Kevin O'Connor. Recorded 28 April. Duration: 42 minutes 56 seconds. RTE sound archive accession no. 138/7.
    Friends and acquaintances of the poet discuss the man and his work, including Leland Bardwell, Anthony Cronin, Martin Green, Katherine Kavanagh, Priscilla MacNamara, Richard O'Riordan, Alan Smith, and James

Smith. Describes Kavanagh's attitude to London as a "counter-world." Bardwell discusses his relationship with Katherine Kavanagh, Green recalls Kavanagh at the 1967 Poetry International.

17 ——. "The London Years of Patrick Kavanagh." *Irish Press* (29 April):9. UCD Archive.

Reproduces material from radio program (1976.16). Describes commemorative plaque to Kavanagh outside The Plough, a public bar in Bloomsbury, marking the spot where the poet once urinated. Discusses Kavanagh's relationship with London, where he intermittently lived over a period of thirty years.

18 "Review." *Sunday Independent* (12 September). UCD Archive.
Review of Anthony Cronin, *Dead as Doornails*. Brief references to Kavanagh.

19 SEYMOUR-SMITH, MARTIN. *Who's Who in Twentieth Century Literature*. London: Weidenfeld & Nicholson, p. 194.
Biographical entry on the poet.

20 Untitled. *Irish Independent* (29 November). UCD Archive.
Brief description of annual Kavanagh commemoration.

21 WALL, MERVYN. "Radio." *Evening Press* (8 May). UCD Archive.
Refers to the recent broadcasting of an "Arts feature devoted to [Kavanagh's] life in London, last week."

1977

1 Broadcast. *Radio Times* (25 June–1 July). UCD Archive.
Announces forthcoming broadcast of Andy O'Mahony's interview with Katherine Kavanagh.

2 CRONIN, ANTHONY. "Old Sores." *Irish Times* (3 June):10.
Responds critically to O'hAodha (1977.38).

3 ——. "Viewpoint: Kavanagh Assessed." *Irish Times* (18 November):10.
Despite consensus about Kavanagh's "greatness," there has been little detailed examination of his work. Perhaps his poetry does not lend itself to academic literary criticism. What can the critic discuss? Kavanagh's poetry does not apparently project a philosophical view of life or "weltanschauung." His attitude to nature seems very simple. However, the poetry expresses "social passion," and is characterized by "profundity, intensity, seriousness."

1977

The poetry demonstrates "fierce originality," especially in his later work, although his early poems seem derivative, except for "Inniskeen Road: July Evening."

4 ——. "Viewpoint: Kavanagh Concluded." *Irish Times* (25 November):10.
Kavanagh would not have become famous had he only written *Ploughman and Other Poems*. Partly, he failed as a nature poet because he does not describe nature "in such a way that the reader shares his experience of it." He tends to describe "the feeling engendered" rather than the object in nature. His work should be regarded as a "personal epic," characterized by opposition to Irish society, a sense of survival, humor, cynicism, and fidelity to "the importance of the humble." His later satires combine personal hatred and social passion.

5 CROWLEY, JEANANNE. "Living On." *Radio Times* (28 May–3 June). UCD Archive.
Preview of a new series on the spouses of famous authors. References to Katherine Kavanagh, with photo.

6 DEANE, SEAMUS. "Unhappy and at home: Interview with Seamus Heaney." *Crane Bag* 6, no. 1:61–67.
Brief discussion of Kavanagh and Yeats as antithetical opposites in the Irish tradition.

7 DONOGHUE, DENIS. "The Brothers Kavanagh: Two Autobiographies." *Hibernia* (23 December):29.
Review of Peter Kavanagh, *Beyond Affection. An Autobiography*. Praises Peter Kavanagh's "generosity" and energy in being his "brother's keeper," but argues that he is condescending, vain, and filled with spleen and bitterness. *Beyond Affection* is the vehicle of this bitterness. "It is a pity that it carries little else." Claims Peter Kavanagh's mind is "spontaneous" but not thoughtful about the subject matter of which he writes. Praises the author's descriptions of shoe-making and scythe-making, but laments his erratic, careless writing.

8 FALLER, KEVIN. "Struggling Kavanagh was a poet delivering a statement of the gods." *Evening Herald* (4 November). UCD Archive.
Review of *By Night Unstarred*.

9 FALLIS, RICHARD. *The Irish Renaissance*. Syracuse: Syracuse University Press, pp. 118, 229, 237, 244, 256–263, 282.
Claims Kavanagh's influence on modern Irish poetry has been "enormous." Considers Kavanagh "the opposite of the patrician, private (Austin) Clarke," although, like Clarke, he was a satirist. Claims *Kavanagh's Weekly*

was "in the best tradition of eighteenth-century satiric pamphleteering." Discusses *The Great Hunger*, which he considers to be not quite a great poem because it is "too long, too repetitious, and sometimes self-indulgent." Discusses Tarry Flynn as an "almost Maguire-like figure." Discusses Kavanagh's "return to simplicity" in his work after his lung operation. Claims Kavanagh liberated Irish poetry from Yeats's ghost.

10 FOLEY, DONAL. "The Saturday Column. A Miscellany. Kavanagh Industry." *Irish Times* (3 December):12.

Predicts that the Kavanagh industry "has a rosy future." Briefly discusses recent TV debate on Kavanagh featuring Denis Donoghue, who claimed Kavanagh was "genuine" but minor, and Anthony Cronin, who called Kavanagh a "remarkable poet." Quotes a four-line ditty Kavanagh wrote for Foley in 1950.

11 GILLESPIE, ELGY. "Elgy Gillespie talked to Katherine Kavanagh." *Irish Times* (30 November): 8.

Reading Dostoevsky's widow's biography of her husband made Katherine Kavanagh wish to be interviewed about her late husband, Patrick. Claims that various scholars have sent her theses on Kavanagh but she regrets that she did not reply to them very politely. She was always attracted to rebellious people (her parents were active Irish Republicans), but Patrick Kavanagh was "the greatest rebel of them all." Describes her life in London when she met Patrick. Claims he loved Dublin, despite rumors to the contrary. Describes their marriage and her role in his work. "I typed his letters and did his correspondence and yet never thought of myself as his secretary." Claims she was the bread-winner of the family. Discusses Kavanagh's drinking habits.

12 HARMON, MAURICE. *An Irish Studies Handbook for Anglo-Irish Literature and its Backgrounds: A Select Bibliography*. Dublin: Wolfhound, p. 127.

Cites two Kavanagh bibliographies: Peter Kavanagh (1972.19), and Nemo (1973.31).

13 ———. "'Cobwebs Before the Wind': Aspects of the Peasantry in Irish Literature from 1800 to 1916." In *Views of the Irish Peasantry, 1800–1916*. Edited by Daniel Casey and Robert Rhodes. Hamden, Conn.: Archon Books, p. 131.

Brief reference to Kavanagh's depiction of the peasantry.

14 ———. "Irish Poetry After Yeats." *Études Irlandaises* no. 2 (New Series), (December):45–62.

Kavanagh's writings represent "the first intimate and authoritative response to rural life in poetry," which links him to the Gaelic poets of the

1977

eighteenth century. Discusses *The Great Hunger*. Kavanagh's poems express an openness to "joy in life" and delight in nature. They express love but also a sense of loss. His poetry also contains "a note of mariolatry." Kavanagh serves as a model for later rural poets, including Montague and Heaney.

15 "It's Paddy Kavanagh's 'missing' novel." *Sunday Independent* (13 February). UCD Archive.

Desmond Egan explains why Goldsmith intends to publish Kavanagh's unpublished novel, *By Night Unstarred*.

16 JORDAN, JOHN. "The Brothers Kavanagh: Two Autobiographies." *Hibernia* (23 December):29.

Review of *By Night Unstarred*. Suggests that the two fragments which comprise *By Night Unstarred* might have been published separately. Speculates that Kavanagh might not have written anything of worth had he stayed in Inniskeen.

17 KAVANAGH, KATHERINE, and O'MAHONY, ANDY. "Literary Widows." BBC radio broadcast. Sound archive, Ulster Folk and Transport Museum, no. BBE22/160U922. Transmitted 23 October. Duration: 29 minutes 30 seconds.

Andy O'Mahony interviews Katherine Kavanagh, widow of the poet. Discusses Kavanagh's life and work, including his work at *Envoy*, his days in Pembroke Road, the success of *Come Dance with Kitty Stobling*, and his relationship with Katherine. Claims Kavanagh really understood women. Expresses annoyance that people came to like Kavanagh's work after he died, not before. Recalls that he liked Ian Paisley.

18 KAVANAGH, PETER. *Beyond Affection: An Autobiography*. New York: Kavanagh Hand Press, 201 pp.

Characterizes his attitude as a young man to Patrick as one of admiration and worship. Discusses family background, Patrick's early reading habits and literary efforts, and the death of their father. Examines his own relationship to Patrick and the vicissitudes of Patrick's and his own career. Describes the foundation of the Hand Press and the publication of *Lapped Furrows*. Recalls the events leading up to and immediately after Patrick's death and outlines his own publishing ventures since then.

19 ——. Introduction and Epilogue to *By Night Unstarred: An Autobiographical Novel*. Edited by Peter Kavanagh. Newbridge, Ireland: Goldsmith Press, pp. 7–22, 187–199.

In "Introduction" discusses the origins of *By Night Unstarred*, which became two incomplete autobiographical novels. Discusses Kavanagh's early

1977

life and career up to the mid-1940s. In "Epilogue," discusses aspects of Kavanagh's later career, including his relationship with John Charles McQuaid, Kavanagh's apartment in Pembroke Road, the production of *Kavanagh's Weekly*, the court case concerning the *Leader* profile of the poet, the lung operation, the job at UCD, Kavanagh's love of New York, the Peter Kavanagh Hand Press, and Kavanagh's 1965 appearance at Northwestern University. Claims the poet was "an intense Catholic, almost a mystic."

20 "Kavanagh Poetry Award." *Irish Times* (26 November):3.
    Announcement of 1977 Kavanagh Poetry Award. Thomas McArthy is to receive prize at commemoration in Inniskeen, 27 November.

21 KEARNEY, COLBERT. *The Writings of Brendan Behan*. Dublin: Gill and Macmillan, p. 42.
    Describes the widespread publicity Brendan Behan received as a result of his appearance in court during Kavanagh's libel action against the *Leader* magazine. Kavanagh believed that Behan had been the author of the famous "Profile" in that paper.

22 KENNEDY, MAEV. "Poet's Progress." *Irish Times* (5 November):13.
    Review of *By Night Unstarred*. Claims Kavanagh has almost deified himself in the book as a "noble-spirited poet." Finds the two fragments of the book "not a novel in any possible sense of the word." Peter Kavanagh has joined the two parts together "by an extraordinarily clumsy link passage." The best portions of the book are to be found in part one, "in the early sections of Peter Devine's life, where the unwavering venom has a horrible fascination." States that the landscape of part one is "*Tarry Flynn* territory, but without the irrepressible joy and humor that lifted that book." The description of Peter Devine is heavy-handed, but "there are flashes of splendid if bloodyminded description."

23 KROLL, JACK. "Lily Tomlin: Funny Lady." *Newsweek* (28 March): 64.
    Uses Kavanagh's remarks on the nature of comedy as a comment on the actress Lily Tomlin.

24 LONGLEY, MICHAEL. "Epitaph. In Memoriam Patrick Kavanagh." *Irish Times* (26 March):8.
    Elegy for Kavanagh.

25 "Major Award for Unknown Poet." *Sunday Independent* (16 October). UCD Archive.
    Announcement that Thomas McArthy won the Kavanagh Poetry Award.

1977

26 MCCARTHY, COLMAN. "Patrick Kavanagh: Ireland's Countryman Poet." *Washington Post* (17 March):A17.

Admires the "poetic realism" and simple language of Kavanagh's writing. Kavanagh is not well known in the U.S.A., "though he will be." His current American audience "is small but passionate." Claims Kavanagh understood failure so well because "he sometimes considered himself to be one." Describes the Kavanagh Hand Press and its publications.

27 MCHALE, JOHN. "Kavanagh. Another 10 Novels." *Sunday Independent:* (13 February). UCD Archive.

Peter Kavanagh describes some of the unpublished manuscript material Patrick Kavanagh left behind, including an unfinished novel, *By Night Unstarred*.

28 MORROW, LARRY [The Bellman.] "Meet Mr. Patrick Kavanagh." In Nemo (1977.29), pp. 71–77. Reprint of Morrow (1948.5).

29 NEMO, JOHN. Patrick Kavanagh Number. *Journal of Irish Literature* 6, no. 1 (January):176 pp.

Contains Morrow (1977.28), Nemo (1977.30, 31), O'Connor (1977.35), and O'Faolain (1977.36), as well as a number of essays by Kavanagh, briefly introduced by Nemo.

30 ———. "Patrick Kavanagh: Notes Toward a Critical Biography." In Nemo (1975.29), pp. 4–21.

Biographical essay. Claims most critics judge Kavanagh by his character rather than his work. Argues that Kavanagh always felt like an "outsider," an emotion of estrangement which he explores in *Tarry Flynn*. Discusses his early reading and writing, his trip to Dublin in the thirties, and the Gogarty law suit. Believes *The Green Fool* is "neither stage-Irish nor a lie," despite the poet's rejection of the work. Observes that Kavanagh's "purposeful cultivation of pomposity" alienated those who might have helped him. He had a self-debilitating concern with his image. Discusses *Leader* profile, pointing out that it was more complimentary than Kavanagh acknowledged, and discusses the trial and Kavanagh's ill health. After his "rebirth" in 1955, he lost his "crusading spirit," which was replaced by a renewed pastoralism. Discusses *Come Dance with Kitty Stobling*, Kavanagh's most successful book, and *Self-Portrait*, 1963, which shows his "preference for viewing life not as it is but as he would like it to be."

31 ———. Preface to Nemo (1975.29), p. 3

Notes that Kavanagh's reputation as poet has "steadily increased" since his death.

1977

32 "New novel by Patrick Kavanagh." *Irish Times* (5 November):6.
Announces publication of *By Night Unstarred*. Briefly describes the Shelbourne Hotel launching of the book on November 4th. Peter Kavanagh "made a short bitter speech in which he castigated the lack of response to his brother's work during the late poet's lifetime." A photograph by Paddy Whelan of Peter Kavanagh at the book launching is reproduced on the front page of this issue of the newspaper.

33 NISBET, TOM. "Weekly Competition, no. 410. Confrontations." *Irish Times* (14 February):8.
Three humorous poems about imaginary confrontations with Kavanagh, by Tom Nisbet, James Evans and B. Herbert.

34 NOWLAN, KEVIN. "The birth and growth of the new states." In *The Irish World*. Edited by Brian de Breffny. London: Thames and Hudson, p. 272.
Brief reference to Kavanagh.

35 O'CONNOR, P.J. *Tarry Flynn*. In Nemo (1977.29), pp. 81–155.
Adaptation of *Tarry Flynn* for the stage, with brief preface by John Nemo.

36 O'FAOLAIN, SEAN. "Poetry in Ireland Today." In Nemo (1977.29), pp. 50–51.
Reprint of O'Faolain (1948.6).

37 O'FARRACHAIN, ROIBEARD. "Letters. The Casting Out of Patrick Kavanagh." *Irish Times* (24 May):9.
Critical response to O'hAodha (1977.38).

38 O'HAODHA, MICHEAL. "The Casting Out of Patrick Kavanagh." *Irish Times* (20 May):8.
Essay review of Nemo (1977.29). Argues that since Kavanagh never had a steady job and was always poor, his peers did not trust him and "shared the views of the ordinary suspicious citizen when considering a case of prolonged failure." Claims the essays on Kavanagh in the *JIL* communicate a sense of pathos, sorrow and personal tragedy. Contrasts the bohemianism of Brendan Behan and Oscar Wilde with Kavanagh's poverty. Notes that Kavanagh's contemporaries found him ungrateful. Discusses the spleen of *Kavanagh's Weekly*, and mentions Kavanagh's tendency to judge his fellow writers brutally. Posits that "there is little social criticism or comment" in Kavanagh's writings. Recalls the last time he spoke to Kavanagh, in 1966.

1977

39 RUSHE, DESMOND. "Patrick Kavanagh Remembers." *Irish Independent* (4 November):12. UCD Archive.

Review of *By Night Unstarred*. Speculates that Kavanagh was continually rebuffed by Irish society during his life because he lacked social graces and was too scornful of Irish institutions. Discusses Kavanagh's efforts, as recounted in *By Night Unstarred*, to secure a job as public relations officer of an Irish plastics firm.

40 SHEERIN, PATRICK H. "Some Themes in Patrick Kavanagh's *The Great Hunger*." University of Valladolid (Spain), pp. 395–411.

Claims Kavanagh's fame "rests alone on *The Great Hunger*." Contrasts the poem's "tragic realism" with the naïveté and sentimentality of the early poetry. Claims Kavanagh abandoned realism in the later work. Kavanagh established his independence from "the overpowering influence of Yeats." Discusses the poem as a study of psychological development, and considers Maguire's relationship to his mother as "sado-masochistic." Discusses the poem's significance in light of the six-year "economic war" with Britain during the 1930s.

41 SOMMER, PIOTR. *Literatura Na Swiecie* (Warsaw), pp. 208–214.

Polish translations of ten Kavanagh poems.

42 "The Great Hunger." *Sunday Independent* (12 June). UCD Archive.

Announces opening of a fast-food restaurant called "The Great Hunger," on Dublin's Canal Bank, opposite the Kavanagh memorial seat.

43 "The Simplicity of Return." *Radio Times* (26 June). UCD Archive.

Notice of forthcoming radio broadcast. "John Miller presents a picture of Kavanagh's life which shows how his bitterness and difficulties were resolved in a return to that simplicity of celebration."

44 "Topic. Programme on Death of Patrick Kavanagh." RTE Radio broadcast. Dubbed 22 June (recorded in 1967). Accession no. BB1863. Duration: 28 minutes 7 seconds.

Friends and contemporaries of Kavanagh remember the poet, including John Ryan, Seamus Heaney, Liam Miller, Lady (Christine) Longford, Tomas MacAnna, and Con O'Houlihan. Heaney discusses how Kavanagh influenced him as poet, although he did not meet him personally "until three months ago" (in 1967). Claims reading Kavanagh's poetry was "like reading into my own life," and that *The Great Hunger* "nearly took the top of my head off."

45 TUOHY, FRANK. "Dublin's Depressive." *Times Literary Supplement* (16 December):1467.

Compares Peter Kavanagh's role as "brother's keeper" to that of Stanislaus Joyce. Review of *By Night Unstarred*, in which the portrait of the Devines in part one is "Kavanagh at his best, economical, lyrical and mercifully free from any political context." In part two, "the prevalent tone is depressive." Although "irritating and unsatisfactory," the book demonstrates Kavanagh's talent.

46 Untitled. *Sunday Press* (24 July). UCD Archive.
   Claims the French Ambassador to Ireland, Comte Pierre de Menthon, is fond of Kavanagh's poetry. He says it is "easy for foreigners to appreciate."

1978

*1 ARGOFF, JEANNE J. *The Hearth, the Field and the Road. The countryman in the works of Yeats and Kavanagh*. Ph.D. thesis, UCD.
   Thesis on Kavanagh and Yeats

2 BOURKE, BRIAN. Drawings on magazine cover. *Era* no. 4.
   Cover drawings of Kavanagh.

3 BOYD, WILLIAM. "Dug Up." *New Review* 4, no. 47 (February):52.
   Review of *By Night Unstarred*, which mostly avoids the romanticism and mysticism which marred *Tarry Flynn* and *The Green Fool*. Claims parts one and two of the book should not have been joined, but published separately, since they are so different. Claims part one is more successful, because the more autobiographical second part is spoiled by the author's bitterness and self-pity. Praises the steadfastness of the ironic gaze in part one, which is compared to *Madame Bovary*.

4 BOYLAN, HENRY. *A Dictionary of Irish Biography*. Dublin: Gill & Macmillan, p. 165.
   Biographical entry for Kavanagh.

5 BURNHAM, RICHARD. "'Where the Road from Laracor Leads': On F. R. Higgins." *Eire* 13, no. 1 (Spring):139–149.
   Brief reference to Kavanagh, who held Higgins's poetry in high esteem.

6 COFFEY, BRIAN. "Excerpts from 'Concerning Making.'" *Lace Curtain* 6 (Autumn):31–37.
   Brief reference to *The Great Hunger*. Complains that few libraries stocked the poem in the 1940s and 1950s: "someone slipped up there, depriving poets in Ireland of what should have been their common good."

1978

7 CRONIN, ANTHONY. "Viewpoint. Evil We Ain't." *Irish Times* (23 June):10.
   Discussion of "the Catholic Novel," with passing references to Kavanagh.

8 DURCAN, PAUL. Foreword to *Lough Derg*. London: Martin Brian & O'Keeffe, pp. vii–ix.
   Claims Kavanagh is a major poet "of profound verbal sophistication and high voltage religious sensibility," although modern academic readers cannot understand him. Predicts that many "memorable monographs" on the poet will result from the publication of *Lough Derg*, in which Kavanagh was attempting to read the Irish soul. Claims the poem's narrative style suggests it was written "with wireless and/or film in mind."

9 EGAN, DESMOND. "At Patrick Kavanagh's Grave: Ten Years Later." *Era* 4:35.
   Poem addressed to Kavanagh.

10 FLEMING, RONNIE. "Patrick Kavanagh." *Irish Times* (18 November).
   Letter announcing that *Lough Derg* will be published in Ireland by the Goldsmith Press on 2 November 20, 1978. The introduction will be by Peter Kavanagh, .

11 GARVEY, JOSEPH B. Review of Peter Kavanagh, *Beyond Affection*. *Era* 4:31.
   Claims it is "a great book," told with great honesty. It "chronicles the dedication, the faithfulness, the awesome discipline with which (Peter) carried out what he saw as his mission in life."

12 GRENNAN, EAMON. "View from the Bridge." *Eire* (Fall):141–147.
   Discusses the publication of *By Night Unstarred*, "two unfinished novels by [Peter Kavanagh's] brother Patrick that he has roughly bandaged together." Claims that 1977, the tenth anniversary of Patrick's death, "was in a special way [Patrick] Kavanagh's [year]. No other writer, living or dead, received more critical or publishing attention." Criticizes Peter Kavanagh's "sour antics" in promoting the poet's reputation.

13 HARMON, MAURICE. Review of *By Night Unstarred*. *Era* 4:30.
   Describes the book's two parts, claiming the second is connected to the first "somewhat clumsily."

14 HIRST, DESIREE. "The Poetic Scene in Ireland Today." *Anglo-Welsh Review*, no. 62:89–112.

1978

Claims Kavanagh was "an imperfect poet" but very influential and "seminal." Claims that he was both religious and yet anticlerical, impatient with provincialism, and "hating the slick fashionable intellectualism" of contemporary literary circles.

15 IGOE, VIVIEN. "Patrick Kavanagh's Dublin." *Irish Times* (17 January):8.
Lists Kavanagh's many Dublin addresses from 1939 to 1965 and the pubs in which he drank. Parson's bookstore was "his refuge, his home from home." Mentions Kavanagh commemorative seat by Grand Canal between the Baggot Street and Leeson Street Bridges: "The seat was made of ancient oak from Meath; granite from the Dublin mountains was used for the uprights, and Liscarra slabs from the Burren form the surrounding paving."

16 JORDAN, JOHN. "Encounter with P. K." *Drumlin* (Autumn):77–79.
Describes first reading *The Green Fool* and *The Great Hunger* in 1946, and first meeting Kavanagh in 1948. Mentions Kavanagh's affiliations with *Envoy*, his 1950 trip to Rome, and other key moments in his later career. When he last saw Kavanagh in June 1967, he "spoke eloquently and quite irrationally."

17 JUDE THE OBSCURE [pseud.]. "Patrick Kavanagh." *Honest Ulsterman*, no. 60 (July/October):60–80.
Claims that Kavanagh's three long poems, *The Great Hunger*, *Why Sorrow,* and *Lough Derg* demonstrate the influence of T. S. Eliot. Argues that *Lough Derg* is "the finest long poem to come out of Ireland." These poems, as well as *By Night Unstarred*, reflect a naturalist aesthetic reminiscent of Flaubert and Zola. Recalls a recent visit to Inniskeen, and noticed the lounge bar called "Kavanagh's Hideout" and "The Green Fool Snack Bar." One local man remarked, "But there's them as is making a power of money out of Kavanagh, a power of money."

18 KAVANAGH, PETER. *A Guide to Patrick Kavanagh Country*. The Curragh, Ireland: Goldsmith. 67 pp.
Reprint of Kavanagh (1978.21).

19 ———. "A Biography of Patrick Kavanagh." Letter to *Irish Times* (8 November).
Request for information on Patrick Kavanagh for a biography of the poet.

20 ———. Introduction to *Lough Derg*. Goldsmith Press, p.7.
Claims Patrick Kavanagh was a Catholic mystic, although he went to Lough Derg not as a mystic, but as a writer. Argues that *Lough Derg* is better than *The Great Hunger*.

1978

21 ——. *Savage Rock. Inniskeen, the History of a Parish.* New York: Peter Kavanagh Hand Press. 67 pp.

Discusses history of Inniskeen and Patrick Kavanagh's childhood there. Also discusses folklore associated with county Monaghan, the history of the Kavanagh house, the decline of Gaelic in Monaghan, and the Famine. Kavanagh's grandfather was a teacher at Kednaminsha school in 1849, which Peter and Patrick Kavanagh also attended. Describes Patrick's early writing habits, his knowledge of Gaelic, and his athleticism. Discusses local reception of *Ploughman and Other Poems* and *The Green Fool*, and describes Patrick's last years.

22 ——. "Ten Years Later: An Address Given by Peter Kavanagh at the Graveside of His Brother, Patrick Kavanagh, November 1977." *Era* (Dublin) 4:3–6.

Describes Kavanagh's death in Dublin and Peter's response to the news. Claims poets are gifted and unique, with visionary capabilities, and society should therefore honor them. Discusses his compilation of all the letters written by his brother and himself, which became *Lapped Furrows* (1969.6). Claims this timely publication prevented issue of a memoir written by someone else. Refers to the subsequent publication of *November Haggard, Collected Poems, Garden of the Golden Apples,* and *By Night Unstarred,* and argues that *The Green Fool* is an immature work, not the poet's authentic autobiography.

23 "Kavanagh the poet." Program for "Kavanagh Week," Inniskeen (2–10 September). UCD Archive.

Brief biographical sketch of the poet.

24 "'Kavanagh Week' at Inniskeen." *Irish Times* (5 September):11.

Announces that Senator Eoin Ryan officially opened the "Kavanagh Week" in Inniskeen. Mrs. Catherine Kavanagh and three local *Teachta Dala* (members of Parliament) were among the attendees.

25 "Kavanagh Week Planned." *Irish Times* (28 August):10.

Announces that Seamus Heaney, Brendan Kennelly, John Ryan, and Alan Warner will give lectures on Kavanagh at the forthcoming Inniskeen Kavanagh Week from September 3 to September 10.

26 KELLEHER, JOHN V. "The Ireland that was." *New Republic* (18 February):25–28.

Remembers meeting Patrick Kavanagh and other Irish writers, including Samuel Beckett, Austin Clarke and Frank O'Connor in 1946. Kavanagh said deprecating things about Kelleher's recent article in *Atlantic*. Kelleher's conversations with living Irish writers made his Harvard courses in literature seem simplistic. Jack Coughlin's portrait of Kavanagh accompanies article.

27 "Lectures on Kavanagh for Inniskeen Festival." *Irish Times* (7 September):8.
Announces lectures by John Ryan and Brendan Kennelly at the "Kavanagh Week" in Inniskeen.

28 LIDDY, JAMES. "Ulster Poets and the Catholic Muse." *Eire* 13, no. 4 (Winter):126–137.
Brief references to Kavanagh. Claims that Heaney's pastoral landscapes are described, "but not felt," in the way Kavanagh portrays the Ulster landscape in his poetry.

29 MCDONNELL, PETER J. "Patrick Kavanagh." Letter to *Irish Times* (9 June):11.
Response to Paul Potts's letter of June 3 (1978.32). Claims *Lough Derg* has, in fact, been published in Ireland, both in *Collected Poems* and *November Haggard*.

30 O'BRIEN, CONOR CRUISE. Preface to *A Prose and Verse Anthology of Modern Irish Writing* Edited by Grattan Freyer. Dublin: Irish Humanities Center, pp. xii–xiv.
Refers to "nightmare of Catholic poverty" in *The Great Hunger*.

31 O'DULAING, DONNCHA. "Highways and Byways. On Patrick Kavanagh." Produced by Cathal O'Griofa, presented by Donncha O'Dulaing. RTE radio. Accession no. AA693. Transmitted 6 August. Duration: 54 minutes 55 seconds.
Interviews friends and neighbors of Kavanagh at Inniskeen, during Kavanagh Week. Discusses local performance of *Tarry Flynn*, first performed there in 1972. An elderly neighbor discusses Kavanagh's prowess as a young football player. Discusses local reaction to *The Green Fool*, which was not well received initially. Some locals felt they had been slighted by his work.

32 POTTS, PAUL. "Patrick Kavanagh." Letter to *Irish Times* (3 June):15.
Claims *Lough Derg* is a greater poem than *The Great Hunger*, but has been published only in America. Suggests it should be published in Ireland.

33 SMITH, SYDNEY BERNARD. "Camera Obscura." *Books Ireland* (March):35–36.
Review of *By Night Unstarred*. Finds the book interesting because of the "growing reputation of the poet." The section on the Dublin years demonstrates Kavanagh's "obsessive" sense of injury, but the reviewer "seeks in

1979

vain in his work the realisation that there were perhaps others whose situation was even less fortunate than his."

34 T., A. "Poet in prose." *Observer* (London), (15 January):28.
Brief review of *By Night Unstarred*. Admires Kavanagh's "jaunty prose."

35 THOMPSON, RICHARD J. "In the Balance: 'The Books of My Numberless Dreams': A Basic Booklist in Irish Studies." *Choice* 15 (December): 1317–1333.
Briefly mentions Kavanagh's *Collected Pruse* as "highly amusing and reflective of the spirit of the age."

1979

1 BROWN, TERENCE. "After the Revival: The Problem of Adequacy and Genre." *Genre* 12, no. 4 (Winter):565–589.
Examines the "anxiety of influence" felt by young Irish writers in the twenties and thirties, and in particular their quarrel with the Irish Revival, including Clarke, Kavanagh, O'Connor, and O'Faolain.

2 CHARLTON, HUGH. "Lough Derg." *Hibernia* (15 February):3.
Letter about how William Carleton influenced Kavanagh.

3 DAVIES, DIANE. Review of *Lough Derg*. *Poetry Wales* 15, no. 1, (Summer):139–145.
Claims that the poem is that of the Kavanagh whose mystical Catholicism was "frequently at odds with both organised religion and the materialism of the age." The poem's blend of "compassion and satire" echoes a "Chaucerian vision." Despite Kavanagh's attraction to "the pagan," the poem avers that "God will reach anyone by the special channels analogous to poetry."

4 DEANE, SEAMUS. "Talk with Seamus Heaney." *New York Times* (2 December):47.
Brief reference to Kavanagh's influence on Heaney.

5 DE BREFFNY, BRIAN. *The Land of Ireland*. London: Thames and Hudson, pp. 13, 41.
Brief references to Kavanagh.

6 EAGLETON, TERRY. "Recent Poetry." *Stand* 21, no. 1:70–74.
Review of recent Irish poetry, including *Lough Derg*: "one of Patrick Kavanagh's undoubtedly finest poems." Praises poem's blend of sacred and

secular and its "range of tones, rhythms and verbal registers." Notes Kavanagh's religious ambivalence in the poem. Admires poem's sense of place, in contrast with "the bland flattening of historical complexities" in Eliot's *Four Quartets*.

7 FISHER, EMMA. "Migrations." *Spectator* (17 February), pp. 25–26.
   Review of several books, including Kavanagh's *Lough Derg*. Notes that the poem was excluded from the 1964 *Collected Poems*, although it was written in 1942. Claims Kavanagh's understanding of Irish Catholicism in *Lough Derg* is "hideously accurate." Although satirical and pleasingly realistic, the poem is "also a good text for students of purgatorial fire."

8 FLECK, RICHARD F. "A Glance at Patrick Kavanagh." *Paintbrush* (Laramie, Wyoming) 6, no. 12, (Autumn):41–46.
   Compares the sections of *The Great Hunger* to the stations of the cross.

9 FOLEY, DONAL. "The Saturday Column. Kavanagh Evening." *Irish Times, Weekend Supplement* (30 June):4.
   Announces that the U.S. Irish Embassy held "commemorative evening" for Kavanagh on June 29, and the event was introduced by Democrat Eugene McCarthy.

10 FOSTER, JOHN WILSON. "Patrick Kavanagh." In *Great Writers of the English Language: Poets*. Edited by James Vinson. New York: St. Martin's Press, pp. 546–547.
   Biographical essay on the poet and bibliography of his principal primary works. Admires some of the early poems, which exhibit "unashamed paganism," although the weaker ones display "a cloying devotionalism and piety." Considers *The Great Hunger* a "justly famous poem," and believes Kavanagh was in error to later reject the poem as "vulgar." Considers his later satirical poetry to have sunk into "invective and doggerel." The satire failed because it sprang from self-pity. Claims that "at least a score of Kavanagh's poems" will be remembered by posterity.

11 ———. "The Poetry of Patrick Kavanagh: A Reappraisal." *Mosaic: A Journal for the Interdisciplinary Study of Literature* 12, no. 3 (Spring):139–152.
   Considers Kavanagh's poetic reputation "uncertain," despite the fact his *Collected Poems* was first published in 1963 and has been available on both sides of the Atlantic since 1973. Claims younger Irish poets "have championed Patrick Kavanagh at the expense of Yeats." Argues that Kavanagh was a "discoverer" rather than "fashioner" of poems: "The unpredictability of magical lines is part of Kavanagh's gauche charm." Kavanagh's belief in the "mystical" charge of poetry was anti-Movement, and an echo of Dylan Thomas's

1979

poetic. Discusses Kavanagh's influence on Heaney. Claims Kavanagh "misread" the Revival writers, O'Casey, Synge, and Yeats, "in order to make room for himself." Discusses *The Great Hunger* as a poem about "sexual famine." The poem's pathos is "stiffened" by the narrator's "outspokenness." Claims Kavanagh had a good eye for detail. "Kavanagh used to notice things Yeats simply did not see," but the later satires are merely "uncooked invective," based on self-pity, not real indignation. Kavanagh was, in part, a "comic scapegoat."

*12 FRAZIER, ADRIAN WOODS. *Under Ben Bulben: Irish Poetry After Yeats.* Ph.D. dissertation, Washington University, St Louis. 210 pp. See DAI-A 40/02 (August):842.

Explores the responses of Irish poets to Yeats, whom they admire but from whom they seek creative distance. Kavanagh's work "exposes the pretentiousness" of many nationalists and Protestant Revival writers, who were self-consciously trying to cultivate connections with native Irish life.

13 ——. "Irish Poetry After Yeats." *Literary Review* 22, no. 2 (Winter): 133–144.

Some overlaps with Frazier's dissertation (1979.12). Kavanagh and Clarke were the most important Irish poets in the generation after Yeats. Kavanagh shunned Clarke's stress on Irishness, although Kavanagh was "inescapably Irish in a way that Clarke, who grew up in Dublin and worked many years in London could never be." Kavanagh wrote *The Great Hunger* in response to urban condescension to "the bog poet." Cites a Canal Bank sonnet as example of the later, authentic voice, in contrast to much of the poet's later "doggerel." Mentions Kavanagh's "moral vocabulary" with which he judged insincere and stage-Irish poetry. By the fifties, Kavanagh had "cleared the air of literary nationalism," having paved the way for Kinsella and Montague.

14 HAFFENDEN, JOHN. "Meeting Seamus Heaney." *London Magazine* (June):6–28.

Brief reference to Kavanagh's influence on Heaney.

15 HARMON, MAURICE. Introduction to *Irish Poetry After Yeats.* Dublin: Wolfhound, and Boston, Toronto: Little, Brown & Co., pp. 9–30.

Kavanagh refused to use the "mythic method," but his antimythic style "did not always appeal to later poets." His playing the role of poet as fool is "a cunning deflation of the Yeatsian personality." Compares John Hewitt's and Seamus Heaney's with Kavanagh's deliberate parochialism. A descendant of the eighteenth-century Gaelic poets, Kavanagh accepted "the ordinary, the parochial, the limited mind, the Catholic conscience," and celebrated "the plenitude of the earth and its seasonal flowering, its great natural processes." His vision is "based on a sense of joy in life, of delight in the natural world."

There is also "a note of mariolatry" in his vision of union with "the feminine earth." His work serves as model for rural poets like Montague and Heaney.

16 HEANEY, SEAMUS. "Kavanagh of the parish." *Listener* (26 April):577–579.

Essay on the poet based on the script of a BBC television program broadcast in the summer of 1977. Examines Kavanagh's poetry as the effort to articulate the world of rural labor which had not found expression before, "the voice of a hidden Ireland." Discusses Kavanagh's awe at his own creativity and his sense of being alone in a community which did not value poetry. Argues that Kavanagh stayed true to his religious faith from childhood, that he "was not an intellectual," and that he attempted in his poetry to recreate the image of Edenic innocence. *Tarry Flynn* is "a summer book," a comedy, whereas *The Great Hunger* is a dark, winter book, "a great howl of grief, the voice of a man not so much crying *in* the wilderness as crying *for* the wilderness." Explores Kavanagh's response to illness and recovery, which released in him "a mood of almost Franciscan love."

17 HOBSBAUM, PHILIP. *Tradition and Experiment in English Poetry*. London: Macmillan, Totowa, New Jersey: Rowman and Littlefield, pp. 325–330.

Claims Kavanagh had a good eye for detail as well as a sense of poetic form. His descriptive writing forms part of a generic tradition stretching back to Cowper, Dryden, Goldsmith, Langhorne, and Pope. Kavanagh was probably most influenced by Pope and Clare. His use of the "loose quatrain" produced effects "similar to those of the English poetic realists." *The Great Hunger*, which is "a masterpiece of structure," portrays Kavanagh as he might have become had he stayed in Inniskeen. Its achievement will probably not be repeated. Kavanagh's poetry transcends the pastoral of Heaney and Mackay Brown, because he avoids simplification and the backward look. His work is a contribution to "the poetry of barbarism."

18 HOLLAND, JACK. "After Yeats." *Hibernia* (23 August):16.

Review of *Irish Poetry After Yeats* (ed. Maurice Harmon). Claims Kavanagh's poetry often had "a blustering, bullying tone," and a "grandiose smugness" in "Epic." *The Great Hunger* is "sloppy," like a rough draft.

19 JORDAN, JOHN. "Pilgrimages." *Irish Press* (8 March) 6.

Review of both editions of *Lough Derg* (Martin Brian & O'Keeffe, and Goldsmith), and Peter Kavanagh's *Patrick Kavanagh Country*. Claims Kavanagh's poem is "at once more naked and more cagey" than Denis Devlin's poem on Lough Derg. Discusses the textual variants between the two editions of the poem (e.g., "bullfrog's hind paws" instead of "bulldog's hind paws"). Discusses Paul Durcan's introduction to the Martin Brian & O'Keeffe edition. Claims that Peter Kavanagh's introduction to the Goldsmith edition contains "near-nonsensical generalizations." Despite some reservations about

1979

the poem, Jordan praises *Lough Derg* as "a notable contribution to the confessional verse of our time."

20 "Kavanagh Ceremony." *Irish Times* (26 November):5.
Brief description of annual commemoration, at which Kavanagh's sister, Josephine Markey, laid a wreath.

21 KAVANAGH, PETER. *Sacred Keeper: A Biography of Patrick Kavanagh*. The Curragh, Ireland: Goldsmith Press. 403 pp.
Biography of the poet by his brother, containing personal memoirs and a detailed examination of Patrick's relationships with family members and the wider community.

22 "Kavanagh poetry prize increased." *Irish Times* (15 June):5.
Describes annual Kavanagh poetry award for Irish poets, begun in 1972, which has been increased to 250 pounds.

23 KENNELLY, BRENDAN. "On Language and Invention. Interview with Brendan Kennelly." *Literary Review* 22, no. 2 (Winter):197–204.
Contrasts Kavanagh with Yeats and alludes to his parody of Yeats's "Under Ben Bulben." Denies that Kavanagh "was immeasurably inferior to Yeats as a poet," although he lacked Yeats's discipline, professionalism, and dedication. His poetry was "an inspiration to a generation in need of a paradigm of such humanity."

24 ———. "Patrick's Pilgrimage." *Irish Times* (27 January):11.
Review of *Lough Derg*, which is primarily concerned with "spiritual poverty, and its purgation, real and imagined." Admires the "energetic thrust" of the writing. The poem is "something of a rich Homeric utterance." Claims Kavanagh's influence will continue to grow because of his moral candor and his faith in a "gay, creative God." In his poetry, he does not escape from personality as did Eliot, Yeats, and David Jones, but gives full expression to it.

25 KIBERD, DECLAN. "The Fall of the Stage Irishman." *Genre* 12, no. 4 :451–472.
Claims Kavanagh reacted against the Yeatsian idealization of peasant life, and that Kavanagh would have agreed with Marx's remarks on "the idiocy of rural life." Compares Kavanagh's view of peasant life with that of Joyce's Stephen Dedalus. Compares *The Great Hunger* with Shaw's *John Bull's Other Island* and Flann O'Brien's *An Beal Bocht*. Claims that in his prose, Kavanagh recognized but finally rejected the temptation to play the Stage-Irish fool. Warns that Ireland has not yet escaped Stage-Irishry.

1979

26 ——. *Synge and the Irish Language*. Dublin: Gill & Macmillan, pp. 11–12.
Discusses "Memory of Brother Michael."

27 LIDDY, JAMES. "Ulster Poets and the Protestant Muse." *Eire* 14, no. 2 (Summer):118–127.
Kavanagh is "the finest Irish poet since Yeats." Notes Kavanagh's low regard for Ulster writers, especially MacNeice.

28 LUBY, TOM. "Patrick Kavanagh's Purgatory." *Hibernia* (11 January):32.
Discusses the two different publications of *Lough Derg* (Martin Brian & O'Keeffe, and Goldsmith). Discusses arguments over copyright.

29 LUCY, SEAN. "Irish Poetry in English, 1978." *Irish University Review* 9, no. 1 (Spring):142–162.
Claims no poet from before 1950 "commands active and fairly continuous attention" since the deaths of Kavanagh and Clarke. Kavanagh spoke in a natural voice, rejected the past and portrayed Irish countryside and town by means of "a passionate new realism which transforms ordinary experience." Kavanagh's work voiced "real speech and that wider experience which makes for better poetry," and which appeals to a wider audience. Because he projected his own voice into poetry, Kavanagh is among "the most useful and inspiring presences" in poetry today.

30 ——. "Irish Poetry in English 1978." In *Image and Illusion: Anglo-Irish Literature and its Contexts. A Festschrift for Roger McHugh*. Edited by Maurice Harmon. Dublin: Wolfhound, pp. 142–162.
Reprint of Lucy (1979.29).

31 MAHON, DEREK. "Pilgrim Poet." *Hibernia* (25 January):13.
Review of *Lough Derg*. Compares and contrasts the Martin, Brian and O'Keefe edition of the poem (introduction by Paul Durcan) with the Goldsmith Press edition of the poem. Prefers the former. Notes that the poet had a low opinion of *Lough Derg*, which was unpublished in his lifetime. Discusses the tradition of Irish writing about St Patrick's Purgatory. Claims Kavanagh had a mystical strain, but it is his religious ambivalence that makes this poem "the confused and oddly touching piece of work that it is." Claims the poem formally resembles *The Great Hunger*. Finds that Durcan overestimates Kavanagh's importance in his introduction to the poem, and argues that the poet is not first rate, but "a poet of the *second* importance, which is not, of course, bad going." Prefers Denis Devlin's poem on Lough Derg to Kavanagh's.

1979

32 MATTHEWS, AIDAN. "Modern Irish Poetry: A Question of Covenants." *Crane Bag* 3, no. 1:48–57.

   Brief discussion of Kavanagh. Claims that it is wrong to construe Kavanagh merely as a poet of religious celebration, because "that intuition of supernumerous existence contends at every moment against a truculent sarcasm which is formidable."

33 MCARDLE, JOHN. "Patrick Kavanagh and Monaghan." *Midlands* (Dublin), (Spring):55.

   Claims Kavanagh's attitude to Monaghan changed during the course of his life. The "land-love of his earlier poems is followed by rejection as he decides he wants to leave Monaghan." Argues that *Tarry Flynn* is the comic obverse of the tragic *The Great Hunger*, and "Innocence" is a rejection of "Stony Grey Soil."

34 MONTAGUE, JOHN. "Global Regionalism. Interview with John Montague." *Literary Review* (Winter):153–174.

   Contrasts Frost with Kavanagh. "The essential heart of Frost does not seem to me to belong to (the farming life) as Patrick Kavanagh did, *inescapably.*" Kavanagh was "the real farmer broken at the age of fifty," but Frost was "the professional farmer, hale and hearty."

35 NEMO, JOHN. *Patrick Kavanagh.* Boston: Twayne. 157 pp.

   Contains six chapters, a chronology and bibliography. Claims there is a real need for an objective evaluation of the poet, since too many critics tend to confuse his character with his poetry. Describes life and career in an introductory chapter, and proceeds to examine his "apprenticeship" (1928–1939), including his composition of *Ploughman* and *The Green Fool*. Considers Kavanagh's finest poem to be *The Great Hunger,* which is rooted in earlier attempts by the poet to describe the rural environment as oppressive. Notes the influence of Joseph Campbell's "Irishry" (1913) on the narrative structure of the poem. Proceeds to examine Kavanagh's commitment in the years 1943–1954 to fiction, criticism, and poetry, and examines the growth of the poet's "public voice" in "Lough Derg" and the satires, and the expression of the "personal voice" in *A Soul for Sale*. Praises the post-trial poems written by the Grand Canal, which "clearly depict his changing mood and his sense of spiritual rebirth." A final chapter considers the critical reception of Kavanagh and speculates on his influence.

36 ———. "Patrick Kavanagh." *Dictionary of Irish Literature*. Edited by Robert Hogan. Westport, Connecticut: Greenwood Press, pp. 340–345.

   Biographical essay and commentary on Kavanagh's writings. Claims Kavanagh has been very influential. His work provides an important portrait of Irish "peasant life." Claims *Tarry Flynn* "lacks the vitality" of *The Green*

Fool and *The Great Hunger* and is flawed by romantic conclusion. The theme of *A Soul for Sale* is personal failure, and his best late poems were the Canal Bank sonnets. His future reputation is assured.

37 ——. "Visions of Self and Society." *Threshold* (Belfast), 30 (Spring):44–71.
Describes poet's life and career. In *The Great Hunger* Kavanagh developed a public voice which finds expression in *Lough Derg*, an inferior poem, and in the satires. The poems of *A Soul for Sale* explore his more private concerns. The last phase of his life was a time of self-examination, in which he came to emphasize the visible over the ideological in his poetry, as in the Canal Bank sonnets, and to reject his earlier writing. Concludes that one of Kavanagh's most serious handicaps to writing verse was "his personality."

38 NI CHUILLEANAIN, EILEAN. Review of *By Night Unstarred* and *Patrick Kavanagh Country*, by Peter Kavanagh. *Irish University Review* (Spring):190–191.
Claims the second part of *By Night Unstarred* demonstrates that Kavanagh "like anyone exiled from his birthplace is tormented by the parallel life he might have lived if he'd stayed at home." Finds the tone of the second section "grimmer" than that of the more sentimental *The Green Fool*. Discusses the role of women in section two. Mentions that Peter Kavanagh uses much of the same material in the introduction and epilogue of *By Night Unstarred* as he used in his book *Patrick Kavanagh Country*.

39 O'DRISCOLL, DENNIS. "Recent Poetry." *Hibernia* (1 March):15.
Review of several books, including *Patrick Kavanagh Country* (Goldsmith). Claims *Tarry Flynn* is "the only account of Kavanagh Country we really need."

40 O'FARRELL, NUALA. "Book News." *Hibernia* (12 July):35.
Discusses the Patrick Kavanagh Poetry Award.

41 ORMSBY, FRANK. Introduction to *Poets from the North of Ireland*. Belfast: Blackstaff, pp. 1–15.
Brief reference to Kavanagh's influence on John Montague.

42 "Patrick Kavanagh commemoration." *Irish Times* (20 November):6.
Announces the upcoming Kavanagh commemorative in Inniskeen, which will include a wreath-laying and a concert.

43 PAYNE, BASIL. "Poet's Testament." Review of Patrick Kavanagh, *Lough Derg*. *Books Ireland*, no. 33 (May):75.
Brief review of *Lough Derg*. Calls Kavanagh "a poet of insight and vision."

1979

44 POTTS, PAUL. "A great Christian poem." *The Tablet* (7 April):346.
   Review of *Lough Derg*. Claims that *Lough Derg*, which the reviewer finds reminiscent of Chaucer's *The Canterbury Tales* and the poems of St John of the Cross, is "going to become the great Christian poem of the age." Claims it is a greater poem than *The Great Hunger*. States that it makes you proud of Ireland.

*45 REILLY, KEVIN PATRICK. *Irish Literary Autobiography: the Goddess that Poets Dream of.* Ph.D. dissertation, University of Minnesota. 265 pp. DAI-A 40/06 (December):3322.
   Examines the autobiographies of Carleton, Kavanagh, Moore, and Yeats as contributions to Irish tradition. Shows how each autobiographer depicts "mother Ireland" as a national goddess, mother, and mistress, and how each author wrote of a particular woman in his life who embodied "mother Ireland." Explores how each author imagines the reader of his autobiography as a composite of lover and nation. Concludes that the "Irish autobiographer insists that his identity cannot be affirmed without reference to the Irish goddess figure."

46 RYAN, JOHN. "Patrick Kavanagh's Dublin." *Midlands* (Dublin), (Spring):52–53.
   Discusses Kavanagh's Dublin years. Recalls twenty years of friendship with the poet, including their time spent together on *Envoy*. Claims Kavanagh was always an outsider in Dublin, and was an "abnormally normal man."

47 SLATTERY, FINBAR. "Patrick Kavanagh's 'Lough Derg.'" *Hibernia* (18 January):2.
   Letter response to Luby (1979.28).

48 STANFORD, DEREK. "Magicians of language." *Books and Bookmen* (September):44–48.
   Review of *Lough Derg* (Goldsmith). Claims it is "one of the most authentic compositions of comparable length to be offered since *The Waste Land*." Sometimes the poetry is "rough-shod." Although it appears to parody Roman Catholicism, the poem contrasts "pure faith" with the "imperfect travesties of it as represented by certain of the laity and the priesthood."

49 THORNTON, WELDON. "Virgin Queen or Hungry Fiend? The Failure of Imagination in Patrick Kavanagh's 'The Great Hunger'." *Mosaic: A Journal for the Interdisciplinary Study of Literature* 12, no. 3 (Spring):153–162.
   Argues that *The Great Hunger* has received more "encomium" than criticism. Examines three aspects of the poem: Its ambiguous attitude to Maguire, its view of the oppressive role of religion in the peasants' lives, and the function of female figures in the poem—the land is bride, Virgin Queen,

and, if unsatisfied, the hungry fiend. Compares Kavanagh's female figures with those of Synge and Yeats.

50 WRIGHT, KATHLEEN. "Kavanagh's Lough Derg." *Hibernia* 1 (February):2.
Letter response to Luby (1979.28). Claims that the royalties for Goldsmith edition will go to Peter Kavanagh.

1980

1 ALEXANDER, ALAN. "The Laughter of Paddy Kavanagh." *Poetry Australia* 73:20–26.
Admires the humor of Kavanagh's verse, and compares his "gaiety" to that of the later Yeats. Claims Kavanagh was a "typical" Irish poet, and "a Monaghan bogman."

2 BRADLEY, ANTHONY. *Contemporary Irish Poetry*. Berkeley: University of California Press, p. 57.
Biographical sketch of the poet. Although Kavanagh's pastoral poetry is bleak it can also be joyful. Praises the later poems, especially "The Hospital."

3 BROWN, TERENCE. "After the Revival: The Problem of Adequacy and Genre." In Schleifer (1980.33), pp. 153–178.
Reprint of Brown (1979.1).

4 DURCAN, PAUL. "Brothers' Keepers." *Irish Times*, Weekend section (16 February):3.
Review of Peter Kavanagh's *Sacred Keeper*. Praises Peter's Kavanagh's efforts to publish Patrick's work and defend his reputation, although he has "allowed his devotion to his brother to turn into an apparent obsession." Discusses Peter Kavanagh's response to Patrick's marriage to Katherine Barry Moloney. Claims *Sacred Keeper* is "depressing" and "transgresses most of the fundamental rubrics of biography and historiography."

5 ———. "Researching Kavanagh." *Irish Times* (4 April):13.
Review of Nemo (1979.35). Claims Nemo's view of Kavanagh is "polluted with the received caricature of Kavanagh as handed down by Larry Morrow, and others still living."

6 FRAZIER, ADRIAN WOODS. "The Sincerity of Patrick Kavanagh." *Malahat Review* 53 (January):110–131.
Contrasts Kavanagh's attitude to art with that of Irish nationalists, comparing him to Stephen Dedalus, who wished to express himself before his

1980

nation. Argues that only those unsure of their Irishness, such as "former colonials," sought to identify with Irish culture during the Revival. Kavanagh, however, who rejected the Revival, was "the real thing." Claims his main qualities are "sincerity, originality, authenticity."

7 HEANEY, SEAMUS. "From Monaghan to the Grand Canal: The Poetry of Patrick Kavanagh." In *Preoccupations: Selected Prose, 1968–1978*. New York: Farrar, Straus & Giroux, pp. 115–130.
Reprint of Heaney (1975.12).

8 ———. "The Sense of Place." In *Preoccupations: Selected Prose, 1968–1978*. New York: Farrar, Straus & Giroux, pp. 131–150.
Claims Patrick Kavanagh's place is known by the illiterate, unconscious part of the self as well as by the literate, conscious part, and the two parts contend. There was tension within Kavanagh between the two ways of looking at place. Contrasts Yeats's nationalism with Kavanagh's parochialism. Discusses reasons for Kavanagh's popularity and his validity as exemplar for poets today. Examines "Iniskeen Road, July Evening," and contrasts Kavanagh's sense of "the hidden Ulster" with that of John Montague.

9 JONES, PETER, and MICHAEL SCHMIDT. Introduction to *British Poetry Since 1970: a Critical Survey*. Manchester: Carcanet, 257 pp.
Contains Meir (1980.19) and Morrison (1980.21).

10 KARRER, WOLFGANG. "Patrick Kavanagh: Dichter und literarischer Markt" ("Patrick Kavanagh: the Poet and the Literary Market"). In *Einführung in die zeitgenössische irische Literatur*. Edited by Joachim Kornelius, Erwin Otto, Gerd Stratman. Heidelberg: (Winter):197–210. German language article.
Divides Kavanagh's career into three stages: "Simplicity (1904–1939)," "Complexities and Anger (1939–1955)," and "Return to Simplicity (1955–1967)." Claims the early poems were written in isolation from the literary world, although "Ploughman" was influenced by the Revival. Upon visiting AE, his "eyes were opened." Discusses the formal device in *The Great Hunger* of mixing short jazzlike lines with long epic lines. In *A Soul For Sale*, Kavanagh shows his hatred of everyday life, yet also his hope that the individual can be liberated within the everyday. Argues that *Tarry Flynn* is "Kavanagh's most important offering on the problem of what it is to be a poet in Ireland." Claims *Come Dance with Kitty Stobling* is "a collection of pastiche," based on nostagia, and the later poems seem to be "quick sketches." Concludes that Kavanagh's work contains the tension between convention and realism, rural and urban. Poses the question, how does cultural dependence on England affect Irish poetry?

1980

11 KAVANAGH, PETER. "Villiers de L'Isle Adam." *Era* 5:16–18.
    Brief reference to Patrick Kavanagh.

12 KIBERD, DECLAN. "The Fall of the Stage Irishman." In Schleifer (1980.33), pp. 39–60.
    Refers to Kavanagh's unsentimental depiction of the peasantry, which is "closer to Joyce than to Yeats." Compares the depictions of Ireland in *The Great Hunger* and Shaw's *John Bull's Other Island*.

13 KILFEATHER, J. B. "Patrick Kavanagh in Belfast." *Threshold* 31 (Autumn/Winter):64–66.
    Recalls inviting Kavanagh to dinner in Belfast in 1947 and the lively conversation of the evening. Remembers Kavanagh's remarks about O'Faolain, na gCopaleen, Saroyan, and *Tarry Flynn*. Describes the poet's voice.

14 LYONS, J. B. *Oliver St. John Gogarty. The man of many talents*. Dublin: Blackwater, pp. 196, 232.
    Briefly discusses Gogarty's libel action against Kavanagh.

15 MCARDLE, J. ARDLE. "What did you do in the fifties, daddy? A ballade of lost opportunities." *Hibernia* (17 April):20.
    Humorous poem, with references to Patrick Kavanagh.

16 McCLUSKEY, FINBARR. Review. *Journal of Irish Literature* 9, no. 3, (September):109–110.
    Review of Nemo (1979.35), a "tedious addition to the rapidly accumulating mound of commentary" on Kavanagh.

17 MCGLINCHY, MARY. "The Missing Bride." *Hibernia* (14 February):6.
    Letter in response to O'Keeffe (1980.25). Corrects a factual error concerning the so-called "missing bride" in Kavanagh's wedding photo, and defends Peter Kavanagh.

18 MCNAMARA, JAMES. "Tending an ancient flame." *Times Literary Supplement* (13 June):681.
    Review of Peter Kavanagh's, *Sacred Keeper* (1979.21), which he claims is "a faithful recording of repeated failure." Wonders how did Kavanagh, for whom "poetry was an ancient sacred flame," survive such a hard life, and why he did not get more recognition when alive.

19 MEIR, COLIN. "The poetry of R. S. Thomas." In Jones and Schmidt (1980.9), pp. 1–13.
    Discusses influence of "The Great Hunger" on R. S. Thomas.

1980

20 MONTAGUE, JOHN. "Collecting Kavanagh." *Irish Times* (5 and 8 February):8 (on both dates).

Recalls his acquaintance with Kavanagh in Dublin in the 1950s and 1960s. Recounts several anecdotes about the poet. Describes circumstances by which he came to edit MacGibbon & Kee *Collected Poems* and refers to the complications involved in the process. Discusses the "suffering and isolation" of Kavanagh and other writers in the postwar period. Examines Kavanagh's mysticism, and his influence on the poet R. S.Thomas.

21 MORRISON, BLAKE. "Speech and Reticence: Seamus Heaney's *North*." In Jones and Schmidt (1980.9), pp. 103–111.

Mentions Kavanagh's influence on early Heaney.

22 O'CASEY, SEAN. *The Letters of Sean O'Casey, 1942–1954*. Vol. II. Edited by David Krause. New York: Macmillan, pp. 10, 20, 229, 388, 499–500, 516, 659, 847, 867, 928, 1070.

Includes letters by O'Casey which make reference to Kavanagh. In 1942, O'Casey praises *The Great Hunger*, printed in *Horizon:* "With a bit of luck, he'll outdo O'Connor and O'Faolain." In 1945, he refers to some scandalous rumors about Kavanagh, which he disbelieves. In 1948, he replies to a letter of Kavanagh's, and tries to persuade him to contact the American critic David Greene. In 1951, he refers to Kavanagh and Myles "boxing with each other in the *Irish Times*." In 1957, he speculates on the beneficent effects which the UCD lectureship may have on Kavanagh's personality.

23 O'CONNOR, ULICK. "Patrick Kavanagh." *Sunday Independent* (9 March). UCD Archive.

Review of *Sacred Keeper*. Recalls seeing Kavanagh in 1948 at a Dublin athletic event, and remembers Kavanagh's views on pole-vaulting. Compares Peter Kavanagh to Stanislaus Joyce, brother of James, because he has "devoted his life to keeping the flame of Patrick's genius alive." Praises *Sacred Keeper* for capturing the life of Patrick. Peter has "raised a monument to his brother."

24 O'FAOLAIN, NUALA. "Book News. Kavanagh Cornucopia." *Hibernia* (10 January):16.

Describes Peter Kavanagh's efforts to "set the record straight" about Patrick, in various publications, including *Love's Tortured Headland* and *Sacred Keeper*, which expresses the "bitter, rancorous view of the poet by the man who possibly knew him, and certainly loved him best." Claims there is "some overlapping of material in this cornucopia of autobiographies" (i.e., in Peter's various publications about Patrick). Also reviews John Nemo's *Patrick Kavanagh* (1979.35). Praises Nemo's bibliography and contrasts this with Peter Kavanagh's.

1980

25 O'KEEFFE, TIMOTHY. "Brothers Can't be Choosers." *Hibernia* (7 February):16.
Review of *Sacred Keeper*. Claims Patrick Kavanagh would not have liked or admired this portrait of him by his brother.

26 ———. "The Missing Bride." *Hibernia* (28 February): 6.
Response to McGlinchy (1980.17). O'Keeffe claims that Peter Kavanagh "excised the face of Mrs. Kavanagh from the photo taken at Patrick Kavanagh's wedding."

27 PAULIN, TOM. "Brother's Keepsake." *Sunday Times* (London) (10 February):42.
Review of *Sacred Keeper*, "a portrait which has an extraordinary quality of absolute verisimilitude." Kavanagh was "difficult," but innocent. He was, in part, "the victim of the partition of Ireland—like Cavan and Donegal, his native Monaghan was severed from the rest of Ulster and cast into a kind of historical limbo." Compares relationship of Patrick and Peter to "the mutual dependency of James and Stanislaus Joyce."

28 "Poet seen as man of vision." *Irish Times* (14 February). 5.
Reports the launching of Peter Kavanagh's *Sacred Keeper* at a reception in Dublin, hosted by the *Irish Farmer's Journal*.

29 POTTS, PAUL. "The War Years in Ulster, 1939–1945." *Honest Ulsterman* 64 (September 1979–January 1980):56.
Expresses surprise that "none of the Ulster poets thought much of Patrick Kavanagh." Retracts his claim that Kavanagh was a major poet since he is not esteemed by the English and Americans, "and to be a great poet one has to be universal."

30 REILLY, KEVIN P. "Re-Membering: *Irish Poetry After Yeats*." *Eire* 15, no. 3 (Fall):120–126.
Review of special Irish issue of *Literary Review*. Discusses contemporary Irish poets' sense of tradition and why most prefer Kavanagh as model to Yeats. Claims contemporary authors are sympathetic to Kavanagh's dissatisfaction with Irish society. Kavanagh symbolizes the tenacity of Irish tradition, "a kind of human bog cotton."

31 RICE, GERARD. Review of *Sacred Keeper*. *Era* 5:54–55.
Sacred Keeper is "rooted in the mystery of one man's life and reveals it to the reader by way of what seems almost direct experience." The book is "rich, casual, objective."

1981

32 SCHIRMER, GREGORY A. "Seamus Heaney's 'Salvation in Surrender.'" *Eire* 15, no. 4 (Winter):139–146.
    Discusses Kavanagh's concept of the parochial, and his influence on Heaney.

33 SCHLEIFER, RONALD. *The Genres of the Irish Literary Revival*. Norman, Oklahoma: Pilgrim Books, and Dublin: Wolfhound.
    Contains Brown (1980.3) and Kiberd (1980.12).

34 SHARE, BERNARD. "Two Noble Kinsmen." *Books Ireland* 42 (April):75–77.
    Review of *Sacred Keeper*. Discusses publication of *Kavanagh's Weekly* in 1952 and his personal meetings with the Kavanaghs at that time. Suspects the biography is not as comprehensive as it might have been, regretting that "apart from the reiterated assertion that the man was a genius (both brothers agreed on this) [the book] offers little in the way of critical evaluation."

35 SHEERIN, PATRICK H. "Stony soil, the country and countryman in Campos de Castilla and the Poetry of Patrick Kavanagh." In *E. S. publicaciones del Departmento de Ingles* 10. Valladolid: University of Valladolid (Spain), pp. 259–288.
    Compares and contrasts the image of the rural world in *Campos de Castilla* by Antonio Machado and the poems of Kavanagh. Each of the two poets "is the first great nature poet of his country and each wrote realistically of the land and the people who worked it." Compares the poets' depiction of climatic conditions, flora and fauna, and farmyard implements. Machado is a much greater poet than Kavanagh, although the latter wrote a dozen good poems.

1981

1 BOLAND, EAVAN. "Memories of Kavanagh." *Irish Times* (20 November):10.
    Describes first meeting Kavanagh at a café in Dublin, and praises his gallantry on that occasion. Although scornful of his generation, Kavanagh admired MacNeice, who he said was "like an eagle with a retinue." Claims Kavanagh was "a primitive with many of the faults of the primitive."

2 BRADLEY, ANTHONY G. "Pastoral in Modern Irish Poetry." *Concerning Poetry* 14, no. 2 (Fall):79–96.
    Discusses Kavanagh, Montague, and Heaney as literary realists and "native Irish insiders," in contrast with the more romantic "Anglo-Irish out-

1981

siders" of the Irish Revival. Kavanagh's rejection of Revivalism resembles that of Padraic Fallon. Compares *The Great Hunger* to Michael Hartnett's portrayal of "the constriction of life in rural Ireland."

3 BROWN, TERENCE. *Ireland: A Social and Cultural History, 1922–1979.* Glasgow: Fontana Paperbacks, pp. 23, 169, 174, 186–187, 193, 208, 210, 212, 228, 318.
   Numerous brief references to Kavanagh, whose work has been considered to be an accurate representation of aspects of the social and cultural life of modern Ireland. *The Great Hunger* is "an antenna that sensitively detects the shifts of consciousness that determine a people's future."

4 CRONIN, ANTHONY. "The 85-day wonder." *Irish Press* (1 October):6. UCD Archive.
   Review of Goldsmith reprint of *Kavanagh's Weekly*, which is "sad and irritating." The writing in the weekly is inferior to Kavanagh's diary in *Envoy* and lacking in specificity and detail. Concludes that the weekly was Patrick Kavanagh's plea for help.

5 DENMAN, PETER. "Man into Myth: The Figure of Yeats in the Poetry of His Successors." *Gaeliana* (Caen, France), no. 2, pp. 11–22.
   Describes the portrayal of Yeats in modern Irish poetry, including Kavanagh's late poem, in which he attacks the poet "not so much for his poetry but for what he was and how he lived."

6 FARRELL, WILLIAM E. "About New York. A Printer with the Proper Respect for the Poet's Art." *New York Times* (14 February):26.
   Short article based on an interview with Peter Kavanagh. Claims he is currently compiling the thirteen issues of *Kavanagh's Weekly* for publication in Ireland.

7 GARRATT, ROBERT F. "Patrick Kavanagh and the Killing of the Irish Revival." *Colby Quarterly* 17, no. 3 (September):170–183.
   Describes the response of writers of the thirties and forties, stifled by Irish Revival mythology, to what seemed a "stale" literary culture. Considers Kavanagh to have been the most aggressive opponent of Revival aesthetics, who wrote not only in the shadow of Yeats, whom he partly admired, partly hated, but also of the condescension of Dublin's literati. Considers *The Great Hunger* to have been "the death blow" to the Irish Revival, and examines the influence of Joyce's urban realism upon Kavanagh. Argues that Kavanagh wrote six good poems.

1981

8 GRENNAN, EAMON. "Pastoral Design in the Poetry of Patrick Kavanagh." *Renascence: Essays on Value in Literature* 34, no. 1 (Autumn):3–16.

Argues that Kavanagh tended to describe his life as a journey from Eden to a new innocence, and that this "pastoral design" provides a useful model for describing his poetic development. Kavanagh moves from the Edenic "Christian pastoral" of the early verse, through the "tragic pastoral" of *The Great Hunger*, to the rebirth by the Grand Canal after 1955, which led to a period of Edenic "stillness."

9 HOUSIN, SEVERIN, ed. *Feathers and Bones: Ten Poets of the Irish Earth*. Sacramento: Halcyon Press, 96 pp.

The book is dedicated to Patrick Kavanagh. In preface, there are several references to Kavanagh. States that "in the manner of Kavanagh, these poets have mostly freed themselves of Yeats," and Housin has written a biographical sketch of Kavanagh. Includes poems by Philip Casey, Desmond Egan, Peter Fallon, James Liddy, Gearoid O'Brien, Maurice Scully, and Eithne Strong. Each poet has written a paragraph on what Kavanagh means to him/her.

10 KAVANAGH, PETER. *The Dancing Flame: A Documentary Drama of the Poet in Society*. New York: Peter Kavanagh Hand Press. 38 pp.

A play based upon the 1954 libel suit against the *Leader*.

11 KENNELLY, BRENDAN, ed. A Note to the Second Edition of *Penguin Book of Irish Verse*, 2d edition, pp. 40–42.

Stresses the importance of Kavanagh for modern Irish writing, and claims his poetry is "increasingly read and appreciated." Praises *Lough Derg* in particular.

12 KENNY, FERGUS. Letter to the editor. *Journal of Irish Literature* 10, no. 2 (May):134–135.

Response to McGlinchy (1980.17). Defends Nemo's book against McCluskey's criticism.

*13 LEONARD, NICHOLAS. *Odium, Ridicule and Contempt. An entertainment from the trial and works of Patrick Kavanagh*, UCD Kavanagh Archive (Kav/B/72), 97 pp.

A play based on the 1954 *Leader* trial. Typescript copy of script.

14 LUCAS, JOHN. "Bar-Room Bluster." *Times Literary Supplement* (31 July):886.

Review of Goldsmith reprint of *Kavanagh's Weekly*, the tone of which was largely dictated by Patrick, although Peter paid printing and publishing costs. The weekly was "brash, school-boyish, nose-thumbing," although it lacked all factual detail, "it simply isn't precise enough," and it was hardly worth reprinting. Because most of the weekly's contemporary references are obscure, unreadable or lost, suggests it should have been annotated.

*15 MCMAHON, NANCY CURRAN. *The Theme of Art in the Poetry of Four Twentieth Century Irish poets: Clarke, Kavanagh, Kinsella, Heaney.* M.A. thesis, Cleveland State University.
Thesis on Kavanagh and others.

16 MURPHY, MAUREEN. Review of John Nemo, *Patrick Kavanagh. College Literature* 8, no.1:104–105.
Claims Nemo's book "demonstrates the close relationship between Kavanagh's creative and critical writing, a relationship not always beneficial to Kavanagh's poetry and prose." Mentions Kavanagh's influence on Montague and Heaney.

17 O'HAODHA, MICHEAL. "Kavanagh's Last Hurrah." *Irish Times* (22 August):10.
Reviews Goldsmith reprint of *Kavanagh's Weekly*—"Kavanagh's Last Hurrah before he was laid low with lung cancer." Praises the weekly as expression of Kavanagh's belief in a "mission to redeem the soul of his country." Claims Kavanagh's collected prose contains "little serious social criticism."

18 O'SHEA, HELEN. "Interview with Seamus Heaney." *Quadrant* (September):12–17.
Brief references to Kavanagh's influence on Heaney.

19 O'TUARISC, EOGHAN. "At the Kavanagh Trial." In *Sidelines: Poems 1951–1974*. Dublin: Raven, p. 25.
Poem in response to the 1954 *Leader* trial.

20 "Poet Honoured." *Irish Times* (30 November):8.
The Kavanagh Society announces intention of opening a Kavanagh summer school in Inniskeen.

21 RAFROIDI, PATRICK. Review. *Etudes Irlandaises* 6:254.
Review of *Sacred Keeper*.

22 REILLY, KEVIN P. "Irish Literary Autobiography: The Goddesses that Poets Dream Of." *Eire* 16, no. 3 (Fall):57–80.
Brief references to Kavanagh, who is compared to Carleton.

1982

23 RUSHE, DESMOND. "Tatler's Parade. Kavanagh's Weekly is re-launched." *Irish Independent* (3 July):2. UCD Archive.
Review of *Kavanagh's Weekly*. Describes the typical contents of the paper as iconoclastic, abrasive, and eccentric.

24 SISSON, C. H. *English Poetry, 1900–1950: An Assessment*. Manchester: Carcanet, pp. 251–254.
Reprint of Sisson (1971.31).

25 WARD, A. C., ed. Revised by MAURICE HUSSEY. *Longman Companion to Twentieth Century Literature*. Third Edition. London: Longman, p. 293.
Brief biographical sketch of Kavanagh.

26 WARNER, ALAN. "Patrick Kavanagh." *Guide to Anglo-Irish Literature*. Dublin: Gill and Macmillan, pp. 89–97.
Describes the poet's life and career, from the "thin lyricism" of the early verse, to *A Soul for Sale*, which contains "some of his best known and best loved 'Monaghan' poems." Compares Kavanagh to Dr. Johnson, and contrasts him to Yeats, but concludes he is "an uneven and, at times, a careless poet."

1982

1 BAIRD, G. H. M. BRIAN. "'The Other Man Concealed': Patrick Kavanagh's Cultural Criticism: A Cryptic Autobiography?" In Kosok (1982.14), pp. 357–367.
Argues that the personal tone of Kavanagh's criticism makes it a form of "cryptic autobiography." Examines the growth of Kavanagh's reputation as a very harsh critic of Irish writers, beginning with a 1945 essay in which he dismissed Clarke, Higgins, Farren, and McDonough, and continuing with his 1947 sallies against Higgins and O'Connor. Examines the autobiographical meaning of his criticism in *Kavanagh's Weekly* and *Envoy*. By defining his enemies, Kavanagh "was aided in the process of self-realisation."

2 BLAMIRES, HARRY. *Twentieth Century English Literature*. New York: Schocken Books, pp. 184–185, 259.
Gives brief account of poet's career.

3 FODASKI-BLACK, MARTHA. "Patrick Kavanagh." In *Encyclopaedia of World Literature in the Twentieth Century*, vol. 2. Edited by Leonard S. Klein. New York: Frederick Ungar, pp. 566–567.
Biographical entry on the poet.

1982

4 GREEN, MARTIN. "Pen and Sword." *Irish Times* (7 April):12.
Review of reprint of *Kavanagh's Weekly*.

5 GUNTON, SHARON R. and STINE, JEAN. "Patrick (Joseph Gregory) Kavanagh: 1905–1967." *Contemporary Literary Criticism*, vol. 22. Detroit: Gale Research Co., pp. 234–245.
Prints excerpts from articles on Kavanagh by eleven critics, namely V. S Pritchett (1938.7), Padraic Colum (1947.1), TLS (1960.1), Louise Bogan (1965.2), Richard Murphy (1965.15), Robin Skelton (1965.22), Brendan Kennelly (1970.12), Alan Warner (1973.46), Darcy O'Brien (1975.25), Frank Tuohy (1977.45), and Derek Stanford (1979.48).

6 HARMON, MAURICE, and ROGER MCHUGH. *A Short History of Anglo-Irish Literature*. Totowa, N.J.: Barnes and Noble, pp. 227–230, 237, 318.
Discusses "primitive power" of *The Great Hunger*, which is Kavanagh's best work. The satirical poetry failed because Kavanagh "lacked the exact rational control of language it demands." His later work was mostly inferior. Discusses his dislike of the Revival, and his preference for Barker and Hughes.

7 HOBSBAUM, PHILIP. "Craft and Technique in Wintering Out." In *The Art of Seamus Heaney*. Edited by Tony Curtis. Bridgend, Mid-Glamorgan; Chester Springs: Poetry Wales; Dufour, pp. 37–43.
Briefly discusses Kavanagh's influence on Heaney.

8 HOOKER, JEREMY. *The Poetry of Place: Essays and Reviews 1970–1981*. Manchester: Carcanet Press, pp. 72, 117, 189.
Compares Heaney's rural poetry with *The Great Hunger*. Contrasts Edward Thomas with Kavanagh. Cites Kavanagh's definition of "the parochial" in discussion of *Faber Book of Poems and Places*.

9 JEFFARES, A. NORMAN. *Anglo-Irish Literature*. New York: Schocken Books, pp. 147–148, 171, 191–194, 201.
Describes poet's life and career. Argues that a sense of craftsmanship is lacking in some of Kavanagh's middle period poems, when "he went through a period of bitter ironic realism." *The Great Hunger* presents "an over-dark, hopeless picture." Kavanagh was always an outsider both in the city and the country.

10 KAVANAGH, PETER. "The Patrick Kavanagh Archive." *Era* 6 (Summer):2–3.
Describes how he began collecting material for a biography of Patrick Kavanagh in 1964, and lists some of the contents of his collection. Outlines how he collected letters, photos, and press cuttings that were kept in a scrap-

1982

book and later laminated. Speculates that the archive will end up in a U.S. library. Reproduction of portrait of Patrick by Alex Sadkowsky.

11 "Kavanagh Remembered." *Irish Times* (29 November):15.
    Describes annual graveside commemoration at Inniskeen and presentation of Kavanagh poetry award to Peter Sirr.

12 KIBERD, DECLAN. Review of *Sacred Keeper*. *Irish University Review* (Spring):108.
    In contrast with Stanislaus Joyce's *My Brother's Keeper*, Peter Kavanagh's memoir is "a work of fraternal love and piety."

13 KILROY, THOMAS. "The Irish Writer: Self and Society, 1950–1980." In *Literature and the Changing Ireland*. Edited by Peter Connolly. Gerrards Cross, England; Totowa, N.J.: Colin Smythe; Barnes & Noble, pp. 175–187.
    Compares and contrasts Kavanagh with Francis Stuart, claiming both are figures of freedom with self-abnegating dedication to art. Both paid a high price in personal terms for their dedication. Kavanagh is "the last of our authentic voices out of a rural Ireland that was already changing beyond all recognition."

14 KOSOK, HEINZ, ed. *Studies in Anglo-Irish Literature*. Bonn: Bouvier. 496 pp.
    Contains Baird (1982.1) and Natterstad (1982.22).

15 KRAUSE, DAVID. *The Profane Book of Irish Comedy*. Ithaca, London: Cornell University Press, pp. 35, 44, 247.
    Brief references to Kavanagh.

16 MCCARTIN, JAMES T. "Patrick & Peter's Irreverent Weekly." *Irish Literary Supplement* (Fall):17.
    Review of Goldsmith's facsimile edition of *Kavanagh's Weekly*. Praises the weekly's "healthy iconoclasm," although claims Patrick expressed his opinions illogically and unreasonably. The essays in the weekly are filled with abuse and self-pity.

17 MCCAULEY, JAMES. Review of Housin (1981.9). *Era* 6:40.
    Claims the book "falls quite flat" as memorial to Kavanagh. Kavanagh's writing should be appreciated for what it is, "and let's leave off trying to make him an Influence, in heaven's name!"

18 MCKENNA, JAMES. "Kavanagh's Weekly, Thirty Years Later." *Era* 6: 27–28.

1982

Review of Goldsmith Press facsimile edition of *Kavanagh's Weekly*. McKenna was student at College of Art when the weekly was first published. Claims Kavanagh "had a sense of grandeur, which he had to submit to the acid of the appalling deprivation, cultural and social, which he saw about him." He was neither a republican nor socialist, but was "a Joyce who stayed behind and awakened slowly." Praises Kavanagh's courage and iconoclasm.

19 MEIR, COLIN. "Narrative Verse in Yeats, Clarke and Kavanagh." *Gaeliana* (Caen, France), no. 4, pp. 219–236.

Claims *The Great Hunger* was as innovative in Ireland as *The Waste Land* was in England. Explores the role of the poem's poet-narrator and praises the variety of the poem's technique.

20 MIKHAIL, E. H. *Brendan Behan: Interviews and Recollections*, vol. I. Totowa, N.J.: Barnes & Noble, pp. 26, 56, 76, 222, 259, 303, 323, 326.

Reprints anecdotes concerning Behan and Kavanagh from Cronin (1976.3) and Ryan (1975.30). Owen Quinn claims Behan once upset Kavanagh by calling him a failure to his face. Reprints Kiely (1965.7).

21 MORRISON, BLAKE. *Seamus Heaney*. London and New York: Methuen, pp. 14, 28–29, 36, 54.

Mentions Kavanagh's influence on Heaney.

22 NATTERSTADT, J. H. "Francis Stuart: The Artist as Outcast." In Kosok (1982.14), pp. 338–344.

Brief discussion of Stuart's essay on Kavanagh (1975.33). Stuart found in Kavanagh "a spiritual counterpart," a "paradigm" for the artist in the modern world.

23 NEMO, JOHN. "A Brother's Keeper." *Irish Literary Supplement* (Spring):2.

Review of *Sacred Keeper* (Goldsmith Press). Protests that Peter Kavanagh "looms too large" in the biography, and that it doesn't offer much new information to the Kavanagh reader.

24 OWENS, COILIN. "Patrick Kavanagh." In *Critical Survey of Poetry*, vol. 4. Edited by Frank N. Magill. Englewood Cliffs, N.J.: Salem Press, pp. 1535–1541.

Describes poet's life and career, and his reaction to the Revival. Argues that he is of the "second generation" of the Revival, who has had a significant influence on the "third generation." Although he disliked being called "Irish poet" his work displays recognizably Irish qualities. Claims his work is "uneven," although he has had a great impact on the nation's cultural life. Discusses *The Great Hunger*, "Shancoduff," and the Canal Bank sonnets.

1983

25 Review of *The Dancing Flame: A Documentary Drama of the Poet in Society*. *Era* (Summer):42.
    Review of the play based on the 1954 libel trial.

26 RUSHE, DESMOND. "Patrick Kavanagh Archives." *Irish Independent* (8 September). UCD Archive.
    Discusses the Kavanagh archive.

27 SEALY, DOUGLAS. "Irish Poetry During the Last Decade." *Crane Bag* 6, no. 1:74–84.
    Claims Michael Hartnett has been influenced by Kavanagh.

28 VELDHUIS, THEO. "Bound to Soil: Patrick Kavanagh's The Great Hunger." *Dutch Quarterly Review* 12, no. 4:279–289.
    Discusses Kavanagh's idea of the national "bucklep" (stage Irishness in literature). Considers *The Great Hunger*, which is "a rural version of 'The Waste Land,'" his most enduring statement against buckleppin." Claims the poem attacked the misrepresentation of rural life, rather than rural life itself. Argues that numerous theatrical references in the poem suggest it is a kind of play, and an "ironic allusion" to Synge's peasant drama. Praises the visual impact of the poem, comprising brief scenes which are "like *tableaux vivants*."

29 WALSH, CAROLINE. "In the Bookshops—6. Parsons of Baggot Street Bridge." *Irish Times* (2 March):8.
    Describes Parsons bookshop and its proprietor, Miss May O'Flaherty. Mentions its distinguished customers, and claims Kavanagh was "the king pin" of the literary patrons. Claims he would sit for hours on a stool in the shop, and used to propose on a regular basis to a young girl who worked there.

30 ———. *The Homes of Irish Writers*. Dublin: Anvil Books, pp. 23, 32.
    Describes Kavanagh's home in Mucker.

1983

*1 "Between the Canals: Dublin in the '50s." RTE TV program. Transmitted 14 December 1983. RTE archive accession no. P485/83. Duration: 50 minutes 31 seconds.
    Documentary essay on Dublin in the 1950s, including footage of Kavanagh.

1983

2 BRADLEY, ANTHONY. "Landscape as Culture: The Poetry of Seamus Heaney." *Contemporary Irish Writing*. Boston: Twayne, pp. 1–14.
Brief references to Kavanagh's influence on Heaney.

3 CANTALUPO, CATHERINE. "Patrick Kavanagh (21 October 1904–November 1967)." In *Dictionary of Literary Biography*, vol. 20: British Poets, 1914–1945. Edited by Donald E. Stanford. Detroit: Gale Research Co., pp. 192–201.
Describes poet's life and career, which resulted in "an intelligent, robust, and ultimately mystical body of work." The early poetry was influenced by the Imagists and by AE, but was marred by abstraction and sentimentality. *The Great Hunger* was modernist, because "it tends uncharacteristically towards nihilism." Admires "religious heat" of the later poetry. Believes Kavanagh's admirers "are mainly Irish." He is disliked by those who prefer "cosomopolitan" poetry. Concludes his work will last, although he "has not yet gained wide recognition."

4 CLINES, FRANCIS X. "Poet of the bogs." *New York Times Magazine* (13 March):43–104.
Brief reference to Kavanagh's notion of parochialism.

*5 COLLINS, JAMES. *Patrick Kavanagh: Reassessment of the Middle Period*. M.A. thesis, New University of Ulster.
Thesis on Kavanagh.

6 CRONIN, ANTHONY. "Patrick Kavanagh: Alive and Well in Dublin." In *Heritage Now: Irish Literature in the English Language*. New York: St Martin's, pp. 185–196.
Comments on failure of critics to explain Kavanagh's alleged greatness, perhaps because the poetry lacks the philosophical depth or coherence to discuss in critical terms. Despite Kavanagh's "primitive" flavor, his early poems were very literary, even derivative, except for "Iniskeen Road, July Evening." Claims the work has epic scope, with a "confessional" tendency. Kavanagh, "an Emersonian Transcendentalist," wrote "a chapter in the moral history of his country."

7 DAWE, GERALD. "Brief Confrontations: Convention as Conservatism in Modern Irish Poetry." *Crane Bag* 7, 2:143–147.
Claims the "instability of his artistic achievements" is the reason for Kavanagh's failure to invent a strong "literary identity" for himself. Argues that Kavanagh updated without transforming the conventional myth of the Irish Poet, inherited from Yeats. Yet Kavanagh remains "the most important figure in Irish poetry of the last three decades."

1983

8 DEANE, SEAMUS. "The Artist and the Troubles." *Ireland and the Arts: A Special Issue of Literary Review*. Edited by Tim Pat Coogan. London: Namara Press, pp. 42–51.
   Claims Kavanagh was the "artistic voice" of the Free State, since he replaced the Yeatsian nation with the parish, and wrote a body of literature that "bears witness to the spectacle of the ordinary, but still miraculous world."

9 EGAN, DESMOND. "Lying Awake in a Sleeping Bag." *Desmond Egan. Collected Poems*. Orono: National Poetry Foundation, p. 189.
   Poem dedicated to Peter Kavanagh. Refers to Patrick.

10 FITZGERALD, MARY M. "Modern Poetry." In *Recent Research on Anglo-Irish Writers: A Supplement to Anglo-Irish Literature: A Review of Research*. Edited by Richard J. Finneran. New York: MLA, pp. 299–334.
   Provides a detailed review of research on modern Irish poetry, with a substantial, although not comprehensive, section on Kavanagh, to 1980, who is characterized as "the most important figure in Irish poetry among the generation after Yeats, especially to the younger poets whom his example liberated from the shadow of the master." Argues that much of the scholarly treatment of Kavanagh's work concentrates on "its historical rather than its literary importance."

11 FITZ-SIMON, CHRISTOPHER. *The Irish Theatre*. London: Thames and Hudson, p.186.
   Refers to O'Connor's 1966 stage adaptation of *Tarry Flynn*.

*12 FLEISCHMANN, RUTH. *Novels of Irish Country Life of the Twentieth Century. A study of Canon Sheehan, Brinsley McNamara and Patrick Kavanagh*. Ph.D. thesis, UCD.
   Thesis on Kavanagh and others.

13 FRAZIER, ADRIAN. "John Montague's Language of the Tribe." *Canadian Journal of Irish Studies* 9, no. 2:57–76.
   Briefly compares Montague to Kavanagh.

14 HEANEY, SEAMUS. "Poetry: Family. Explorations II." BBC Radio. Produced by David Hammond, compiled and presented by Seamus Heaney. Transmitted 25 January. Sound archive, Ulster Folk and Transport Museum. Duration: 18 minutes 9 seconds.
   Discusses group of poems about family life, including Kavanagh's "Memory of My Father."

1983

*15 KEATING, MARIA. "Ireland's Eye. Great Hunger at the Peacock." RTE TV program. Accession no. P290/83. Transmitted 24 May.
   Maria Keating visits the Peacock Theatre, Dublin, while Tom MacIntyre's *Great Hunger* is under rehearsal.

16 KENNER, HUGH. *A Colder Eye.* New York: Knopf, pp. 238, 293–299, 303–307.
   Discusses Kavanagh's life and his relationships with other Dublin writers. Discusses *The Great Hunger*, and contrasts the early with the later "bitter" poems. Mentions Kavanagh's rejection of Yeats and contrasts their respective views of peasant life. Claims Kavanagh's best work resembles "faux naif." Compared to Yeats, the poems seem "amateurish," but Kavanagh's poetic looseness was liberating for younger poets because he "could suggest a domain WBY hadn't pre-empted."

17 KLEJS, LENE. "Seed Like Stars: Kavanagh's Nature." *Eire* 18, no. 1 (Spring):98–108.
   Claims Kavanagh's poetry expresses two very different conceptions of nature: poems like *The Great Hunger* and "Stony Grey Soil" project an image of nature as dead, infertile and stultifying, whereas most of Kavanagh's poems—including "Father Mat" and "To the Man after the Harrow," which are singled out for discussion—project an image of nature as life-affirming, suffused with divine spirit, and are witness to Kavanagh's "Christian Pantheism." Claims Kavanagh later rejected *The Great Hunger* because he realized that he had depicted nature as dead, whereas in most of his work he had showed nature alive.

18 MATTHEWS, JAMES. *Voices. A Life of Frank O'Connor.* New York: Atheneum, pp. 106, 109, 187, 190, 236–238, 361, 375–376.
   Examines Kavanagh's expressed opinion of O'Connor that he had been hindered by following Yeats. Discusses O'Connor's kindness to Kavanagh and their mutual admiration for each other's work, each of them "in exile" in Ireland and, at times, poverty-stricken. Discusses O'Connor's review of Kavanagh's *Collected Poems*. Claims that at O'Connor's funeral, Kavanagh recited Yeats's poem, beginning, "I knew a phoenix in my youth."

*19 MCLAUGHLIN, PHILIP J. *"A Profound and Holy Faith": the Poetry of Patrick Kavanagh.* M.A. thesis, New University of Ulster.
   Thesis on Kavanagh.

*20 MORROW, G. *The Poetry of Austin Clarke and Patrick Kavanagh: Two Major Departures in Anglo-Irish Poetry from the Tradition Established by W. B. Yeats.* M.Phil. thesis, Ulster Polytechnic.
   Thesis on Kavanagh.

1983

21 NEMO, JOHN. "Patrick Kavanagh (21 October 1904–1930 November 1967)." In *Dictionary of Literary Biography*, vol. 15: British Novelists, 1930–1959. Part 1: A–L. Edited by Bernard Oldsey. Detroit: Gale Research, pp. 241–246.

   Biographical and critical essay. Praises Kavanagh's use of local subject matter in *Tarry Flynn* and *The Green Fool*, which has been influential on later writers. Discusses Kavanagh as an outsider who had more enemies than friends. Claims *The Green Fool* is not "stage-Irish," as Kavanagh thought. Examines the history of the drafts of *Tarry Flynn*, a significant novel, although sometimes maudlin, full of pleasing detail and vivid dialect. Discusses the novel Kavanagh began writing after *Tarry Flynn*, about a group of "youthful cobblers." Considers both parts of *By Night Unstarred* inferior to the earlier fiction. Claims Kavanagh's reputation has "grown steadily" since his death: "More of his writing is currently in print in England, Ireland, and America than at any time during his life."

*22 O'REILLY, DAVID. *Kavanagh's Weekly: A Survey*. Ph.D. dissertation, New University of Ulster.

   Thesis on Kavanagh.

23 SCHIRMER, GREGORY. *The Poetry of Austin Clarke*. University of Notre Dame Press; Portlaoise: Dolmen, pp. 4–5, 6–7, 24.

   Discusses Kavanagh's notion of the provincial and parochial.

24 SEALY, D. H. "To You, Ewart Milne, Failte." In *Ewart Milne: For His 80th Birthday*. Skye and Louth: Aquila, p. 7.

   A poem. Brief reference to Kavanagh.

25 STAPLETON, MICHAEL. *Cambridge Guide to English Literature*. Cambridge: Cambridge University Press, p. 473.

   Biographical entry on the poet.

*26 WARREN, LORNA. *Out of the Shadow of Yeats: The Poetry of Clarke and Kavanagh*. M.Phil. thesis, Ulster Polytechnic.

   Thesis on Kavanagh.

27 WELCH, ROBERT. "Language as Pilgrimage: Lough Derg Poems of Patrick Kavanagh and Denis Devlin." *Irish University Review* 13, no 1 (Spring): 54–66.

   Analyzes Kavanagh's and Devlin's poems about Lough Derg, both of which are very experimental attempts "to find authentic speech." Kavanagh's poem is "a kind of diastole to the systole of 'The Great Hunger' published in the same year," and an expression of Kavanagh's Romantic desire to speak out to the common man. Compares Kavanagh to Lady Gregory in his belief in the links between art and community. Contrasts Kavanagh's tone of sympathy with Devlin's hermeticism.

1984

1 AGNEW, ART. "Patrick Kavanagh Poetry Award." Letter to *Irish Times* (10 July):9.
    Invites entries for the Kavanagh award.

2 ANNWN, DAVID. *Inhabited Voices: Myth and History in the Poetry of Geoffrey Hill, Seamus Heaney and George Mackay Brown.* Frome, Somerset: Bran's Head Books, pp. 79, 85, 91, 95.
    Brief remarks on Heaney's interest in Kavanagh.

3 BROWNE, VINCENT. "Wigmore." *Magill* (March):62.
    Gives an account of a humorous anecdote by Ronnie Drew on the subject of his last meeting with Kavanagh.

4 DALSIMER, ADELE. "Hell and Parnassus by the Canal Bank: Patrick Kavanagh's Dublin." In Harmon (1984.7).
    Discusses Kavanagh's search for "Parnassus," claiming he depicted Dublin as either infernal or Parnassian, corresponding to the pain and joy he experienced there. Examines motives for departure from Monaghan in light of "Temptation in Harvest" sequence, in which Dublin becomes Parnassian ideal. Kavanagh later hated Dublin and transformed it into a hell, until 1955, when it became Parnassian and he felt reborn. However, during the final stages of his illness, he hated Dublin again. See Dalsimer (1989.9).

5 DAWE, GERALD. "The Permanent City: The Younger Irish Poets." In Harmon (1984.7), pp. 181, 184.
    Brief references to Kavanagh.

6 DE BREADUN, DEAGLAN. "Iniskeen has busy Kavanagh weekend." *Irish Times* (26 November):7.
    Describes Kavanagh's Yearly at Carrickmacross and Inniskeen, and annual graveside commemoration. The Abbey Players performed *Pennies of Time*, a compilation of Kavanagh's work.

7 HARMON, MAURICE, ed. *The Irish Writer and the City.* Edited by Maurice Harmon. Gerrards Cross, Bucks: Colin Smythe, and Totowa, N.J.: Barnes & Noble, 203 pp.
    Contains Dalsimer (1984.4) and Dawe (1984.5).

1984

8 HEANEY, SEAMUS. "Poet to Poet: Seamus Heaney on Patrick Kavanagh. A Poet's Blessing." *Listener* (19 April):13–14.
   Examines Kavanagh's life and background, and discusses "A Christmas Childood," "Iniskeen Road: July Evening," "Epic," and *The Great Hunger*. Discusses also the comic, "anti-heroic stance" of the later Kavanagh—"a poetry which names rather than blames the world." Claims Kavanagh gave him his "blessing" when they met in a Dublin pub in 1966, shortly after the publication of Heaney's first book. Kavanagh said yes to the offer of a drink "with an acceptance that I like to think was an acceptance of more than a drink."

9 ——. "Station Island, V." *Station Island*. London: Faber, pp. 73–74.
   A brief meeting with Kavanagh's ghost.

10 KAVANAGH, PETER. *Sacred Keeper: A Biography of Patrick Kavanagh*. Orono: National Poetry Foundation, University of Maine at Orono. 404 pp.
   Reprint of Peter Kavanagh (1979.21).

11 "Kavanagh weekend programme." *Irish Times* (18 September):6.
   Announces forthcoming Kavanagh's Yearly at Carrickmacross.

12 "Kavanagh's Yearly." *Irish Times* (18 December): 10.
   Describes the Yearly at Carrickmacross.

13 KEANE, MICHAEL JAMES. *Private and Public Voices in Irish Poetry: W. B. Yeats, Patrick Kavanagh and Seamus Heaney*. Ph.D. dissertation, University of Michigan. See DAI-A 45/07 (January 1985):2097.
   Examines Kavanagh's rejection of Yeats's aesthetic by deliberately cultivating parochialism. Shows how Kavanagh influenced subsequent poets, especially Heaney.

14 MCMAHON, SEAN. *A Book of Irish Quotations*. Dublin: O'Brien Press, pp. 81–82.
   Contains eighteen quotations from Kavanagh's poetry and fiction.

15 NEMO, JOHN. "Patrick Kavanagh." In *Dictionary of Irish Literature*. Edited by Robert Hogan. Dublin: Gill and Macmillan, pp. 340–345.
   Reprint of Nemo (1979.36).

16 O'CONNOR, ULICK. "Patrick Kavanagh." In *A Critic At Large*. Dublin and Cork: Mercier Press, pp. 21–24.
   Reprint of O'Connor (1980.23).

1985

17 PAULIN, TOM. "A New Look at the Language Question." In *Ireland and the English Crisis*. Newcastle: Bloodaxe, p. 191.
    Refers approvingly to Kavanagh's use of dialect word, "gobshite."

18 TREVOR, WILLIAM. *A Writer's Ireland: Landscape in Literature*. London: Thames and Hudson, pp. 160, 173.
    Refers to *Lough Derg* and "Shancoduff." "Kavanagh belonged to Ulster's border country, to the limbo-lands of Monaghan."

19 WATERS, MAUREEN. "Patrick Kavanagh and Tarry Flynn." In *The Comic Irishman*. Albany: State University of New York Press, pp. 137–148.
    Praises Kavanagh's plain style, his skill in representing rural speech in the fiction, and his eye for small details. Discusses the satiric humor of *Tarry Flynn*, in which "romantic conventions about rustic life" are mocked, and compares Kavanagh to Carleton. Examines Jansenistic Catholicism, sexual frustration, and the domineering mother in both the novel and *The Great Hunger*. Compares Tarry with "the figure of the poet-fool" in ninth- and twelfth-century Irish literature.

1985

1 ANDREWS, ELMER. "The Gift and the Craft: An Approach to the Poetry of Seamus Heaney." *Twentieth Century Literature* 31, no. 4 (Winter):368–379.
   Makes occasional references to Kavanagh as influence on Heaney.

2 BOLD, ALAN. *Longman Dictionary of Poets*. Harlow, Essex: Longman, p. 146.
   Brief biographical sketch of Kavanagh.

3 BRADY, ANNE M., and BRIAN CLEEVE. *A Biographical Dictionary of Irish Writers*. Mullingar: Lilliput Press, p. 117.
   Brief biographical profile. Claims that "doubt exists as to the extent of his (Patrick Kavanagh's) authorship" of *By Night Unstarred*.

4 BROWN, STEPHEN J., and DESMOND CLARKE, eds. *Ireland in Fiction: A Guide to Irish Novels, Tales, Romances and Folklore*, vol 2. Cork: Royal Carbery Books, p. 131.
   Gives short biographical account of Kavanagh's life. Briefly discusses *Tarry Flynn*.

*5 CAGHILL, LIAM. "News Bulletin. Plaque to Patrick Kavanagh." RTE TV program. Accession no. N155/85A. Duration: 2 minutes 15 seconds. Transmitted 4 June. Voice-over by Liam Caghill.

1985

Film of the unveiling of a commemorative plaque to Kavanagh at the Irish Congress of Trade Unions building, Raglan Road, Dublin.

6 DAWE, GERALD. "Solitude and Participation: A Look at Irish Poetry, Public and Publishing." *Crane Bag* 9, 1:105–108.
Brief reference to Kavanagh's *Self Portrait*.

7 DEANE, SEAMUS. *Celtic Revivals: Essays in Modern Irish Literature, 1880–1980*. London: Faber, pp. 11, 15, 16, 37, 135, 145, 146–147, 152, 154, 175, 176.
Occasional passing references to Kavanagh, including acknowledgment of his influence on contemporary Irish poetry, generally, and Heaney and Montague, in particular.

8 DILWORTH, THOMAS. "Wordsworth and Lewis Carroll in Patrick Kavanagh's *The Great Hunger*." *Review Of English Studies* 36, no. 144:541–543.
Finds *The Great Hunger* uneven, especially section 8, which is very repetitive. Traces the "sitting on a wooden gate" section to Lewis Carrol's *Through the Looking Glass*, when the White Knight talks to an old man sitting on a gate, which, in turn, is a parody of Wordsworth's "Resolution and Independence." Kavanagh's allusion suggests his approval of Carroll's parody, thus he "attacks Wordsworth indirectly."

9 DODSWORTH, MARTIN. "Heaney's Poetry: Ambiguous Space." *PN Review* 46:38–40.
Brief reference to Kavanagh's "ghost" in *Station Island*.

10 DRABBLE, MARGARET, ed. *The Oxford Companion to English Literature*. Fifth Edition. Oxford University Press, p. 526.
Biographical and critical entry on Kavanagh.

11 DUFFY, P. J. "Carleton, Kavanagh and the South Ulster Landscape, ca. 1800–1950." *Irish Geography* no. 18:25–37.
Describes how Carleton's and Kavanagh's writings throw light on the personality of the South Ulster landscape, rural population and community. Claims South Ulster seems to have changed little from Carleton's time to Kavanagh's. *The Great Hunger* is a comment on "the social tyranny of land ownership in the small farmlands" of the region. Discusses Kavanagh's depiction of the social activity and behavior in the rural landscape. Mentions the value for social and regional geographers of the study of creative writing.

12 "Funds sought to buy poet's papers." *Irish Times* (14 September):17.
Announces Dublin launching of Kavanagh archive campaign.

1985

13 GILLESPIE, ELGY. "Kavanagh plaque unveiled in Dublin." *Irish Times* (5 June):7.
Describes Kavanagh plaque unveiled at poet's old lodging house on Raglan Road, where he lived for three years.

14 GREVER, GLENN. "Exciting Kavanagh's Clay-Heavy Mind." In *Hopkins Among the Poets: Studies in Modern Responses to Gerard Manley Hopkins*. Edited by Richard F. Giles. Hamilton, Ontario: International Hopkins Association, pp. 69–71.
Discusses presence in Kavanagh's early poetry of Hopkins-like poetic techniques, especially the "combining of words through hyphenation." Kavanagh was excited by the mystical linkage of God and nature in Hopkins's poetry, and by his startling poetic techniques. As with Hopkins, "Kavanagh's love is an outpouring to the God whom [sic] he saw everywhere in nature."

15 HARMON, MAURICE. "The Era of Inhibitions, 1920–1960." In *Irish Writers and Society At Large*. Irish Literary Studies 22. Edited by Masaru Sekine. Gerrards Cross, Bucks.: Colin Smythe, Totowa, N.J.: Barnes & Noble, pp. 31–41.
Describes the forces preventing or discouraging creative writing in post-revolutionary Ireland, and argues that Kavanagh's poetry "protests against those repressive forces."

16 HOBSBAUM, PHILIP. "Craft and Technique in Wintering Out." In *The Art of Seamus Heaney*. Edited by Tony Curtis. Bridgend, mid-Glamorgan; Chester Springs: Poetry Wales, 1985, pp. 37–43.
Compares Heaney's *Wintering Out* to *The Great Hunger*.

*17 JACKSON, ALASDAIR. "News Bulletin. Patrick Kavanagh Poetry Awards." RTE TV program. Accession no. N329/85A. Reported by Alasdair Jackson. Transmitted 25 November. Duration 1 minute 7 seconds.
Film of Kavanagh's grave and of the Poetry Awards ceremony.

18 JEFFARES, A. NORMAN. "The Realist Novel, 1900–1945." In Martin (1985.24), pp. 42–52.
Discusses contrast between dream and reality in *Tarry Flynn*.

19 JOHNSTON, DILLON. *Irish Poetry After Joyce*. Notre Dame, Indiana: University of Notre Dame Press & Mountrath, Ireland: Dolmen Press, pp. 4, 10, 32–33, 41–42, 121–166, 182.
Examines Kavanagh's role in Irish literary history, arguing that Kavanagh's Dublin poetry provided Irish poetry with a new urban landscape, reminiscent of Joyce's Dublin. Discusses Joyce's influence on Kavanagh, and Kavanagh's influence on contemporary Irish poets. Examines some of his

1985

major themes, including the poet's relationship to his audience, the movement from childhood innocence to radical, adult innocence, his rejection of the nationalist myth of the pure peasant and his ambivalent relationship with Yeats's work. Contrasts Kavanagh's early poetry with the idyllic pastoral of Padraic Colum. Praises *The Green Fool* and *Tarry Flynn*, but finds unevenness in tone in *The Great Hunger* and *Lough Derg*. Argues that Irish writers have found the early and later Kavanagh most exemplary, and that Kavanagh freed modern Irish poetry from Yeats, much as Williams freed modern American poetry from Eliot.

20 KILROY, THOMAS. "The Autobiographical Novel." In Martin (1985.24), pp. 67–75.
    Brief discussion of *Tarry Flynn*. Praises its comedy.

21 MARTIN, AUGUSTINE. "Fable and Fantasy." In Martin (1985.24), pp. 110–120.
    Brief reference to "Kavanagh's doctrine of 'the habitual, the banal.'"

22 ———. "Peter Kavanagh: Sacred Keeper." *Irish Times* (1 August):10.
    Recalls first meeting with Peter Kavanagh in New York and compiling an inventory of the Kavanagh archive, preserved in boxes in a New Jersey bungalow. Describes contents of archive. Praises *Sacred Keeper* and *Beyond Affection*.

23 ———. "A Visit to Iniskeen." *Irish Times* (2 August):10.
    Describes visiting Iniskeen with Peter Kavanagh, where he met neighbors who knew Patrick. Argues the need to bring Peter's papers to Dublin for safekeeping. Peter wants to sell them to UCD (the only Irish university to have given Patrick employment) for 100,000 pounds, although UCD, at present, can offer only ten thousand pounds. Announces intention of writing Kavanagh's biography.

24 ———, ed. *The Genius of Irish Prose*. Edited by Augustine Martin. Dublin: Mercier Press. 174 pp.
    Contains Jeffares (1985.18), Kilroy (1985.20) and Martin (1985.21).

25 MCENEANEY, KEVIN T. "Elegy for Patrick Kavanagh" (poem). *An Gael* 3, no. 1 (Summer):38–39.
    Claims "the begrudgers" killed Kavanagh, although his "wit" survives.

26 "Move to buy poet's papers." *Irish Times* (11 September):7.
    Announces Belfast launching of Kavanagh archive campaign.

1985

27 MURPHY, BRUCE. "Patrick Kavanaugh's [sic] Parnassus." *An Gael* 3, no. 1 (Summer):34–37.

Claims the long poem was Kavanagh's real medium, as *The Great Hunger*, *Lough Derg*, and *Why sorrow?* demonstrate, and he is as much a virtuoso as the "modern masters of the long poem." His poems chart his development from childhood simplicity to adult simplicity. Discusses "Canal Bank Walk" and the "almost Eastern" peacefulness of the Canal Bank sonnets, which are "the zenith" of his work.

28 MURPHY, DANIEL J. "Apocalypse of Clay: Religion in Patrick Kavanagh's Poetry." *Studies* 74, no. 293 (Spring):47–65.

Discusses importance of religious mysticism in Kavanagh's work in relation to four main subjects: "the Genesis of the Word," "childhood innocence," "life-affirming morality," and "mystical contemplation and prayer." Compares *The Great Hunger* to Blake's *Songs of Innocence and Experience*, and Eliot's *Four Quartets*, although the note of tragedy dominates in Kavanagh.

29 MYERS, KEVIN. "An Irishman's Diary." *Irish Times* (6 December):13.

Discusses forthcoming auction at Newman House of Kavanagh memorabilia to raise funds for Kavanagh archive, which so far has raised 40,000 pounds.

30 O'CLEIRIGH, GEAROID. "Paddy Gaelach Kavanagh" (Irish Language article). *Comhar* 44, no. 5:22–25.

Claims Kavanagh's main objective was to celebrate in his poetry his inheritance and native land, although he had no interest in protecting the Irish language itself. Indeed, he once wrote: "Irish is the badge of our nationality but a lion has no need of a badge to roar." Claims that Ireland and its native culture will die unless we begin to treat the past with the dignity it deserves. Kavanagh may not have fully understood this.

31 O'LOUGHLIN, MICHAEL. *After Kavanagh: Patrick Kavanagh and the Discourse of Contemporary Irish Poetry*. Dublin: Raven Arts Press. 38 pp.

Agrees with Seamus Deane that Kavanagh is more influential on Irish writing than Yeats, despite the fact he is often considered "minor" by English critics. Argues that Kavanagh was the first modern Irish poet to have an uncomplicated relationship with Irish nationality. He is "the first fully-fledged Irish poet in the English language." "His angle of vision and sense of poetic rightness" is rooted in Irish oral traditions which he shares with Irish-language ballad writers. He has access to Gaelic culture not through translations but through his cultural origins. Claims his realistic treatment of rural life has influenced Montague and Heaney, and his mystical, "Parnassian" tone has influenced Durcan.

1985

32 O'TOOLE, FINTAN. "Going West: The Country versus the City in Irish Writing." *Crane Bag* 9, no. 2:116.
   Kavanagh's *The Great Hunger*, along with Flann O'Brien's *The Poor Mouth* and the plays of Tom Murphy, attack "the synthetic notions of the country in the name of genuine rural experience."

33 "Patrick Kavanagh Poetry Award." *Irish Times* (17 August):18.
   Announces annual Kavanagh award.

34 PAULIN, TOM. "Life Sculpture: Patrick Kavanagh." In *Ireland and the English Crisis*. Newcastle: Bloodaxe, pp. 103–105.
   Reprint of Paulin (1980.27).

35 QUINN, ANTOINETTE. "A rediscovered Patrick Kavanagh manuscript." *Long Room* (Friends of Trinity College Library, Dublin), 30:36–37.
   Draws attention to "a holograph collection of poems donated by Patrick Kavanagh to the National Library in 1950," overlooked for years because it was miscataloged. Seven of the forty-two poems are unpublished, and there are variant versions of others.

36 RIORDAN, MAURICE. "Eros and History: On Contemporary Irish Poetry." *Crane Bag* 9, 1:49–55.
   Discusses *The Great Hunger* and Kavanagh's reaction against the Revival. Explores the poem's shortcomings, "a stereotyped mother and sister" and a thinly-drawn protagonist, whose motivation is inadequately examined. Yet Kavanagh is "the first Irish poet to see the Irish landscape with a lover's intensity." Compares and contrasts Kavanagh with John Montague.

37 ROWLEY, ROSEMARIE. "Poetic Challenge." Letter to *Irish Times* (22 August):9.
   Brief references to Kavanagh's preference for the country over the city.

38 SCHIRMER, GREGORY A. "Biased biography only distorts image of complex Irish poet." *Christian Science Monitor* (22 May):22.
   Review of *Sacred Keeper*, which is "not the book that Kavanagh's readers, looking for a clarifying, definitive image of the man, might have hoped for." Claims the author is too biased.

39 ———.*The Poetry of Austin Clarke*. Notre Dame, Indiana: University of Notre Dame Press, and Mountrath, Ireland: Dolmen, pp. 4–6, 24.
   Discusses Kavanagh's concept of the parochial.

40 SEYMOUR-SMITH, MARTIN. *New Guide to Modern World Literature.* London: Macmillan. First American edition, New York: Peter Bedrick Books, p. 337.

Kavanagh entry is a reprint of Seymour-Smith (1973.42).

41 TOLLEY, A. T. *The Poetry of the Forties in Britain.* Ottawa: Carleton University Press, pp. 121, 165, 166–169, 182, 283, 292.

Examines Kavanagh's work as a reaction against the Revival, and compares his concept of parochialism with Norman Nicholson's definition of provincialism as long residence in a native region. Contrasts Kavanagh's realistic poetic with the "visionary" poetic popularized in the '40s. Praises *The Great Hunger* as "the outstanding regional poem of the 1940s" and the Canal Bank poems as highly individual. Claims Kavanagh only became "widely celebrated" posthumously, although well known in the '40s.

42 WATSON, GEORGE. "The Narrow Ground: Northern Poets and the Northern Ireland Crisis." In *Irish Writers and Society at Large.* Edited by Masaru Sekine. Gerrards Cross, Bucks.: Colin Smythe, Totowa N.J.: Barnes & Noble, pp. 207–224.

Uses quotation from Kavanagh on the folly of writing about "an important thing," in the context of a discussion of Tom Paulin's poems about Ulster, suggesting that "Northern Irish Protestant culture needs its own Patrick Kavanagh."

*43 WERNE, A. *Patrick Kavanagh: vision and realism: the poet-artist in relation to Irish tradition and society.* M.A. thesis, University of Exeter. See Aslib *Index to Theses* 1985.

Describes the development of Kavanagh's work, from the early "visionary mysticism" to the later "critical response to Irish society." Discusses the early poetry and fiction, *The Great Hunger, Kavanagh's Weekly*, the later poetry and *Lough Derg*. Kavanagh's attitude to his native Monaghan wavered between "visionary love" and contempt.

1986

1 ABBOTT, VIVIENNE, "God in Woman in Kavanagh's Writing." In Kavanagh (1986.28), pp. 301–310.

Examines the presentation of women in Kavanagh's fiction and poetry. Claims Kavanagh sees women as redeeming and "at the centre of all life, of hope, of sanity." Men in Kavanagh are dependent on women. Discusses Tarry Flynn's relationship to his mother and the stultifying, enforced chastity of Catholic Ireland, which resulted in low marriage rates. Discusses Kavanagh's

1986

chauvinistic attitude toward women writers. Claims Kavanagh does not question women's position in Irish society.

2 ARDEN, JOHN. "Literary Emperor." In Kavanagh (1986.28), pp. 283–284.
Recalls first seeing Kavanagh in a Dublin pub in the 1950s. Speculates that Kavanagh left his Monaghan farm in order to escape atmosphere of feuding, although in Dublin, he became "a savage warrior, Cuchulain at the ford." He was both self-protective and assertive of his right to be a poet and became one of Ireland's "mutilated heroes."

3 BARRY, SEBASTIAN. Introduction to *The Inherited Boundaries: Younger Poets of the Republic of Ireland*. Edited by Sebastian Barry. Mountrath, Portlaoise: Dolmen, pp. 13–29.
Invokes Kavanagh's distinction between the parochial and the provincial, claiming that the younger Irish poets are neither parochial nor provincial, just Irish.

4 BLOOM, HAROLD, ed. Introduction to *Seamus Heaney*. New York: Chelsea House Publishers, pp. 2, 10.
Brief references to Kavanagh's influence on Heaney.

5 BOYLAN, FRANCIS. "Patrick Kavanagh." In Kavanagh (1986.28), pp. 387–422.
Reprint of Boylan (1972.7).

6 CORCORAN, NEIL. *Seamus Heaney*. London: Faber, pp. 20, 47, 49, 53, 98, 100, 143, 159, 161, 167.
Discusses Kavanagh's influence on Heaney.

7 CREELEY, ROBERT. "A True Poet." In Kavanagh (1986.28), pp. 311–314.
Praises the "insistent particularity" of Kavanagh's writing. Recalls first reading Kavanagh in 1967, on the recommendation of Charles Olson, who had heard Kavanagh read in London that year. Claims Kavanagh's poetry is true to the spoken voice and is comparable to Auden, Burns, Tristan Corbière, Heine, Irving Layton, Skelton, and Villon.

8 DEANE, SEAMUS. *A Short History of Irish Literature*. London: Hutchinson, and Notre Dame, Indiana: Notre Dame Press, pp. 195, 210, 227, 228, 230, 232–235, 237, 238, 240, 242, 246.
Claims Kavanagh is "father figure" for Northern Irish poets, especially Heaney, since he released himself and them from "bondage" to Yeats and Joyce, by a life of "iconoclastic battlings and manoeuvreings." Kavanagh was "poet laureate of the Free State," opposed to the Revival's heroic mythology. Claims his influence is stronger than his "uneven" output would suggest,

which makes it hard to gauge his importance. Admires *The Green Fool, Tarry Flynn, The Great Hunger*, and Canal Bank sonnets.

9 DEVINE, BRIAN, "One Brave Gesture." In Kavanagh (1986.28), pp. 315–321.
   Claims that the need for individual vision is central to Kavanagh's poetry and criticism. Argues that Kavanagh was priest-like and his writings have a spiritual dimension. Discusses his technique and his later philosophy of "not-caring."

10 DEVITT, JOHN. "Paulin's and Muldoon's Choices." *Irish Literary Supplement* (Fall):27.
   Discusses Paul Muldoon's choice of Kavanagh's poetry in his edition of the *Faber Book of Contemporary Irish Poetry*.

11 DILLON, J. Interview with Michael Longley. In *Irish Literary Supplement* (Fall): 22.
   Longley claims that for Derek Mahon and himself, Kavanagh was, to some extent, an early influence.

12 DONLEAVY, J. P. *J. P. Donleavy's Ireland*. New York: Viking Penguin, pp. 102, 105–107, 138, 189, 211, 218.
   Claims that, in the 1950s, Kavanagh appeared large and powerful in Dublin, and "walked the streets like a battleship plunging through the waves." Describes a meeting with Kavanagh in the *Envoy* magazine office, in which Kavanagh accused Donleavy, who was farming a small plot in Wicklow, of "phoniness."

*13 DOYLE, OWEN. "From Simplicity back to Simplicity: Patrick Kavanagh's Poetic Vision." *CAE* (Collection of articles and essays), Hankuk University of Foreign Studies, Korea, 19:517–534.
   Essay on Kavanagh.

14 DUFFY, PATRICK J. "Patrick Kavanagh's Landscape." *Eire* 21, no. 3 (Fall):105–118.
   Somewhat revised version of Kavanagh section in Duffy (1985.11).

15 EGAN, DESMOND. "Homer's Ghost." In Kavanagh (1986.28), pp. 197–213.
   Stresses the need to separate the poet from the man who gained a reputation for being an outrageous "character." Argues that he reintroduced into Irish poetry "the world of the ordinary." Contrasts Kavanagh with Yeats. Claims he has had many imitators, including those who use "proper names" in poetry, a hallmark of his verse. Argues that he did not revise his poems, and thus they appear rough-hewn and informal. However, his poems express a

1986

"sensuous richness unequalled in English verse since John Keats." Kavanagh is a master of tone: his poetry expresses the speaking voice. Discusses Kavanagh's technique, use of rhyme, enjambment, and slang. He is "the least 'literary' of poets" and thus has not had the critical attention he deserves.

16 FARRELL, PATRICK. "A Memoir." In Kavanagh (1986.28), pp. 163–167.
    Recalls first meeting Kavanagh in 1956 at a press conference at the Algonquin Hotel, New York. Claims McCandlish Phillips's subsequent interview for the *New York Times* with Kavanagh was suppressed. Describes meetings with Kavanagh at other occasions in New York and Rome.

17 FRIBERG, HEDDA. "Irish Writing in the Late 20th Century: A Report of a Conversation with Two Irish Critics." *Moderna Sprak* 80, no. 3:210–220.
    Interview with Fintan O'Toole and Declan Kiberd. O'Toole discusses *The Great Hunger* as an anti-Revivalist text.

18 "Fundraising Hop." *Irish Times* (9 April):9.
    Announces fund-raising in Dublin for Kavanagh archive.

19 GARRATT, ROBERT F. *Modern Irish Poetry: Tradition and Continuity from Yeats to Heaney*. Berkeley: University of California Press, pp. 16, 41, 54, 57, 118, 137–166, 259.
    Examines Kavanagh's position in Irish literary history, claiming that he rejected Yeats's cultural politics and admired Joyce. Explores Kavanagh's reaction against the Revival and nationalism as a literary theme. Claims he had to contend with not only Yeats but also a condescending Dublin literati. Much of his criticism can be read as a reaction against them. Examines the influence of Joyce's writing on the growth of Kavanagh's "poetic realism" and on his search for the universal particular. Dislikes the satires, praises the Canal Bank sonnets, and dispraises the late poems, which lack precision and technique.

20 GILLESPIE, ELGY. "Kavanagh papers acquired by UCD." *Irish Times* (5 November):11.
    Announces the presentation of Kavanagh papers by Peter Kavanagh to Augustine Martin in New York. Describes the papers.

*21 GOODBY, JOHN. *Inner Emigres: A Study of Seven Irish Poets (1955–1985)*. Ph.D. dissertation, Leeds University.

22 GREACEN, ROBERT. "Bumping into Kavanagh." *Books Ireland* 102 (April):67.
    Mentions Kavanagh's *Complete Poems* and O'Loughlin (1985.31). Recalls meetings with Kavanagh, including period of residence at guest house

in Ballsbridge. Discusses Kavanagh's hunger for news, his distrust of Austin Clarke, his talent for making enemies. Compares Kavanagh to Johnson and Swift. Discusses publishing history of *The Green Fool*.

23 ——. "In a Genteel Guest House." In Kavanagh (1986.28), pp. 87–88.
Greacen once stayed in same guest house as Kavanagh near Ballsbridge. Recalls that he was respectful of women, and "in my presence emphasised his belief in God and Mother Church." He praised only Auden, among poets. He had "strong rapport" with his brother, Peter. He loved news, "devoured news of all kinds, political, racing, gossip—with avidity."

24 GRENNAN, EAMON. "A Piecemeal Meditation on Kavanagh's Poetry." Kavanagh (1986.28), pp. 339–350.
Finds two idioms in Kavanagh's early poetry: (1) "visionary-transcendent mode," influenced by AE; and (2) conversational, colloquial mode, influenced by James Stephens. The two idioms are blended in *A Soul for Sale* and *The Great Hunger*, and the mystical idiom later becomes elegiac, mourning the loss of innocence. Discusses the two idioms in *Tarry Flynn* and *The Great Hunger*. The language of the Canal Bank sonnets is that "of pure presence, of possession and being possessed." Discusses the love poems—"usually dismal failures"—and Kavanagh's masterful use of syntax. Discusses his influence on Irish poetry, and concludes with poem about the poet, "Kavanagonistes."

25 HEANEY, SEAMUS. "Three Irish Poets to Watch." *Irish Literary Supplement* (Spring):1.
Review of O'Loughlin, *After Kavanagh* (1985.31).

26 JENCKES, NORMA. "The Rocky Road to Dublin: Patrick Kavanagh's Apprenticeship, 1930–1939." In Kavanagh (1986.28), pp. 371–381.
Kavanagh's career shifts from "bucolic innocence" to "a survivor's reclamation of self in the natural world." Describes Kavanagh's walk from Monaghan to Dublin as "an emblem of a personal, poetic, and psychological journey." Praises the early lyrics for their "spare exactness," influenced as they were by Georgians and Imagists. Argues that anxiety about his poetic identity and a sense of "poetic isolation" haunts Kavanagh's early poems. Discusses his devotion to freeing poetry from the style of the Literary Revival and his desire to marry spiritual vision and the quotidian. Examines "Memory of My Father."

27 "Kavanagh weekend opens in Monaghan." *Irish Times* (29 November):3.
Announces forthcoming Kavanagh's Yearly at Carrickmacross.

1986

28   KAVANAGH, PETER, ed. *Patrick Kavanagh: Man and Poet*. Orono: National Poetry Foundation, University of Maine. 499 pp.
Contains Abbott (1986.1), Arden (1986.2), Boylan (1986.5), Creeley (1986.7), Devine (1986.9), Egan (1986.15), Farrell (1986.16), Greacen (1986.23), Grennan (1986.24), Jenckes (1986.26), Kavanagh (1986.29–33, 35), Kilfeather (1986.38), Liddy (1986.40), Martin (1986.47), McEneaney (1986.49), Milne (1986.51), Morrow (1986.52), George O'Brien (1986.53), Margaret O'Brien (1986.54), O'hAodha (1986.56), Rafroidi (1986.59), Rice (1986.60), Sealey (1986.61), Simpson (1986.63), Stuart (1986.65), Warner (1986.67).

29   ———. "Annotated Bibliography of Patrick Kavanagh." In Kavanagh (1986.28), pp. 425–486.
Annotated bibliography of primary and secondary sources, with preface, describing origins and parameters of bibliography.

30   ———. Introduction to Kavanagh (1986.28), pp. 15–29.
Provides brief biographies of Kavanagh's grandfather, father, and mother. Describes Kavanagh's youth and early education, and his work as shoemaker and farmer. Discusses his ill health (typhoid and thrombosis of the leg), his attendance at Gaelic classes, and other details of his personal life.

31   ———. "Kavanagh Case." In Kavanagh (1986.28), pp. 141–156.
Describes history of 1954 libel action and prints "extracts from the newspaper reports" on the trial.

32   ———. "Kavanagh Country." In Kavanagh (1986.28), pp. 49–65.
Overlaps with Peter Kavanagh's *Guide to Patrick Kavanagh Country* (1978.18). Describes parish and village of Inniskeen, as well as Slieve Gullion, and Shancoduff. Lists local Irish place-names with derivations. Describes family home and its history, the Kednaminsha school and the Big House at Rocksavage. Provides history of region, especially during 1798 and the famine years.

33   ———. "Kavanagh's Weekly." In Kavanagh (1986.28), pp. 123–140.
Describes origins, funding and production of *Kavanagh's Weekly*. Also prints "digest of *Kavanagh's Weekly* with primary emphasis on Patrick's contribution."

34   ———. *Sacred Keeper: A Biography of Patrick Kavanagh*. Orono: National Poetry Foundation, University of Maine. 403 pp.
Reprint of Kavanagh (1979.21).

35 ——. "Writer." In Kavanagh (1986.28), pp. 77–85.
   Describes the poet's writing career, from 1928 to his death, and provides many biographical details about him and his brother. For Peter, Patrick was "a mystic."

36 KIBERD, DECLAN. "Beckett and Kavanagh: Comparatively Absurd?" *Hermathena: A Trinity College Dublin Review* 141 (Winter): 45–55.
   Compares Kavanagh with Beckett. Argues that, although usually treated as a minor "transitional figure" in literary history, Kavanagh's opposition to Irishness links him with European modernists like Beckett and Devlin. Like Beckett, he promoted a comic vision, and made laughing at his own failure his main subject. Discusses Kavanagh's essay on *Waiting for Godot*. For Kavanagh, since God existed, humans could develop "not-caring" as a philosophy of life. He is "our first and only Christian absurdist."

37 KILEY, FREDERICK. "Book Reviews." *Eire* 21, no. 3 (Fall): 155–157.
   Review of *Sacred Keeper*. Finds it disappointing, distorted, and reverent: "It protects more than it reveals." Regrets that poet's relationships with women are not discussed.

38 KILFEATHER, RENEE and JOHN KILFEATHER. "Romantic." In Kavanagh (1986.28), pp. 95–99.
   Renee Kilfeather recalls visiting Kavanagh in Dublin in 1948, when he was film critic for the *Standard*. Although sometimes rude, he was humorous and gentle. John Kilfeather recalls Kavanagh visiting Belfast for a weekend. After dinner, they had a "marathon question and answer session." Claims his manners were "old-fashioned and punctilious." Overlaps with Kilfeather (1980.13).

39 KINSELLA, THOMAS. Introduction to *The New Oxford Book of Irish Verse*. Oxford University Press, pp. xxiii–xxx.
   Contrasts Clarke's and Kavanagh's attitudes toward literary tradition.

40 LIDDY, JAMES. "A Memoir of Parnassus." In Kavanagh (1986.28), pp. 295–300.
   Imagines the conversation between Kavanagh, Joyce and Tom Moore in Heaven. Praises Kavanagh's technique. Although from Monaghan, he was "born too soon for the Ulster poetry bash." Believes Kavanagh was a Christian: "He had the secret quality of real traditional religion." Compares him to Mandelstam. Claims Kavanagh told him he would sabotage the Northwestern University Yeats symposium in 1967: "He vowed to break it up in half an hour." Discusses Kavanagh's contribution to the symposium.

1986

41 LONGLEY, EDNA. *Poetry in the Wars*. Newcastle: Bloodaxe Books. 264 pp.
    Contains Longley (1986.42–44).

42 ——. "'Inner Emigré' or 'Artful Voyeur'? Seamus Heaney's *North*." In Longley (1986.41), pp. 140–169.
    Discusses *The Great Hunger* in relation to Heaney's "At a Potato Digging."

43 ——. Introduction to Longley (1986.41), pp. 9–21.
    In a discussion of links between poetry and clichés, argues that Kavanagh "smashed both the Yeatsian and the Irish Nationalist icon of the peasant."

44 ——. "'Worn New': Edward Thomas and English Tradition." In Longley (1986.41), pp. 47–77.
    Quotes from Kavanagh's essay on the parish in a consideration of Edward Thomas's sense of place.

45 MAGUIRE, AISLING. *York Notes. Selected Poems, Seamus Heaney*. Harlow, Essex: Longman, pp. 8–9.
    Mentions Kavanagh's influence on Heaney.

46 MARTIN, AUGUSTINE. "Anglo-Irish Poetry: Moore to Ferguson." *Canadian Journal of Irish Studies* 12, no. 2 : 84–104.
    Briefly contrasts Kavanagh's attitude toward the Anglo-Irish Literary Revival with that of Austin Clarke.

47 ——. "The Apocalypse of Clay: Technique and Vision in *The Great Hunger*." In Kavanagh (1986.28), pp. 285–293.
    Kavanagh steered Irish poetry away from Yeatsian mythologizing, replacing myth with a poetics of realism. The realism of *The Great Hunger* exemplifies Kavanagh's eye for detail, although its cinematic narrative style also demonstrates the influence of film on the poet. The poem is "theatrical" in structure, but is antidramatic ("the drama of non-event"), and anti-Revivalist in its assumptions about peasant life. The Canal Bank sonnets establish Kavanagh as Ireland's best religious poet.

*48 MCCULLOUGH, ALAN. "News Bulletin. Patrick Kavanagh's Manuscripts." RTE TV program. Reported by Alan McCullough. Accession no. BN/356/86E. Transmitted 22 December. Duration: 1 minute 49 seconds.
    Bulletin concerning return of Kavanagh's papers to Ireland. Interview with Gus Martin and John Bruton, Minister of Finance.

1986

49 MCENEANEY, KEVIN T. "Patrick Kavanagh: His Trinity." In Kavanagh (1986.28), pp. 269–282.

Claims Kavanagh had three private obsessions—"authority, honesty and universality." Discusses *Kavanagh's Weekly* and the 1954 trial proceedings— "a valuable and uproarious record of Kavanagh's wit." Discusses his use of rhyme and the prevalence of the pronoun "I" in his poems. Draws parallels between Kavanagh, Blake, and Baudelaire, although claims that Kavanagh was too original to have been influenced by anybody. Discusses his religious poetry, the Canal Bank sonnets, and *Lough Derg*.

50 MCGUINN, NICHOLAS. *Seamus Heaney: A Student's Guide to the Selected Poems 1965–1975*. Leeds: Arnold-Wheaton, p. 29.

Briefly discusses Kavanagh's influence on Heaney.

51 MILNE, EWART. "London Encounter 1955." In Kavanagh (1986.28), pp. 157–159.

Reprinted from *Sacred Keeper*. Recalls meeting Kavanagh with his brother, Peter, in London in 1955, when the poet seemed like "a startlingly correct picture of a lumping stage-Irishman." Describes the encounter. Claims Kavanagh appeared ill.

52 MORROW, LARRY (THE BELLMAN). "Meet Patrick Kavanagh." In Kavanagh (1986.28), pp. 117–122.

Reprint of Morrow (1948.5).

53 O'BRIEN, GEORGE. "The Walk of a Hundred Years: Kavanagh and Carleton." In Kavanagh (1986.28), pp. 351–357.

Draws a series of parallels between William Carleton and Kavanagh. Claims the forebears of some characters in *Tarry Flynn* may be found in Carleton's *Traits and Stories of the Irish Peasantry*. Compares the two writers' sense of place: both thought of the parish as "an imaginative unit," although Kavanagh's sense of place was "much more specific" than Carleton's. Claims Carleton was attracted to the grotesque; Kavanagh to the refined.

54 O'BRIEN, MARGARET T. "With Living Eyes." In Kavanagh (1986.28), pp. 329–337.

Recalls first meeting Kavanagh in New York in 1957, when he appeared very ill. Claims he hated "chauvinistic patriotism" and "popular piety." Although his honesty made him isolated and lonely, he lacked self-pity. Discusses the "symbolism" of the poetry, including "A Wind," "Blind Dog," and "To a Child." His early poems adumbrated "transcendental poetic vision," but his later work became more ironic.

1986

55 O'CALLAGHAN, KATE. "Seamus Heaney. A Poet of his People." *Irish America* (May):24–30.
   Brief reference to Kavanagh's early influence on Heaney.

56 O'HAODHA, MICHAEL. "The Casting Out of Patrick Kavanagh." In Kavanagh (1986.28), pp. 367–370.
   Reprint of O'hAodha (1977.38).

57 "Patrick Kavanagh Poetry Award." *Irish Times* (30 June):12.
   Announces annual Kavanagh award, the annual graveside commemoration at Inniskeen, and Kavanagh's Yearly.

58 PYLE, FERGUS. "Kavanagh Comes Home for Christmas." *Irish Times* (23 December):8.
   Describes press conference at UCD following the arrival in Dublin of Kavanagh papers. Describes various contributors to the Kavanagh archive fund, including Samuel Beckett. The Ministry of Finance contributed 25,000 pounds to fund.

59 RAFROIDI, PATRICK. "Patrick Kavanagh: A French Tribute." In Kavanagh (1986.28), pp. 323–327.
   Claims the later poems of Kavanagh translate best into French, although little of his poetry has been translated. Discusses reasons for Kavanagh's relative popularity in France. Partly, it's his sincerity, but partly, it's because the French love writing about rural subject matter. Compares Kavanagh to Jean Giono, Paul Leautaud, and Voltaire.

60 RICE, GERARD. "The Kavanagh Years." In Kavanagh (1986.28), pp. 67–76.
   Describes social, political, and economic background of life in Ireland when Patrick Kavanagh was alive. Describes how the troubles in the 1920s impinged on life in County Monaghan and Dundalk, and how it was reported by the local press. Describes the continuities and changes in civil service, the Catholic Church, railways, workhouses, and education. The Irish state changed little from 1920 to 1960: "The founders of the Irish state had effected a successful political revolution but failed with any kind of social revolution." *Kavanagh's Weekly* expressed widespread midcentury disillusionment. Kavanagh was the "historian" of "the Catholic Ireland of the Kavanagh years." Compares Kavanagh's moral vision to that of Thucydides. His rural poetry expresses an almost medieval world in modern Monaghan, and his vision resembles that of "nature poets of early Christian Ireland." Kavanagh, not Joyce, was "the forger of the uncreated conscience of his race."

1986

61 SEALY, DOUGLAS. "As a Balladeer." In Kavanagh (1986.28), pp. 361–366.

Explores Kavanagh's relationship with the ballad tradition, in light of the fact family members sang many ballads at home. Examines his use of ballad form for satirical purposes, and discusses "Raglan Road" and "If Ever You Go to Dublin Town."

62 SHIELDS, KATHLEEN. "Irish Poetry Publishing (1950–1980)." *Gaeliana* (Caen, France), no. 8:229–238.

Whereas Kavanagh and other Irish poets in the fifties had to support themselves with journalism, poets today can depend on universities and arts councils for support.

63 SIMPSON, LOUIS. "An Irish Poet" (poem). In Kavanagh (1986.28), pp. 359–360.

Poem about Kavanagh, first published in *Poetry East* (New York, 1980). Recalls meeting the poet at a party in New York. Imagines him sitting at his habitual seat by the Dublin Canal.

64 SLOAN, BARRY. *Pioneers of Anglo-Irish Fiction 1800–1850*. Irish Literary Studies, 21. Gerrards Cross: Colin Smythe; Totowa, N.J.: Barnes and Noble, pp. 30, 171, 252.

Discusses Maria Edgeworth's *Ormonde* in relation to Kavanagh's distinction between the parochial and the provincial. Mentions Kavanagh's admiration for Carleton's "authentic dialect."

65 STUART, FRANCIS. "Earthy Visionary." In Kavanagh (1986.28), pp. 383–386.

Reprint of Stuart (1975.33).

66 TAPSCOTT, STEPHEN. "Poetry and Trouble: Seamus Heaney's Irish Purgatorio." *Southwest Review* 71 (Autumn):519–535.

Brief references to Kavanagh, whose rural Catholicism is compared to Heaney's.

67 WARNER, ALAN. "Remembering Patrick Kavanagh." In Kavanagh (1986.28), pp. 175–181.

Describes his first meetings with Kavanagh and his attempts to secure permission from the poet to write a book about him. Claims Kavanagh was initially willing and then suddenly, mysteriously, very unwilling to oblige. Reprints correspondence between himself and the poet concerning these matters. Argues that Kavanagh was "the last peasant poet."

1987

*1 "After all those Late Late Shows: 1967." RTE TV program. Accession no. BP30/2314. Transmitted 31 December.
Film footage of noteworthy news events in 1967, including Kavanagh's funeral.

2 BARKER, JONATHAN. "One Barker to Another." *Agenda* 25, no. 2:71–79.
Briefly invokes Kavanagh's distinction between the Comic Muse and Tragedy (see *Collected Pruse*) in relation to the poetry of George Barker.

3 BONACCORSO, RICHARD. *Sean O'Faolain's Irish Vision*. Albany: SUNY Press, pp. 27, 56, 116, 123–125.
Claims Kavanagh and O'Faolain were part of "a new breed of peasant-born writers." Compares O'Faolain's work to Kavanagh's. Discusses *The Great Hunger* as "an eloquent ally to the efforts of O'Faolain, who as editor of *The Bell* was also trying to shake Irish people out of their moral complacency."

4 COLGAN, MAURICE. "Exotics or Provincials? Anglo-Irish Writers and the English Problem." In Zach and Kosok (1987.45), pp. 35–40.
In *Tarry Flynn* and *The Green Fool* Kavanagh gives us "profound insights into rural life in the 20th century," giving us "a window into the pre-industrial, pre-urban world we have lost."

5 COSTELLO, PETER, and PETER VAN DE KAMP. *Flann O'Brien: An Illustrated Biography*. London: Bloomsbury, pp. 15–20, 81, 104, 106.
Describes Dublin's Bloomsday celebrations in 1954. Mentions Kavanagh's need to write for newspapers to make a living. Discusses Kavanagh's 1954 libel suit. Kavanagh and O'Nolan were invited to the Literary and Historical Society at UCD to discuss Irish newspapers—"one as victim; the other as a master of attack." When O'Nolan's mother died in 1956, Kavanagh told him "there is only one real death in your life and that's your mother's." Includes photographs of Kavanagh.

6 DUDDY, BRENDAN, S.J. Review of *Complete Poems* and *Patrick Kavanagh: Man and Poet*. *Studies* 76, no. 304 (Winter):493–495.
Claims Kavanagh is "a harsh prophet who, like a good surgeon, will not shirk exposing the nerve and slicing the diseased parts to the very bone." Discusses impact of Kavanagh's iconoclasm on Dublin's smug literary world. Although seemingly anti-intellectual, Kavanagh had "a powerful and original mind."

1987

*7 DUNNE, LEE. "On the Town." RTE TV program. Accession no. BP20/3631. Transmitted 4 December. Duration: 2 minutes, 36 seconds.
   Lee Dunne asks Anne Doyle and Noel Sheridan at Jury's Hotel about their impressions of the recent RTE film documentary on Kavanagh, "Gentle Tiger" (1987.27).

8 DURCAN, PAUL. "What Shall I Wear, Darling, to *The Great Hunger?*" In *Going Home to Russia*. Belfast: Blackstaff, p. 23.
   Satirical poem about a wealthy and narcissistic Dublin socialite's visit to the Peacock Theatre, to watch the dramatic adaptation of the poem.

9 FLEISCHMANN, RUTH. "Old Irish and Classical Pastoral Elements in Patrick Kavanagh's *Tarry Flynn*." In Zach and Kosok (1987.44), pp. 311–321.
   Argues that *Tarry Flynn* has much in common with the Gaelic literary tradition, in its attention to the detail of Irish speech and natural landscape. In this respect, Kavanagh had more in common than is usually thought with the writing of the Celtic Revival which he so often attacked.

10 FOSTER, JOHN WILSON. *Fictions of the Irish Literary Revival. A Changeling Art*. Syracuse: Syracuse University Press; Dublin: Gill & Macmillan, pp. 144, 242, 290.
    Brief references to Kavanagh.

11 HEANEY, SEAMUS. "The Placeless Heaven: Another Look at Kavanagh." *Massachusetts Review* 28, no. 3 (Autumn):371–380.
    Contrasts Kavanagh's early and late poetry. The early poetry is like a physical tree. It concerns real places, whereas the later resembles the space left after the tree has fallen—"a placeless heaven rather than a heavenly place." The self of early poetry is "absorbed by scene," but the landscape of later poetry is "inside himself." Discusses liberating impact on Heaney, when young, from reading Kavanagh. "In Memory of My Mother" is a pivotal poem; "Auditors In" exemplifies the late style. Compares early Kavanagh to Millet, the later to Chagall, "afloat above his native domain." The later poetry is self-generating, the "poetry of inner freedom." Revises his claim that Kavanagh "ate his heart out" (1975.12); rather, he "cleared a space" within himself.

12 HIRST, DESIREE. "Modern Writing in English from Ireland and Wales: A Comparative Study." In Zach and Kosok (1987.44), pp. 149–159.
    Kavanagh's work influenced Heaney's pastoral realism. Kavanagh is "a Christian poet," as shown by his poem *Lough Derg*.

1987

13 ——. "The Sequel to 'The Irish Renaissance.'" *Canadian Journal of Irish Studies* 13, no. 1:17–42.

   Briefly discusses Kavanagh's work, including *The Great Hunger* and *Lough Derg*. Claims Kavanagh's influence caused "a minor revolution in Irish poetry."

14 HITCHENS, CHRISTOPHER. "American Notes." *Times Literary Supplement* (9 January):36.

   Discusses sale of Kavanagh archive to UCD. "It's extraordinary to think of a haul like that leaving America instead of being shipped here." Speculates that Kavanagh's work is little known in U.S.A. because the Irish-American community "sensed a lack of propriety in his attitude toward the motherland."

15 HOWARD, BEN. "The Pressed Melodeon." *Kenyon Review* 9, no. 1 (Winter):33–49.

   Examines a number of contemporary Irish poets, and mentions Kavanagh's influential notion of the parochial and provincial. Discusses "Shancoduff" and "Canal Bank Walk."

16 ——. "Selective Laurels." *Sewanee Review* 95, no. 3:505–511.

   Review of Thomas Kinsella, *The New Oxford Book of Irish Verse*. Claims Kavanagh and MacNeice are often seen as "near opposites," and as patrons of Southern and Northern poetry respectively, but argues that they have more in common than is usually thought. Their influence is felt among poets today.

17 JAQUIN, DANIELLE. "Translations." In *Poesies d'Irlande*, edited by Denis Rigal. Marseilles, Sud: Domaine Etrager.

   French translations of eight Kavanagh poems.

18 JOHNSTON, MICHEAL. "Appraisal. Kavanagh's Yearly." RTE Radio broadcast. Accession no. AA4167. Produced by Micheal Johnston and presented by Des Hickey and Micheal Johnston. Transmitted 3 December. Duration: 24 minutes, 20 seconds.

   Interviews participants at the Kavanagh's Yearly celebration at Inniskeen, including Bernard Loughlin (of Tyrone Guthrie Centre), Art Agnew (President of Kavanagh Society), Clinton O'Rourke (Kavanagh Museum), John Morrow, who recalls Kavanagh in Dublin in the 1950s, and Michael Kane, who grew up in the Baggott Street area when Kavanagh lived there and who talks about his Dublin exhibition of paintings "Homage to Kavanagh."

1987

*19 KAVANAGH, PETER. "Brother Commemorate Me. A Conversation with Peter." RTE TV program. Recorded 6 July. Accession no. B90/1354. Duration: 39 minutes.
   Professor Augustine Martin interviews Peter Kavanagh.

*20 ——. "Brother Commemorate Me. Peter Kavanagh Interview." RTE TV program. Directed by Paul Fitzgerald, designed by Suzanne Murphy, produced by Tom McArdle. Recorded 24 November, transmitted 28 November. Accession no. HX30/815. Duration: 28 minutes, 5 seconds.
   Professor Augustine Martin interviews Peter Kavanagh. Possibly a shortened version of Kavanagh (1987.19).

21 KELLY, MICHAEL J. "Kavanagh's Roots." Letter to *Irish Times* (17 September):9.
   Discusses origins of Kavanagh's grandfather.

22 KENNELLY, BRENDAN. "Kavanagh as Comic, Mystic and Balladeer." *Sunday Tribune* (26 April). UCD Archive.
   Review of *Patrick Kavanagh: Man and Poet* (1986.28). The book is "well worth reading and re-reading." Describes general contents of the book, and praises, in particular, contributions by Rafroidi, Martin, and annotated bibliography by Peter Kavanagh. Patrick Kavanagh is "a myriad-minded poet," whose poetry has "a kind of spiritual electricity." He is "a symbolic figure for many Irish poets," and his influence on Irish poets is deepening.

23 ——. "Patrick Kavanagh: 20 Years On." *Irish Times* (30 November):12.
   Discusses the continuing appeal and growing reputation of Kavanagh's poetry. Although not very polished technically, his poetry is "immediate and clear, and it echoes in the mind." Claims Kavanagh's view of Tragedy as "underdeveloped Comedy" is appealing to the young, who "want a poet who recognises the tragedy of life but is not overwhelmed by it."

24 KIBERD, DECLAN. "State of the Art: Declan Kiberd on Patrick Kavanagh." *Irish Times*, Weekend Supplement (23 May):5.
   Review of *Patrick Kavanagh: Man and Poet*, which he considers a "hugely entertaining book." Although Kavanagh was not "a systematic thinker," he had an "incisive mind." Indeed, the best essays in the book are by Kavanagh himself. Discusses contributions by Kavanagh, John Arden and Francis Stuart.

25 LIDDY, JAMES. "Patrick Kavanagh's Dublin." *A White Thought in a White Shade*. Dublin: Kerr's Pinks, p. 107.
   Reprint of Liddy (1964.15).

1987

26 MADDEN-SIMPSON, JANET. "Haunted Houses: The Image of the Anglo-Irish in Anglo-Irish Literature." In Zach and Kosok (1987.45), pp. 41–46.
   Quotes Kavanagh's remarks (*Irish Farmer's Journal* [3 June 1961]) on the inhabitants of a local big house who pretended to "keep up a front," despite their own poverty.

*27 MCARDLE, TOM. "Gentle Tiger. Patrick Kavanagh Documentary." RTE TV program. Accession no. B90/1238. Produced by Tom McArdle, designed by Molly Molloy. Adviser: Augustine Martin. Transmitted 30 November. Duration: 85 minutes.
   Documentary film on the poet, broadcast on the twentieth anniversary of his death, featuring interviews with family members, friends and critics.

*28 MCLOUGHLIN, D.J. *Tradition and Nationality in the Work of Three Irish poets: W. B.Yeats, Patrick Kavanagh and Seamus Heaney*. M.Phil. dissertation. University of Manchester. See Aslib *Index to Theses* 1987.
   Discusses the influence of Yeats on Kavanagh, and of Kavanagh on Heaney. Examines the three poets' sense of place, their relationships to Irish society, and the influence upon those who are not Irish writers.

29 MOLINO, MICHAEL R. "Heaney's 'Singing School': A Portrait of the Artist." *Journal of Irish Literature* 16, no. 3 (September):12–17.
   Discusses Heaney's invocation of Kavanagh in the poem "Singing School." Claims that Kavanagh "typifies the Irish writer whose consciousness is molded by his ties to his native land and his hatred of British control."

30 MOORE, JOHN REES. "Irish Story. *Sewanee Review* 95, no. 3:494–505.
   Review of Seamus Deane's *Short History of Irish Literature* and Denis Donoghue's *We Irish*. Considers *The Great Hunger* "the most impressive protest poem of its decade."

31 MURPHY, DANIEL. "Apocalypse of Clay: Religion in Patrick Kavanagh's Poetry." In *Imagination and Religion in Anglo-Irish Literature, 1930–1980*. Blackrock, Co. Dublin: Irish Academic Press, pp. 25–51.
   Slightly revised version of Murphy (1985.28).

32 MURPHY, MAUREEN O'ROURKE, and MACKILLOP, JAMES, eds. *Irish Literature: A Reader*. Syracuse University Press, p. 308.
   Brief biographical and critical introduction to Kavanagh.

33 O'NEILL, CHARLES L. *Circumventing Yeats: Austin Clarke, Thomas Kinsella, Seamus Heaney*. Ph.D. dissertation, New York University. See DAI-A 48/03 (September): 655.
   Discusses Kavanagh's influence on Heaney in his poems "A Cart for Edward Gallagher," "Death of a Naturalist," "The Seed Cutters," "Harvest

Bow" and others. Suggests that Heaney hopes to unite the virtues of Kavanagh and Yeats in his own poetry.

34 O'NEILL, MICHAEL. *Indexes to Envoy*. M.A. thesis, QUB.
Subject index and contributor index to the twenty issues of *Envoy*, with an introduction based upon an interview with John Ryan. Introduction includes several references to Kavanagh's contribution to the journal, and he is cataloged in indexes.

35 OREL, HAROLD. "William Carleton: Attitudes toward the English and the Irish." In Zach and Kosok (1987.45), pp. 85–93.
Briefly cites Kavanagh's remark that Carleton had used Protestantism for self-aggrandizement.

36 "Patrick Kavanagh commemoration." *Irish Times* (18 March):8.
Describes commemoration of poet at Canal Bank memorial seat.

37 PERKINS, DAVID. "The Poetry of Ireland." In *A History of Modern Poetry: Modernism and After*. Cambridge, Mass.: Belknap, Harvard University Press, pp. 471–485.
In a consideration of several poets, describes Kavanagh's life and career, praising *The Great Hunger* as his greatest poem and comparing it to R. S. Thomas's poems about Welsh farmers. Kavanagh's less successful poems are marred by "flat and clichéd phrasing, and rhythmic collapse."

38 PYLE, FERGUS. "Sleuthing after clues to Kavanagh's loves." *Irish Times* (12 September):2.
Discusses Augustine Martin's task as biographer of the poet. Martin considers Kavanagh archive at UCD "a biographer's dream." Describes contents of the archive, currently on exhibit at UCD.

39 "Remembering Kavanagh." *Irish Times*, Weekend Supplement (21 November):11.
Announces forthcoming annual Kavanagh's Yearly at Carrickmacross. It will be "neither ball-breakingly scholarly nor arse-achingly dull," in the words of organizer Bernard Loughlin.

40 ROBERTS-BURKE, ROBIN J. *The Country of the Mind: Homeland Symbolism in Twentieth Century Hebrew and Irish Poetry (Greenberg, Kavanagh, Ratosh, Heaney)*. Ph.D. dissertation, UCLA. 2 vols. 503 pp. See DAI-A 49/03 (September): 502.
Compares the sense of belonging to a national community and the need for individuation in modern Irish and Israeli poetry. Explores the poet's relationship to home nation and colonizer in terms of an Oedipal relationship

1988

between child, mother, and father respectively. Discusses Kavanagh's revolt against the Revival, his love-hate relationship with the soil, his comic vision, and his influence on Heaney. Compares Kavanagh's "peasant mythos," with which he sought to free himself from the soil, with the "Zionist mythos" and with Israeli poets Ratosh and Greenberg.

41 RUSSELL, NOEL. "Heaney turns up the lantern." *Irish News* (2 July):6.
    Brief reference to Kavanagh's influence on Heaney.

42 RYAN, JOHN. *Remembering How We Stood: Bohemian Dublin at the Mid-Century*. Dublin: Lilliput. 168 pp.
    Reprint of Ryan (1975.30).

43 "The Kavanaghs." *Irish Times*, Weekend Supplement (11 April):5.
    Brief description of *Patrick Kavanagh: Man and Poet*, by Peter Kavanagh, published by Goldsmith that week.

44 ZACH, WOLFGANG, and KOSOK, HEINZ, eds. *Literary Interrelations: Ireland, England and the World: Comparison and Impact*. Vol. 2. Tübingen: Gunter Narr. 370 pp.
    Contains Fleischmann (1987.9) and Hirst (1987.12).

45 ——, eds. *Literary Interrelations: Ireland, England and the World: National Images and Stereotypes*. Vol. 3. Tübingen: Gunter Narr. 244 pp.
    Contains Colgan (1987.4), Madden-Simpson (1987.26), Orel (1987.35).

1988

1 ANDREWS, ELMER. *The Poetry of Seamus Heaney. All the Realms of Whisper*. London: Macmillan, pp. 2, 3, 9, 19, 34, 54, 116, 127, 147, 156, 158, 162–165, 195.
    Discusses Kavanagh's influence on Heaney, particularly with regard to views on place and parochialism. Compares Heaney's and Carleton's responses to Lough Derg with Kavanagh's, and examines the appearance of Kavanagh's ghost in *Station Island*. Attributes Heaney's trope of floating in some lyrics in *Station Island* to Kavanagh's "longing for weightlessness."

2 "Appraisal. Abbey Theatre in Russia." RTE Radio broadcast. Accession no. AA3876. Transmitted 25 February. Duration: 29 minutes, 2 seconds.
    Documentary program on the Abbey Players performing Tom MacIntyre's *Great Hunger* in Leningrad and in the 1400-seat Moscow Arts

Theatre, with simultaneous translation by Natasha Alexeva. Interviews actors Niall Tobin and Tom Hickey and directors Ben Barnes, Patrick Mason, and Vincent Dowling. Russians were puzzled by the play. Michael Sheridan claims the small gestures of the actors were lost in such a large theater.

3 BOYLAN, HENRY. *A Dictionary of Irish Biography*. Second Edition. Dublin: Gill & Macmillan, p. 179.
   Biographical sketch of Kavanagh.

4 BRADLEY, ANTHONY. Introduction to *Contemporary Irish Poetry*. New and Revised Edition. Berkeley: University of California Press, pp. 1–9, 57.
   Revised version of Bradley (1980.2). Makes brief remarks about *The Great Hunger*. Prints thirteen poems by Kavanagh, and gives biographical introduction to the poet.

5 ———. "Literature and Culture in the North of Ireland." In Kenneally (1988.34), pp. 36–72.
   Occasional references to Kavanagh. Claims the image of the hedge school, found in the works of Heaney, Friel, and Montague, derives from Kavanagh. Alludes to Kavanagh's notion of the parochial, which produces poetic realism, which, in turn, "gives expression to a way of life that had not really been expressed before."

6 BRANDES, RANDY. "Seamus Heaney: An Interview." *Salmagundi* 80 (Fall):4–21.
   Briefly discusses what Kavanagh meant to Heaney.

7 BROWN, TERENCE. *Ireland's Literature: Selected Essays*. Dublin: Lilliput, Totowa, N.J.: Barnes & Noble. 262 pp.
   Contains Brown (1988.8–10).

8 ———. "After the Revival: Sean O'Faolain and Patrick Kavanagh." In Brown (1988.7), pp. 91–116.
   Reprint of Brown (1979.1), (1980.3).

9 ———. "The Church of Ireland and the Climax of the Ages." In Brown (1988.7), pp. 49–64.
   Kavanagh's long poem, *Why Sorrow* (1942), is part of a tradition in modern Irish writing of representing the struggle between the individual and an oppressive church.

10 ———. "Thomas Moore: A Reputation." In Brown (1988.7), pp. 14–28.
    Briefly refers to Kavanagh's poem on Moore's statue.

1988

11 CAHALAN, JAMES M. *The Irish Novel: A Critical History*. Dublin: Gill & Macmillan, pp. 91, 181, 182, 184, 191, 196–197, 236, 239, 300.
    Brief references to Kavanagh. Discusses *Tarry Flynn* as a "bildungsroman or *Kunstlerroman*." Compares Tarry to Yeats's John Sherman.

12 CAHILL, EILEEN. *An Intentional Echo: Translation in the Poetry of Medieval Lyricists, William Wordsworth and Seamus Heaney*. Ph.D. dissertation, SUNY Buffalo, pp. 180, 285. See DAI-A 48/10 (April 1988):2633.
    Notes that Heaney "celebrates Kavanagh" as an inspiration.

13 CAIRNS, DAVID, and RICHARDS, SHAUN. *Writing Ireland: Colonialism, Nationalism and Culture*. Manchester University Press, pp. 136, 138.
    In *The Great Hunger*, Kavanagh "powerfully indicted" the "inequalities of wealth and opportunity" in Ireland.

*14 CONOLLY, COLM. "RTE News. *Great Hunger* in Moscow." RTE TV program. Recorded 24 February. Accession no. BN447/88.
    Colm Connolly interviews cast and audience at performance of Tom MacIntyre's *Great Hunger* in Moscow.

15 CRONIN, ANTHONY. *The End of the Modern World*. Dublin: Raven, p. 88.
    Poem about Kavanagh.

16 DANTANUS, ULF. *Brian Friel*. London: Faber, p. 26
    Quotes Kavanagh's notion of parochialism as universal with reference to Friel.

17 DUBREUX, JEAN-LUC. "Traduction." *Études Irlandaises* 13, no. 2 (December): 13.
    Translation of Kavanagh's "Inniskeen Road: July Evening."

18 DURCAN, PAUL. "Passage to Utopia." In *Across the Frontiers: Ireland in the 1990s*. Edited by Richard Kearney. Dublin: Wolfhound, pp. 192–196.
    Claims the Italian philosopher Gianni Vattimo's views on "a free, non-fanatical, postmodern attitude to our myths" resemble Kavanagh's views on an art of "complete casualness." Claims he is more interested in Kavanagh's views than in Irish nationalism or the 1916 rising. Claims he and Kavanagh shared an interest in Jack Kerouac, the Stones, and Bob Dylan, and he once "wrote out all the words of Dylan's 'Desolation Row' for Kavanagh."

19 Editor's Preface to Kavanagh and MacIntyre (1988.32), p. vii.
    Compares MacIntyre's adaptation of Kavanagh's poem to Yeats's dramatization of the Cuchulain tales. "He [MacIntyre] pursues a similar objective in seeking to unite the old and the new."

1988

20 FOSTER, JOHN WILSON. "Post-War Ulster Poetry: A Chapter in Anglo-Irish Literary Relations." In Kenneally (1988.34), pp. 154–171.
    Brief references to Kavanagh. Discusses his ambivalence toward English critics and the Movement poets, who were generally unimpressed by his work.

21 FOSTER, R. F. *Modern Ireland, 1600–1972*. London: Allen Lane, Penguin, p. 539.
    Gives biographical sketch of Kavanagh. Briefly discusses *The Great Hunger* as an indirect expression of "discontent with the de Valera vision."

22 GREEN, MARTIN. "The Great Hunger." Letter to *Times Literary Supplement* (26 August):931.
    Letter concerning *Great Hunger: Poem into Play* (1988.32).

23 ———. "The Great Hunger." Letter to *Times Literary Supplement* (16 December):1395.
    Response to Quinn (1988.48).

24 GUSSOW, MEL. "'Great Hunger,' A Dearth of Words." *New York Times*, Section L (18 March): C3
    Review of Tom MacIntyre's stage adaptation of *The Great Hunger*, directed by Patrick Mason and staged by the Abbey players at the Triplex Theater, at the Borough of Manhattan Community College. Dismisses it as an incomprehensible work of performance art: "There are some words in the play, but they are insistently and boringly repetitive."

25 HEANEY, SEAMUS. "The Pre-Natal Mountain: Vision and Irony in Recent Irish Poetry." *Georgia Review* (Fall):465–480.
    Briefly discusses Kavanagh's term "bucklep," and examines Kavanagh's views on F. R. Higgins.

26 HEWSON, PAUL (BONO). "The White Nigger." In *Across the Frontiers: Ireland in the 1990s*. Edited by Richard Kearney. Dublin: Wolfhound, p. 189.
    Claims U2's lyrics are more influenced by Kavanagh than by Woody Guthrie.

27 HORNBY, RICHARD. "Theater: Shakespeare at the Public Theater." *Hudson Review* 41, no. 2 (Summer):339–347.
    Discusses Abbey's New York performance of *The Great Hunger*. Dislikes the dialogue, the actors, and the setting: "Patrick Kavanagh fans, if there are any, will probably be moved to sue."

1988

28 HOUSTON, DOUGLAS. "Landscapes of the Heart: Parallels in the Poetries of Kavanagh and Auden." *Studies: An Irish Quarterly Review* 77, no. 308 (Winter):445–459.

  Compares Kavanagh with Auden, noting that their lives parallel one another chronologically; they both demonstrated stubborn independence of thought; they both write about a homeland while in exile; and they both wrote of a mythic Edenic place. Describes Kavanagh's admiration for Auden and the influence of the latter on the former's poetry, including *The Great Hunger*, "Possessing Eden," and "Canal Bank Walk."

29 HURLEY, VINCENT. "*The Great Hunger*: A Reading." In Kavanagh & MacIntyre (1988.32), pp. 71–83.

  Discusses figure of the peasant in European literature generally, and in *The Great Hunger*. Examines MacIntyre's adaptation of the poem in Peacock Theatre, which subsequently toured in the U.S. and Russia, to "mixed and frequently turbulent responses." Compares MacIntyre's "non-linear" dramatic technique with that of modern film directors, including Bunuel, Cocteau, Fellini, Godard, Herzog, Pasolini, and Tarkovsky. Describes influence of MacIntyre's Cavan background on his production of *The Great Hunger*. Kavanagh would have liked the adaptation.

30 JACOBSEN, KURT. "An Interview with John Ryan." *Journal of Irish Literature* 17, no. 1 (January):5–15.

  Ryan describes target of Kavanagh's Diary in *Envoy* as: "everybody. Particularly what he thought were phonies." Kavanagh hated attitudinizing and political correctness, and had particular distaste for Austin Clarke, Sheehy-Skeffington, and Behan. He admired Myles, however. Concludes that Kavanagh was always "totally pessimistic," because he lost his childhood faith.

31 JOHNSTON, DILLON. "The Go-Between of Recent Irish Poetry." In Kenneally (1988.34), pp. 172–185.

  Claims Kavanagh is one of many Irish writers who have tried to escape "anachronistic myths" of Irishness. Refers to Kavanagh's ghost in Heaney's *Station Island*.

32 KAVANAGH, PATRICK, and MACINTYRE, TOM. *The Great Hunger: Poem Into Play*. Mullingar: Lilliput. 83 pp.

  Contains Editor's Preface (1988.19), Hurley (1988.29), MacIntyre (1988.39), Mason (1988.42), Quinn (1988.47).

33 "Kavanagh's hardy annual." *Irish Times*, Weekend Supplement (19 November):5.

  Announces the fifth Kavanagh's Yearly at Carrickmacross.

1988

34 KENNEALLY, MICHAEL, ed. *Cultural Contexts and Literary Idioms*. Totowa, N.J.: Barnes & Noble. 250 pp.

Contains Bradley (1988.5), Foster (1988.20), Johnston 1988.31), O'Toole (1988.46), Roche (1988.49).

*35 KENNELLY, BRENDAN. "Bookside: Brendan Kennelly." RTE TV program. Transmitted 2 November. Accession no. P308/88. Duration: 5 minutes, 15 seconds.

Anne Roper interviews Kennelly about his favorite book, Kavanagh's *Collected Poems*.

36 LEONARD, AOIFE. "No Earthly Estate." Kavanagh Exhibition Catalog, University College Dublin Library, May, 10 pp.

Provides detailed list of contents of UCD Kavanagh exhibition in May-June, including photographs, personal and family documents, letters, manuscripts, and page proofs,

37 ———. "University College Dublin Library: Kavanagh Collection. Descriptive list compiled by Aoife Leonard." 76 pp.

Describes the contents of the Kavanagh archive.

38 MACGOUGH, FREDA. "Appraisal." RTE Radio broadcast. Accession no. AA4001. Produced by Patrick O'Gorman, Presented by Freda MacGough. Transmitted 8 September. Duration: 8 minutes, 20 seconds.

Discusses "Mucker," a one-man Kavanagh show by Paul O'Hanrahan of the Balloonatics Theatre Company.

39 MACINTYRE, TOM. "*The Great Hunger*: Play." In Kavanagh & MacIntyre (1988.32), pp. 29–68.

The script of MacIntyre's dramatic adaptation of the poem.

40 MCARDLE, KATHY. Introduction to Kavanagh Exhibition Catalog. University College Dublin Library, May, 2 pp.

Brief appreciation of the poet.

41 MARTIN, AUGUSTINE. "Desmond Egan. Universal Midlander." *Études Irlandaises* 13, no. 2 (December):81–84.

Claims Egan and Kavanagh have in common "a sensuous feeling for nature, especially for its humbler, intimate manifestations."

42 MASON, PATRICK. "Director's Note." In Kavanagh and MacIntyre, (1988.32), pp. 69–70.

Describes evolution of the original script of the play into the final performing script, printed in this edition.

1988

43 MURPHY, MIKE. "Arts Show. Patrick Kavanagh." RTE Radio broadcast. Produced by Colin Morrison, presented by Mike Murphy. Accession no. AA4121. Transmitted 29 November. Duration: 44 minutes, 30 seconds.

Documentary on fifth "Kavanagh's Yearly" at Inniskeen. Interviews Gene Carroll (Inniskeen Drama Group), Anthony Cronin, Tony Glavin, Brendan Kennelly, Michael Longley, Bernard Loughlin, Medbh McGuckian, Peter Murphy, John Ryan, and Fr. Tom Stack. Cronin opened the festivities. Ryan remarked that Kavanagh would have loved the "Yearly." Glavin gives lecture, "Close encounters in an Ulster parish." Kennelly claims Kavanagh is a mystic.

44 O'BRIEN, DARCY. "Piety and Modernism: Seamus Heaney's 'Station Island.'" *James Joyce Quarterly* 26, no. 1 (Fall):51–67.

Brief references to Kavanagh.

45 O'GRADY, THOMAS. "High Anxiety: Flann O'Brien's Portrait of the Artist." *Studies in the Novel* (Denton, Tex.) 21, no. 2 (Summer):200–207.

Brief references to *Tarry Flynn*.

46 O'TOOLE, FINTAN. "Island of Saints and Silicon: Literature and Social Change in Contemporary Ireland." In Kenneally (1988.34), pp. 11–35.

Discusses Kavanagh's attack on notion of the happy peasant, and mentions James Simmons's and Michael Longley's depictions of the Irish peasant. Argues that *The Great Hunger* was landmark in Irish attitude toward sexuality. Maguire's relationship to the earth is "a nightmarish and surreal miscegenation."

47 QUINN, ANTOINETTE. "Textual Note." In Kavanagh & MacIntyre (1988.32), pp. 27–28.

Describes textual history of *The Great Hunger*. The entire poem was published by Cuala Press in 1942, although the 1964 *Collected Poems* differed from the Cuala edition. Gives details of the variations between the 1942 and 1964 versions.

48 ———. "The Great Hunger." Letter to *Times Literary Supplement* (16 September):1017.

Response, on behalf of Lilliput Press, to Green (1988.22). Insists that, contrary to what Green claims, Lilliput Press had printed the original Cuala Press version of the poem, which the *Collected Poems* did not print.

49 ROCHE, ANTHONY. "Ireland's *Antigones:* Tragedy North and South." In Kenneally (1988.34), pp. 221–250.

Briefly notes that Kennelly's *Cromwell* is no more a historical study of Cromwell than Kavanagh's *The Great Hunger* was a historical study of the Great Famine.

50 RYAN, JOHN. "Patrick Kavanagh." *Some Dublin Writers*. Dublin: Dublin Corporation, 1988, pp. 34–37.
Brief biography of the poet.

51 SAUNDERS, NORAH, and A. A. KELLY. *Joseph Campbell: Poet and Nationalist 1879–1944*. Dublin: Wolfhound, p. 138.
Claims the publication of *The Great Hunger* demonstrates that the censorship of poetry was less rigorous in Ireland than the censorship of fiction.

52 SCRUTON, JAMES ALBERT. *A Vocable Ground: The Poetry of Seamus Heaney*. Ph.D. dissertation, University of Tennessee, pp. 2, 18, 132, 206. See DAI-A, 49/11 (May 1989):3361.
Mentions Kavanagh's influence on Heaney's poetry.

53 SIMON, JOHN. "Strictly From Hunger." *New York Magazine* 28 (March):108–109.
Review of MacIntyre's adaptation of *The Great Hunger*, performed at the Triplex Theater. Praises the poem but dislikes the play which is regarded as disorganized and incoherent.

54 SIMPSON, LOUIS. "The Poet's Theme." *Hudson Review* 41, no. 1 (Spring):93–141.
Recalls meeting Kavanagh in New York. Praises the social criticism of *The Great Hunger* and the poet's intimate knowledge of his subject, and contrasts this with the socially-aware, left-wing poetry of Auden and Spender in the 1930s. *The Great Hunger* demonstrates that "poems that move one to feel some social injustice keenly may not be overtly political."

55 WATERS, MAUREEN. "Heaney, Carleton and Joyce on the Road to Lough Derg." *Canadian Journal of Irish Studies* 14, no. 1:55–65.
Discusses literary treatment of Lough Derg, with references to Kavanagh's ghost in Heaney's *Station Island*.

56 ZACH, WOLFGANG. "Brian Friel's *Translations*, National and Universal Dimensions." In *Medieval and Modern Ireland*. Edited by Richard Wall. Gerrards Cross, Bucks: Colin Smythe, p. 76.
Refers to Tom MacIntyre's stage version of *The Great Hunger* as an example of a contemporary Irish history play.

1989

1 ALLEN, MICHAEL, and WILCOX, ANGELA, eds. *Critical Approaches to Anglo-Irish Literature.* Gerrards Cross, Bucks: Colin Smythe, and Totowa, N.J.: Barnes & Noble. 193 pp.
Contains Hughes (1989.20) and Kenneally (1989.25).

2 ARKINS, BRIAN. "Too Little Peace: The Political Poetry of Desmond Egan." In *Irish Writers and Politics*, edited by Okifumi Komesu. Gerrards Cross, Bucks: Colin Smythe, p. 289.
Brief reference to Kavanagh's influence.

3 BONO. "Which Poems Most Impressed You during Your School-Days and Why? A Sounding." *Poetry Ireland Review*, no. 26 (Summer):20.
Bono, from the rock group U2, claims he was influenced by "the stony grey soil of Kavanagh's ordinary madness."

4 BRADLEY, ANTHONY. "The Irishness of Irish Poetry after Yeats." In *New Irish Writing. Essays in Memory of Raymond J. Porter.* Edited by James D. Brophy and Eamon Grennan. Boston: Iona College Press (Twayne), pp. 1–12.
Discusses the modern poetic treatment by Kavanagh and others of "the unpicturesque rural areas" of Ireland. Compares Kavanagh's *The Great Hunger* to Joyce's *Dubliners* and Clarke's poems: all are satires on modern Irish life.

5 BROWN, TERENCE, and NICHOLAS GRENE, eds. *Tradition and Influence in Anglo-Irish Poetry.* Totowa, N.J.: Barnes & Noble. 201 pp.
Contains Dawe (1989.11), Heaney (1989.18), Longley (1989.27), and Quinn (1989.34).

6 "Confusion delays Kavanagh burial." *Irish Times* (21 August):10.
Announces delay in the burial of Katherine Kavanagh.

7 CONNELLY, FRANK. "'Brutal Business' of Poetic Justice in Kavanagh Case." *Sunday Tribune* (20 August). UCD Archive.
Announces burial of Katherine Kavanagh at Inniskeen on August 19. Discusses bitter legal battle with Goldsmith and Peter Kavanagh over control of publication of Kavanagh's writings.

8 CRONIN, ANTHONY. *No Laughing Matter. The Life and Times of Flann O'Brien.* London: Grafton, pp. 90, 94, 108–110, 134, 144, 153, 165, 171–172, 184, 189, 190–196, 205, 218, 234, 245.
Numerous references to Kavanagh. Discusses Kavanagh's relations with Flann O'Brien. Describes Kavanagh's relationship with literary Dublin

as comic, "with tragic undertones." Examines Kavanagh's career as journalist with *Envoy* and *Kavanagh's Weekly*. Discusses 1954 Bloomsday pilgrimage in Dublin, and an unfulfilled plan that O'Brien and Kavanagh should visit the USSR in 1954.

9   DALSIMER, ADELE. "The Priest and the Parnassian: The Religious Dimension of Patrick Kavanagh's 'Canal Bank Sonnets.'" *Canadian Journal of Irish Studies* 15, no. 1 (July):58–67.

Discusses Kavanagh's view of art as sacred, which is based on "Catholic ritual and the legacy of Church doctrine." Yet he had a "dual aesthetic vision" and also believed in the ideal of the poet's Parnassian distance from his subject matter. The notions of poet as Parnassian and as priest converge in his poetry, especially in the Canal Bank sonnets, which illustrate the poet's "belief in the religious nature of poetry and the supernatural power of the poet." See Dalsimer (1984.4).

10 DAVIE, DONALD. *Under Briggflatts: A History of Poetry in Great Britain, 1960–1988*. University of Chicago Press, pp. 248, 251.

Expresses surprise that Heaney prefers Kavanagh to Clarke.

11 DAWE, GERALD. "An Absence of influence: Three Modernist Poets." In Brown and Grene (1989.5), pp. 119–142.

In a concluding section of the essay, examines Kavanagh's example by way of contrast with Devlin, Coffey, and Kinsella. Claims Kavanagh realized there was no poetic community for him in Ireland, and so he had to create one—"an heroic task for any man." Kavanagh has had a major influence on contemporary Irish poetry, unlike the three modernist poets under discussion.

12 DICK, SUSAN, DECLAN KIBERD, DOUGALD MCMILLAN, and JOSEPH RONSLEY. "Richard Ellmann: The Critic as Artist." In *Essays for Richard Ellmann. Omnium Gatherum*. Kingston and Montreal: McGill-Queen's University Press, p. xvi.

Claims Richard Ellmann believed Kavanagh's poem "Who Killed James Joyce?" alluded to Ellmann himself.

13 ETHERTON, MICHAEL. *Contemporary Irish Dramatists*. London: Macmillan, p. 46.

Discusses *The Great Hunger*, staged by Tom MacIntyre in 1983, and toured in 1986 in Ireland and London.

14 FOSTER, THOMAS C. *Seamus Heaney*. Boston: Twayne, pp. 3, 14, 21, 27, 37, 41, 66, 96, 120.

Discusses Kavanagh's influence on Heaney.

1989

15 GARRATT, ROBERT F. "'Non Serviam:' James Joyce and Modern Irish Poetry." In *James Joyce and His Contemporaries*. Edited by Diana A. BenMere and Maureen Murphy. New York: Greenwood Press, pp. 121–129.
    Occasional references to Kavanagh. Claims the poet adopted "Joycean realism" in preference to "Yeatsian romance."

16 GOTHBERG, HELEN. "Literature." *School Library Journal* 35, (November):71.
    Review of *The Abbey Reads*, a recording of Irish poetry by actors at the Abbey, including some of Kavanagh's poems.

17 GRENNAN, EAMON. "'Of So, and So, and So': Re-Reading Some Details in Montague." *Irish University Review* 19, no. 1 (Spring):110–128.
    "Intense attention lodging in plain speech is one of the principal legacies Kavanagh left to Irish poets." Discusses influence of Kavanagh on John Montague.

18 HEANEY, SEAMUS. "The Placeless Heaven: Another Look at Kavanagh." In *The Government of the Tongue: Selected Prose, 1978–1987*. New York: Farrar, Straus & Giroux, pp. 3–14. Also in Brown and Grene (1989.5), pp. 181–193.
    Reprint of Heaney (1987.11).

19 ———. "In the midst of the force field." *Irish Times* (28 January).
    Essay on Yeats, which makes reference to Kavanagh's influential denunciation of Yeats's romantic Ireland.

20 HUGHES, EAMONN. "The Political Unconscious in the Autobiographical Writings of Patrick Kavanagh." In Allen and Wilcox (1989.1), pp. 103–110.
    Examines the theme of identity in Irish autobiography and Irish writing, generally, in light of Jameson's theory of the political unconscious. Claims one of Kavanagh's main themes is failure, which is linked to the fact he lived in a state of "anoeses, a condition of experience without understanding." His writing charts his struggle to understand experience. *By Night Unstarred* was the only Kavanagh book about success, but he was unable to write an autobiography about success.

21 KAVANAGH, PETER. *Piling Up the Ricks: A Sequel to "Beyond Affection"*. Brigantine, N.J.: Peter Kavanagh Hand Press. 181 pp.
    As the title suggests, a continuation of *Beyond Affection*. Consisting of three sections. Discusses childhood, family life, early education in Inniskeen, and his relationship with Patrick. Includes chapter on Patrick as a football player and memoirs of Patrick and Peter by their sister, Celia. Sections two

and three mainly concern the author's life in New York, his family life, his trips home to Inniskeen since the 1960s and his relations with Francis Boylan, Desmond Egan, Augustine Martin, and others. Describes circumstances surrounding publication of *Sacred Keeper, By Night Unstarred, The Dancing Flame, Complete Poems, Patrick Kavanagh: Man and Poet*, and the correspondence with Katherine Kavanagh over copyright. Describes sale of Kavanagh archive to UCD. Recalls deaths of various family members.

22 "Kavanagh time." *Irish Times*, Weekend Supplement (18 November):5.
   Announces forthcoming Kavanagh's Yearly celebration at Carrickmacross.

23 "Kavanagh's widow and publisher dispute copyright." *Irish Times* (29 July):4.
   Discusses Katherine Kavanagh's legal dispute with Goldsmith Press over control of publication of Kavanagh's work.

24 "Kavanagh's widow dies." *Irish Times* (17 August):11.
   Announces death of Katherine Kavanagh.

25 KENNEALLY, MICHAEL. "The Autobiographical Imagination and Irish Literary Autobiographies." In Allen and Wilcox (1989.1), pp. 111–131.
   Describes how the autobiographer may wish to revise an identity established earlier, as for example in the case of Kavanagh's rejection of *The Green Fool* in his *Self Portrait*. Also, briefly discusses the sense of place in *The Green Fool*.

26 KIBERD, DECLAN. "Irish Literature and Irish History." In *Oxford Illustrated History of Ireland*. Edited by R. F. Foster. New York: Oxford University Press, pp. 275–337.
   Compares Synge's *Playboy of the Western World* to *The Great Hunger* as Irish antipastoral. Kavanagh rediscovered in the Baggott Street area the pastoral landscapes he abandoned in his youth—"and *that* version of Ireland proved far more attractive to poetry-readers among the New Dubliners than had Kavanagh's savage indictment of rural torpor in 'The Great Hunger.'" Kavanagh's long poem was an "anti-travelogue and anti-pastoral, which opens by rejecting Yeats's beloved image of *soil*."

27 LONGLEY, EDNA. "Poetic Forms and Social Malformations." In Brown and Grene (1989.5), pp. 153–181
   Explores the "liberating influence" of Kavanagh, especially of *The Great Hunger* and *Lough Derg*, on later Irish poets, including Paul Durcan, Seamus Heaney, Brendan Kennelly, and Paul Muldoon.

1989

28 MATTHEWS, STEVEN. *"When Centres Cease to Hold": "Locale" and "Utterance" in Some Modern British and Irish Poets.* D.Phil. dissertation, University of York (England), pp. 34, 141–142, 147, 164, 176.
    Refers to Kavanagh's influence on Heaney and to the use of *The Great Hunger* and *Lough Derg* as models for *Station Island*.

29 MAYS, J. C. C. Introduction to *Collected Poems of Denis Devlin.* Dublin: Daedalus Books, pp. 23–25.
    Dublin in the 1930s was dominated by Yeats and his circle on one hand, and by Clarke and Kavanagh on the other, who were "intent on modifying the agenda set by their elders."

30 MCLOUGHLIN, DEBORAH. "An Ear to the Line: Modes of Receptivity in Seamus Heaney's Glanmore Sonnets." *Papers on Language and Literature* 25, no. 2 (Spring):210–216.
    Notes Kavanagh's influence on Heaney.

31 MONTAGUE, JOHN. "Patrick Kavanagh: A Speech from the Dock." In *The Figure in the Cave and Other Essays.* Edited by Antoinette Quinn. Syracuse: Syracuse University Press, pp. 136–146.
    Reprint of Montague (1980.20).

*32 NI NUADHAIN, MAIREAD. "Iris. Eigse Carlow." RTE TV program. RTE archive accession no. P192/89. Transmitted 1 July. Duration: 26 minutes, 52 seconds.
    Mairead Ni Nuadhain reports from Carlow arts festival. Brief film footage of John and Tommy McArdle performing stage adaptation of *The Green Fool*.

33 O'DRISCOLL, DENNIS. "For Larkin, Read Kavanagh." *PoetryR* 79, no. 1:38–40.
    Claims that "it is mandatory in any discussion of Irish poetry to quote Patrick Kavanagh as frequently as possible." His voice is now more authoritative than Yeats's in Ireland.

34 QUINN, ANTOINETTE. "Patrick Kavanagh's Parish Myth." In Brown and Grene (1989.5), pp. 97–118.
    Examines the effect upon Kavanagh of severance from his childhood home in Inniskeen after thirty five years of residence there. Compares Kavanagh's grief to that of Hardy over his first wife and to Tennyson's grief over the death of Hallam. Describes the poet's admiration for the three "parishioners," Moore, Carleton, and Joyce, and claims his notion of the parochial is related to his "programmatic return to Inniskeen as poetic theme."

Explores the parish myth, which was an "attempt to establish a separatist Irish Catholic literary tradition," in relation to "Epic," "Shancoduff," *The Great Hunger*, and *Tarry Flynn*. Stresses the link between parochialism and Irish separatism.

35 ——. "The Great Hunger." Letter to *Times Literary Supplement* (3 February):109.
Response to Green (1988.23), concerning the version of *The Great Hunger* used in *Collected Poems*.

36 SCHNEIDER, JURGEN, and RALF SOTSCHECK. *Irland. Eine Bibliographie selbständiger deutschsprachiger Publikationen 16. Jahrhundert bis 1989*. Verlag der Georg Buchner Buchhandlung, pp. 8, 67, 314. (German language.)
Brief reference to Kavanagh's influence on Heaney, and to Tom MacIntyre's *The Great Hunger*.

37 TODD, LORETTO. *The Language of Irish Literature*. London: Macmillan Education, pp. 8, 112, 186.
Briefly discusses Kavanagh's use of short and long lines in *The Great Hunger*.

1990

1 ALLEN, BARBARA, and MICHAEL KANE. Portraits of Kavanagh. In *Faces in a Bookshop. Irish Literary Portraits*. Introduction by Gerald Dawe. Galway: Kenny's Bookshop, pp. 17, 66, 142.
Reproductions of portraits of Kavanagh by Barbara Allen and Michael Kane. Includes brief biographical sketch of the poet.

2 BLACK, CIARAN. "Kavanagh's chair." Letter to *Irish Times* (1 August):11.
Letter protesting the removal of Kavanagh's Canal Bank seat, his "Chair of Poetry," by the Office of Public Works. See "Paddy Kavanagh loses his seat" (1990.28) and see further letters from Thomas Bryan (14 August, p. 11), F. A. Coffey (7 August, p. 11), Dara McKenna (3 August, p. 13), Jimmy Murphy (28 July, p. 7), Tom Nisbet (30 July, p. 11), Oliver Nulty (22 August, p. 11), and Diana B. Perry (3 August, p. 13).

*3 BLANKENSHOP, E. DOUGLAS. *Take Five*. M.F.A. thesis, University of Alaska, Anchorage. 82 pp. See MAI 28/04 (Winter), p. 502.
A collection of original poems with attached essay, explaining the influence upon the poet of several writers, including Kavanagh.

1990

4 BURRIS, SIDNEY. *The Poetry of Resistance: Seamus Heaney and the Pastoral Tradition*. Athens: Ohio University Press, pp. 24–26, 52, 60, 81.
   Discusses Kavanagh's influence on Heaney, and compares and contrasts the poets' treatment of rural subject matter.

5 CARROLL, JOE. "'Bottomification' Name of Game at Kavanagh Love-In." *Irish Times* (26 November):2.
   Review of "Kavanagh's Yearly." Polish writer Nina Witoszek argued that Kavanagh's critics had "bottomified" him. Claims the audience disliked Seamus Deane's lecture on the absence of nationalism in Kavanagh's poetry. Belfast poet Sinead Morrisey won the annual Kavanagh poetry award.

6 CRONIN, JOHN. *The Anglo-Irish Novel: Vol. 2, 1900–1940*. Belfast: Appletree; Savage, Maryland: Barnes & Noble, pp. 19, 108.
   Considers Brinsley MacNamara's *The Valley of the Squinting Windows* (1918) a forerunner to *The Green Fool* and *Tarry Flynn*.

7 EGAN, DESMOND. *The Death of Metaphor*. Gerrards Cross, Bucks: Colin Smythe. 170 pp.
   Contains Egan (1990.8–1990.13).

8 ——. "Mairtin O'Direain." In Egan (1990.7), pp. 93–94.
   Compares the achievement of O'Direain to that of Kavanagh.

9 ——. "Meeting Beckett." In Egan (1990.7), pp. 101–112.
   Claims Beckett was impressed by Kavanagh's capacity for alcohol when he met the poet in the sixties.

10 ——. "The Death of Metaphor." In Egan (1990.7), pp. 13–20.
   In a discussion of eating in Ulster poetry, claims Kavanagh is "the most sensuous poet" since Keats. Mentions "Restaurant Reverie" and "Spraying the Potatoes."

11 ——. "The Poetry of Patrick Kavanagh." In Egan (1990.7), pp. 21–39.
   Reprint of Egan (1986.15).

12 ——. "The Room Upstairs: Poetry in Modern Society." In Egan (1990.7), pp. 71–77.
   Briefly refers to Kavanagh's poverty as an example of the poverty of poets in general.

13 ——. "The Writer and Religion." In Egan (1990.7), pp. 132–135.
   Unlike Yeats, Kavanagh is a great writer. Praises the mysticism in Kavanagh's poetry.

1990

14 FAINLIGHT, RUTH. "A Discussion with Patrick Kavanagh (about his 'Intimate Parnassus')." In *The Knot*. London: Hutchinson, pp. 59–60.
   Poem about Kavanagh.

15 FALLON, PETER, and DEREK MAHON. Introduction to *Penguin Book of Contemporary Irish Poetry*. London: Penguin, pp. xvi–xxii.
   Claims Kavanagh and MacNeice are the major Irish poets after Yeats, but "more than MacNeice, more than Yeats, Kavanagh may be seen as the true origin of much Irish poetry today." Discusses "Epic" in light of Kavanagh's notion of parochialism.

16 HEGARTY, NOIRIN. "Plaque unveiled to poet." *Irish Independent* (2 February).
   Describes unveiling of Kavanagh plaque at 62 Pembroke Road.

*17 HUGHES, E. *Nation and Self: A Study of Four Modern Irish Literary Autobiographies*. Ph.D. dissertation, Leicester University. See Aslib *Index to Theses* 1990.
   Provides readings of four autobiographies, including Kavanagh's *The Green Fool*, focusing on "the problems of identity faced by autobiographers in a period when the issue of national identity had been apparently settled by the establishment of the Irish state."

18 JAQUIN, DANIELLE. "L'Etudiant d'*At Swim Two Birds* et le paysan de *Tarry Flynn* sur les chemins de la liberté." (The student of *At Swim Two Birds* and the peasant of *Tarry Flynn* on the paths to freedom.) *Études Irlandaises* 15 (June):85–96. (French language.)
   Compares and contrasts Tarry Flynn with the protagonist of *At Swim Two Birds*, with regard to how they seek emancipation from their respective emotional and environmental constraints. Explores each character's relationship with the figure of the uncle, and argues that O'Brien's character, who is an experimental novelist, is more intellectual and sophisticated than the intuitive Tarry, although they have in common a tendency to be silent, turning to the written word for emancipation.

19 LONGLEY, EDNA. *From Cathleen to Anorexia: The Breakdown of Irelands*. Lip Pamphlet. Dublin: Attic Press. 24 pp.
   Brief allusion to Kavanagh's reservations about Irish sentimentality in the context of discussing Irish nationalism's reliance on "its own outdated propaganda."

1990

20 LOUGHLIN, BERNARD. "November Songs." Letter to *Irish Times* (5 December):15.

Concerns Joe Carroll's coverage in the *Irish Times* of the Yearly. Claims Raymond Deane's musical cycle based on Kavanagh's poems "got a rapturous reception from an audience of over 250 people."

21 MARTIN, AUGUSTINE. "Patrick Kavanagh." Letter to *Irish Times* (5 September):11.

Announces intention of writing Kavanagh's biography and requests information.

22 MAYS, J. C. C. "Flourishing and Foul: Ideology, Six Poets and the Irish Building Industry." *Irish Review* 8 (Spring):7.

Dublin bookseller Fred Hanna claims Kavanagh's *Complete Poems* is very popular and is selling "the way Corn Flakes do."

23 MURI, ALLISON. "Paganism and Christianity in Kavanagh's *The Great Hunger*." *Canadian Journal of Irish Studies* 16, no. 2 (December):66–78.

Examines the incorporation of and ultimate rejection of certain pagan and Christian concepts in *The Great Hunger*. Discusses the depiction of Catholicism as repressive in the poem. Examines the presentation of the two mothers, Mrs. Maguire and mother Earth, as harsh and unyielding, which leads to the stifling of Maguire's sexuality. Discusses the prominence of triads in the poem, and an appendix provides detailed list of triads of images and phrases.

24 "New Plaque for Kavanagh." *Irish Press* (2 February).

Describes unveiling of Kavanagh plaque at 62 Pembroke Road.

25 O'DEA, TOM. "About Poets." RTE Radio broadcast. Produced and presented by Padraic O'Neill. Transmitted 12 September. Accession no. BB3724. Duration: 14 minutes, 2 seconds.

Interviews Tom O'Dea on Kavanagh. Discusses "Stony Grey Soil" and other poems. Claims the drumlin soil of Monaghan is a watery clay which is unpleasant to work with. Expresses surprise that Kavanagh became a poet at all, given the limitations of his background.

26 O'GRADY, THOMAS B. "At a Potato Digging: Seamus Heaney's Great Hunger." *Canadian Journal of Irish Studies* 16, no. 1 (July):48–58.

Discusses the antiromantic influence of Kavanagh's "Spraying the Potatoes" and *The Great Hunger* on Heaney's "At a Potato Digging," and explores the differences between the poetic outlooks of the poets.

1990

27 ORMSBY, FRANK. Introduction to *Poets from the North of Ireland.* New Edition. Belfast: Blackstaff, pp. 1–20.
     Revised edition of Ormsby (1979.41). Brief references to Kavanagh's influence on Montague and Heaney.

28 "Paddy Kavanagh loses his seat." *Irish Times* (23 July):1.
     Describes the removal by the Office of Public Works of the Canal Bank seat on which Kavanagh wrote his sonnets because it was thought to be in dangerous disrepair. Brendan Kennelly protested that Kavanagh's Baggot Street area deserves preservation "as much as Yeats's Coole Park."

29 "Patrick Kavanagh." *New Encyclopaedia Britannica.* 15th Edition. Vol. 6. Chicago: Encyclopaedia Britannica, p. 769.
     Biographical entry on the poet.

30 PINE, RICHARD. *Brian Friel and Ireland's Drama.* London, New York: Routlege, p. 52.
     Brief reference to Kavanagh's notion of parochialism.

*31 REDMOND, JOHN. *Irish Poetry after Auden: The Influence of W. H. Auden on Patrick Kavanagh, Derek Mahon, and Paul Muldoon.* M.A. thesis, UCD. See Aslib *Index to Theses* 1990.
     Argues that *The Great Hunger* may have escaped the influence of Yeats, but the poem is an uneasy response to Auden's 1930s poetry, and the later Kavanagh was fighting with Auden's influence. Traces this influence also in Mahon and Muldoon.

32 VANCE, NORMAN. *Irish Literature: A Social History. Tradition, Identity, Difference.* Oxford: Blackwell, pp. 102, 211, 213–214, 222, 243–244, 250.
     Discusses Kavanagh's influence on Heaney. Claims that Kavanagh is admired in Ireland but is considered minor in England.

33 WOODWORTH, PADDY. "Composing to Kavanagh." *Irish Times*, Weekend Supplement (24 November):5.
     Describes Raymond Deane's musical cycle, "November Songs," based on Kavanagh's poems, to be performed at the "Yearly."

34 ——. "Kavanagh's hardy annual." *Irish Times*, Weekend Supplement (17 November):5.
     Announces names of participants in "Kavanagh's Yearly" at Inniskeen, including Raymond Deane, Seamus Deane, Nell McCafferty, Kevin McAleer, the McCabe family, Jimmy McCarthy, John McGahern, Fiona Pitt-Kethley, and the Charabanc Theatre Company.

1991

35 ———. "Tarry Revived." *Irish Times*, Weekend Supplement (6 October):5.
Discusses revival of *Tarry Flynn* at the Tivoli Theatre, Dublin. Claims Kavanagh admired the 1966 revival.

1991

*1 AGNEW, UNA B. *The Word Made Flesh: Christian Mysticism in the Works of Patrick Kavanagh*. Ph.D. dissertation, UCD.
Examines Kavanagh's work in light of his religious beliefs. Using archive materials and personal interviews with friends of the poet, explores his biographical background and the "agrarian history" of the family farm. Describes the poet's mysticism, his struggle between hope and despair, and traces the sacramental imagery in the Canal Bank sonnets. See Aslib *Index to Theses* 1991.

2 BATTERSBY, EILEEN. "Seated Statue of Kavanagh Unveiled." *Irish Times* (12 June):2.
Describes unveiling by President Mary Robinson of life-size bronze statue of the poet sculpted by John Coll and located by the Grand Canal. Mary Robinson claimed Kavanagh "suffered the blindness of a society and the tendency of a settled establishment to regard any artist as a nuisance who disrupts its peace." Photograph of statue printed on front page.

3 BERTHA, CSILLA. "Thomas Murphy's Psychological Explorations." In *More Real Than Reality. The Fantastic in Irish Literature and the Art* edited by Donald E. Morse and Csilla Bertha. New York: Greenwood Press, pp. 179–190.
Brief reference to Tom MacIntyre's *The Great Hunger*.

4 BROWN, TERENCE. "The Counter-Revival 1930–1965: Poetry." In Deane (1991.9), pp. 129–134.
Notes that Kavanagh had a "phobia" about Yeats. Describes his life and career, his early education, and his dismissal of the Revival. *The Great Hunger* offered a "realistic riposte to the Revival's romantic pastoralism." Kavanagh believed Joyce, not Yeats, had given a voice to the Irish mind.

5 BYRNE, ART, and SEAN MCMAHON. "Patrick Kavanagh 1904–1967." *Great Northerners*. Dublin: Poolbeg, pp. 114–115.
Biographical sketch of the poet.

*6 COLL, JOHN. "News Bulletin. Weekly Arts Review." RTE TV program. Accession no. BN144/910. Transmitted 24 May. Duration: 6 minutes, 42 seconds.
Interview with John Coll, sculptor of the Kavanagh bronze statue at the Grand Canal.

1991

7 CRONIN, ANTHONY. "Three Irish Writers." *Arena*. BBC2 TV program. Transmitted Friday 15 March. Written and presented by Anthony Cronin, researched by Rosemarie Bradford, produced by Kate Maynell and Rosemary Wilton.
    Documentary film on Kavanagh, Brendan Behan, and Flann O'Brien in Dublin in the forties and fifties. Interviews people in the Baggott Street area who knew Kavanagh.

8 DAWE, GERALD. *How's the Poetry Going? Literary Politics & Ireland Today*. Belfast: Lagan Press, pp. 26–32.
    Describes clichés about the poet in Ireland, and how Kavanagh fought those clichés. Disapproves of the way certain sectors of Irish society treated Kavanagh during his lifetime and of the "graceless manoeuvrings literally over his grave."

9 DEANE, SEAMUS, ed. *Field Day Anthology of Irish Writing*. Vol. 3. Derry: Field Day Publications. 1483 pp.
    Contains Brown (1991.4) and Kiberd (1991.18).

10 DURCAN, PAUL. "The Levite and His Concubine At Gribeah." *Crazy About Women*. Dublin: National Gallery of Ireland, pp. 45–47.
    Humorous poem in which the speaker is Mrs. Kerr of Dundalk. Refers to Kavanagh. Quotes first line of "Kerr's Ass."

11 FOSTER, JOHN WILSON. "The Poetry of Patrick Kavanagh." In *Colonial Consequences: Essays in Irish Literature and Culture*. Dublin: Lilliput, pp. 97–113.
    Reprint of Foster (1979.11).

12 GREACEN, ROBERT. "Encounters with Kavanagh." In *Brief Encounters: Literary Dublin and Belfast in the 1940s*. Dublin: Cathair Books, pp. 39–47.
    Recalls his acquaintance with Kavanagh in the forties.

*13 ——. "Sunday Miscellany. Patrick Kavanagh." RTE Radio broadcast. Accession no. D00717. Transmitted 3 November. Duration: 7 minutes, 18 seconds.
    Robert Greacen recalls Kavanagh as a fellow boarder in a boarding house in Raglan Road.

14 HIRSCH, EDWARD. "The Imaginary Irish Peasant." *PMLA* 106, no. 5 (October):1116–1133.
    Examines Kavanagh's rejection of the Revival, arguing that he came to the literary world "with a furious sense of belatedness." Kavanagh's distinc-

1991

tion between provincialism and parochialism influenced all his later work. The most important Irish poet since Yeats, he provided a model for younger Irish poets, especially in the sixties.

*15 HOWLETT, MICHAEL. *The Human Condition in the Writings of Patrick Kavanagh (1904–1967): A Theological Exploration.* Th.D. dissertation, Pontificia Universitas Gregoriana (Vatican). 684 pp. See DAI-C 53/04 (Winter 1992):619.

Describes Kavanagh's career and achievement in light of the poet's reflection on the meaning of human life. Argues that, for Kavanagh, humans are born in tragedy but may find rebirth in a state of openness to God.

16 JORDAN, JOHN. *Collected Poems.* Dublin: Dedalus Press.

Includes several poems which make reference to Kavanagh, including "Wordsworth Was Right" (p.44), "Abbey Press Lunch" (p.199), "Patrick (1904–1967)" (p.120), "P.K" (p.120), and "Two Years Ago" (p.129).

17 "Kavanagh's Yearly." *IrishTimes*, Weekend Supplement (16 November):5.

Announces forthcoming annual Kavanagh celebration at Inniskeen (November 22–24), including Declan Kiberd's keynote address, "Kavanagh: Criticism and the National Bucklep."

18 KIBERD, DECLAN. "Contemporary Irish Poetry." In Deane (1991.9), pp. 1309–1316.

Discusses the "sense of anticlimax" in Ireland after the deaths of Yeats and Joyce and the struggle of the new generation of writers, including Kavanagh, against insular provincialism. Claims Kavanagh and others in the fifties sought to "interrogate the mythic with the quotidian banal." The influence of Auden was felt in Irish poetry through the work of Kavanagh.

19 KIELY, BENEDICT. *Drink to the Bird. A Memoir.* London: Methuen, p. 151.
Recalls first reading about Kavanagh in a newspaper article.

20 KINOULTY, JOHN CHARLES. *A Biographical Dictionary of Ireland. From 1500.* Belfast: Kinoulty family, p. 350.
Biographical entry on the poet.

21 MCDONALD, PETER. "History and Poetry: Derek Mahon and Tom Paulin." In *The Poet's Place*, edited by Gerald Dawe and John Wilson Foster. Belfast: Institute of Irish Studies, pp. 193–208.
Brief reference to Kavanagh's influence on Heaney.

1991

22 MCGUINNESS, ARTHUR. "Seamus Heaney: The Forging Pilgrim." *Essays in Literature (Macomb, IL)* 18 (Spring):46–67.
Briefly discusses Kavanagh's ghost in *Station Island*.

*23 "News Bulletin. Patrick Kavanagh Statue." RTE TV program. Accession no. BN162/91T. Transmitted 11 June. Duration: 30 seconds.
Film of President Mary Robinson unveiling John Coll's statue of Kavanagh at the the Grand Canal.

24 O'BRIEN, MARGARET. "William Carleton: the Lough Derg Exile." In *Irish Writing: Exile and Subversion*, edited by Paul Hyland and Neil Sammells. London: Macmillan, pp. 82–97.
Contains brief discussion of intertextual relations between Carleton's, Kavanagh's, and Heaney's treatments of Lough Derg.

25 O'BYRNE, ROBERT. "Savouring the Poetic Spirit: Skipping over the Buckleps." *Irish Times* (27 November):10.
Describes both academic and social activities at the Kavanagh's Yearly at Carrickmacross, which featured guest speakers Declan Kiberd, Antoinette Quinn, Sean MacMathuna, and Desmond O'Grady. Writers Dermot Healey, Julie O'Callaghan, and Frank Ormsby read from their work. The poetic spirit was savored late into the night at the Nuremore Hotel, Carrickmacross.

26 O'LOUGHLIN, MICHAEL. "Frank Ryan: Journey to the Centre." In *Letters from the New Island*. Edited by Dermot Bolger. Dublin: Raven Arts Press, pp. 56–72.
In the course of a general meditation on Frank Ryan and the Spanish Civil War, discusses Ireland's place in Europe during the war years in relation to Kavanagh's *Lough Derg*. Claims the poem is "a profoundly political document, showing the moral price that had to be paid for neutrality."

27 POPOWICH, BARRY. "Patrick Kavanagh's Space Beyond Time." *Canadian Journal of Irish Studies* 17, no. 2:31–38.
Argues that Kavanagh has an acute sense of the spatial, whereas Clarke, MacNeice and Yeats are more interested in temporal or historical perspectives in their poetry. Discusses Heaney's essay "A Placeless Heaven." Examines Kavanagh's spatial thinking in *The Great Hunger* and *Tarry Flynn*.

28 PRITCHETT, V. S. *Dublin*. London: Hogarth Press, pp. 13, 32.
A few brief references to Kavanagh.

1991

29   QUINN, ANTOINETTE. *Patrick Kavanagh: Born-Again Romantic*. Dublin: Gill & Macmillan. 493 pp.
   Consists of eleven chapters plus conclusion and select bibliography. Chapter one considers the poetry to 1939, which, given the poet's social and educational background, reflects a "triumph over almost insuperable odds." Considers the poet's development in the thirties to have been "spasmodic." Chapter two examines *The Green Fool* as autobiographical fiction and as a work of art. Argues that the book reflects a tension between Revival aesthetics and local realism, although the realist mode is dominant. Claims the expansive genre of prose fiction allowed Kavanagh to break free from lyric constraints, which led to the narrative verse of the longer poems. Chapter three considers the poems, 1939–1942, which were "glorious years for his poetry," during which time he developed the tones of "sociological narrative." In a number of poems, including "Stony Grey Soil," the poet anticipates the stance of *The Great Hunger*, which is the subject of the fourth chapter. Offers a close, sustained reading of the poem. Chapter five explores Kavanagh's upholding of Irish Catholic culture as a bulwark against Ascendancy literary culture, up to and including the composition of *Lough Derg*, which is examined in light of Kavanagh's interest in Catholic pilgrimage as a blend of sacred and secular. Chapter six examines Kavanagh's parish myth, drawing upon Quinn's earlier essay on the subject (1989.34), and including consideration of *Tarry Flynn*. Chapter seven looks at the poet as cultural critic and verse satirist in Dublin, 1942–1956, arguing that his decision to channel his talent into these roles was "brave but foolhardy." In chapter eight, discusses Kavanagh's "urban self-image" in the poetry, and in chapter nine, examines the "new introversion" of the poems after 1950, when he foregrounds the distinction between public persona and private poet and develops the trope of Parnassus in his work. During this period, Kavanagh is "an introverted rural exile." Chapter ten deals with the cancer operation and the subsequent recuperative period when he produced the Canal Bank poems, *Come Dance with Kitty Stobling*, and eventually the automythologizing of *Self Portrait*. Examines the poet's construction of the myth of his life as journey and hegira. In the eleventh chapter, discusses his poetry of the sixties. Concludes that Kavanagh is a "born-again Romantic," manifesting the egotism and sublimity of Romantic poetry in a modern Irish poetic.

30   ———. *Patrick Kavanagh: A Critical Study*. Syracuse: Syracuse University Press. 493 pp.
   American edition of Quinn (1991.29).

31   VAN DE KAMP, PETER. "Desmond Egan: Universal Provincialist." In *The Crows Behind the Plough. History and Violence in Anglo-Irish Poetry and Drama*. Edited by Geert Lernout. Amsterdam and Atlanta, Ga.: Rodopi, pp. 143–158.

Alludes to Kavanagh's stress on the universality of the local and the influence of this outlook on Egan, who has "acknowledged Kavanagh as a predecessor."

32 WATSON, GEORGE. "Landscape in Ulster Poetry." In *The Poet's Place. Ulster Literature and Society. Essays in Honour of John Hewitt, 1907–1987*, edited by Gerald Dawe and John Wilson Foster. Belfast: Institute of Irish Studies, pp. 1–15.

Discusses the sense of place and the image of the land in Ulster poetry, and contrasts Kavanagh's neutral landscape with the archetypal, archaeological landscape of Heaney.

1992

1 ALLEN, MICHAEL. "'Holding Course': *The Haw Lantern* and its Place in Heaney's Development." In Andrews (1992.4), pp. 193–207.

Brief reference to Kavanagh's notion of the parish, in connection with Heaney's "folk values." Also, detects a "Kavanagh-like rural muse" in Heaney's poem "Making Strange."

2 ANDREWS, ELMER, ed. *Contemporary Irish Poetry. A Collection of Critical Essays*. London: Macmillan. 344 pp.

Contains Andrews (1992.3), Kearney (1992.19), McDonald (1992.25), Ni Chuilleanain (1992.27), and Welch (1992.37).

3 ———. Introduction to Andrews (1992.2), pp. 1–24.

Claims that Kavanagh "has the greatest influence of all on contemporary Irish poetry." He did for the representation of rural life what Joyce did for the depiction of the urban. Compares Kavanagh's regionalism to that of Hewitt and McFadden.

4 ———, ed. *Seamus Heaney: A Collection of Critical Essays*. London: Macmillan. 273 pp.

Contains Allen (1992.1), Andrews (1992.5), Lucas (1992.22), Simmons (1992.33), and Simpson (1992.34).

5 ———. "The Spirit's Protest." In Andrews (1992.4), pp. 208–232.

Uses the early Heaney poem "Honeymoon Flight" to illustrate how Heaney was intrigued by Kavanagh's notion of "weightlessness" in poetry.

6 ARKINS, BRIAN. *Desmond Egan: A Critical Study*. Little Rock, Arkansas: Milestone Press, pp. 14, 17, 18, 20, 21.

Briefly refers to Kavanagh's concept of the parochial.

1992

7 BEHAN, BRENDAN. *Letters of Brendan Behan*. Edited by E. H. Mikhail. London: Macmillan, and Montreal & Kingston: McGill—Queen's University Press, pp. 49–50, 53–57, 69–73, 202.
   Includes letter to *Kavanagh's Weekly* in 1952, and a letter in which he calls Kavanagh "the wanker poet and peasant." Refers to Kavanagh's "disciples" in the bars of Dublin. An unpublished letter to the *Irish Times* concerns Kavanagh's lectures at UCD, in which he calls Kavanagh "our border Proust."

8 BELL, BRIAN, ed. *Insight Guides: Ireland*. Dublin: APA publications, pp. 102, 253.
   Brief references to Kavanagh.

9 BORAN, PAT. "Shadows and Apples." *Colby Quarterly* 28, no. 4 (December):220–226.
   Discusses influence of Kavanagh and Yeats on Irish poetry.

*10 BYRNE, GAY. "Late Late Show." RTE TV program. Accession no. HX90/3240. Transmitted 6 March. Duration: 58 minutes.
   Gay Byrne interviews John and Tom McArdle about Kavanagh.

11 CORCORAN, NEIL, ed. *The Chosen Ground: Essays on the Contemporary Poetry of Northern Ireland*. Chester Springs, Pa.: Dufour Editions, and Bridgend, Wales: Seren Books. 288 pp.
   Contains McDonald (1992.26), O'Donoghue (1992.28), and Smith (1992.35).

12 DENMAN, PETER. "Ghosts in Anglo-Irish Literature." In Welch (1992.36), pp. 62–74.
   Compares the appearance of Homer's ghost in "Epic" to the appearance of Plato's Ghost in Yeats's poetry and other manifestations in Kinsella and Heaney.

13 DONOVAN, STEWART. "Finn in Shabby Diggs: Myth and the Reductionist Process in *At Swim-Two-Birds*." *Antigonish Review*, number 90 (Summer): 147–155.
   Briefly discusses Kavanagh's poem "In Memory of Brother Michael" as representative of the "anger, frustration and disillusionment" shared by Irish writers from 1933 to 1955.

14 EGAN, DESMOND. *For Sam Beckett on His 80th Birthday*. In Welch (1992.36), p. 193.
   Poem containing brief reference to Kavanagh.

15 ——. "Religion?" In Welch (1992.36), pp. 190–192.
   References to Kavanagh as religious poet.

1992

16 GOODBY, JOHN. "Irish Bards and English Reviewers: The Reception of Contemporary Irish Poetry in England." In *The Internationalism of Irish Literature and Drama* (Irish Literary Studies 41), edited by Joseph McMinn. Savage, Maryland: Barnes & Noble, pp. 171–180.

   Discusses the contemporary popularity, or otherwise, of rural poetry. Notes that "Kavanagh, the most 'rural' of all modern Irish poets, has made very little headway in the popularity stakes," whereas the urbane Paul Muldoon is very popular.

17 GRENNAN, EAMON. "Contemporary Irish Poetry." *Colby Quarterly* 28, no. 4 (December):184.

   Claims Kavanagh is the "indispensable forerunner" of contemporary Irish poetry.

18 HART, HENRY. *Seamus Heaney: Poet of Contrary Progressions*. Syracuse: Syracuse University Press, pp. 7, 10, 12, 21, 160, 170–171, 177.

   Discusses Heaney's essays on Kavanagh and his presentation of the poet in *Station Island*. Compares Heaney's view of Lough Derg with Kavanagh's.

19 KEARNEY, RICHARD. "Myth and Modernity in Irish Poetry." In Andrews (1992.2), pp. 41–62.

   Discusses Kavanagh's animus against Revivalist myth-making, based on his belief in the "comic spirit," which "scorned the self-importance of Grand Narrative."

20 KIBERD, DECLAN. "Fathers and Sons: Irish-Style." In *Irish Literature and Culture*, edited by Michael Kenneally. Savage, Maryland: Barnes & Noble, pp. 127–157.

   Discusses Maguire's relationship with his mother in *The Great Hunger* with regard to the Irish cliché of the smothering, "clutching" mother who prevents her son from leaving her. If this became a common Irish literary theme, Kavanagh described the cost of such love in his poem.

21 LONGLEY, EDNA. "Weekend: Books. Forget Me Not." *Irish Times* (18 January):9.

   Review of Antoinette Quinn, *Patrick Kavanagh: Born-Again Romantic* (1991.29). Claims it is "the authoritative critical study for which lovers of Kavanagh's poetry have been waiting."

22 LUCAS, JOHN. "Seamus Heaney and the Possibilities of Poetry." In Andrews (1992.4), pp. 117–138.

   Brief references to Heaney's essays on Kavanagh. Compares Heaney's "Changes" to Kavanagh's "Kerr's Ass."

1992

23 MACMONAGLE, NIALL, ed. *Lifelines: Letters from Famous People about Their Favourite Poems.* Dublin: Town House and Wesley College, pp. 57, 123, 132, 165, 171, 159, 245, 268.

   The following name a Kavanagh poem as their favorite poem, briefly explaining their choices: Alicia Boyle, Anne Boyle, Cyril Cusack, Mary Harney, Sr. Stanislaus Kennedy, James Plunkett, Annie Taylor, and Martin Waddell.

24 MARTIN, AUGUSTINE. "That Childhood Country. Extracts from a Biography of Patrick Kavanagh." *Irish University Review* 22, no. 1 (Spring):107–126.

   Describes Kavanagh's school years, his teachers, his copybooks, his first encounters with poetry, and his English textbooks and their early influence on him. Discusses the influence of Catholic doctrine and the cult of Mary on the boy's thought, his time as an altar boy, and his later ideas about the priestly vocation of the poet. Explores the impact of world and national events on county Monaghan: the Great War, the Home Rule crisis and the 1918 General Election, the "Troubles," 1919–1921.

25 MCDONALD, PETER. "History and Poetry: Derek Mahon and Tom Paulin." In Andrews (1992.2), pp. 86–106.

   Discusses Paul Muldoon's attitude toward political poetry in light of Kavanagh's caveat about "the important thing" in art.

26 ———. "Michael Longley's Homes." In Corcoran (1992.11), pp. 65–86.

   Brief reference to Kavanagh's use of a place-name in "Kerr's Ass" in the context of a discussion of Longley's use of naming places in order to create a sense of home.

27 NI CHUILLEANAIN, EILEAN. "Borderlands of Irish Poetry." In Andrews (1992.2), pp. 25–40.

   Argues that Kavanagh noticed a problem between poets and their audience in Ireland, and in his work he explored this problematic relationship. Claims his demythologizing aesthetic was welcomed in the sixties, when people had a critical relationship to the state, which was associated with censorship, and wanted to escape myth, to "make the present real." Kavanagh's fame grew simultaneously with mounting opposition to Yeats. Discusses Kavanagh's Catholicism and marriage. Holds that the debate about parochialism "seems finally exhausted."

28 O'DONOGHUE, BERNARD. "Involved Imaginings: Tom Paulin." In Corcoran, (1992.11), pp. 171–188.

Claims Kavanagh was "championed by the *Honest Ulsterman* in the early 1970s as a martyr to the perfidy of Flann O'Brien and the southern capital Dublin."

29 O'GRADY, DESMOND. "Patrick Kavanagh in Rome, 1965: A Personal Memoir." Part I. *Poetry Ireland Review* no. 34, pp. 14–24.

Account of Kavanagh's visit to Rome in 1965, to take part, as a representative of Ireland, in a general meeting of the European Community of Writers, under the presidency of Giuseppe Ungaretti. Describes Kavanagh's stay with O'Grady and family.

30 ——. "Patrick Kavanagh in Rome, 1965: A Personal Memoir." Part II. *Poetry Ireland Review* no. 35, pp. 118–128.

Describes the European Writers Conference, where Kavanagh was frequently photographed and his physiognomy admired. Discusses reception at Russian Embassy and Kavanagh's meeting with Hungarian author Istvan Vas. When Kavanagh met Jean-Paul Sartre, "the two of them got along together like two old cowboys." Expresses gratitude to Kavanagh who encouraged him as a writer.

31 OWENS, COILIN. "Patrick Kavanagh." In *Critical Survey of Poetry*. English Language Series. Revised Edition. Vol. four. Edited by Frank Magill. Salem Press, pp. 1761–1768.

Reprint of Owens (1982.24).

32 PEACOCK, ALAN. "Received Religion and Secular Vision: MacNeice and Kavanagh." In Welch (1992.36), pp. 148–168.

Claims Kavanagh is the "antithesis" of MacNeice, although they both share certain stylistic features, such as a conversational style and "conversational artlessness." During his Canal Bank period, Kavanagh was "like a down-at-heel Beckett character." Discusses Kavanagh's search for the universal in the particular.

33 SIMMONS, JAMES. "The Trouble with Seamus." In Andrews (1992.4), pp. 39–66.

Finds, in general, that Heaney does not measure up as a poet to Kavanagh and Yeats. Mentions influence of Kavanagh on "At a Potato Digging" and "Bog Oak," which is seen as "a companion poem" to Kavanagh's "Memory of Brother Michael."

34 SIMPSON, LOUIS. "Irish Ghosts: 'Station Island.'" In Andrews (1992.4), pp. 139–149.

Claims that Kavanagh is "as humorous and satiric in death as he was in life" in Heaney's poem *Station Island*.

1993

35 SMITH, STAN. "Seamus Heaney: The Distance Between." In Corcoran (1992.11), pp. 35–64.
   Discusses Heaney's treatment of Kavanagh in his essay "The Sense of Place" and mentions influence on Heaney of Kavanagh's concept of the parish. Holds that "The Old Team" is Heaney's "most Kavanaghish poem [sic]."

36 WELCH, ROBERT, ed. *Irish Writers and Religion.* Irish Literary Studies 37. Gerrards Cross, Bucks: Colin Smythe, and Totowa, N.J.: Barnes & Noble. 250 pp.
   Contains Denman (1992.12), Egan (1992.14–15), Peacock (1992.32).

37 ———. "'A Rich Young Man Leaving Everything He Had': Poetic Freedom in Seamus Heaney." In Andrews (1992.2), pp. 150–181.
   In *Station Island*, Kavanagh is Heaney's "Zen master." Discusses the sense of spiritual clarity in Heaney's "Clearances," which he learned from Kavanagh.

1993

*1 AGNEW, UNA. "Religious Themes in the Work of Patrick Kavanagh: Hints of a Celtic Tradition." *Studies* 82, no. 327:257–275.
   Essay on Kavanagh.

*2 ANDERSSON, ERIK. "Svarta Kullar, Gronskande Kanal: Introduktion till Patrick Kavanagh (1904–1967)." *Ord Och Bild* (Frolunda, Sweden) 102, no. 3:19–24.
   Essay on Kavanagh.

3 BERTHA, CSILLA. "The Fantastic In Irish Drama." In *A Small Nation's Contribution to the World: Essays on Anglo-Irish Literature and Language.* Edited by Donald Morse, Csilla Bertha, Istvan Palffy. Gerrards Cross: Colin Smythe, and Debrecen: Lajos Kossuth University Press, pp. 28–42.
   Discusses MacIntyre's adaptation of *The Great Hunger*.

4 BOLAND, EAVAN. "Continuing the Encounter." In *Ordinary People Dancing: Essays on Kate O'Brien.* Edited by Eibhear Walshe. Cork: Cork University Press, p. 20.
   Refers to Kavanagh's attack on the Revival and on Anglo-Irish metropolitan literary culture, with reference to the woman writer.

5 BOLGER, DERMOT. *The Picador Book of Irish Contemporary Fiction.* London: Picador, pp. vii–xxvi.
   Kavanagh is "Ireland's most important poet after Yeats."

1993

6 BOURKE, EOIN. "Poetic Outrage: Aspects of Social Criticism in Modern Irish Poetry." In *A Small Nation's Contribution to the World: Essays on Anglo-Irish Literature and Language*, edited by Donald Morse, Csilla Bertha, and Istvan Palffy. Gerrards Cross, Bucks: Colin Smythe, and Debrecen: Lajos Kossuth University Press, pp. 88–106.
   Refers to Kavanagh's indictment of religion and capitalism in *The Great Hunger*.

7 CAHALAN, JAMES M. *Modern Irish Literature and Culture: A Chronology*. New York: G. K. Hall, pp. 17, 228–229, 233, 238, 243, 249, 251, 253, 268, 274, 275, 295.
   Biographical entry on poet, and reference to Kavanagh's contributions to the journals *Irish Writing*, *Envoy*, *The Bell*, and *Arena*. Briefly refers to publication of each of the major works.

8 CAULFIELD, MAX. *Ireland*. Dublin: Gill & Macmillan, pp. 19, 28.
   Brief references to Kavanagh.

9 CORCORAN, NEIL. *English Poetry since 1940*. London, New York: Longman, pp. 180, 184.
   Describes the influence of Kavanagh on Irish poetry as "the strategic filling-in of a gapped Irish tradition."

10 FLEMING, DEBORAH. "The Common Ground of Eamonn Grennan." *Eire* 28, no. 4 (Winter):133–149.
   Occasional references to Kavanagh. Grennan claims Kavanagh "made contemporary Irish poetry possible."

*11 HEDLAND, MAGNUS. "Tre Processer: En Sammanstallning." *Ord Och Bild* 102, no. 3:85–90.
   Discusses Kavanagh's *The Green Fool*, as well as works by Gogarty and Beckett.

12 KENNELLY, BRENDAN. Introduction to *Between Innocence and Peace: Favourite Poems of Ireland*. Dublin: Mercier Press, pp. 9–11.
   Explains why he loves Kavanagh's work, which is as "fresh" to him now as it was forty years ago. Claims Kavanagh "wrote out of humility" and his poetry often reached "sublimity."

13 MERRILL, THOMAS F. Review of Quinn, *Patrick Kavanagh: A Critical Study* (1991.30). *Journal of Irish Literature* 22, no. 1 (January):62–63.
   Claims Kavanagh is not popular in America. Praises Quinn's book.

1993

14 MILLER, KARL. *Rebecca's Vest*. London: Hamish Hamilton, pp. 160–161.
Briefly recalls meeting Kavanagh ("Irish poet and misanthrope"), at a soccer game in Battersea Park, London.

15 MOORMAN, CHARLES W. "Kavanagh, Heaney, and the Anti-Revival in Poetry." *The Celtic Literature of Defeat: An Extraordinary Assortment of Irregularities*. Lewiston, N.Y.; Queenston, Ontario; Lampeter, Wales: Edwin Mellen Press, pp. 111–130.
Argues that all Irish literature reflects a heritage of cultural defeat. Discusses Kavanagh's part in the counter-Revival and the rejection of Yeats's noble peasant in *The Great Hunger*. Compares and contrasts Beckett to Kavanagh, arguing that their common Irish background produces a similarity of cadence in their poetic language. Compares Kavanagh to Heaney.

16 NEWMANN, KATE (compiler). *Dictionary of Ulster Biography*. Belfast: Institute of Irish Studies, p. 123.
Biographical entry on the poet.

17 PARKER, MICHAEL. *Seamus Heaney: The Making of the Poet*. Iowa City: University of Iowa Press, pp. 24, 29, 30–36, 39, 47, 62, 69–71, 74, 76, 79, 88, 146, 167, 183, 192, 193, 194, 198, 199.
Recurrent allusions to Kavanagh's influence on Heaney, particularly in relation to *The Green Fool*, *The Great Hunger*, and *A Soul For Sale*. Discusses Heaney's essays on Kavanagh, his view of Kavanagh's idea of the parish, and echoes of *The Great Hunger* in "At a Potato Digging." Examines an early Heaney poem about a character called "Mackenna," supposedly based on Kavanagh's Maguire.

18 SAMPSON, DENIS. *Outstaring Nature's Eye: The Fiction of John McGahern*. Dublin: Lilliput, pp. 12, 78, 245.
Refers to Kavanagh's sense of local place in "Epic." Compares McGahern's potato-picking scene in *Amongst Women* with details in *The Great Hunger*.

19 WELCH, ROBERT. *Changing States: Transformations in Modern Irish Writing*. London and New York: Routledge, pp. 104, 153, 266–268.
Makes several brief references to Kavanagh. Attributes the later Heaney's sense of metaphysical clarity to Kavanagh's influence.

20 WHELAN, KEVIN. "The Bases of Regionalism." *Culture in Ireland. Regions: Identity and Power*. Edited by Proinsias O'Drisceoil. Belfast: Institute of Irish Studies, pp. 5–63.

1994

In a wide-ranging examination of Irish regionalism, discusses Kavanagh's "Epic" as "the classic celebration of the townland's centrality." Alludes to Kavanagh's notion of parochialism.

1994

*1 BARNES, RITA MARLENE. *Patrick Kavanagh and the Materials of Modern Irish Poetry.* Ph.D. dissertation, University of Massachusetts. 320 pp. See DAI-A 55/11 (May 1995):3506.

Argues that Kavanagh has been variously called an asocial realist and a Romantic lyricist, and that his "varied and often mixed literary strategies responded satirically to his cultural milieu throughout his career."

2 BETJEMAN, JOHN. *John Betjeman: Letters. Vol. One: 1926 to 1951.* Edited by Candida Lycett Green. London: Methuen, pp. 271, 297, 300, 330.

Occasional references to Kavanagh ("who used JB [John Betjeman] mercilessly to help him promote his work.") In letter of December 30, 1941, addressed to Cyril Connolly, Betjeman praises *The Great Hunger.* "The total effect is grand." Alludes to Kavanagh's poverty.

3 DAWE, GERALD. "'And Then—The Spring!': Brendan Kennelly's *Breathing Spaces.*" In Pine (1994.21), pp. 59–65.

Explores the influence on Kennelly of Kavanagh's sense of a lack of a poetry audience in Ireland.

4 FOLEY, MICHAEL. "Sitting with Kavanagh by the Grand Canal." *Insomnia in the Afternoon.* Belfast: Blackstaff, pp. 98–100.

Humorous poem about the commercialization of the Pembroke Road area where Kavanagh lived, and about John Coll's ICI-funded bronze statue of the poet by the Grand Canal.

5 HART, HENRY. "What is Heaney seeing in *Seeing Things?*" *Colby Quarterly* 30, no. 1 (March):33.

Briefly discusses the influence of Kavanagh on the later poetry of Heaney.

6 KAVANAGH, P. J. *Voices in Ireland: A Traveller's Literary Companion.* London: John Murray, pp. 46–47, 83, 85–87, 144, 290, 298.

Brief references to the poet and to "Kavanagh country."

7 KENNELLY, BRENDAN. "Patrick Kavanagh's Comic Vision." In *Journey Into Joy.* Edited by Ake Persson. Newcastle: Bloodaxe, pp. 109–126.

Reprint of Kennelly (1970.12).

1994

8   LONGLEY, EDNA. *The Living Stream: Literature and Revisionism in Ireland*. Newcastle: Bloodaxe. 302 pp.
    Contains Longley (1994.9–13).

9   ———. "Defending Ireland's Soul: Protestant Writers and Irish Nationalism after Independence." In Longley (1994.8), pp. 130–149.
    Discusses Hubert Butler's reaction to Kavanagh's dismissal of the Revival.

10 ———. "From Cathleen to Anorexia: *The Breakdown of Irelands*." In Longley (1994.8), pp. 173–195.
    Reprint of Longley (1990.19).

11 ———. "Introduction: Revising 'Irish Literature.'" In Longley (1994.8), pp. 9–68.
    Brief references to Kavanagh. Compares his "A Christmas Childhood" with Louis MacNeice's "Carrickfergus" as parish poems.

12 ———. "Progressive Bookmen: Left-wing Politics and Ulster Protestant Writers." In Longley (1994.8), pp. 109–129.
    Brief references to Kavanagh. Contrasts MacNeice's stress on "community" with Kavanagh's stress on "parish."

13 ———. "Poetic Forms and Social Malformations." In Longley (1994.8), pp. 196–226.
    Reprint of Longley (1989.27).

14 ———. "Poetry in Ireland, Scotland, and Wales, 1920–1990." *Columbia History of British Poetry*. Edited by Carl Woodring. New York: Columbia University Press, pp. 605–642.
    Compares Kavanagh to MacNeice, MacDiarmid, Muir, and Dylan Thomas, all of whom were, in their own way, antipuritanical poets. Examines Kavanagh's parochialism, antipastoralism, his opposition to Revival aesthetics, and his objections to "the totalizing Nationalist myth of Ireland." Claims *The Great Hunger* "savages the pastoral idioms" popular in Kavanagh's time.

15 MARTIN, AUGUSTINE. "Technique and Territory in Brendan Kennelly's Early Work." In Pine (1994.21), pp. 36–49.
    Briefly examines Kavanagh's impact on the literary scene in the sixties, which were Kennelly's formative years as a poet. Mentions the influence of "Shancoduff" on Kennelly's poem "My Dark Fathers." Kennelly approved of Kavanagh's impatience with "gallivanting" and "buckleppin."

1994

16 MERCIER, VIVIAN. *Modern Irish Literature: Sources and Founders.* Oxford: Oxford University Press, pp. 327–328.

Questions Kavanagh's distinction between parochial and provincial outlooks, claiming some writers, like Joyce, appear to have both outlooks at once.

17 O'DONOGHUE, BERNARD. "Patrick Kavanagh." In *Oxford Companion to Twentieth Century Poetry.* Edited by Ian Hamilton. Oxford, New York: Oxford University Press, pp. 267–268.

Biographical entry for the poet, who "gave Irish poetry a salutary shift towards reality, away from its Celtic high ground."

18 O'GRADY, THOMAS B. "At the Crossroads With Carleton and Joyce: Patrick Kavanagh's *Tarry Flynn*." *Eire* 29, no. 3 (Fall):22–36.

Compares and contrasts *Tarry Flynn* with Joyce's *Portrait* in light of Kavanagh's claims that his novel was the only authentic account of modern Irish life. Claims there are themes common to both novels, and in each case the protagonist rejects his home. However, Kavanagh has less critical distance from his protagonist than Joyce has from his. Claims *Tarry Flynn* recalls the rustic fiction of Carleton.

19 PERSSON, AKE. Introduction to Brendan Kennelly, *Journey Into Joy: Selected Prose.* Edited by Ake Persson. Bloodaxe, pp. 1–22.

Briefly discusses Kennelly's views on Kavanagh.

20 ———. "The Critic: Towards a Literary Credo." In Pine (1994.21), pp. 148–167.

Briefly discusses "A Man I Knew," Kennelly's poem to Kavanagh (1968.23), and Kennelly's essay on Kavanagh (1970.12).

21 PINE, RICHARD, ed. *Dark Fathers Into Light: Brendan Kennelly.* Newcastle: Bloodaxe. 224 pp.

Contains Dawe (1994.3), Martin (1994.15), Persson (1994.20), and Roche (1994.22).

22 ROCHE, ANTHONY. "*The Book of Judas*: Parody, Double-Cross and Betrayal." In Pine (1994.21), pp. 91–113.

Mentions the influence of Kavanagh's "passionate transitory" on Kennelly's work.

1995

1 ALLEN, MICHAEL. "The Parish and the Dream: Heaney and America, 1969–1987." *Southern Review* 31, no. 3 (Summer):726–738.

Includes passing references to Kavanagh's influential "parochial aesthetic" and its importance for Heaney.

2 BOLAND, EAVAN. "Writing the Political Poem in Ireland." *Southern Review* 31, no. 3 (Summer):485–498.

In a general discussion of political poetry in Ireland, discusses Kavanagh's resistance to politicization and objectification by the Revival, and his insistence on the private vision of poetry. Compares plight of Kavanagh as objectified peasant to plight of Irish women poets, who feel politicized and silenced simultaneously.

3 GLAVIN, ANTHONY. "Parish life, synomonous with real values." *Sunday Tribune Magazine* (1 January):15.

Discusses Kavanagh's view of the parish and the sense of place. Claims Ireland is less insular than America.

4 GRENNAN, EAMON. "Wrestling with Hartnett." *Southern Review* 31, no. 3 (Summer):655–675.

Passing references to Kavanagh's influence on Hartnett.

5 KIBERD, DECLAN. "Underdeveloped Comedy: Patrick Kavanagh." *Southern Review* 31, no. 3 (Summer):714–725.

Compares Kavanagh to Samuel Beckett, arguing that both wrote about economic, religious, and intellectual underdevelopment, as exemplified by *The Great Hunger*. For Beckett, modernity made conventional tragedy impossible; for Kavanagh, tragedy was "underdeveloped comedy," and God's existence made humanity comical. Contrasts Kavanagh's and Beckett's views on God. Kavanagh was a "genuinely postcolonial thinker and poet."

6 KINSELLA, THOMAS. *The Dual Tradition: An Essay on Poetry and Politics in Ireland*. Manchester: Carcanet. 129 pp.

In chapter entitled "Modern Irish Poetry" (pp. 92–110), discusses Beckett, Clarke, Kavanagh, and Irish publishing. Argues that Kavanagh's work was "uneven," his persona "hysterical." Admires a number of poems, including *The Great Hunger* and "Shancoduff," and some of his essays, which contain "a number of profound statements." Kavanagh was indebted to Joyce in formulating distinction between parochialism and provincialism.

1995

7 LONGLEY, EDNA. "Irish Bards and American Audiences." *Southern Review* 31, no. 3 (Summer):757–771.
   Includes brief references to Kavanagh.

8 MILLER, KARL. "When Auden Was Young." *Raritan* 14, no. 4 (Spring):144–152.
   Briefly recalls, in a review of an edition of Auden's juvenilia, Kavanagh's envious assessment of Auden's "well-stocked mind." Argues that Kavanagh's critical remarks "are worth recalling, for all their crafty country-fellow's poor mouth."

9 ROSENTHAL, M. L. "Modern Irish Poetry: Some Notes by an Outsider." *Southern Review* 31, no. 3 (Summer):696–713.
   Discusses Kavanagh's career, paying attention to the influence of his idea of parochialism.

Author Index

A
Abbott, Vivienne, **1986**.1
Adams, Michael, **1968**.2
Agnew, Art, **1984**.1
Agnew, Una, **1991**.1; **1993**.1
Ahern, A.C., **1940**.3
Alexander, Alan, **1980**.1
Allen, Barbara, **1990**.1
Allen, Michael, **1975**.1; **1989**.1; **1992**.1; **1995**.1
Alvarez, A., **1960**.2; **1964**.1
Anders, Jaroslaw, **1976**.1
Andersson, Erik, **1993**.2
Andrews, Elmer, **1985**.1; **1988**.1; **1992**.2-5
Annwn, David, **1984**.2
Arden, John, **1986**.2
Argoff, Jeanne, **1978**.1
Arkins, Brian, **1989**.2; **1992**.6
Armstrong, Robert, **1960**.3
Arnold, Bruce, **1971**.2
'Art Lover,' **1941**.2

B
B., V. A., **1949**.1
Babler, O.F., **1937**.1
Barid, Brian, **1982**.1
'Bandar-Ka-Bai,' **1940**.3
Bardwell, Leland, **1970**.2
Barker, Jonathan, **1987**.2
Barnes, Rita Marlene, **1994**.1
Barrett, Mary, **1960**.4
Barry, Sebastian, **1986**.3
Bates, David R., **1972**.4
Battersby, Eileen, **1991**.2
Behan, Brendan, **1992**.7
Bell, Brian, **1992**.8
Bence-Jones, Mark, **1966**.2
Bertha, Csilla, **1991**.3; **1993**.3

Betjeman, John, **1994**.2
Black, Ciaran, **1990**.2
Blamires, Harry, **1982**.2
Blankenshop, Douglas, **1990**.3
Bloom, Harold, **1986**.4
Bodkin, Thomas, **1960**.5
Bogan, Louise, **1965**.2
Boland, Eavan, **1965**.3; **1967**.2-3; **1970**.3; **1971**.3; **1973**.2; **1981**.1; **1993**.4; **1995**.2
Boland, John, **1971**.4; **1972**.5-6; **1973**.3; **1975**.2
Bold, Alan, **1985**.2
Bolger, Dermot, **1993**.5
Bonaccorso, Richard, **1987**.3
Bonner, H., **1975**.3
Bono, **1988**.26; **1989**.3
Boran, Pat, **1992**.9
Bourke, Brian, **1978**.2
Bourke, Eoin, **1993**.6
Boyd, William, **1978**.3
Boylan, Francis, **1972**.7; **1986**.5
Boylan, Henry, **1978**.4; **1988**.3
Boyle, Alicia, **1992**.23
Boyle, Annie, **1992**.23
Boyle, Patrick, **1972**.8
Bracken, T., **1967**.4
Bradley, Anthony, **1980**.2; **1981**.2; **1983**.2; **1988**.4-5; **1989**.4
Brady, Anne, **1985**.3
Brandes, Rand, **1988**.6
Brazil, David, **1974**.2
Braybrooke, Neville, **1965**.4
Breit, Harvey, **1950**.1
Breslin, Jimmy, **1966**.3
Briscoe, H.V., **1940**.3
Brown, Harold, **1940**.3
Brown, Malcolm, **1972**.9
Brown, Stephen, **1985**.4

Author Index

Brown, Terence, **1975**.5; **1979**.1; **1980**.3; **1981**.3; **1988**.7–10; **1989**.5; **1991**.4
Browne, Vincent, **1984**.3
Brownlow, Timothy, **1968**.3
Bryan, Thomas, **1990**.2
Burgess, Anthony, **1967**.5
Burnham, Richard, **1978**.5
Burris, Sidney, **1990**.4
Butler, Hubert, **1951**.1
Buttel, Robert, **1975**.6
Byrne, Art, **1991**.5
Byrne, Gay, **1992**.10
Byrns, Ruth Katherine, **1951**.2

C

C., N., **1940**.3
Caghill, Liam, **1985**.5
Cahalan, James, **1988**.11; **1993**.7
Cahill, Eileen, **1988**.12
Cahill, Susan, and Thomas, **1973**.5
Cairns, David, **1988**.13
Callaghan, Barry, **1966**.4
Callinan, Brian, **1970**.4
'Candida,' **1967**.6
Cantalupo, Catherine, **1983**.3
Carew, Rivers, **1968**.3
Carey, Edward Pat, **1951**.3
Casey, Daniel J., **1976**.2
Carroll, Joe, **1990**.5
Carroll, Niall, **1966**.5
Carruth, Hayden, **1962**.1
Cassen, Bernard, **1968**.4
Cassidy, Whit, **1940**.3
Caulfield, Max, **1993**.8
Chambers, Harry, **1972**.10
Charlton, Hugh, **1979**.2
Childs, Sister Maryanna, **1968**.5
Clarke, Austin, **1938**.1; **1961**.1; **1968**.6; **1971**.6
Clarke, Desmond, **1985**.4
Cleeve, Brian, **1967**.7; **1985**.3
Clifford, Judy, **1940**.3
Clines, Francis X., **1983**.4
Coffey, Brian, **1978**.6
Coffey, F.A., **1990**.2
Colgan, Maurice, **1987**.4
Coll, John, **1991**.6
Collins, James, **1983**.5
Colum, Padraic, **1947**.1; **1962**.2
Connelly, Frank, **1989**.7
Connolly, Colm, **1988**.14
Conroy, Harry, **1940**.3
Cooper, William, **1971**.7
Corcoran, Neil, **1986**.6; **1992**.11; **1993**.9

Costello, Peter, **1987**.5
Coughlan, Denis, **1975**.7
Craven, Jim, **1967**.8; **1973**.36
Creeley, Robert, **1986**.7
'Critic,' **1949**.3
Cronin, Anthony, **1956**.1; **1960**.6; **1971**.8–9; **1973**.7; **1976**.3–4; **1977**.2–4; **1978**.7; **1980**.4; **1983**.6; **1988**.15; **1989**.8; **1991**.7
Cronin, John, **1990**.6
Cronin, Sean, **1968**.7
Crowley, Jeananne, **1977**.5
Curtayne, Alice, **1966**.6
Curtis, Niall O'Leary, **1941**.2
Cusack, Cyril, **1992**.23
'CUS04,' **1940**.3

D

Dalsimer, Adele, **1984**.4; **1989**.9
Dantanus, Ulf, **1988**.16
Davie, Donald, **1989**.10
Davies, Diane, **1979**.3
Dawe, Gerald, **1983**.7; **1984**.5; **1985**.6; **1989**.11; **1991**.8; **1994**.3
De Breadun, Deaglan, **1984**.6
De Breffny, Brian, **1979**.5
Deale, Edgar, **1959**.1
Deane, Seamus, **1975**.9; **1977**.6; **1979**.4; **1983**.8; **1985**.7; **1986**.8; **1991**.9
Delahanty, James, **1960**.7; **1962**.3,
Denman, Peter, **1981**.5; **1992**.12
Devine, Brian, **1986**.9
Devitt, John, **1986**.10
Dick, Susan, **1989**.12
Dillon, J., **1986**.11
Dilworth, Thomas, **1985**.8
Dodsworth, Martin, **1985**.9
Donleavy, J.P., **1986**.12
Donoghue, Denis, **1958**.1; **1971**.7
Donovan, Stewart, **1992**.13
Downey, Gerry, **1976**.5
Downey, P.K., **1971**.10; **1973**.8
Doyle, Owen, **1986**.13
Drabble, Margaret, **1985**.10
Druska, John Andrew, **1974**.3
Dubreux, Jean-Luc, **1988**.17
Duddy, Brendan, **1987**.6
Duffy, P.J., **1985**.11; **1986**.14
Dunn, Douglas, **1975**.10
Dunne, Lee, **1987**.7
Durcan, Paul, **1968**.16; **1973**.36; **1978**.8; **1980**.4–5; **1987**.8; **1988**.18; **1991**.10

Author Index

E
Eagleton, Terry, **1978**.6
Egan, Desmond, **1973**.36; **1977**.15; **1978**.9; **1983**.9; **1986**.15; **1990**.7–13; **1992**.14–15
Ellmann, Richard, **1974**.4
Etherton, Michael, **1989**.13

F
Fahey, William, **1969**.1
Fainlight, Ruth, **1990**.14
Faller, Kevin, **1968**.11; **1977**.8
Fallis, Richard, **1977**.9
Fallon, Padraic, **1938**.2–3; **1964**.2
Fallon, Peter, **1973**.36; **1990**.15
Farrell, Patrick, **1986**.16
Farrell, William, **1981**.6
Farren, Robert, **1948**.1
Felton, Keith, **1972**.12
Figgis, F.R., **1944**.1
Finneran, Richard J., **1976**.6
Fisher, Emma, **1979**.7
Fisher, Jonathan, **1967**.15
Fitts, Dudley, **1947**.2
Fitzgerald, Mary M., **1983**.10
Fitz-Simon, Christopher, **1968**.12; **1983**.11
Fleck, Richard, **1979**.8
Fleischmann, Ruth, **1983**.12; **1987**.9
Fleming, Deborah, **1993**.10
Fleming, Ronnie, **1978**.10
Fodaski-Black, Martha, **1982**.3
Foley, Donal, **1967**.16; **1974**.5; **1977**.10; **1979**.9
Foley, Michael, **1969**.2; **1972**.13; **1994**.4
Foster, John Wilson, **1979**.10–11; **1987**.10; **1988**.20; **1991**.11
Foster, R.F., **1988**.21
Foster, Thomas, **1989**.14
Frazier, Adrian, **1979**.12–13; **1980**.6; **1983**.13
Freyer, Grattan, **1960**.9; **1968**.13
Friberg, H., **1986**.17

G
Galvin, Patrick, **1958**.2
Ganley, R. B., **1941**.2
Garratt, Robert, **1981**.7; **1986**.19; **1989**.15
Garvey, Joseph, **1978**.11
Gerard, Paul, **1950**.3
Gilbert, Stephen, **1941**.2
Gill, Brendan, **1975**.11
Gillespie, Elgy, **1977**.11; **1985**.13; **1986**.20

Gogan, L. S., **1941**.2
Glavin, Anthony, **1995**.3
'Goldwyn Girls,' **1964**.4
Gonella, Aurora, **1973**.36
Goodby, John, **1986**.21; **1992**.16
Gothberg, Helen, **1989**.16
Grant, Damian, **1973**.9
Greacen, Robert, **1942**.2; **1947**.3; **1969**.3; **1976**.7; **1986**.22–23; **1991**.12–13
Green, Martin, **1968**.15–16; **1972**.14; **1973**.36; **1982**.4; **1988**.22–23
Gregory, Horace, **1948**.2
Grene, Nicholas, **1989**.5
Grennan, Eamon, **1978**.12; **1981**.8; **1986**.24; **1989**.17; **1992**.17; **1995**.4
Grever, Glenn, **1973**.10; **1985**.14
Griffith, H.B., **1951**.5
Grubb, Frederick, **1960**.10
Guinness, Bryan, **1948**.6
Gunton, Sharon, **1982**.5
Gussow, Mel, **1988**.24

H
H., J.R., **1940**.3
H., T., **1964**.5
Haffenden, John, **1979**.14
Hall, Donald, **1960**.11
Halpern, Susan, **1974**.6
Hamburger, Michael, **1973**.11
Hamilton, Iain, **1965**.5
Hand, Michael, **1968**.17; **1970**.7; **1973**.12–13
Harman, M.A., **1964**.6
Harmon, Maurice, **1968**.18; **1974**.7; **1977**.12–14; **1978**.13; **1979**.15; **1982**.6; **1984**.7; **1985**.15
Harney, Mary, **1992**.23
Harsch, Sandol, **1966**.7
Hart, Henry, **1992**.18; **1994**.5
Hartnett, Michael, **1968**.19; **1970**.3
Harvey, Francis, **1973**.36
Harvey, N.S., **1940**.3
Hayman, Ronald, **1967**.19
Harrity, Richard, **1949**.4
Heaney, Seamus, **1963**.1–2; **1970**.3; **1972**.15; **1974**.9; **1975**.12–14; **1979**.16; **1980**.7–8; **1983**.14; **1984**.8–9; **1986**.25; **1987**.11; **1988**.25; **1989**.18–19
Hedland, Magnus, **1993**.11
Hegarty, Noirin, **1990**.16
Hennigan, Aidan, **1969**.4
Hewitt, John, **1961**.3

Author Index

Hewson, Paul (Bono), **1988**.26; **1989**.3
Higgins, Brian, **1964**.7
Hirsch, Edward, **1991**.14
Hirst, Desiree, **1978**.14; **1987**.12–13
Hitchens, Christopher, **1987**.14
Hobsbaum, Philip, **1979**.17; **1982**.7; **1985**.16
Hogan, James, **1969**.5
Hogan, Robert, **1968**.20
Hogan, Thomas, **1950**.4
Holland, Jack, **1979**.18
Holloway, John, **1961**.4
Holohan, Leo, **1962**.4; **1967**.20
Holzapfel, Rudi, **1973**.36
Hooker, Jeremy, **1982**.8
Horgan, John, **1964**.8; **1967**.21
Hornby, Richard, **1988**.27
Housin, Severin, **1981**.9
Houston, Douglas, **1988**.28
Howard, Ben, **1987**.15–16
Howlett, Michael, **1991**.15
Hughes, Eamon, **1989**.20; **1990**.17
Hunter, Francis L., **1949**.5
Hurley, Vincent, **1988**.29
Hutchins, Patricia, **1976**.8

I
Igoe, Vivien, **1978**.15
Iremonger, Valentin, **1946**.1
'Isotta Degli Atti,' **1940**.3

J
J., F. L., **1940**.3
Jackson, Alasdair, **1985**.17
Jackson, John S. **1941**.2
Jacob, T. F. Harvey, **1941**.2
Jacobsen, Kurt, **1988**.30
James, Hilaire, **1950**.5
Jaquin, Danielle, **1987**.17; **1990**.18
Jeffares, A. Norman, **1982**.9; **1985**.18
Jenckes, Norma, **1986**.26
Johnston, Dillon, **1985**.19; **1988**.31
Johnston, Jennifer, **1973**.14
Johnston, Michael, **1987**.18
Jones, Frank F. Prenton, **1940**.3
Jones, K., **1974**.14
Jones, Peter, **1980**.9
Jordan, John, **1960**.12; **1964**.11; **1967**.25; **1968**.21; **1970**.9; **1971**.12 -14; **1973**.15; **1974**.15; **1977**.16; **1978**.16; **1979**.19; **1991**.16
Joyce, Trevor, **1970**.29–30
'Jude the Obscure,' **1972**.17; **1978**.17

K
Kane, Michael, **1970**.10; **1990**.1
Karrer, Wolfgang, **1980**.10
Kavanagh, Katherine, **1977**.17
Kavanagh, P.J., **1994**.6
Kavanagh, Patrick, **1965**.6; **1988**.32
Kavanagh, Peter, **1952**.3; **1960**.13; **1969**.6; **1971**.15; **1972**.18–**19**; 1973.**19**; 1974.**16**; 1977.**18**–19; **1978**.18–22; **1979**.21; **1980**.11; **1981**.10; **1982**.10; **1984**.10; **1986**.28–35; **1987**.19–20; **1989**.21
Keane, John B., **1967**.28
Keane, Michael James, **1984**.13
Kearney, Colbert, **1977**.21
Kearney, Richard, **1992**.19
Keating, Maria, **1983**.15
Kehoe, Kieran, **1976**.10
Kell, Richard, **1960**.14
Kelleher, John V., **1978**.26
Kelleher, Terry, **1972**.22
Kelly, A. A., **1988**.51
Kelly, James W., **1967**.29
Kelly, Michael J., **1987**.21
Kenneally, Michael, **1988**.34; **1989**.25
Kennedy, Maev, **1977**.22
Kennedy, Maurice, **1964**.12
Kennedy, Sr. Stanislaus, **1992**.23
Kennelly, Brendan, **1964**.13; **1966**.9; **1968**.23–24; **1969**.7–8; **1970**.12–13; **1971**.16; **1972**.23–24; **1973**.22,36; **1974**.17; **1979**.23–24; **1981**.11; **1987**.22–23; **1988**.35; **1993**.12; **1994**.7
Kennelly, T.B., **1967**.30
Kenner, Hugh, **1983**.16
Kenny, Fergus, **1981**.12
Kenny, Herbert, **1974**.18
Kerr, Theresa, **1939**.5
Kersnowski, Frank, **1975**.17; **1976**.11
Kiberd, Declan, **1979**.25–26; **1980**.12; **1982**.12; **1986**.36; **1987**.24; **1989**.12; **1989**.26; **1991**.18; **1992**.20; **1995**.5
Kiely, Benedict, **1950**.6; **1956**.2; **1965**.7; **1971**.17–18; **1973**.23; **1991**.19
Kiley, Frederick, **1986**.37
Kilfeather, John, **1980**.13; **1986**.38
Kilfeather, Renee, **1986**.38
Kilroy, Thomas, **1982**.13; **1985**.20
King, Richard, **1938**.5
Kinoulty, John Charles, **1991**.20
Kinsella, Thomas, **1960**.15; **1965**.6;

Author Index

1965.8; **1973**.24; **1974**.19; **1976**.12; **1986**.39; **1995**.6
Klejs, Lene, **1983**.17
Kosok, Heinz, **1982**.14
Krause, David, **1960**.16; **1975**.18; **1982**.15
Kroll, Jack, **1977**.23

L
L., P., **1975**.19
Lambert, Hugh, **1974**.20
Lambkin, W.H., **1940**.3
Lennon, Anthony, **1965**.9
Lennon, Peter, **1974**.21
Leonard, Aoife, **1988**.36–37
Leonard, Hugh, **1975**.20
Leonard, Nicholas, **1981**.13
Liddy, James, **1962**.6; **1963**.3; **1964**.14–15; **1965**.10; **1969**.9; **1971**.19; **1973**.36; **1974**.22; **1978**.28; **1979**.27; **1986**.40; **1987**.25
Loftus, Richard, **1964**.16
Longley, Edna, **1975**.21; **1986**.41–44; **1989**.27; **1990**.19; **1992**.21; **1994**.8–14; **1995**.7
Longley, Michael, **1968**.25; **1977**.24
Loomis, Laird, **1976**.11
Loughlin, Bernard, **1990**.20
Love, Oscar, **1940**.3; **1941**.2
Luby, Tom, **1979**.28
Lucas, John, **1981**.14; **1992**.22
Lucy, Sean, **1973**.25–26; **1979**.29–30
Lyons, J.B., **1980**.14

M
M., H.L., **1949**.6
M., L., **1952**.4
M., S., **1967**.31
MacAonghusa, Proinsias, **1967**.32–33; **1969**.10
MacCaig, Norman, **1960**.17
MacDonnell, James, **1950**.7
MacDonagh, Donagh, **1936**.1; **1944**.3; **1945**.1; **1958**.3
MacDonald, E. A., **1940**.3
MacGlynn, Lochlinn, **1947**.4
MacGonicle, Ewart, **1940**.3
MacGoris, Mary, **1971**.21
MacGough, Freda, **1988**.38
MacIntyre, Tom, **1988**.32; **1988**.39
MacKillop, James, **1987**.32
MacLiammoir, Micheal, **1960**.18
Macm., F., **1937**.2
Macm., M. J., **1947**.5

MacMilcho, Caitlin, **1954**.15
MacMonagle, Niall, **1992**.23
MacMurchadha, Eoin T., **1940**.3
Madden-Simpson, Janet, **1987**.26
Maguire, Aisling, **1986**.45
Mahon, Derek, **1968**.26–27; **1973**.36; **1979**.31; **1990**.15
Mahon-Smith, Walter, **1975**.22; **1976**.13
Mannin, Ethel, **1950**.8
Manning, John F., **1940**.3
Manning, Mary, **1939**.7
Marcus, David, **1948**.3
Martin, Augustine, **1965**.12; **1967**.34–35; **1973**.27; **1985**.21–24; **1986**.46–47; **1988**.41; **1990**.21; **1992**.24; **1994**.15
Mason, Patrick, **1988**.42
Matthews, Aidan, **1979**.32
Matthews, James, **1970**.15; **1983**.18
Matthews, Steven, **1989**.28
'Max,' **1966**.10
Mays, J.C.C., **1989**.29; **1990**.22
McAlernon, Don, **1960**.19; **1962**.7
McArdle, J. Ardle, **1980**.15
McArdle, John, **1979**.33
McArdle, Kathy, **1988**.40
McArdle, Tom, **1987**.27
McCaffey, Angelina, **1941**.2
McCarthy, Colman, **1977**.26
McCarten, John, **1971**.22
McCartin, James, **1982**.16
McCartney, Dorothy W., **1973**.36
McCauley, James, **1982**.17
McClusky, Finbarr, **1980**.16
McCullough, Alan, **1986**.48
McDonald, Peter, **1991**.21; **1992**.25–26
McEneaney, Kevin T., **1985**.25; **1986**.49
McGlinchy, Mary, **1980**.17
McGowan, Garrett, **1967**.36
McGuinn, Nicholas, **1986**.50
McGuinness, Arthur, **1991**.22
McGuinness, Norah, **1941**.2
McGurk, Tom, **1968**.28; **1969**.11; **1973**.28; **1974**.23
McHale, John, **1977**.27
McHugh, Roger, **1982**.6
McInern, **1974**.24; **1976**.14
McInerny, Michael, **1974**.24; **1976**.14
McKenna, Dara, **1990**.2
McKenna, James, **1982**.18
McKeown, Patrick D., **1968**.29
McLaughlin, Philip J., **1983**.19
McLaughlin, Tom, **1969**.12
McLoughlin, D.J., **1987**.28

203

Author Index

McLoughlin, Deborah, **1989**.30
McMahon, Bryan, **1973**.29
McMahon, Nancy Curran, **1981**.15
McMahon, Sean, **1965**.13; **1966**.11; **1968**.30; **1984**.14; **1991**.5
McMillan, Dougald, **1989**.12
McNamara, James, **1980**.18
McNeice, W.G., **1967**.37
Meir, Colin, **1980**.19; **1982**.19
Mercier, Vivien, **1947**.6; **1962**.8; **1994**.16
Meredith, David, **1940**.3
Merrill, Thomas F., **1993**.13
Mikhail, E. H., **1982**.20
Miller, Cecilia Parsons, **1973**.36
Miller, Karl, **1993**.14; **1995**.8
Miller, Liam, **1970**.3; **1972**.25
Milne, Elizabeth, **1941**.2
Milne, Ewart, **1940**.3; **1941**.2; **1947**.7; **1948**.4; **1950**.9; **1956**.3; **1986**.51
Molino, Michael, **1987**.29
Montague, John, **1957**.1; **1958**.4; **1959**.2; **1960**.20; **1965**.14; **1966**.12; **1967**.38; **1968**.31; **1972**.26; **1973**.30; **1974**.25; **1976**.15; **1979**.34; **1980**.20; **1989**.31
Montgomery, Niall, **1940**.3
Mooney, Donal, **1962**.9
Moore, John Rees, **1966**.13; **1987**.30
Moorman, Charles W., **1993**.15
Moraes, Dom, **1960**.21
Morgan, Matthew, **1951**.6
Morrison, Blake, **1980**.21; **1982**.21
Morrow, G., **1983**.20
Morrow, Larry, **1948**.5; **1977**.28; **1986**.52
Mulligan, Arthur, **1956**.4
Mulvaney, Terence, **1940**.3
Muri, Alison, **1990**.23
Murphy, Bruce, **1985**.27
Murphy, Daniel, **1985**.28; **1987**.31
Murphy, Hayden, **1973**.36
Murphy, Jimmy, **1990**.2
Murphy, Maureen, **1981**.16; **1987**.32
Murphy, Mike, **1988**.43
Murphy, Richard, **1965**.15
Murray, Gerard Majella, **1949**.7
Myers, Kevin, **1985**.29

N

Na Gcopaleen, Myles, **1950**.10
Natterstadt, J.H., **1982**.22
Needham, Wilbur, **1939**.8
Nemo, John, **1971**.24; **1973**.31; **1974**.26; **1975**.23–24; **1977**.29–31; **1979**.35–37; **1982**.23; **1983**.21; **1984**.1

Newman, Kate, **1993**.16
Newton, J.M., **1965**.16
'Nichevo,' **1951**.5
Ni Chuilleanain, Eilean, **1979**.38; **1992**.27
Nicolson, Harold, **1938**.6
Ni Nuadhain, Mairead, **1989**.32
Nisbet, Tom, **1977**.33; **1990**.2
Nowlan, Kevin, **1977**.34
Nulty, Oliver, **1990**.2
Nye, Robert, **1973**.32

O

Obarn, F. McEwe, **1940**.3
O'Beolain, Art, **1968**.33
O'Brien, Conor Cruise, **1978**.30
O'Brien, Darcy, **1975**.25; **1988**.44
O'Brien, Eamon, **1973**.33
O'Brien, F., **1940**.3; **1941**.2
O'Brien, George, **1986**.53
O'Brien, Margaret, **1986**.54; **1991**.24
O'Byrne, Robert, **1991**.25
O'Callaghan, Kate, **1986**.55
O'Cascy, Scan, **1975**.26; **1980**.22
O'Cleirigh, Gearoid, **1985**.30
O'Conaill, Donal, **1962**.10
O'Connor, Frank, **1942**.3; **1942**.4; **1964**.17; **1967**.41
O'Connor, Kevin, **1976**.16–17
O'Connor, Lir, **1940**.3
O'Connor, Miss "Alas" Luna, **1940**.3
O'Connor, P. J., **1977**.35
O'Connor, Patricia, **1948**.6
O'Connor, Ulick, **1966**.14; **1970**.16; **1972**.27; **1980**.23; **1984**.16
O'Dea, Tom, **1990**.25
O'Donnell, Donat, **1949**.8
O'Donoghue, Bernard, **1992**.28; **1994**.17
O'Donoghue, Florence, **1965**.18
O'Driscoll, Dennis, **1979**.39; **1989**.33
O'Dulaing, Donncha, **1978**.31
O'Faolain, Nuala, **1967**.42; **1980**.24
O'Faolain, Sean, **1935**.1; **1948**.6; **1962**.11; **1977**.36
O'Farrachain, Roibeard, **1942**.5; **1947**.9; **1977**.37
O'Farrell, Mairin, **1964**.18–19
O'Farrell, Nuala, **1979**.40
O'Glaisne, Risteard, **1964**.20
O'Grady, Desmond, **1968**.34; **1973**.36; **1992**.29–30
O'Grady, Thomas, **1988**.45; **1990**.26; **1994**.18
O'hAodha, Micheal, **1966**.15; **1967**.43; **1977**.38; **1981**.17; **1986**.56

O'Keeffe, Timothy, **1970**.17; **1980**.25–26
O'Laoghaire, Colm, **1951**.7
O'Loughlin, Clement, **1939**.10
O'Loughlin, Michael, **1985**.31; **1991**.26
O'Madan, The, **1940**.3
O'Mahony, Andy, **1976**.17
O'Muirithe, Diarmuid, **1967**.44
O'Neill, Charles, **1987**.33
O'Neill, Michael, **1987**.34
O'R., B.M., **1939**.11
O'Reilly, David, **1983**.22
O'Reilly, P.O., **1964**.21
O'Ruddy, Jno., **1940**.3
O'Shea, Helen, **1981**.18
O'Sheel, Sheamus, **1939**.12
O'Sullivan, T.F., **1973**.34
O'Toole, Fintan, **1985**.32; **1988**.33
O'Tuarisc, Eoghan, **1981**.19
Olden, G.A., **1954**.21
Orel, Harold, **1987**.35
Ormsby, Frank, **1979**.41; **1990**.27
Osborne, Charles, **1971**.26
Owens, Coilin, **1982**.24; **1992**.31

P
P., B., **1960**.22
P., F., **1939**.13
Parker, Michael, **1993**.17
Paulin, Tom, **1980**.27; **1984**.17; **1985**.34
Payne, Basil, **1960**.23; **1962**.12–13; **1964**.22–23; **1965**.19; **1971**.27; **1973**.36; **1979**.43
Peacock, Alan, **1992**.32
Perkins, David, **1987**.37
Perry, Diana B., **1990**.2
Persson, Ake, **1994**.19–20
Philips, McCandlish, **1958**.5
Pine, Richard, **1990**.30; **1994**.21
Platt, Eugene, **1973**.36
Plunkett, James, **1952**.7; **1992**.23
Pollack, Adnrew, **1973**.37
Popowich, Barry, **1991**.27
Potts, Paul, **1960**.24; **1961**.5; **1963**.4; **1967**.54; **1968**.36–37; **1970**.24; **1973**.38; **1978**.32; **1979**.44; **1980**.29
Press, John, **1969**.13
Pritchett, V.S., **1938**.7; **1991**.28
'Pro-Quidnunc,' **1968**.38
'Punch,' **1940**.3
Pyle, Fergus, **1986**.58; **1987**.38

Q
Q., F. M., **1940**.3
'Quidnunc,' **1966**.16; **1967**.57; **1971**.29; **1972**.29; **1975**.29
Quigley, Isabel, **1972**.31
Quinn, Antoinette, **1985**.35; **1988**.47–48; **1989**.34–35; **1991**.29–30
Quinn, Owen, **1950**.11

R
R., E. O., **1968**.39
Rafroidi, Patrick, **1972**.32; **1981**.21; **1986**.59
Redmond, John, **1990**.31
Redshaw, T.D., **1973**.36
Reid, Forrest, **1938**.8
Reilly, Kevin Patrick, **1979**.45; **1980**.30; **1981**.22
Reynolds, Horace, **1939**.16; **1950**.12
Rice, Gerard, **1980**.31; **1986**.60
Richards, Shaun, **1988**.13
Richardson, Kenneth, **1969**.14
Ricks, Christopher, **1964**.24
Riordain, John, **1950**.13
Riordain, Maurice, **1985**.36
Roberts, Michael, **1973**.36
Roberts-Burke, Robin J., **1987**.40
Robertshaw, Joan, **1948**.6
Robinson, Lennox, **1958**.3
Roche, Anthony, **1988**.49; **1994**.22
Roche, Emer, **1964**.25
Rogers, W. R., **1972**.34
Ronsley, Joseph, **1989**.12
Rosenfield, Ray, **1968**.41–42
Rosenthal, M.L., **1967**.58; **1995**.9
Rowley, Rosemarie, **1985**.37
Rushe, Desmond, **1972**.35; **1973**.40; **1977**.39; **1981**.23; **1982**.26
Russell, Noel, **1987**.41
'Rustic,' **1968**.43
Ryan, John, **1948**.10; **1950**.14; **1967**.59; **1968**.44–46; **1975**.30; **1979**.46; **1987**.42; **1988**.50
Ryan, Stephen P., **1959**.4

S
S., R.H., **1940**.3
S., T.J.M., **1962**.14
Salkeld, Blanaid, **1948**.6
Salomon, I.L., **1947**.12
Sampson, Denis, **1993**.18
Sampson, George, **1973**.41
Sandrock, Mary, **1949**.11
Saunders, Norah, **1988**.51
Schirmer, Gregory A., **1980**.32; **1983**.23; **1985**.38–39
Schleifer, Ronald, **1980**.33
Schmidt, Michael, **1980**.9

Author Index

Schneider, Jurgen, **1989**.36
Scott, Kingsley, **1944**.4
Scruton, James, **1988**.52
Sealey, Douglas, **1965**.21; **1966**.17; **1967**.60; **1982**.27; **1983**.24; **1986**.61
Seymour-Smith, Martin, **1973**.42; **1976**.19; **1985**.40
Shannon, S., **1942**.6
Share, Bernard, **1972**.36; **1980**.34
Sheedy, Larry, **1962**.15
Sheehy, Michael, **1968**.47
Sheehy-Skeffington, Hannah, **1938**.9
Sheerin, Patrick H., **1977**.40; **1980**.35
Sheridan, John D., **1950**.15
Sherwin, F.X., **1973**.36
Shields, Kathleen, **1989**.62
Simmons, James, **1964**.15; **1973**.43; **1992**.33
Simon, John, **1988**.53
Simpson, Louis, **1986**.63; **1988**.54; **1992**.34
Sissman, L.E., **1968**.48; **1973**.36
Sisson, C.H., **1971**.31; **1981**.24
Skelton, Robin, **1965**.22
Slattery, Finbar, **1970**.28; **1979**.47
Slevin, Gerard, **1968**.50
Sloan, Barry, **1986**.64
Smith, Michael, **1970**.29–30; **1971**.32–33; **1974**.29; **1975**.32
Smith, Peter Duvall, **1964**.26
Smith, Sidney Bernard, **1978**.33
Smith, Stan, **1992**.35
Snodgrass, W. D., **1965**.6
Sommer, Piotr, **1976**.1; **1977**.41
Sotscheck, Ralf, **1989**.36
'South American Joe,' **1940**.3
Sowton, Ian, **1961**.7
Speaight, Robert, **1944**.5
Spender, Stephen, **1965**.6
Spinks, C. W., **1976**.11
Stanford, Derek, **1979**.48
Stapleton, Michael, **1983**.25
Stern, James, **1949**.13
Stuart, Francis, **1962**.16; **1975**.33; **1986**.65
Sullivan, Kevin, **1969**.16
Sullivan, Sam, **1940**.3
Summerfield, Henry, **1975**.34
Swan, Desmond, **1975**.35
Swan, Thomas D., **1960**.27
Sweeney, Maurice, **1971**.34
Swift, Patrick, **1951**.8
Szanto, Piroska, **1974**.30

Sylvester, Harry, **1939**.17

T
T., A., **1978**.34
T., P.C., **1937**.3
Tapscott, Stephen, **1986**.66
Taubman, Robert, **1965**.23
Taylor, Annie, **1992**.23
Taylor, Geoffrey, **1942**.7
Tessier, Thomas, **1973**.36
Thompson, Richard, **1978**.35
Thornton, Weldon, **1979**.49
Thwaite, Anthony, **1964**.27
Todd, Loretto, **1989**.37
Tolley, A.T., **1985**.41
Torchiana, Donald, **1964**.28; **1965**.24
Tracy, Honor, **1958**.6; **1971**.35
Trevor, William, **1984**.18
Tuohy, Frank, **1977**.45

U
Upshott, Hilda, **1940**.3

V
Van De Kamp, Peter, **1991**.31
Vance, Norman, **1990**.32
Veldhuis, Theo, **1982**.28

W
W., B., **1947**.14; **1948**.7
W., M., **1936**.2
Waddell, Martin, **1992**.23
Wakeman, John, **1975**.36
Walker, Dorothy, **1971**.36
Walker, Martin, **1973**.45
Wall, Mervyn, **1976**.21
Walsh, Caroline, **1975**.37; **1982**.29–30
Ward, A.C., **1970**.31; **1981**.25
Warner, Alan, **1964**.29–30; **1968**.53; **1969**.17–18; **1973**.46–47; **1981**.26; **1986**.67
Warren, Lorna, **1983**.26
Waters, Maureen, **1984**.19
Watson, George, **1985**.42; **1991**.32
Webb, E.T., **1973**.48
Webb, W.L., **1967**.66
Weber, Richard, **1956**.6; **1958**.7; **1963**.5–6
Welch, Robert, **1983**.27; **1992**.36–37; **1993**.19
Werne, A., **1985**.43
Weygandt, Cornelius, **1937**.4; **1969**.19
Whelan, Kevin, **1993**.20

Author Index

White, Jack, **1954**.24
White, Terence de Vere, **1962**.18; **1965**.26; **1967**.67
Wilcox, Angela, **1989**.1
Wollman, Maurice, **1963**.7
Woodworth, Paddy, **1990**.33–35

Wright, David, **1968**.54; **1973**.36
Wright, Kathleen, **1979**.50

Z

Zach, Wolfgang, **1987**.44–45; **1988**.56

Subject Index

A

Abbey Theatre, **1941**.1; **1966**.15, 18; **1967**.17, 55, 64; **1975**.19; **1984**.6; **1988**.1, 24, 27; **1989**.16
A.E., **1939**.7, 16; **1940**.1–2; **1964**.17; **1967**.33; **1972**.34; **1973**.10; **1975**.34; **1980**.10; **1983**.3
Agnew, Art, **1987**.18
Alexeva, Natasha, **1988**.2
Alvarez, Al, **1965**.12
Allen, Barbara, **1990**.1
America, **1966**.7–8; **1974**.18; **1977**.26; **1987**.14; **1993**.13; **1995**.3
Amongst Women (John McGahern), **1993**.18
An Beal Bocht (Flann O'Brien), **1979**.25
Aran Islands (Synge), **1939**.12
Arnold, Matthew, **1975**.1
At Swim-Two-Birds (Flann O'Brien), **1990**.18
Auden, W.H., **1947**.12; **1956**.3; **1964**.7; **1986**.7, 23; **1988**.28, 54; **1990**.31; **1991**.18; **1995**.8
Austen, Jane, **1968**.53

B

Baggott Street, Dublin, **1968**.7, 31; **1978**.15; **1987**.18; **1989**.26; **1990**.28; **1991**.7
Bailey, The (pub), **1968**.19; **1971**.20
Balloonatics Theatre Company, **1988**.38
Balzac, Honoré, **1972**.9
Bardwell, Leland, **1976**.16
Barker, George, **1964**.3, 7; **1966**.4; **1982**.6; **1987**.2
Barnes, Ben, **1988**.2
Barron, Brian, **1970**.18
Barry, Kevin, **1967**.50
Barry, Paul, **1970**.14
Battersea Park (London), **1965**.25; **1993**.14
Baudelaire, Charles, **1950**.10; **1962**.16; **1975**.33; **1986**.49
Beatles, The, **1966**.5
Bell, The, **1968**.33; **1973**.15; **1987**.3; **1993**.7
Beckett, Samuel, **1956**.2; **1971**.32; **1975**.25, 33; **1978**.26; **1986**.36, 58; **1990**.9; **1992**.32; **1993**.11, 15; **1995**.5
Behan, Brendan, **1958**.1; **1962**.7; **1965**.7; **1967**.39; **1970**.16; **1971**.6; **1972**.29; **1974**.5; **1975**.8; **1976**.3; **1977**.21, 38; **1982**.20; **1988**.30; **1991**.7
Betjeman, John, **1969**.1; **1975**.30; **1976**.4
Blake, William, **1947**.6; **1968**.34, 37, 41; **1969**.7; **1985**.28; **1986**.49
Bloomfield, Robert, **1942**.7
Bloomsday, **1987**.5; **1989**.8
Bodley, Seoirse, **1972**.11
Boland, Eavan, **1967**.22
Bourke, Jimmy, **1974**.8
Bourniquel, Camille, **1964**.22
Boylan, Francis, **1989**.21
Boy Scout Movement, **1940**.3
Brendan, William, **1939**.2
Brennan, Senator Joseph, **1951**.3
Breughel, Peter, **1939**.12; **1942**.7
British Arts Council, **1967**.53, 65
British Broadcasting Corporation (BBC), **1964**.26; **1972**.34; **1974**.9; **1975**.24; **1976**.5; **1977**.17; **1979**.16
Brown, George Mackay, **1979**.17
Browne, Garech, **1968**.9
Bruton, John, **1986**.48
Bunuel, Luis, **1988**.29

Subject Index

Burgess, Anthony, **1973**.47
Burns, Robert, **1938**.6; **1939**.11–12, 14; **1968**.7, 42; **1969**.1, 18; **1986**.7
Butler, Hubert, **1973**.47; **1994**.9

C

Campbell, Joseph, **1973**.10; **1979**.35
Campbell, Roy, **1964**.7
Canal Bank Seat, Dublin **1968**.1, 22, 31, 35, 38; **1971**.22; **1973**.34; **1977**.42; **1978**.15; **1986**.63; **1987**.36; **1990**.2, 28; **1991**.29
Canterbury Tales, The (Geoffrey Chaucer), **1979**.44
Carleton, William, **1960**.7; **1969**.16; **1974**.26; **1975**.24; **1979**.2, 45; **1981**.22; **1985**.11; **1986**.53, 64; **1987**.35; **1988**.1; **1989**.34; **1991**.24; **1994**.18
Carlow Arts Festival, **1989**.32
"Carrickfergus" (Louis MacNeice), **1994**.11
Carrickmacross, **1984**.6, 11, 12; **1986**.27; **1987**.39; **1988**.33; **1989**.22; **1991**.25
Carroll, Gene, **1988**.43
Carroll, Joe, **1990**.20
Carroll, Lewis, **1985**.8
Casey, Philip, **1981**.9
Cassidy, Frank, **1970**.7
Catholicism (*see also* Mysticism, Religion), **1939**.11, 17; **1951**.1; **1960**.23, 25; **1965**.23; **1967**.20, 47; **1968**.5, 36–37; **1977**.19; **1978**.7, 20, 28, 30; **1979**.3, 7, 15, 48; **1984**.19; **1986**.1, 60, 66; **1989**.9, 34; **1990**.23; **1991**.29; **1992**.24, 27
Cavan, county, **1949**.11; **1980**.27; **1988**.29
Chagal, Marc, **1987**.11
Charabanc Theatre Company, **1990**.34
Chaucer, Geoffrey, **1979**.3, 44
Christie's (London), **1967**.15
Churchill, Winston, **1956**.4
Claddagh Records, **1968**.9
Clare, John, **1938**.7; **1968**.37
Clarke, Austin, **1959**.4; **1963**.2–3; **1965**.12; **1967**.41; **1968**.3, 5; **1969**.16; **1970**.15; **1972**.30; **1973**.10, 27; **1974**.4, 7; **1977**.9; **1978**.26; **1979**.1, 13, 29; **1981**.15; **1982**.1; **1986**.22, 39, 46; **1988**.30; **1989**.4, 10, 29; **1991**.27
Cocteau, Jean, **1972**.7; **1988**.29
Coffey, Brian, **1971**.32; **1989**.11

Cole, William, **1972**.12
Coll, John, **1991**.2, 23; **1994**.4
Collins, Patrick, **1964**.28
Colum, Padraic, **1965**.21; **1985**.19
Comedy, **1970**.12; **1971**.3; **1977**.23; **1979**.16; **1982**.15; **1985**.20; **1987**.23; **1992**.19; **1994**.7; **1995**.5
Comic, **1950**.6; **1957**.1; **1962**.8; **1965**.15; **1967**.33; **1968**.54; **1970**.12–13; **1971**.3; **1974**.3; **1975**.3, 12; **1979**.11, 33; **1984**.8, 19; **1986**.36; **1987**.2, 22, 40; **1989**.8; **1992**.19; **1994**.7; **1995**.5
Connolly, Colm, **1988**.14
Connolly, Cyril, **1971**.2; **1976**.4; **1994**.2
Coole Park, **1990**.28
Corbiere, Tristan, **1986**.7
Corkery, Daniel, **1975**.21
Costello, John A., **1954**.24; **1974**.21, 23; **1976**.14
Coughlin, Jack, **1978**.26
Cowper, William, **1979**.17
Crabbe, George, **1964**.24, 29
Cromwell (Brendan Kennelly), **1988**.49
Cronin, Anthony, **1974**.23; **1975**.17; **1976**.16, 18; **1977**.10; **1988**.43
Cronin, Sean, **1968**.9
Cuala Press, **1943**.7; **1972**.25; **1988**.47
Cuchulain, **1986**.2; **1988**.19

D

Dante, **1968**.37
Davitt, Michael, **1968**.34, 37
De Valera, Eamon, **1988**.21
Deane, Raymond, **1990**.20, 33–34
Deane, Seamus, **1987**.30; **1990**.5, 34
Dedalus, Stephen, **1979**.25, **1980**.6
Deserted Village, The (Goldsmith), **1956**.6; **1964**.29; **1972**.26; **1973**.46
"Desolation Row" (Bob Dylan), **1988**.18
Devlin, Denis, **1971**.32; **1972**.30; **1973**.10; **1979**.31; **1983**.27; **1989**.11
Donegal, county, **1980**.27
Donleavy, J.P., **1986**.12
Donnelly, Charles, **1971**.32
Donoghue, Denis, **1987**.30
Dostoevesky, **1977**.11
Dowling, Vincent, **1988**.2
Doyle, Anne, **1987**.7
Drew, Ronnie, **1984**.3
Dryden, John, **1979**.17
Dublin Magazine, **1968**.11
Dubliners (Joyce), **1989**.4
Duck, Stephen, **1961**.3

Subject Index

Dunn, Lee, **1987**.7
Durcan, Paul, **1974**.20; **1979**.19, 31; **1985**.31; **1989**.27
Dylan, Bob, **1988**.18

E
Edgeworth, Maria, **1986**.64
Egan, Desmond, **1981**.9; **1988**.41; **1989**.21; **1991**.31
Einstein, Albert, **1968**.37
Eisenhower, President, **1956**.4
Eliot, T. S., **1968**.13, 37; **1969**.9; **1972**.7; **1973**.10;**1978**.17; **1979**.6, 24; **1985**.19, 28
Ellmann, Richard, **1989**.12
Emerson, Ralph Waldo, **1967**.50; **1983**.6
Ennis, John, **1975**.27, 29
Envoy (Dublin), **1950**.2–5, 7–11, 13–15; **1951**.1, 3–8; **1964**.30; **1967**.67; **1968**.53; **1976**.3–4; **1977**.17; **1978**.16; **1979**.46; **1981**.4; **1982**.1; **1986**.12; **1987**.34; **1988**.30; **1989**.8; **1993**.7
Esmonde, Sir John, **1954**.3
Evans, James, **1977**.33

F
Faber Book of Irish Verse, **1974**.4
Faber Book of Poems and Places, **1982**.8
Faber Book of Contemporary Irish Poetry, **1986**.10
Fallon, Padraic, **1981**.2
Fallon, Peter, **1981**.9
Farmer Boy, (Bloomfield), **1942**.7
Father Ralph (Gerald O'Donovan), **1942**.3
Faulkner, William, **1975**.1
Fellini, **1988**.29
Fitzgerald, Paul, **1987**.20
Flaubert, **1978**.17
Football, **1967**.31; **1970**.8; **1989**.21; **1993**.14
Four Quartets (T. S. Eliot), **1979**.6; **1985**.28
French Ambassador, **1975**.15, 29, 31; **1977**.46
Friel, Brian, **1988**.5
Frost, Robert, **1979**.34

G
Gaelic (language and culture), **1949**.11; **1971**.14; **1977**.14; **1978**.21; **1979**.15; **1985**.30, 31; **1986**.30; **1987**.9
Galway, **1968**.29; **1971**.27; **1972**.14

"Gamble No Gamble" (Ballet), **1961**.6
"Gentle Tiger" (RTE), **1987**.7
Gide, André, **1971**.12
Giono, Jean, **1986**.59
Glavin, Anthony, **1988**.43
Godard, Jean Luc, **1988**.29
Gogarty, Oliver St. John, **1939**.2–4; **1971**.7, 30; **1973**.40; **1980**.14; **1993**.11
Goldsmith, Oliver, **1956**.6; **1964**.29; **1972**.26; **1973**.46; **1979**.17
Goldsmith Press, **1978**.10; **1989**.7, 23
Goodbye to All That (Robert Graves), **1965**.21
Grand Canal, Dublin, **1967**.6, 64; **1979**.35; **1980**.1, 22; **1981**.8; **1991**.2, 6, 23; **1994**.4
Graves, Robert, **1965**.21
"Great Hunger, The" (restaurant), **1977**.42
Great Hunger, The (Tom MacIntyre), **1988**.2, 14, 19, 22–24, 27, 29, 53, 56; **1989**.13, 36; **1991**.3; **1993**.3
Great Southern Hotel, Galway, **1971**.27
Green, Martin, **1976**.16
Greenberg (Israeli poet), **1987**.40
Greene, David, **1980**.22
Gregory, Lady Augusta, **1975**.26
Gresham Hotel, Dublin, **1954**.11
Guthrie, Woody, **1988**.26

H
Hallam, Arthur, **1989**.34
Hand, Michael, **1973**.13
Hannah, Fred, **1971**.33; **1990**.22
Hardy, Thomas, **1975**.1; **1989**.34
Harmon, Maurice, **1979**.18
Hartnett, Michael, **1975**.17; **1981**.2; **1982**.27; **1995**.4
Healey, Dermot, **1991**.25
Healey, Shay, **1968**.52
Heaney, Seamus, **1966**.6; **1967**.16; **1968**.4; **1969**.13; **1973**.9; **1974**.25; **1975**.1, 6, 17, 37; **1977**.14, 44; **1979**.4, 11, 14–15, 17; **1980**.21, 32; **1981**.2, 15, 16, 18; **1982**.7, 21; **1983**.2; **1984**.2; **1985**.1, 7, 9, 16, 31; **1986**.4, 6, 8, 42, 45, 50, 55, 66; **1987**.11, 28–29, 33, 41; **1988**.1, 5, 6, 12, 31, 52, 55; **1989**.10, 14, 27, 30, 36; **1990**.4, 26–27, 32; **1991**.18, 24, 32; **1992**.1, 5, 12, 18, 22, 33–35, 37; **1993**.15, 17, 19; **1994**.5; **1995**.1
Heine, **1986**.7

Subject Index

Herbert, B., **1977**.33
Herbert, George, **1968**.37
Herzog, Werner, **1988**.29
Hewitt, John, **1946**.1; **1975**.17; **1979**.15; **1992**.3
Hickey, Tom, **1988**.2
Hidden Ireland, The (Daniel Corkery), **1975**.21
Higgins, F.R., **1978**.5; **1982**.1; **1988**.25
Holden Caulfield, **1968**.30
Holohan, Leo, **1967**.16
Homeric, **1979**.24; **1992**.12
Honest Ulsterman (Belfast), **1973**.43; **1992**.28
Hopkins, Gerard Manley, **1968**.13; **1985**.14
Horizon (London), **1976**.7; **1980**.22
Huckleberry Finn, **1968**.30
Hughes, Ted, **1982**.6
Hyde, Douglas, **1947**.1

I

Ibsen, Henrik, **1968**.53
Imagists, **1983**.3; **1986**.26
Inniskeen, **1954**.21; **1968**.32, 54; **1970**.5, 7, 8, 11, 18, 20; **1971**.18; **1972**.3, 6, 16, 20–21, 28, 40; **1973**.4–5, 12, 17; **1975**.15, 27–29; **1976**.8; **1977**.20; **1978**.21, 24, 27, 31; **1979**.42; **1981**.20; **1982**.11; **1984**.6; **1985**.23; **1986**.32, 57; **1987**.18; **1989**.7, 34; **1990**.34; **1991**.17
Inter-Cert Examinations (Ireland), **1967**.62
Irish Congress of Trade Unions (ICTU), **1985**.5
Irish Embassy (London), **1969**.4
Irish Farmers Journal, **1980**.28; **1987**.26
Irish nationalism (*see also* Irishness), **1951**.1; **1964**.16; **1971**.32; **1973**.10; **1974**.26; **1975**.9, 25; **1979**.12–13; **1980**.6, 8; **1985**.19, 30; **1986**.19, 43; **1988**.13, 18, 51; **1990**.5, 19; **1992**.24; **1994**.14
Irish Poetry After Yeats (Maurice Harmon), **1979**.18
Irish Republican Army (IRA), **1956**.4
Irishness, **1973**.26; **1979**.13; **1980**.6; **1990**.17
Islandman, The (Tomas O'Crohan), **1939**.12
Israel, **1987**.40
Iveagh, Earl of, **1975**.30

J

Jameson, Frederic, **1989**.20
John Bull's Other Island (G.B. Shaw), **1979**.25; **1980**.12
Johnson, Dr., **1968**.54; **1971**.13; **1976**.7; **1981**.26; **1986**.22
Jones, David, **1979**.24
Jonson, Ben, **1954**.2
Jordan, John, **1973**.16
Joseph, Michael, **1939**.2
Joyce, James, **1942**.3; **1962**.11; **1965**.5; **1968**.53; **1970**.9–10; **1974**.26; **1979**.25; **1980**.12, 23, 27; **1981**.7; **1982**.18; **1985**.19; **1986**.8, 19, 40, 60; **1989**.4, 15, 34; **1991**.18; **1992**.3; **1994**.16, 18; **1995**.6
Joyce, Stanislaus, **1980**.23, 27; **1982**.12
Jury's Hotel, Dublin, **1987**.7

K

Kafka, Franz, **1950**.6
Kane, Michael, **1987**.18; **1990**.1
Kavanagh, Anne, **1972**.21
Kavanagh, Celia, **1969**.6; **1989**.21
Kavanagh, Katherine (*see also* Katherine Barry Moloney), **1976**.16; **1977**.1, 5, 11, 17; **1978**.24; **1989**.6, 7, 21, 23–24
Kavanagh, P.J., **1967**.57
Kavanagh, Patrick,

WORKS BY:
"Advent," **1974**.29
Almost Everything (LP Record), **1965**.9, 19; **1969**.15
"Auditors In," **1957**.1; **1972**.7; **1987**.11
"Beech Tree," **1965**.16
"Blind Dog," **1986**.54
By Night Unstarred, **1977**.8, 15–16, 19, 22, 27, 32, 39, 45; **1978**.3, 12–13, 17, 22, 33–34; **1979**.38; **1983**.21; **1985**.3; **1989**.20, 21
Canal Bank sonnets, **1968**.13; **1969**.1; **1970**.12; **1971**.3; **1972**.7; **1973**.10, 46; **1976**.2; **1979**.13; **1982**.24; **1985**.27, 41; **1986**.19, 47, 49; **1987**.15; **1988**.28; **1989**.9; **1991**.1
"Candida," **1947**.14
"Christmas Childhood, A" **1947**.14; **1984**.8
Collected Poems, **1964**.1–3, 11, 13, 17, 24, 27; **1965**.15, 17, 20; **1973**.32, 43; **1978**.29; **1979**.7, 11; **1980**.20; **1983**.18

Subject Index

Collected Pruse, **1967**.3, 5, 24, 25, 34, 42, 60; **1971**.12; **1973**.47; **1974**.21; **1978**.35; **1988**.47–48
Come Dance with Kitty Stobling, **1960**.1–6, 8, 10–12, 14–15, 17–20, 23, 25; **1961**.3–4, 7; **1962**.1; **1963**.1; **1964**.28; **1965**.21–22; **1968**.54; **1969**.1; **1974**.19; **1976**.2; **1977**.17, 30; **1980**.10; **1991**.29
Complete Poems, **1972**.23; **1986**.22; **1989**.21; **1990**.22
"Epic," **1966**.11; **1968**.54; **1975**.13; **1979**.18; **1984**.8; **1989**.34; **1990**.15; **1992**.12; **1993**.18, 20
"Father Mat," **1983**.17
"Goat of Slieve Donard, The" **1937**.1
Great Hunger, The, **1942**.6–7; **1944**.5; **1963**.1; **1964**.1–2, 10–11, 13, 17, 24, 27, 29; **1965**.15–16, 21; **1966**.4, 13; **1967**.2, 19, 32–33, 38, 40–41, 66–67; **1968**.13, 16, 30, 33, 47, 54; **1969**.1, 13, 14–18, **1970**.3, 12–13, 15, 17; **1971**.3, 19, 31; **1972**.7, 25–26; **1973**.10, 24, 42, 46, 48; **1974**.3, 25; **1975**.1, 5–6, 12, 17, 23, 33, 35; **1976**.1–2, 5, 7; **1977**.9, 14, 40, 42, 44; **1978**.6, 16–17, 20, 30, 32; **1979**.8, 10–11, 13, 16, 17–18, 25, 31, 33, 35–37, 44, 49; **1980**.10, 19, 22; **1981**.2, 3, 7–8; **1982**.6, 8–9, 19, 24, 28; **1983**.3, 15–17, 27; **1984**.8, 19; **1985**.8, 11, 16, 27–28, 32, 36, 41, 43; **1986**.8, 17, 24, 42, 47; **1987**.3, 8, 13, 30, 37; **1988**.4, 13, 21–24, 27–29, 39, 46–47, 49, 51, 53–54, 56; **1989**.4, 26–28, 34–35, 37; **1990**.23, 26, 31; **1991**.4, 27, 29; **1992**.20; **1993**.6, 15, 17–18; **1994**.2, 14; **1995**.5–6
Green Fool, The, **1938**.1–9; **1939**.1–2, 4, 6–17; **1964**.10; **1971**.5, 7, 11, 25, 28, 35; **1972**.1, 4, 8, 13–15, 31; **1973**.14; **1975**.4; **1976**.2; **1977**.30; **1978**.3, 16, 22, 31; **1979**.35–36; **1983**.21; **1985**.19; **1986**.8, 22, 24; **1987**.4; **1989**.25, 32; **1990**.6, 17; **1991**.29; **1993**.11, 17
"Hospital, The," **1964**.29; **1968**.54; **1980**.2
"If Ever You Go to Dublin Town," **1986**.61
"In Memory of My Mother," **1968**.13; **1987**.11
"Inniskeen Road: July Evening," **1977**.3; **1980**.8; **1983**.6; **1984**.8; **1988**.17
"Innocence," **1971**.3; **1973**.46
Kavanagh's Weekly, **1952**.1–6, 9–10; **1964**.30; **1965**.20; **1967**.6, 67; **1968**.13, 53; **1972**.36; **1973**.47; **1977**.9, 38; **1980**.34; **1981**.4, 6, 14, 17, 23; **1982**.1, 4, 16, 18; **1983**.6; **1984**.8; **1985**.43; **1986**.33, 49, 60; **1989**.8; **1992**.7
"Kerr's Ass," **1991**.10; **1992**.22, 26
Lapped Furrows, **1969**.6; **1970**.7, 17; **1973**.20; **1975**.7; **1977**.18; **1978**.22
"Lay of the Crooked Knight, The," **1975**.23
"Long Garden, The," **1974**.9
Lough Derg, **1978**.8, 10, 17, 20, 29; **1979**.6–7, 19, 24, 28, 31, 37, 43–44; **1981**.11; **1984**.18; **1985**.19, 27, 43; **1986**.49; **1987**.12–13; **1988**.1, 55; **1989**.27–28; **1991**.24, 26, 29; **1992**.18
"Memory of Brother Michael," **1947**.5, 9; **1964**.16; **1966**.11; **1973**.26; **1979**.26; **1992**.13
"Memory of My Father," **1983**.14; **1986**.26
November Haggard, **1971**.16; **1978**.29
"Old Peasant, The," **1942**.1, 5
"Paddiad, The," **1949**.12; **1966**.2; **1971**.19; **1976**.2
"Peace," **1973**.46
"Pegasus," **1947**.14; **1976**.2
"Plough Horses," **1969**.1
"Ploughman," **1969**.1, 18; **1973**.46; **1980**.10
Ploughman and Other Poems, **1936**.1–2; **1938**.2–3; **1947**.4; **1973**.10; **1975**.26; **1977**.4; **1979**.35
"Possessing Eden," **1988**.28
"Prelude," **1957**.1
"Primrose," **1947**.2
"Pygmalion," **1971**.3
"Raglan Road," **1986**.61
Recent Poems, **1959**.2
"Restaurant Reverie," **1990**.10
Self Portrait, **1962**.10, 14, 17; **1964**.5, 10, 20, 22, 24; **1966**.13; **1967**.25; **1969**.1; **1977**.30; **1985**.6; **1989**.25
"Shancoduff," **1969**.1; **1973**.46; **1976**.1–2; **1982**.24; **1984**.18; **1987**.15; **1989**.34; **1994**.15; **1995**.6

Subject Index

Soul for Sale, A, **1947**.1–2, 5–6, 9–14; **1948**.2–3; **1958**.2; **1960**.12, 23; **1961**.3; **1962**.8; **1964**.27–28; **1965**.21; **1968**.29; **1970**.12, 15; **1973**.10; **1976**.2; **1979**.35–37; **1980**.10; **1981**.26; **1986**.24; **1993**.17
"Sower, The," **1935**.1
"Spraying the Potatoes," **1990**.10, 26
"Stony Grey Soil," **1964**.17; **1979**.35; **1983**.17; **1989**.3; **1990**.25; **1991**.29
Tarry Flynn, **1948**.9; **1964**.30; **1965**.13, 23; **1966**.10, 18; **1967**.17, 20, 24; **1968**.7, 12, 14, 29–30, 40, 42, 51–52, 54; **1971**.3; **1972**.9, 13; **1973**.11, 23, 42; **1974**.24; **1975**.12; **1976**.2; **1977**.9, 22, 30; **1978**.3, 31; **1979**.16, 33, 36; **1980**.10, 13; **1983**.11, 21; **1984**.19; **1985**.4, 18–20; **1986**.1, 8, 24, 53; **1987**.9; **1988**.11, 45; **1989**.34; **1990**.6, 18; **1991**.27, 29; **1994**.18
"Temptation in Harvest," **1947**.14; **1984**.4
"Thank You, Thank You," **1972**.6
"To a Blackbird," **1976**.2
"To a Child," **1986**.54
"To a Late Poplar," **1937**.3
"To the Man After the Harrow," **1983**.17
"Who Killed James Joyce?", **1974**.18; **1989**.12
"Why Sorrow?", **1978**.17; **1985**.27; **1988**.9
"Wind, A," **1986**.54
"Yeats," **1981**.5
Kavanagh, Peter, **1968**.10, 32, 39; **1969**.6; **1970**.7, 17–18; **1971**.12; **1972**.23; **1975**.7; **1977**.7, 22, 26–27, 32, 45; **1978**.11–12; **1979**.19; **1980**.4, 17–18, 23–25, 27–28, 31, 34; **1981**.6, 14; **1982**.23; **1983**.9; **1985**.23; **1986**.32; **1987**.19–20; **1989**.7
WORKS BY:
Beyond Affection, **1977**.7; **1978**.11; **1985**.22; **1989**.21
Dancing Flame, The, **1989**.21
Garden of the Golden Apples, The, **1972**.18–19, 24; **1978**.22
Guide to Patrick Kavanagh Country, **1979**.19, 38; **1986**.32
Love's Tortured Headland, **1980**.24
Patrick Kavanagh: Man and Poet, **1987**.43; **1989**.21

Sacred Keeper, **1980**.23–25, 27–28, 31, 34; **1981**.21; **1982**.23; **1985**.22, 38; **1986**.37, 51; **1989**.21
Kavanagh Archive (UCD), **1982**.26; **1985**.12, 23, 26, 29; **1986**.18, 20, 58; **1987**.14; **1988**.36–37; **1989**.21
Kavanagh Museum (Inniskeen), **1970**.20, 23; **1973**.12; **1987**.18
Kavanagh Room (Dundalk), **1971**.18
Kavanagh Society, **1970**.1; **1971**.1; **1975**.22; **1981**.20; **1987**.18
Kavanagh's Yearly, **1987**.18, 39; **1988**.33, 43; **1989**.22; **1990**.5, 20, 33–34; **1991**.17, 25
Keats, John, **1968**.41; **1970**.17; **1986**.15; **1990**.10
Kearney, Richard, **1988**.18
Kednaminsha School, **1978**.21
Kennedy, Ludovic, **1971**.12
Kennelly, Brendan, **1968**.4; **1970**.30; **1972**.26; **1975**.17; **1978**.25; **1988**.35, 43, 49; **1989**.27; **1990**.28; **1994**.3, 15, 19–20, 22
Kentucky, **1939**.6, 16
Kerouac, Jack, **1988**.18
Kiberd, Declan, **1986**.17; **1991**.17, 25
Kiely, Benedict, **1972**.6; **1974**.23
Kilcavan, county Wexford, **1968**.50
Kinsella, Thomas, **1966**.17; **1973**.10, 27; **1976**.12; **1979**.13; **1981**.15; **1987**.16; **1989**.11; **1992**.12

L
Langhorne, **1979**.17
Larkin, Philip, **1960**.11
Lawrence, D.H., **1960**.9; **1968**.13, 53
Layton, Irving, **1986**.7
Leautaud, Paul, **1986**.59
Leaving Certificate Examination (Ireland), **1974**.11–12
Leningrad, **1988**.1
Lennon, John, **1970**.27
Liddy, James, **1975**.17, 32; **1981**.9
Lilliput Press, **1988**.48
Listowel Players, **1968**.51
Longford, Lady (Christine), **1977**.44
Longley, Michael, **1973**.44; **1986**.11; **1988**.43, 46; **1992**.26
Loughlin, Bernard, **1987**.18, 39; **1988**.43
Lyric Theatre, Belfast, **1968**.12, 14, 40, 42; **1972**.38

M
MacAnna, Thomas, **1977**.44
MacAonghusa, Proinsias, **1965**.9; **1966**.5

Subject Index

MacDiarmid, Hugh, **1964**.7; **1968**.37; **1994**.14
MacGreevy, Thomas, **1971**.32
MacIntyre, Tom, **1983**.15; **1988**.2, 14, 19, 22–24, 27, 29, 53, 56; **1989**.36; **1993**.3
MacMathuna, Sean, **1991**.25
Macmillan, Harold, **1975**.30
Macmillan, Maurice, **1975**.30; **1976**.4
MacNamara, Brinsley, **1990**.6
MacNamara, Priscilla, **1976**.16
MacNaughten, Justice, **1939**.4
MacNeice, Louis, **1975**.5; **1979**.27; **1981**.1; **1987**.16; **1990**.15; **1991**.27; **1992**.32; **1994**.11, 12, 14
Machado, Antonio, **1980**.35
Madame Bovary (Flaubert), **1978**.3
Magee, Patrick, **1973**.39
Maguire, Patrick (in *The Great Hunger*), **1942**.2; **1944**.5; **1966**.4, 13; **1968**.30; **1970**.15; **1975**.23, 35; **1977**.9, 40; **1988**.46; **1990**.23; **1993**.17
Mahon, Derek, **1975**.17; **1986**.11; **1990**.31
Mandelstam, Osip, **1986**.40
Mangan, James Clarence, **1974**.22
Markey, Josephine, **1979**.20
Markham, Edward, **1966**.13
Martin, Augustine, **1986**.20, 48; **1987**.19, 20, 27, 38; **1989**.21
Marx, Karl, **1979**.25
Matthews, Aidan, **1976**.9
Mason, Patrick, **1988**.2, 24
McAleer, Kevin, **1990**.34
McArdle, John, **1972**.38; **1989**.32; **1992**.10
McArdle, Tom, **1972**.38; **1987**.20, 27; **1989**.32; **1992**.10
McArthy, Thomas, **1977**.19, 25
McCabe, Eugene, **1972**.38
McCabe family, **1990**.34
McCafferty, Nell, **1990**.34
McCarthy, Eugene, **1979**.9
McCarthy, Jimmy, **1990**.34
McCaughney, Barny, **1968**.42
McDaid's pub, **1964**.19; **1966**.3; **1967**.44; **1972**.29; **1974**.1; **1976**.3–4
McDonagh, Donagh, **1946**.1; **1982**.1
McEvoy, Johnny, **1968**.52
McFadden, Roy, **1948**.3; **1992**.3
McGahern, John, **1990**.34; **1993**.18
McGowan, T., **1967**.44
McGuckian, Medbh, **1988**.43
McGurk, Tom, **1973**.8, 28

McKenna, Siobhan, **1968**.46
McKenna, T.P., **1968**.46
McNello's pub (Inniskeen), **1972**.3
McQuaid, Archbishop, **1972**.35, 39; **1977**.19
"Meditations on Lines from Patrick Kavanagh" (Seoirse Bodley), **1972**.11
"Michael" (Wordsworth), **1973**.46
Midnight Court, The, **1972**.26
Miller, John, **1977**.43
Miller, Liam, **1977**.44
Millet, **1987**.11
Milne, Ewart, **1975**.17
Molière, **1968**.21
Molloy, Molly, **1987**.27
Moloney, Katherine Barry (*see also* Katherine Kavanagh), **1967**.50, 52; **1980**.4
Monaghan, **1938**.3; **1967**.24; **1968**.13, 24, 27, 29; **1969**.3; **1970**.6; **1971**.17–18; **1972**.15; **1973**.7, 46; **1975**.12, 34; **1978**.21; **1979**.33; **1980**.1; **1984**.4, 18; **1985**.43; **1986**.2, 26, 40, 60; **1990**.25; **1992**.24
Montague, John, **1966**.17; **1967**.16; **1968**.4; **1970**.3; **1973**.9; **1975**.1, 9; **1977**.14; **1979**.13, 15, 41; **1980**.8; **1981**.2, 16; **1983**.13; **1985**.7, 31, 36; **1989**.17; **1990**.27
Montgomery, Niall, **1971**.32
Moore, George, **1979**.45; **1980**.31; **1989**.34
Moore, Thomas, **1986**.40; **1988**.19
Morrissey, Sinead, **1990**.5
Morrison, Colin, **1988**.43
Morrow, John, **1987**.18
Morrow, Larry, **1980**.5
Moscow, **1988**.1, 14
Movement poets, **1979**.11; **1988**.20
Mucker, **1938**.2; **1960**.16; **1982**.30; **1988**.38
"Mucker" (Paul O'Hanrahan), **1988**.38
Muir, Edwin, **1994**.14
Muldoon, Paul, **1973**.9; **1986**.10; **1989**.27; **1990**.31; **1992**.16, 25
Murphy, Hayden, **1967**.44
Murphy, Peter, **1988**.43
Murphy, Suzanne, **1987**.20
Murphy, Tom, **1985**.32
Mysticism (*see also* Catholicism, Religion), **1937**.2; **1949**.1; **1960**.14; **1975**.25; **1978**.3; **1977**.19; **1980**.20; **1985**.28, 43; **1990**.13; **1991**.1

Subject Index

N

Na Gopaleen, Myles, **1980**.13, 22; **1988**.30
National Film Institute, **1950**.15
National Library, **1985**.35
Nemo, John, **1977**.38; **1980**.5, 16, 24; **1981**.12, 16
New Orleans, **1968**.26
New York, **1967**.39, 50, 55; **1977**.19; **1985**.22; **1986**.16, 20, 54, 63
New Yorker, **1975**.11
Ni Nuadhain, Mairead, **1989**.32
Nicholson, Norman, **1985**.41
Nicolson, Harold, **1969**.18
Nisbet, Tom, **1977**.33
Northwestern University, **1965**.8, 24; **1966**.1, 8; **1967**.67; **1977**.19; **1986**.40
"November Songs" (Raymond Deane), **1990**.33
Nuremore Hotel, Carrickmacross, **1991**.25

O

O'Brien, Conor Cruise, **1968**.37
O'Brien, Flann (*see also* Myles na Gopaleen and Brian O'Nolan), **1970**.29; **1973**.7; **1976**.3; **1979**.25; **1985**.32; **1987**.5; **1989**.8; **1990**.18; **1991**.7; **1992**.28
O'Brien, Gearoid, **1981**.9
O'Brien, Paddy, **1964**.19; **1972**.29; **1974**.1
O'Cadhain, M., **1974**.4
O'Callaghan, Julie, **1991**.25
O'Casey, Sean, **1948**.2; **1965**.5; **1966**.5; **1968**.37; **1974**.5; **1975**.26; **1979**.11; **1980**.22
O'Connor, Frank, **1939**.16; **1967**.41; **1978**.26; **1979**.1; **1980**.22; **1982**.1; **1983**.18
O'Connor, P.J., **1966**.10, 18
O'Connor, Patrick, **1966**.14, 16; **1967**.15
O'Connor, Ulick, **1973**.40
O'Crohan, Tomas, **1939**.12
O'Dalaigh, President Cearbhall, **1976**.9
O'Dea, Tom, **1990**.25
O'Direain, Mairtin, **1990**.8
O'Donnell, Peadar, **1939**.12; **1974**.24
O'Donovan, Gerard, **1942**.3
O'Faolain, Sean, **1939**.17; **1967**.41; **1975**.33; **1979**.1; **1980**.13, 22; **1987**.3
O'Flaherty, May, **1982**.29
O'Grady, Desmond, **1991**.25
O'Hanrahan, Paul, **1988**.38
O'Houlihan, Con, **1977**.44
O'Keeffe, Timothy, **1974**.27; **1980**.17
O'Loughlin, Michael, **1986**.25
O'Nolan, Brian, **1940**.2; **1987**.5
O'Riordain, Dr., **1967**.44
O'Riordan, Richard, **1976**.16
O'Rourke, Clinton, **1987**.18
O'Sullivan, Maurice, **1939**.12
O'Toole, Fintan, **1986**.17
Oldham, Andrew, **1965**.1
Ormonde (Maria Edgeworth), **1986**.64
Ormsby, Frank, **1991**.25
Orpheus, **1950**.2

P

Paisley, Ian, **1966**.5; **1977**.17
Palace Bar, **1976**.3–4
Pan, **1938**.3
Parnell, Charles Stewart, **1968**.37
Parochialism, **1968**.30; **1972**.10; **1975**.1, 9, 56; **1979**.15; **1980**.8, 32; **1982**.8; **1983**.4, 8, 23; **1985**.39, 41; **1986**.3, 44, 64; **1987**.15; **1988**.1, 5, 16; **1989**.34; **1990**.15, 30; **1992**.1, 6, 27, 35; **1993**.17; **1994**.12, 14, 16; **1995**.1, 3, 6, 9
Parson's bookshop, **1975**.20; **1978**.15; **1982**.29
Pasolini, **1988**.29
Pasternak, Boris, **1968**.37
Patrick Kavanagh Bar (Galway), **1972**.14
Paulin, Tom, **1985**.42
Payne, Basil, **1965**.12
Peacock Theatre, **1967**.20; **1983**.15; **1987**.8; **1988**.29
Pearl Bar, **1958**.6; **1969**.10
Pembroke Road, **1976**.4; **1977**.17, 19; **1990**.16, 24; **1994**.4
Penguin Book of Irish Verse, **1970**.30
Pennies of Time, **1984**.6
Phillips, McCandlish, **1986**.16
Piers Plowman, **1973**.23
Pitt-Kethley, Fiona, **1990**.34
Playboy of the Western World (J.M. Synge), **1989**.26
Plough, The (public bar), **1965**.11; **1966**.4; **1973**.6, 18, 35, 37, 45; **1974**.2, 13, 27–28; **1976**.17
Poe, Edgar Allen, **1962**.16; **1975**.33
Poems from Ireland (William Cole), **1972**.12
"Poet's Pub" (Alan Reeve), **1954**.17
Poetry Book Society, **1968**.54
Polish language, **1976**.1; **1977**.41

Subject Index

Poor Mouth, The (Flann O'Brien), **1985**.32
Pope, Alexander, **1979**.17
Portrait of the Artist as a Young Man, A (Joyce), **1942**.3; **1994**.18
"Potato Eaters" (Van Gogh), **1965**.22
Potts, Paul, **1970**.4
Pound, Ezra, **1968**.37; **1972**.7; **1975**.30
Pritchett, V.S., **1976**.4
Proust, Marcel, **1992**.7
Prufrock, J. Alfred, **1970**.15
Pryor, Maureen, **1974**.27

Q
Quinn, Antoinette, **1992**.21; **1993**.13
Quinn, Owen, **1982**.20

R
Radio Telefís Éireann (RTE), **1952**.4; **1962**.17; **1964**.4, 21, 25; **1967**.17, 21, 26; **1973**.27–28; **1976**.16; **1987**.1, 7, 19, 27; **1988**.1, 14, 35, 38, 43; **1990**.25; **1991**.6; **1992**.10
Raglan Road, **1985**.13; **1991**.13
Ratosh (Israeli poet), **1987**.40
Realism, **1938**.1, 8; **1942**.7; **1947**.13; **1948**.6; **1949**.5; **1950**.3; **1961**.1; **1968**.13, 30; **1969**.15; **1975**.33, 35; **1977**.26, 41; **1979**.7, 17, 29; **1980**.10; **1981**.2, 7; **1982**.9; **1985**.43; **1986**.19, 47; **1987**.12; **1988**.5; **1989**.15; **1991**.4, 29; **1994**.1
Reardon, Richard, **1967**.16
Religion (*see also* Catholicism, Mysticism), **1938**.3; **1960**.12, 19, 23; **1964**.2, 23; **1967**.56; **1968**.13, 36, 41; **1979**.3, 49; **1983**.3; **1985**.28; **1986**.40, 47, 49; **1987**.31; **1989**.9; **1990**.13; **1992**.15, 32, 36; **1993**.6
Remembering How We Stood (John Ryan), **1976**.10
"Resolution and Independence" (Wordsworth), **1985**.8
Revival, Irish Literary, **1951**.1; **1959**.4; **1965**.21; **1967**.41; **1969**.12; **1971**.32; **1973**.10; **1975**.12; **1979**.1, 11–12; **1980**.3, 6, 10, 33; **1981**.2, 7; **1982**.6, 24; **1985**.7, 36, 41; **1986**.8, 17, 19, 26, 46–47; **1987**.9–10, 40; **1988**.8; **1989**.19; **1991**.4, 14, 29; **1992**.19, 27; **1993**.4, 15; **1994**.9, 14, 17; **1995**.2
Reynolds, Horace, **1975**.26

Rexroth, Kenneth, **1959**.2
Rimbaud, **1962**.16; **1975**.33
Roberts, G.D., **1939**.2
Robinson, President Mary, **1991**.2, 23
Rolling Stones, **1965**.1; **1988**.18
Rome, **1951**.5; **1978**.16; **1986**.16; **1992**.29
Roper, Anne, **1988**.35
Rough Field, The (John Montague), **1970**.3
Royal Hibernian Academy, **1941**.2
Russia, **1988**.2; **1989**.8
Russian Embassy (Rome), **1992**.30
Ryan, Senator Eoin, **1978**.24
Ryan, John, **1968**.46; **1976**.10; **1977**.44; **1978**.25; **1987**.34; **1988**.43; **1991**.26

S
Sadkowsky, Alex, **1982**.10
Saroyan, William, **1980**.13
Sartre, Jean-Paul, **1992**.30
Schweitzer, Albert, **1959**.1
Scully, Maurice, **1981**.9
Seasons, The (James Thomson), **1964**.29
"September 1913" (W.B. Yeats), **1968**.53
Shakespeare, **1956**.6, **1968**.41; **1976**.2
Shaw, George Bernard, **1979**.25; **1980**.12
Sheehy-Skeffington, **1988**.30
Shelbourne Hotel, Dublin, **1977**.32
Sheridan, Michael, **1988**.2
Sheridan, Niall, **1974**.23
Simmons, James, **1988**.46
Sinatra, Frank, **1948**.5
Sirr, Peter, **1982**.11
Skelton, John, **1986**.7
Slade, G.O., **1939**.2
Sligo, **1968**.13; **1973**.44
Smith, Alan, and James, **1976**.16
Snake Water (Alan Williams), **1965**.4
Songs of Innocence and Experience (Blake), **1985**.28
Spanish Civil War, **1991**.26
Spender, Stephen, **1988**.54
Spinoza, **1968**.37
Stack, Fr. Tom, **1988**.43
Station Island (Seamus Heaney), **1985**.9; **1989**.28; **1991**.22
Stephens, James, **1986**.24
Strong, Eithne, **1981**.9
Stuart, Francis, **1982**.13
Stuart, Jesse, **1939**.6, 16
Swift, Jonathan, **1957**.1; **1962**.8; **1967**.20; **1972**.7; **1986**.22

Subject Index

Swift, Patrick, **1971**.27, 36; **1972**.2
Synge, John Millington, **1939**.12; **1950**.12; **1967**.33; **1968**.53; **1969**.17; **1979**.11, 49; **1982**.28; **1989**.26

T
"Tarry Flynn" (song), **1968**.52
Tarry Flynn (stage play), **1966**.10, 15, 18; **1967**.17, 20, 55; **1968**.12, 14, 20, 29, 40, 42, 51; **1972**.33, 37; **1977**.35; **1990**.35
Tarkovsky, **1988**.29
Teevan, Justice, **1954**.17, 24
Tennyson, Alfred Lord, **1989**.34
Thomas, Dylan, **1948**.5; **1960**.10; **1973**.30; **1975**.30; **1979**.11; **1994**.14
Thomas, Edward, **1969**.17; **1982**.8; **1986**.44
Thomas, R.S., **1960**.11; **1969**.17; **1974**.25; **1980**.19, 20; **1987**.37
Thomson, James, **1964**.29
Thucydides, **1986**.60
Tivoli Theatre (Dublin), **1990**.35
Tobacco Road (Erskine Caldwell), **1949**.11
Toibin, Niall, **1968**.46; **1988**.2
Toibin, Tomas, **1967**.44
Tomlin, Lily, **1977**.23
Tomlinson, Charles, **1960**.11
Tragedy, **1971**.3; **1974**.3; **1977**.39; **1985**.28; **1987**.2, 23; **1991**.15; **1995**.5
Tragic, **1967**.67; **1968**.54; **1981**.8; **1989**.8
Traits and Stories of the Irish Peasantry (Carleton), **1986**.53
Trinity College Dublin, **1941**.1, 3
Triplex Theatre, New York, **1988**.24
Twenty Years A-Growing (Maurice O'Sullivan), **1939**.12
Tyrone Guthrie Centre, **1987**.18

U
U2, **1988**.26
Ulysses (Joyce), **1970**.9
"Under Ben Bulben" (W.B. Yeats), **1979**.23
Ungaretti, Giuseppe, **1992**.29
University College Dublin (UCD), **1955**.9; **1956**.2, 5; **1971**.13; **1972**.7; **1977**.19; **1980**.22; **1982**.26; **1985**.23; **1986**.58; **1987**.5, 14, 37; **1988**.36
USSR, **1989**.8

V
Vail, Sindbad, **1970**.16
Valley of the Squinting Windows (Brinsley MacNamara), **1990**.6
Van Gogh, Vincent, **1965**.22; **1968**.37
Vas, Istvan, **1992**.30
Vattimo, Gianni, **1988**.18
Vaughan, Henry, **1947**.2; **1968**.37
Venus and Adonis, **1956**.6
Villon, **1962**.16; **1975**.33; **1986**.7
Voltaire, **1986**.59

W
Waiting for Godot, **1956**.2; **1986**.36
Walsh, Maurice, **1940**.3
Warner, Alan, **1974**.15, 17; **1978**.25
Waste Land, The, **1943**.7; **1947**.1; **1979**.48; **1982**.19, 28
Way it Was With Them, The, (Peadar O'Donnell), **1939**.12
Welsh, John, **1973**.39
Westland Row Christian Brothers School, **1968**.39
Whitman, Walt, **1967**.50; **1968**.37
Wild Earth (Padraic Colum), **1965**.21
Wilde, Oscar, **1970**.17; **1977**.38
Williams, Alan, **1965**.4
Williams, William Carlos, **1985**.19
Wintering Out (Seamus Heaney), **1985**.16
Witoszek, Nina, 1990.5
Wordsworth, **1947**.2; **1969**.18; **1973**.10, 46; **1985**.8
Wright, David, **1967**.16

Y
Yeats, W.B., **1950**.15; **1954**.23; **1958**.1; **1962**.6, 12–13; **1963**.4; **1964**.22; **1965**.14, 17; **1966**.1; **1967**.3, 33, 36; **1968**.3, 5, 13, 26, 37, 53; **1969**.7–9, 16; **1970**.13; **1971**.19, 31–32; **1972**.7, 30; **1973**.41, 43–44, 47; **1974**.18; **1975**.12, 33; **1976**.2; **1977**.6, 9; **1978**.1; **1979**.11–12, 15, 23–25, 27, 45; **1980**.30; **1981**.5, 9, 26; **1983**.7, 10, 16, 18; **1984**.13; **1985**.19; **1986**.8, 15, 19, 43; **1987**.28, 33; **1988**.11, 19; **1989**.15, 19, 26, 29, 33; **1990**.15, 31; **1991**.4, 14, 18, 27; **1992**.9; **1993**.5, 15

Z
Zionism, **1987**.40
Zola, Emile, **1978**.17

Note on the Author

Jonathan Allison is Associate Professor of English at the University of Kentucky and editor of the Series in Irish Literature, History, and Culture published by the University Press of Kentucky. He was educated at the Queen's University of Belfast, University College London, and the University of Michigan, where he completed his Ph.D. He has published articles on W. B. Yeats, Seamus Heaney, Brendan Kennelly, and Paul Muldoon and edited *Yeats's Political Identities* (University of Michigan Press). He was a Visiting Fellow at the Institute for Advanced Studies in the Humanities, University of Edinburgh, in 1996.

PR 6021 .A74 A55 1996
Allison, Jonathan, 1958-
Patrick Kavanagh

DATE DUE

Demco, Inc. 38-293